The Universal Calibra

Elegant Empowerment

EVOLUTION
OF
CONSCIOUSNESS

Elegant Empowerment: Evolution of Consciousness
Peggy Phoenix Dubro and David P. Lapierre
Copyright © 2002 by Platinum Publishing House
First Edition, First Printing

Published by **Platinum Publishing House**, United States of America.

Foreword by Lee Carroll.

Cover Design by Ilan Wainer
Cover Art (EMF Logo) by Moshe Alembik.
Chapter 1 artwork by Dielle Davin

The EMF Logo is a trademark of the Energy Extension, Inc.
EMF Balancing Technique® is a trademark of the Energy Extension, Inc.
The UCL (Universal Calibration Lattice)® is a trademark of the Energy Extension, Inc.
The UCL (Universal Calibration Lattice)® material and illustrations are copyrighted by the Energy Extension, Inc. 595 W. Main St. PMB 77, Norwich, CT, USA 06360

Editing team: Steve Dubro, Mark Greenia, and Mary Preuss Olsen.   Index by Mark Greenia.
Book production by BookMasters, Inc.

Nothing in this book is meant to replace the advice of your personal medical doctor. The authors do not dispense medical advice nor prescribe the use of any technique as a form of treatment for any medical or physical condition without the advice of a physician. This material is provided for informational use only to help those interested in personal and spiritual growth. Use of this material is the responsibility of the reader.

Library of Congress Cataloging-in-Publication Data

Dubro, Peggy Phoenix; Lapierre, David P.
1. Spirituality/Science 2.Human Potential/Personal growth, 3. Spirit/Mind/Body, 4. Health

ISBN 0-9711074-08

Additional copies of this book may be obtained by calling 1-860-889-3451.
Platinum Publishing House
info@PlatinumPublishingHouse.com
Printed in U.S.A.

Elegant Empowerment

EVOLUTION
OF
CONSCIOUSNESS

By
Peggy Phoenix Dubro
&
David P. Lapierre

Published by
Platinum Publishing House

Dedicated

To you, who know
Reality is more than what is seen
And have the courage to explore what you know.

&

To my husband and teacher Stephen,
With deep gratitude
For your limitless love
And for keeping the vision!

Peggy Phoenix Dubro

This work
is

Dedicated

To my brother Philip who has discovered
The Light in his hands,
& Through brotherly Love,
Supported this project in an inestimable way
During a critical juncture in my life…

To my two sons, Michael & Justyn
Who are destined to discover
An alternate view of reality,
For we are forever connected…

&
To all you who discover this material
In your pursuit of flowing the
Light Of understanding through an
Evolving view of the nature of reality.

David P. Lapierre

 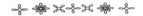

CONTENTS

List Of Illustrations
& Figures

LIST OF ILLUSTRATIONS
& FIGURES CONT'D

LIST OF ILLUSTRATIONS
& FIGURES CONT'D

LIST OF TABLES

Acknowledgments

To be in the resonance of Lee Carroll is a joyful privilege. His obvious love of Creator is the foundation of our kinship. I am filled with unlimited gratitude for the last five years my husband Stephen and I have spent working with Lee Carroll and Kryon. This time together can best be described as a cosmic collegiate learning experience. Lees' drive to know and to learn is undeniable and inspiring. He once said anyone can channel the Kryon. In honor of the unique pattern of his sacred templates and the level of his awakened consciousness, I confidently tell you no one can channel Kryon like Lee Carroll!

When I first met Jan Tober, she told me "the energy of this work was so refined it would take time for others to really see it." It has indeed taken time and Jan has been a friend and consistent supporter of this work. I thank her for the playfulness and love she has so generously shared with Stephen and me.

Trish and Winston Ellis our Australian friends and sponsors who did recognize the resonance of this work at once and have remained in strong support.

Stephen Dubro, who nurtured each concept and steadfastly taught me an appreciation of integrity and clarity that shines throughout all aspects of my life.

David Lapierre, for the brilliant work presented as co-author of this book, your insights will touch the hearts of many.

Mark Greenia, for his admirable editing, swift and to the point.   *Mary Olsen*, for her loving editing skills and contribution to the editing team.   *Dielle*, for her artwork. When I first saw Dielles' lovely work, I felt as though she had been present at some of my truly sacred experiences and then recorded them.   *Joanna Bernstein* who spent many hours listening and helped put the initial words on paper, bringing form to the very first draft of this book.
Tina Pearce, an English woman with a great sense of humour who tried to teach me proper english. *Jacqueline Janes* and *Joy Patton*, two of the wisest and most patient women I know, thank you for our enduring friendship of many years.

Shana, beautiful daughter, for all of your inspiration, hard work, and unconditional support. Krista, beautiful daughter, for your support and "making sure I knew what I was teaching." The resonance of being mother to both of you is an honor and contribution to all that I am.

To all the wonderful EMF "students" throughout the world who have studied with us, a sincere

"thank you,"

for your trust, love, and encouragement, you have been and still are awesome teachers.

And last, but not least
Ahnya

Peggy Phoenix Dubro

FOREWORD

by

Lee Carroll

Dear reader,

It's hard to know what brought your eyes to this page. Perhaps you wanted to find out more about this book before you purchased it. Perhaps you just read forewords? (Many don't.) Whatever the case, I want to give you a sentence to ponder before you put the book down: *If you think you knew about healing, body balancing, and energy work–or perhaps you are one who doesn't believe in any of it–this is different, different, different!*

Today is a new age where physicists are reinventing reality. Astronomers are declaring that much of all the energy of the Universe is "hiding" somewhere (they call it dark energy, because it can't be seen, and at this writing, they don't know where it is). Time as we know it is being examined as something that might not actually exist, and science has now embraced String Theory–an elegant, complex mathematical model that demands that all matter be interdimensional. This is a scientific acknowledgment to all of us that much of our reality is there, but unseen. More and more of the previous "strange and weird" is instead becoming multiple areas of scientific study, and it's a perfect time for the emergence of a new science–the study of previously hidden universal energy, and the ability of Humans to access it directly.

Peggy Phoenix Dubro, along with the support of her husband, Steve, are the forerunners of this science. Throughout history, many have used energy to heal others, to balance the body, and to basically help one another. Some profound metaphysical systems have emerged, and perhaps some of you reading this use them to this day. What is in this book does not compete with anything you know or understand. What the Universal Calibration Lattice and the EMF Balancing Technique are really about is the unfolding story of the expansion of knowledge around the ability of Human beings to access "hidden" universal energy–something that this very year has been acknowledged by science. So whatever you're using, this may be the explanation of its core, and the beginning of a graduate study of what it actually is and where it's going.

Almost everything that is "out there" regarding energy work now begins to be explained by this new science. Peggy and Steve have become stewards of this new information, since they were the first to document how it works, to display ways to access it, and to begin to train other teachers to bring it into the mainstream. Mainstream? Yes. At one time a group of US Navy scientists were so interested in the EMF work, it was even brought to the attention of NASA, and that was because the method gets results, seen by those who measure Human response.

Many have "felt" this energy in these emerging years of the new millennium—almost like it was something being delivered from the Universe, now available in a grander way in this new age. It has unfolded like never before in its profundity, right into the stewardship of Peggy and Steve, who have now become the experts. They steadfastly strive to keep this study and the training of it pure, in keeping with the integrity of their obvious responsibility to everyone concerned. Many have scampered off to find various specialized ways to use it, or to let people "feel" it. It's everywhere, and it's being delivered to us strongly, so it's getting easier to "see" and feel. Some have never heard of Peggy and Steve but are very familiar with this new energy . . . unnamed as yet in their minds, but so powerful that it's easy to access or "feel" in an elementary fashion.

But there is only one comprehensive source of information for the full unfolding and explanation of this new power. It's from the ones who have spent almost all their waking hours interpreting the nuances of it for the last decade. They are also the ones who will manifest the mature use of it, and who are continuing to develop the system to access it in its fullest capacity.

Although Peggy might not allude to it, one of the most difficult things she had to deal with when writing this book was that more and more is being revealed to her each month. When do you stop writing and publish? When is it done? As Peggy and Steve now know, it's never done. This is, therefore, the first textbook. It will be the introduction to something so profound and scientifically significant, that someday we may look back and wonder why we didn't "get it" before now.

Peggy and Steve travel the world with me. I'm a lecturer, not an energy worker. In the beginning, I stood back, unbiased, and watched what happened. Australia, Canada, France, Belgium, Germany, and Israel all looked at Peggy and said, "Oh, yeah, another form of spooky, energy work." Then I saw students' eyes get wide after about a week of training, and now there are branches of this work in every one of those countries. Early critics became their strongest supporters! That's because it works, and the results are very observable. Of course, now I'm biased—I'm biased because this EMF Balancing Technique works!

Join Peggy in her journey as the information of the Universal Calibration Lattice unfolds ... It's about time we understood what's happening around us that enables us to tap in to unseen energy—an energy that until the year 2000 was an "eye-roller" to many. Now it's science . . . and it's different, different, different!

Lee Carroll,
Author of the *"Kryon"* series of books, and co-author of the best-selling
"Indigo Children" series.

FOREWORD

by
Peggy Phoenix Dubro

A spinning planet circles a sun, part of a vast swirling universe. Perhaps we are a little dizzy from all that spinning! Whether we understand it or even realize it, we all exist in this state of motion together. In the midst of this reality, personally and collectively we are co-creating a new paradigm, a reality of paradox. We are simultaneously strengthening our individuality while we develop new levels of respect for one another as we discover how intimately we are all connected.

I originally wanted to write this book to share knowledge about the Universal Calibration Lattice (UCL), a specific system within our energy anatomy, ever mindful that all of the systems in both the physical and energy anatomy are really a unified whole. In order to co-create strong foundations in the new energy dynamics, it is important to understand the function of the UCL. This understanding will help to incorporate the new energy dynamics quickly and clearly in our daily lives. The UCL evolves within our energy anatomy as humanity takes the next evolutionary step and further develops the archetype of the collective whole.

The information I share here comes from my own seeking, finding, teaching and traveling over a period of almost 30 years. These perceptions complement much of our current understanding in the realm of energy work. Working around the world with various cultures and in several languages has revealed new insights about how the UCL works. When working with a translator, I sometimes observe human energy responding even before the words are understood! We communicate in the language of energy all of the time - with one another, the universe, and even with ourselves, right through to the cellular level of our being. It is important to understand the nature of this energetic language - what are we saying and what does it mean?

It is my pleasure to introduce to you David Lapierre, a physicist and geophysicist. Dave is also a practitioner and teacher of the EMF Balancing Technique. As we interacted during the training, we realized that each of us held complementary knowledge regarding the electromagnetic nature of the UCL and the mechanics of the EMF Balancing Technique.

Dave said to me "Your work proves my theories, and my theories prove your work." Eventually I invited him to write an appendix for this book and he agreed. When I read the information he presented and realized the depth of his understanding, I knew it was appropriate to ask him to co-author this book. The ability to apply critical thinking to the understanding of inspired information is of utmost importance for all of us at this time in our evolution. It is my hope that this body of information serves as one of the bridges between the metaphysical and scientific worlds, contributing to the elegant union of science and spirit.

Many people refer to Earth as the "planet of choice," or the "free will zone." We are neophytes in this arena of choice, and this is exciting news. How do we define freedom? How do we define an enlightened life? I often think of one of my ancestors, John Hart, an original signer of the Declaration of Independence, and of the vision of freedom that he and his courageous contemporaries had when they signed that document. The answers to the questions posed here are not political; they are very personal and varied according to each individual's perception of freedom and enlightenment.

I am passionate about everyone's right to know about and demonstrate his or her empowerment. Regardless of the circumstances you may be in at the moment, you have the right to know your empowerment now. If you feel powerless, or want to increase your sense of freedom and independence, the next step is an evolution of consciousness. You are already in a universal partnership. You are already communicating in a reciprocal, holographic manner with the entire universe. If you are consciously living in the powerful resonance of this relationship, keep going! Learn more, and above all, practice what you are learning. We are testing the skills and limits of our ability to co-create.

Please look beyond any words or concepts in this book that may be outside your belief system. I honor your beliefs exactly as they are, and offer this information as a practical guide to assist you in co-creating the most enlightened life you can!

Peace filled empowerment,
Peggy Phoenix Dubro

PREFACE

TO THE READER
by David P. Lapierre

Dear Reader,

Here I am able to speak to you personally, as if we were in the same space and time. Within this text you will encounter several ideas and perceptions that we probably already share in common. Perhaps only the language of expression is different. If you are not already familiar with the terms presented in this book, do not be overly concerned, and do not in any way be discouraged with yourself. Many scholars of Science today, may not relate to them at first either. The Glossary at the end of this text was designed to help us have the same footing, and to enable a maximum of exchange of ideas. The two papers of the Appendix are for the more 'technically' inclined, although some parts read easily in plain language. I have assumed that you do not necessarily possess any background in science...or at least a marginal amount. Accordingly, I have attempted to create for you, a foundation. Your advantage is that you may have no preconceived limitations to the nature of reality! As Robert Monroe said: *"Our greatest illusion is that we have limitations"*.

The effort that you place in working through the material, at your own pace, will be well worth it! In the end, you will have acquired a language of concepts that you will find useful in discourse even with learned individuals of various professions. It is not necessary that you agree with all the ideas, or postulates presented here. We do not have all the answers, and in regards to the unseen reality, we likely never will. However, I assure you, that the overall 'industry' requires a step upwards in concepts if we are to begin to understand a reality in which the likes of *Remote Viewing* is a given; time-travel may be more than speculative; and all the other 'paranormal' phenomena refuse to be swept away under the carpet.

For those of us who feel 'subtle energy', either around ourselves, or with our interactions with others, we do not have to be convinced of its existence. For others, who are prepared to open themselves to the flow through practice, you will find it intriguing to discover that playing with the energy of your hands feels like playing with magnets! Play with magnets, and you are playing in hyperspace! Hyperspace is believed to be the realm of this subtle energy. When you tap into this energy in hyperspace, you are tapping into the Infinite! Then again, each one of us is a reflection of the Infinite!

Peace,
David P. Lapierre

AMIDST
A TIME
OF CHANGE

We occupy unique coordinates in what we define as space, and that we know as time. Like the whale, humanity has "breached" to find itself in the 21st century. This has been more than just a calendar event. In many instances, historical world events of the 20th century carried the probability of placing this planet and its inhabitants on a distinctly different timeline of experience. At times it would have taken no more than the simple twist of the dial or the push of a button to send us there.

Our current timeline of experience marks a triumph for humanity. Collectively we have chosen to experience a path that holds great promise. As we look into the near future, something remarkable for humanity lies in our path. We refer to the "shift" that is upon us [1].

CHANGES UNDERWAY

Changes are underway around us at levels beyond our comprehension. This is reflected in the following statement :

"Because of the geomagnetic changes, profuse solar activity, and the space shift in the space-time continuum, *there has been a change in the natural pulse of the Earth and the Sun which is not electromagnetic, but scalar-takyonic.* We are now absolutely sure that these cosmic changes are being orchestrated/monitored by a supremely advanced extraterrestrial [see editor's note below[1]] intelligence for the evolution of consciousness, humankind and Mother Earth. We mentioned in earlier missives that the fundamental constants of the universe are changing, and the space-time fabric is undergoing a colossal twister-motion or "warp", which is the actual mechanism creating the physical quantum-relativistic cosmic changes. In brief and simple terms, this has tremendous effects on the human mind, psyche and subtle bodies at first, and then on the <u>physical</u> body, especially the brain, central nervous system and DNA-RNA complex...Events are being accelerated, and emotions are being magnified almost a hundredfold" [2].

This statement appeared in the 1999 Publication *Ancient Wisdom & Modern Physics*. The language spoken above sounds like what you would expect to hear if you were an observer on the bridge of the starship *Enterprise*, in the TV series "Star Trek." However, the authors of the statement above are not presenting science fiction. Perhaps only a few scientific minds on this planet really understand what all this scientific terminology means. For the rest of us – the implication and effects this may have on our human organism are spelled out quite clearly!

NEED FOR INTERNAL BALANCE

In his consciousness-raising book *Science And Human Transformation – Subtle Energies, Intentionality And Consciousness*, William A. Tiller, Ph.D., physicist and Professor Emeritus at Stanford University, invites us to consider that we may be under the influence of parameters of change that are influencing our personal energy systems. This he raises in the following:

"Let us suppose, however, that via some energy condition at the spiritual or mental level of the cosmos, a pattern develops which forces the chakras of all members of the human ensemble to spin faster and faster. If such a cosmic condition did develop, people would have their chakras spinning faster and faster, energy imbalances in their body would increase and reveal itself first as enhanced tension and then as neural discharges and other pathway discharges in the body (much like a voltage breakdown phenomena)"[3].

---

[1] Note the use of 'extraterrestrial' as an adjective or descriptive word, & not a noun. The dictionary context defines this as "originating, located or occurring outside Earth". The editor believes the reference is to an intelligence beyond the Earth plane (example- a Spiritual intelligence, All That Is, The Creator etc.).

Professor Tiller explains that should such a circumstance happen, a variety of phenomenon would be experienced by the human organism, some consequential to internal balance "unless they do learn the inner self management and energy balancing techniques..." [4].

In a later chapter, Prof. Tiller raises concerns regarding the Stewardship of the Home Planet. In it he discusses the relationships that humans experience, and he designates these relationships into three categories:

> Man in relationship to the cosmos; Man in relationship to his local
>   self; Man in relationship to society.

As he raises his concerns over the need for transformation at all levels of our relationships, Prof. Tiller leads us to his following insight:

> **"One way of accelerating the desired transformation in individuals and societies is via human energy-field interactions"[5].**

This he explains is possible and beneficial because we all tap into an energy source from the cosmos, and from this energy we ultimately and uniquely build patterns within our energy fields.

> **We have internal mechanisms to transform the cosmic energy into patterns that become an energy signature of who & what we are. These patterns we radiate outward. As our patterns evolve in quality with expanding consciousness, these have a positive impact on those around us.**

As we feel the influences of change within us, and as we work to adjust and adapt our internal mechanisms and circuitry, Professor Tiller gives us hope-raising encouragement. As we raise our individual consciousness we broaden our radiated spectrum and "in this way, each of us may exercise some influence on the transformation of the masses – by our personal radiation fields" [6].

PROFOUND TRANSFORMATION

The path of transformation holds promise of changes at the cellular level involving the DNA. Evidence of this has been discussed regarding our INDIGO CHILDREN. We understand that our DNA is being influenced by outside energy sources. This suggestion is reflected in the following statement by Col. Philip J. Corso after his discussions with researcher Dr. Gislero Flesch during the 1940's:

> **"It was a wild and, I thought, supernatural theory on what he called the filament within each cell. The filament was activated by some cosmic action or form of electromagnetic radiation that bombarded the Earth continuously from outer space and resonated against a constant refresh of electrical activity from the brain"[7].**

Certainly we understand from this statement that outside factors influencing our DNA is not a new idea. Nor was it, apparently, considered outrageous by some scientific minds during the period of Dr. Flesch.

WHAT IS REALITY?

Expanding awareness has everything to do with questioning our sense of reality. To understand earthly affairs we require knowledge of the history and the real events around us. As we perhaps struggle to understand and find truth in our three-dimensional earthy reality, this book will take you into the realm of the invisible and intangible.

> **Human evolution is characterized by "discovering" the existence of "new" dimensions and tunable circuits within our energy dynamics. These dimensions exist as elements of creation and are accessible from within our own multi-dimensional configuration. Expanding awareness encompasses the realization that we can consciously alter our internal architectural dynamics. In doing so, we expand our angular view outward to encompass a greater slice of this creation.**

The human energy field and the Universal Calibration Lattice exist outside of our sense of reality. As we grow in consciousness, we can expect that our concept of reality will extend beyond the current perceptions of Homo Sapiens. In this text we introduce the reader to new aspects of the human energy anatomy. As well, we introduce the notion that we can affect the energy fields of another individual through the human-to-human interaction. This idea is not a suggestion outside of scientific thought. We refer the reader to this remark by T.E. Bearden [8]:

> **"There exists a solid scalar electromagnetic basis --a thoroughly scientific basis-- for the ancient idea of 'healing the aura' or auric bodies"**

Here the term "auric bodies" is used as a more generalized reference to all "subtle" energy body concepts.). Thus is the word from Thomas E. Bearden, major proponent of scalar electromagnetic theory, and inventor of "overunity" energy devices (*extracting energy from virtual space/Dirac sea/Cosmic Lattice*). .T.E. Bearden views the brain as a

> **"Scalar interferometer detector of superluminal quantities. This enables remote viewing, clairvoyance, clairaudience, telepathy, precognition, postcognition, psychokinesis, etc. – indeed, all the phenomenon of classical parapsychology are explainable directly by scalar electromagnetic theory"[9].**

What we now view as paranormal may one day be normal for humans as we learn to exploit and develop the hyperfunctions of our brains, and undergo cellular transformation at all levels of our being.

CONSCIOUSNESS & INTENT AT PLAY

As we move into an era of new theory and new physics, T.E. Bearden and other progressive scientific thinkers like Professor Tiller, tell us that mind and <u>INTENT</u> play a deliberate causative role in our reality. In our text, and within our paradigm of reality, we consider INTENT to be a real force. Our only way to characterize this force is as one being *metaphysical* (*beyond physics*), as such a force is beyond the notion of orthodox physics.

> Within context of a reality that is founded upon unseen organizational patterns within unseen dimensions, INTENT is the force that serves to alter, choose, shape, modify, and organize these primary patterns. As any of these influences occurs, the informational fields that shape the material world are altered. This change precipitates physical change.

As we extend our notion beyond the limiting view of how an "observer" affects the outcome of an experiment in particle physics, we enter the domain of co-creating our reality. Co-creating our reality is the message in the following as we come to understand that

> "The wheels of cyclic Tai Chi's work through unconscious magnetism. This helps to precipitate full-fledged magnetism of conscious possibilities or realities" [10].

This is so aptly described by P. Stephen Petersen, Ph.D., physicist, in his book *The Quantum Tai Chi- Gauge Theory: The Dance of Mind Over Matter.* Stephen Petersen goes on to explain how consciousness interacts with the "blueprint of life" whereat the

> "(Blueprint)...creates a geometry for the life field. This relates to the force that moves the currents of field sources through the body. This matrix also may be programmed in the consciousness or brain through gauge angles (Tai Chi's) relating to specific location in the body"[11].

The matrix, blueprint, lattice, pattern- these are all references to geometric form. Geometry is the basis to the development of all life forms,

"In fact, all life forms *are* these geometrical patterns, but it is not apparent to the causal eye" [12].

This is well explained by Drunvalo Melchizedek, physicist and founder of Flower of Life. What is not apparent to the causal eye is orchestrated from the "implicate order". This is a term used by physicist David Bohm to explain how our reality is an "unfolding" manifestation of an organizing potential and intelligence not immediately visible to us.

"According to Bohm, what happens in space-time is nevertheless determined by what happens in a nonlocal reality beyond space-time" [13].

Amit Goswami, Ph.D., expands on this idea in his book *The Self Aware Universe--How Consciousness Creates The Material World.*

HOLOGRAPHIC CONNECTEDNESS IN A MULTI-DIMENSIONAL REALITY

David Bohm, a physicist who has made immense contribution to the field of quantum Physics, "holographically" connects us to every aspect of matter, consciousness, and both the visible and invisible universes. We are all part of one vast "holomovement". Separation is truly an illusion. According to Bohm, we are fundamentally all "undividedly" connected - despite the illusion we carry that we are separate [14]. This connectedness spans a vast expanse of unseen aspects of a complex, yet elegant, structure of our visible universe. For within the background of this universe is a web that spins throughout untold dimensions. This web links a multi-dimensional fabric together, as if it were a never-ending chain, pulsing with the very life force of all existence. This is so eloquently described by Brian Greene is his statement from *The Elegant Universe*:

"The fabric of our universe is a richly intertwined multi-dimensional labyrinth within which the strings of the universe endlessly twist and vibrate, rhythmically beating out the laws of the cosmos". [15]

PROFOUND CONNECTION

As we raise our awareness we will one-day come to fully appreciate not only the existence of our personal energy fields and our paranormal abilities, but also the multidimensional facets and nature of our being. We will also come to understand our connectedness to the Universe and to each other, and the profound nature of the Human-to-Human connection.

INITIATION INTO THE LIGHT

Peggy's Story

> *It's good to be a seeker,*
> *But sooner or later you have to be a finder...*
> *And then it is right to give what you have found*
> *A gift to the world for those who will accept it.*
> *Jonathan Livingston Seagull*
> *By Richard Bach*

With our first breath we are initiated into the school of life on planet earth.
Breathing deepens our initiation into the sacred school of life.

It all began when....

There are many beliefs surrounding how we incarnate onto this planet. . . from the Grace of God, to standing in line to get here, to a cosmic accident. In my case, I was born so fast the attending nurse did not believe my mother when she called and said I was here. "Your baby can't be here!" the nurse shouted from another room. My astonished mother shouted back, "If my baby can't be here, then what's this?" This dubious welcome to planet earth makes me laugh every time I think about it!

I remember dreaming vividly before the age of five. One could say I had sight, or a great imagination. I was aware of the "company" around me. My best playmates were imaginary luminous beings with whom I talked for hours on end. Once in awhile I saw other luminous beings with some very unfriendly energy. Instinctively, I knew not to bother with them. I had not even a hint of curiosity because their energy repelled me. Sometimes I think about those early experiences and wonder about today's challenges of discernment and non-judgment facing each of us.

At the age of five, I witnessed the senseless trashing of our apartment by my father. As he tore through the place, he came to a wall where my mother had hung some finger paintings I had created in kindergarten that week. In a tirade of uncontrollable anger, my father ripped them down. As he shredded the paintings, something strange happened within me. It felt as though a cocoon of energy began to form around me—closing me off in some way. The "connected" feeling I always had, along with my sight, shut down. It felt like I was left with only a single strand of energy to cling to, one that thankfully contained simple joy and hope.

From this point forward, my father's alcoholism was my constant shadow. This was the mid 1950s, a time when such situations of abuse were kept quiet, so my family struggled to keep itself together as best it could. There were no programs readily available to a poor family and there was no help or support from the community. My father's condition worsened over the years as the alcohol took its toll. Eventually he was diagnosed as a paranoid schizophrenic.

My early years of instruction were spent in Catholic school. On my very first day I was branded a troublemaker, wrongly accused of humming in class. From the start, I had a hard time there. My teacher, one of the nuns from the convent, threatened to put me out of the classroom "so fast my head would spin." I didn't fit in with the other kids; in part because almost everyone there (including the nuns) looked down on my home life, and also because I still spent a lot of time by myself. In third grade, the nun who was our teacher once asked who among us wanted to be a nun when they grew up? To me, being a nun looked like a fabulous way to live. The convent where the sisters lived was like a beautiful mansion to me. I loved being in church and I loved God. Joyfully, I stood up. The teacher glared at me and sharply replied, "You have a long way to go young lady before you ever become a nun!" Humiliated and confused, I wondered what I had done to make her so angry. I did not realize that my family and I had become such a disgrace in the parish due to our conditions at home.

My Mothers' determination to protect and provide for us was indomitable. Against all odds, my mother finally divorced my father, when I was ten years old. He had received some treatment for his illness, and after a bitter legal battle, the court awarded him visitation rights, but only at my discretion. Such a legal decision was highly unusual, considering I was a ten-year-old child. My family had a strong Christian background and was very forgiving. We all wanted to believe that my father had changed, so I agreed to weekly visits with him on Sundays. At first, things seemed to be fine. However, within a short time I began to wonder if everything was as it should be. I wondered if it was really safe for my younger brother and sister and me to visit him. This was not at a time in our culture when children were encouraged to "tell," so when I started to notice alcohol in my father's home, I kept the discovery a secret.

One day when he arrived to pick us up for a visit, I stood at the window in my second-story bedroom, looked out, and saw his energy field! There was something not right about his energy—it felt "unfriendly" to me. I knew that we were not to see him anymore. Without telling anyone what I was about to do, I marched downstairs and walked outside. In the presence of what seemed like the entire neighborhood, I physically removed my brother and sister from the car. I confronted my father and told him that we were not going to see him anymore. Of course he became very angry. My father's last words to me were, "I will get even with you some day, Peggy Ann!" At that moment, the powerful man who would one day become my stepfather came outside to see what all the commotion was about. I felt his presence behind me and I was able to stand strong in my truth.

My father never tried to see us again, and I never looked back. I knew what I had seen. At eleven years old, I recognized that we had all been set free, including my father.

For The Love Of God

These previous events set the stage for the next level of my initiation. Still just eleven years of age, my "sight" started to reopen. I had always been a religious child. Now my interest in God and religion began to increase. Over the next few years I attended several different churches, Episcopalian, Congregational and Methodist. I always sang in the choir, and often played the part of the Christmas angel in the annual Christmas pageants. I was fifteen when I had my first experience of feeling the energy of God. I was in a Christian spiritual group for young women. As I studied the Bible, I read of how God's glory and magnificence make even the mountains pale in comparison. I began to sense the magnitude of His presence. The cells of my body started to vibrate and I felt a strong pulsing sensation through my entire being. I thought that I was preparing to transport to the mountaintop! I was overwhelmed and frightened - I quickly slammed my Bible shut. The energy of Creator was trying to show itself but I wasn't ready yet.

A few years later, I chose to leave home and claim my freedom. Like many teenagers, especially those raised in religious homes, I felt my family was too strict. I graduated from high school, and got married on my eighteenth birthday, making a grand statement to my family that I would follow my own rules from that point forward.

My husband went into the service and did a yearlong tour in Vietnam. Some time after he came home, like many others, I found myself asking the big questions about life. It was the end of the 1960s and the beginning of the 1970s. The Age of Aquarius was upon us. The Vietnam War would soon end, and Self-knowledge was about to become the next step in our collective growth process. While I didn't directly participate in the wild abandon characterized by the sixties, I was certainly influenced by it, and I was about to catch the evolutionary wave that the era incited. By now, I was in my early twenties. My life was finally in my own hands. I was married to my childhood sweetheart, and I had a great job and a lovely apartment. Yet, I knew something was missing; there was an empty place inside.

For all the time I had spent in worship of God, I still did not feel the connection I desired. I had been taught that if one actually saw God's face, he or she would not live. In my youth and naiveté, I believed the warning literally meant death. Nonetheless, my enthusiasm and longing would reach a level of intensity that I could not deny. I was passionate about God, and reasoned that if God were my Father (I didn't know then about Mother Goddess), there must have been a time when I was a part of God. This was my reasoning, and it invited me to remember my union with God - not the God of ancient times - but the God of NOW. I wasn't even sure exactly what that meant. All I knew was that my deepest desire was to know God in my being, in my biology, in this time, in this place, right now in my life. I didn't know then that my craving to know God was also a desire to remember my own spirit. And so I became a seeker.

There was never any question in my mind of God's existence. I was not looking for a sign, I always knew God existed. What I sought was union! How does one experience this union? Looking back, I am not surprised that my first attempt was quite comical. (Ever feel you are cosmic entertainment? You are not alone!) I read a book that recommended sitting in a dark room with a candle. This seemed spooky to me, but as I mentioned earlier ... I really wanted this union. I covered the window with a blanket, lit a candle, turned off the bedroom light and asked God three times, "Are you here?" I thought we should say hello before we entered this state of union. The first two times I asked the question very gently, "Are you here?" Since I had not received the slightest hint of an answer, the third time I asked in a much stronger voice, "Are you here?" Suddenly, I heard three loud knocks, as if someone were banging on my dresser! The blanket I used to make sure the room was really dark fell away from the window, and light poured into the room. I was so startled that I literally ran outside to get away from my apartment. As I stood out in the midday sun I knew that Creator was saying, "Yes, I'm here. And you can stop the spooky stuff!" So I tried another approach.

At that time I knew nothing of meditation or mantras. Nonetheless, I began to continuously repeat to myself, "I remember, I remember, I remember." I focused on Christ, saying, "I and the Father are one." I wanted to experience that oneness with every breath I took.

When I first saw the cobalt-blue light dancing in front of me, the hair on the back of my

Illustration 1.1 **"Creation"**

neck stood up. I was asking to know God - but had I connected with something else by accident? The sparkling blue light became my constant companion. It was with me wherever I went. In time, I moved beyond fear, and curiosity set in. I reached out and touched the light. It felt pleasantly electrical, alive, and very peaceful. I was fascinated by the way it seemed to dance around and through my hands. There was a connection between this light and me. Even though I couldn't understand what it was trying to communicate, it felt right. One night, this light would not let me sleep. As I lay in bed, it hovered over me, sparkling and moving. It was impossible to get any rest with such a light show going on! I slipped out of bed and went into the living room. As the light intensified, I felt some apprehension and instinctively grabbed my Bible to hold close to my heart. Still not sure what I was looking at, a question arose from deep within; not from my head, but from my solar plexus. I asked the light, "What do you have to teach me?" Finally the right question, and an answer. I felt an infusion of joy. I also sensed a celebration around me as the light continued to amplify until it became a great veil of illumination. Then the veil fell away, and energy began to flow from above my head and downward throughout every part of me. Suddenly, I remembered! In an overwhelming burst of energy, I became "no beginning and no end."

This exquisite energy flowed into and out of my body, through every fiber of my being. There was light everywhere, creating the sense that I had stepped outside of time. Infused in this energy and light I felt the unconditional love of God the Creator - no judgment - only infinite love. I knew God was alive and well, and was a very loving God. I experienced a vision of Christ on the cross (due to my strong Christian background). He was radiating powerful energy and speaking words of love to the Creator. The energy intensified and it felt as though all the cells of my body were turned up to full power, and that power had overloaded my circuits. It was like having a 220-volt jolt in a body wired for 110-volts. The ecstasy was excruciating! I cried tears of joy and gratitude. I don't know how long this state lasted, but I did not sleep that night. Life for me was forever changed. Such love, such light. ... and alas, such confusion! .

Yes! God was everything I had suspected and more! God was loving, beyond words! These kinds of exclamations burst from my mouth, and to really make the point, my eyes practically popped out of my head. I quickly gained the reputation as a foaming-at-the-mouth eccentric (or worse). I desperately wanted to understand what had happened within me. I wanted to become comfortable with this new level of awareness, to develop the ability to repeat the experience and then live in it.

Uncertain where to go for answers and guidance, I turned to those people who surely must know - the religious leaders in my life. But their response was not quite the illumination I had hoped for. "How could you have such an experience? Why, you're only 22. You're a product of divorce, and you're from that neighborhood. There is something very strange about you. Why on earth would God talk to you?" Feeling slightly discouraged, but not ready to give up, I finally found someone who really seemed to listen, and might have some answers. "Let's see, this vision began with lights?" she asked. "Yes, yes, beautiful lights!" I answered. She asked a few more seemingly discerning questions and I began to feel that we were making some progress. This person must know something. Then the great Aha! Her conclusion was a warning to me: "Never forget that Satan is the angel of light and the great deceiver." Sigh. I realized, it was time to stop talking about my experience and continue seeking.

CONFUSED BY THE LIGHT

I was determined to experience that state of unconditional love again, and the next time I vowed "I will hold it and not let it slip away." In that spirit, for the next 15 years I studied anything I thought might help to explain—and therefore regain—the intense energy of love I had felt. I immersed myself in a broad and intense study of numerous and diverse understandings and disciplines. I set out to find whatever I could that had some sense or feel of energy to it, some twinkling of that unconditional Divine Love.

Here is a highly abbreviated overview of some of my explorations—I am sure many of you have traveled some of the same paths. I began with books and became the voracious reader initiate. I couldn't stop, I had to have the next book. The books were empowering and contributed a significant sense of personal peace. I realized I was not alone in my quest. People who visit my home today often look at my library and comment that they too have read many of these classic works. It's wonderful to realize now how "in sync" we were in our early years seeking consciousness.

During that time of intense reading I also studied belly dancing. I was determined to move the energy through my body. I wore pale blue when I danced and called myself "Electra." I met a woman in our dance group who introduced me to The Silva Mind Method, which remains to this day one of my most valued courses of study. I became active with groups of like-minded individuals. Some were study groups, some were prayer groups, and some were with people who were physically working with energy.

Next, I turned my attention to Zen Buddhism. Through my studies of Eastern philosophy, I met people who were macrobiotics. I faithfully started chewing brown rice 35 times per mouthful, for maximum digestion. I contemplated basic "ancient" wisdom, such as the meaning of everything having a front and a back. I was fascinated with all I was learning, and the wisdom was like water for my parched soul. I was undaunted by the warning that these understandings would take a lifetime to master.

Eventually, Sufism tugged at my heart and Pir Viliyats' *Toward the One* became my Bible. The practical guidance in that book gave me a substantial direction to deepen my expression as a spiritual being. Then I spent a few years in passionate revival through born-again Christianity. During that time I also experienced Rebirthing and Rolfing. Years in Siddha Yoga and personal interaction with Swami Muktananda followed, providing some of the most precious experiences in my life's journey.

Shamanism then became part of my "schooling." I began my studies with an African shaman, then with a Brazilian shaman. I became very comfortable with Native American wisdom, studying with a Lakota pipe carrier who is also a beautiful woman. I remember the day Little Hawk gently unwrapped her pipe and held it in her hands. She looked at me for a moment and said, "I see you have no need to steal another's energy." She then placed the pipe in my hands and several years of teaching ensued.

I studied the martial arts - Tae Kwon Do, Tai Chi, and Kung Fu. I tried anything to get that wonderful energy consistently active in my life. In fact, all of my studies yielded fine spiritual principles, such as "The truth is within you and so are all the answers," and "We are magnificent beings and capable of Mastery." This gave me hope, but I had a hard time using these tenets in my daily life. They did not produce the intense Love energy that I so wanted to experience once again. I had touched the Unlimited and continued to have profound visions, yet my daily life reflected powerlessness. To tell you the truth, despite the years of effort, my life, my work, and my home were a mess! My frustration deepened, but my love for God and desire to know Him/Her remained.

THE DIVINE FEMININE

So here I was, after 15 years of searching and waiting for the Divine reality that I knew existed. I understood that I had a "power pack," but how could I turn it on? This was the constant question during my years of study and futile attempts for union with God. My heart filled over and over again as I gained some understanding of the ancient truths and the realization that we are all one. However, I still passionately desired to once again hold the electrical charge of that truth. After all that time of seeking and not finding, in sincerity and exasperation, I asked, "If the answers are within me, then I want to know <u>where</u> within me they are - and <u>how</u> do I get to them?" Finally, on the first day of spring in 1988, in a spectacular luminous event, I once again had the joyous experience of no beginning and no end.

This time, there was a tall, dark haired warrior of light who accompanied me throughout the experience. He took me out of body and led me through the maze of the Cosmic Lattice, the unlimited energy of the Universe. I became aware of how vulnerable and naive I was on this ethereal plane, and how appreciative I was of his guidance. We went far out into the cosmos. As I looked back on the universal reality - expecting to see only harmony and symphony - instead, I saw a cacophony of unlimited life forms caught in the struggle between freedom and enslavement. Then we entered a place - a spacious, beautifully furnished room with a stunning view. In front of us was the biggest window I had ever seen. It revealed infinite space. There were several women in this place. They were my friends, and we were all preparing for . . . something.

As I gazed out on the beautiful, black expanse of the universe, the event began to unfold. At the far left of the great window, an exquisite white light began to build. A beautiful horse of white light galloped through the black of space, and on his back was a brilliant feminine form of light. The sight was breathtaking! I turned to speak with my warrior guide and I noticed that he was gone. Now the women surrounded me, and feelings of love and peace were radiating everywhere. I turned back to look at the feminine being of light and found that my warrior guide was out there with her. I laughed as I realized that he was enjoying her beauty. Then, to my surprise, he started to guide the horse she rode in my direction. Next, the women had me partially recline on a luminous couch. The closer my warrior guide and the being of light came, the stronger I felt a complete stillness inside of me. Finally, only the window remained between us. The being of light slid off her horse and gracefully floated through the window as if it weren't even there. She placed her beautiful face of light directly in front of mine. I felt our energies align, and she smiled at me. Her smile was radiant, and I felt pure peace.

Then, the most awesome event took place, one that continues to have a profound influence on me. Slowly and steadily we merged, becoming one being. The energy was intensely powerful and consuming. I knew instantly that the last 15 years had prepared me for this event. The power of the light and energy was so great that I now understood I had not been ready for it until this very moment. As the light being and I became one, my new female friends soothed some of my rising apprehension by singing the sound of "aahh" from their hearts. I was so comforted by this sound. I relaxed and became what seemed like columns and fibers of light and energy as a constant stream of information was transferred to me during this process. I have no idea how long this event went on - such events are "timeless." I do know that when I opened my eyes here on the physical plane, most of the energy from the experience remained present with me. Even though I felt supercharged, I could not move until I had absorbed every bit of this energy into every cell of my body and then, as absurd as it seems, I sat up and wanted someone to sing the happy birthday song to me!

Illustration 1.2 *"Amour"*

Who was this magnificent being of light and energy? She defined herself as the Feminine Always, the Feminine Divine. The Male Divine, or God the Father, is the Yang aspect of Creator. I believe I met and merged with the Yin aspect of Creator. This merger transferred or activated a pattern of light throughout my energy field. I would later understand this energy pattern as the Universal Calibration Lattice ("UCL"). I had become the fibers of light and energy of the UCL and felt the "electrical charge of my truth." This was my first experience of channeling, and it was highly potent. I received a tremendous amount of information in this one momentous event, including additional patterns of energy that would eventually become the EMF Balancing Technique®. Naively, I thought I had arrived spiritually, that this was the transformation I had been waiting for. I thought some marvelous spiritual gate had opened, and that from that point forward, my life would be easy and charmed. I found out however, that this was still a time of old energy dynamics for me, and further trial and initiation were still to come.

A MOMENT OF TRUTH

As I pondered how the opening of this spiritual gate would affect my life, the next test unfolded. I was reading *Crystal Woman*, my fourth or fifth book by Lynn Andrews. I had always set aside time to read her books because I found the stories so powerful, and they often resulted in great realizations or initiations for me. I got to the part in the story where Lynn recognizes that every time she claims her power she becomes very ill. "Gee," I thought, "I can really relate to that." And in that instant, I began to feel ill. "Get a grip, Peg," I thought to myself, "boy are you suggestible."

A few days before, I had gone swimming with the neighborhood kids at the local pool. I contracted a form of pneumonia that is relatively harmless to children, but can be deadly to adults. I became very ill. Ah, the synchronicity of it! I finished the book as quickly as possible. I had to see if Lynn was able to integrate her male and female aspects, and at the end of the book, she did! Now, my test went into full swing. I mused at the co-operation of the Universe. At the time, I couldn't go to all these exotic places I had read about for my spiritual quest, so the Universe brought the quest to me in the little town of Norwich, Connecticut. At the height of this ordeal, I had a 104-degree temperature, my face was deep red, and my heart was racing. I crawled to the bathroom and forced myself to stand up.

I looked up, and there in front of me, bigger than I had ever seen it before, I recognized the Blue White Star, an entranceway to the next dimension. It was sparkling and alive and I knew that I was being offered an opportunity to leave my body and end this lifetime. Instinctively, I closed my eyes, turned my head away and spoke aloud, "No, wait! I want to stay! I will do my work!" I thought to myself, "Where did that come from? What did I mean?" I had two little children of my own and four more kids for whom I cared daily - I was just the neighborhood day-care mom. What "work" was I talking about? This was a moment of truth; the offer to leave had been tempting. I was surprised to find that even after experiencing the Unlimited, I really wanted to stay here on Earth. There were so many blessings to experience here.

When I looked up again, the Blue White Star was gone. During the next few days, I reached a critical turning point, but not until I had passed through the hallucinations of high fever and experienced, in Lynn Andrews-like fashion, an aboriginal man placing crystals in my body. It took months for me to come back from this illness. Although physically I'm very robust, I felt like a stick figure for a long time after this experience. The energy I had absorbed into every cell of my being remained dormant as I recovered from my illness.

It was 1989, and I was still the daycare mom on the block, but I knew from deep within myself that something profound had changed in the essential energy of the planet. Once again my sight and imagination became very active in my life. I became aware of the divine female form of light within my field. There were also luminous beings of golden light present. Perhaps you could call them the angels of this knowledge. There were three beings in particular who stood by my left side. I lovingly thought of them as the three wise guys. The essence of their collective being held an energy pattern that is now the logo of the EMF Balancing Technique® work.

As I continued to care for the children in my charge, I began to use the information from these angels to produce a new kind of energy work. I gave sessions using the additional energy patterns as they had been shown me. It was like tracing crop circle patterns through the human energy field. I was instructed to always follow the patterns as they were given, and the results would vary according to each person's need, or intent. There were occasional physical healings, but these I viewed as side effects. The main focus of this new method, now known as the EMF Balancing Technique®, was to activate and balance the Universal Calibration Lattice.

At the same time, my life and my surroundings began to change dramatically. I started to keep my home neat and clean because the flow of clients kept increasing as word spread of the effectiveness of the work. People reported feeling "different" and "lighter," and they noticed that their lives were more fulfilling. This did not come easily, for there was always more work for each individual to do on their own, but the clients found they had more energy and a stronger will and guidance to follow through on their Soul's next step. By staying consistent and working with one person at a time, the reputation of the work grew.

Through a series of unusual coincidences, a complimentary article was written in the local newspaper about the EMF work. This resulted in my first step into the public arena. I was invited to teach at local adult education programs, and eventually new-age stores, whole-health expos, and mainstream businesses. This was not an easy step for me to take - only one year before the article appeared, I had been living like a hermit for several years. I was still very awkward in social situations and not comfortable with people.

I took the step almost unconsciously; simply following my passion and love for God/Goddess. I really never noticed how much I was changing. Almost in spite of myself, I learned to speak and teach about the Universal Calibration Lattice and the EMF Balancing Technique. These teachings come from my soul like songs and poems flow from others. I was invited to speak on some local radio and TV programs. While it was not always easy, I reached a point where I realized I wanted the process to continue. I started to travel, first throughout New England and then to a few different parts of the country. After a few years, I realized this work was growing into a nationwide business.

While working with the UCL within others, my own body and energy field became stronger, more capable of "holding the full charge of my own being." I now had a place for all that universal energy to circulate, I realized I could hold my own power, and my partnership with God/Goddess came alive! For the first time, I started to feel at home right here on planet Earth.

ONE PLUS ONE EQUALS INFINITY

The intense emotions of fear, pain, and sorrow are powerful teachers. After 23 years of marriage, my first husband, David, and I divorced. We had been walking two different paths for a long time, and we just grew very far apart. I was grateful for the years we had together, our two wonderful daughters, and his tolerance for my many years of spiritual searching. As the marriage neared an end, I overheard one of David's coworkers comment, "Now she will have to get a real job!" My whole world as I knew it had ended and I could not foresee what was to come, but I knew what my real job was, and it had everything to do with my soul's growth. Like everyone else I had some hard lessons to learn.

I left a safe and beautiful home and moved to the more uncertain side of town, all in the name of freedom. The experience made me strong and taught me how to build a life and career one step at a time. I rented a large, old home with an office and parking lot. I was very protective of my two daughters and was committed to remain a stay-at-home mom. I worried about having enough money to pay my bills if I were out of work for a month. I was really on my own, or so I thought.

I had forgotten about my unlimited partner, the one I was so passionate about. The Universal One knows us all, and I had indeed forged a partnership. A wonderful woman called me a day after I started to worry about finances. She told me she had five people who wanted to learn the work and since I just moved, I could teach the class in her home! Instead of spending the money I earned in that class on the new things I wanted for my home, I gratefully put it in the bank. I started to learn to respect the energy of money. Life was challenging and exciting all at once. My private practice continued to grow. I was teaching locally and continued to travel when it was appropriate for my little family. I was able to support us all with my private practice and teaching, and I continued to develop the EMF Balancing Technique®. I dated for a while and had some wild adventures, but no special relationship. Raising my children and doing my work fulfilled me, and I was at peace with being single. I didn't need anyone else to feel complete; I was completing myself. Sometimes, I did muse a little on whether true love really existed on this planet and if it did what would it be like to experience that.

Illustration 1.3 *"Fusion"*

As synchronicity would have it, I was teaching an "Introduction to Energy" class at a local adult education program. There were almost 30 people enrolled and I was amazed to see so many men in the room. Stephen Dubro walked into my classroom and took a seat among the other students. I noticed him right away, and had to keep reminding myself that I was there to do my job, and began to teach the class. A little while later, as I walked around the room to observe my students' energies, I was standing at Stephen's back when he turned around to look at me. I felt a rush of energy go through my whole being, and like a young schoolgirl, I felt flustered. He seemed so familiar. I managed to finish teaching the evening's lesson. He came up to talk with me after class, and we discovered that we knew many of the same people and had lived in neighboring towns for a while during childhood. I could write a romance novel about our relationship and how it grew but I promised my husband I would spare him that embarrassment! Here is the essence of who we are as a couple: Take one human being who knows that he is "Soul becoming," add another human being who also knows herself that way, mix in the growing understanding and love of Creator within, and blend together in the energy of love. The result is infinite possibility!

Eventually, and without hesitation, we married, and we have grown together ever since. I soon realized that Stephen strongly resembled my dark haired warrior, the one who accompanies, guides, and protects me whenever I meet with light beings in other dimensional realities. On this plane, he is the other half of this body of work, providing the vital energies of integrity and stability. The information for Phases III and IV of the EMF Balancing Technique® did not manifest until Stephen and I met and began working as partners. Together, we have promised to be good stewards of the work. He is here to make sure of that, encouraging me to fulfill my potential and providing an ongoing assessment of the quality and integrity of the work as it evolves. We complement each other; in our partnership we feel the enormous potential of what it means to be one plus one equals infinity. We are best friends and have the greatest respect for each other. And, of course, we are husband and wife, in what is a deliciously spiritual marriage.

A LITTLE HELP FROM OUR FRIENDS

After my marriage to Stephen, I continued my private EMF practice. When we met I was operating primarily at survival level, working six and seven days a week. I reasoned that I was in service to my fellow humans, so it was important to always be on call. I was really ready to learn that being in service did not mean that I no longer counted. I was burning out, and even with all my good intentions, I was not living in balance.

Under Stephen's guidance, I rearranged my schedule. Our children required our attention to grow and so did our work. I limited my session work to four days a week and spent the other days tending to the development of our company. We legally incorporated to send a message to the world that even though we are in service, we are also a business. This is our spiritual path, and we walk it together. We developed new skills as we learned to follow the lead of our unlimited partner. Stephen always reminded me that it was not whether we were successful; it was whether or not we gave our best effort. If we gave our best effort and failed, then so be it. We became acquainted with the computer, developed our own advertising, set up training structures for the practitioners and eventually the teachers program. We created the first EMF manuals. All the time we were learning how to cooperate with one another and be a family. (Please note that there is no mention that this was easy!)

Interesting opportunities continued to present themselves and we embraced many of them, learning a great deal along the way. One exciting event came in the summer of 1995. Through a very special friend of ours, Sonalysts, a respected Connecticut-based research and development firm, approached Stephen and me. The producers of C. Everett Koop's video health series, Sonalysts specialized in government contracts. They wanted to collaborate with us to apply for a NASA grant to study the effects of the EMF Balancing Technique®. Our part of the experiment was to provide the training and exercises that we use with our students. The study was "to test the effect of electromagnetic field energy awareness on improving team performance and strengthening the human health maintenance process." In other words, we were to stimulate collective consciousness by integrating spirit and biology! We learned the timing wasn't right then, and were disappointed when Sonalysts did not get the NASA grant. But the experience of compiling the formal 23-page proposal detailing the experiment in conjunction with Navy scientists was such an encouragement from the Universe!

I continued to speak at many whole health expos. Many of those who attended asked if I knew about the Kryon writings of Lee Carroll. When I answered no, the response I usually heard was, "You're saying a lot of the same things he is." I felt a little curious about these writings, but in the realm of curiosity is where it stayed. I had lost interest in books because I was at a stage in my development where I did not want to read any more. I wanted to do and to be, and so I continued on my path of action.

In spring, within three days, I received three copies of the first Kryon book, *The End Times,* from three different sources. All three books were delivered to my front door. Anything that happens in sets of three tends to get my attention, so I thought this was very interesting. Perhaps because it was "channeled," I resisted reading the book, and still wanted time to think about it. Even though much of the channeled information I had been exposed to until that time had been inspiring, I felt that these works sometimes lacked tangible, helpful, practical information. I craved real substance—usable, practical tools and information for our world as it is.

My husband Stephen however, did not ignore the coincidence and started to read the book, deeply touched by its energy and information. He knew it was important material so he started to read parts of the book to me. I was happy to hear some of the information and was very impressed with the clarity of what I heard. However, I still did not pick up the book for myself. One day, Stephen was having a phone conversation with a representative of an agent for a New Age trade magazine. They were discussing the Kryon material in regard to the EMF work. The representative felt it was necessary for us to speak with Lee and gave Stephen his telephone number. Another coincidence.

"This is for you," Stephen said, putting the phone number in my hand. Through synchronicity, I had been experiencing the opportunity to speak with some outstanding leaders in the spiritual field. Here was chance to connect with and say hello to another human being from whom I could learn. Out of respect to Lee Carroll, I knew I should read some of his book before I called. I finally picked the book up and held it in my own hands and planned to do a quick read; instead I read every word! I was elated, I cried, and laughed as I read the words that rang true so deeply within me.

Lee's book provided me with an explanation for what I had experienced in my life and work. I knew something powerful on a very large scale had happened in 1989. This was the year that the UCL became accessible. There are many contributing factors to consider when viewing these kinds of events, and we will look at these later in this book. Specific to this work, the arrival of Kryon into the collective consciousness in 1989 was a key factor in the evolution of the EMF Balancing Technique®, as well as to human evolution in general. During the previous seven years of private practice, facilitating thousands of sessions, I had a front row seat to witness this evolution within our energy anatomy.

When I called and spoke with Lee there was an immediate kinship - it was like talking with an old friend. In the fall of that year in New Hampshire, Stephen and I met Lee, his spiritual partner Jan Tober, and Kryon. In February 1997, we formally became co-workers. Together in sacred partnership we work and travel throughout the world.

The reality of the Universal Calibration Lattice rings true for people around the world. Many people will say they have been seeing parts of a lattice-like structure. In our training seminars, the response to the information regarding the UCL is always very favorable. People are recognizing a part of themselves and are eager to learn how to work with it. When I teach, I watch the fibers of energy through the each person's field respond, making each class unique and interesting. Even when I teach and my words are being translated, I sometimes notice energetic movement before the participants understand the words! There truly is another language.

The EMF Balancing Technique® is the energy procedure specifically designed to work with the Universal Calibration Lattice. The seeds of this work are well planted all over the planet. At the time of this writing, there are practitioners and teachers of the technique in 33 countries throughout the world. The work continues to grow because it is effective in people lives, and this good news travels fast!

AHNYA

One day Stephen and I were discussing my experiences with the female form of light. We wondered if she was an angel. Was she a part of my own being? To me she is a brilliant friend who is always there in a posture of support. We talked about the reality of these beings of light with whom I feel so comfortable. Almost in passing, Stephen wondered aloud, "Do you think she has a name?" The next thing I knew, I sat up straight, my voice deepened and out came the name: Ahnya! She proceeded to speak with both of us for over 30 minutes. Her presence was nurturing and reassuring.

Illustration 1.4 *"Awakening"*

For now, this is my understanding. I have experienced Ahnya as a truly divine feminine energy. She is an aspect of a consciousness that is a genderless, unified whole, but for the sake of convenience I will describe this great being as She. She is a teacher of teachers, part of an entourage, complementing Kryon's planetary changes, and she is a partner in the development of the EMF work. Her focus is on the human-to-human connection and the honor and respect we show each other in this reality. She likes to call me Phoenix and she reminds me to see the Phoenix in others. We all are consumed in the fire of life and one way or another we do rise again. Ahnya has much to say about the Phoenix events of our lives and those teachings will be part of the next level of this work. Whenever I teach, she is present. I am clearly aware that I am the human being doing the work. I am in and out of channel because that is how I prefer it at this time. She is present to offer support whenever and wherever an EMF Balancing teacher presents the work. She is also present whenever an EMF practitioner performs a session. I am still developing an understanding of "us," because I sometimes feel that Ahnya and I are really one. No matter what the reality, I feel a sacred love for her and honor the responsibility of sharing these teachings with my fellow humans.

At one time in my life I was so frightened of people I would rarely leave home. Now we travel all over the world. Our schedule is very demanding and we may teach for up to seven weeks in one trip. Remember how I wanted to remember God? When I teach, I see the face of God/Goddess in everyone!

"It is good to be a seeker ... but sooner or later, you have to be a finder."

Richard Bach, Jonathan Livingston Seagull

CHAPTER TWO

TOWARDS A NEW PARADIGM

Mind, Matter, & Intentionality

As far as the laws of mathematics refer to reality, they are not certain.
And as far as they are certain, They do not refer to reality.

Albert Einstein

Intelligence is present at every point in space,
And can be acted upon through the power of thought.

Nikola Tesla, The Wall of Light

Each one of us is a reflection of the *Infinite*. How then, do we begin to define the structure of what we would call the human dynamic--- the structure and essence of the human being?

As human beings, each one of us is a part of the whole that we outwardly perceive as the Universe. Yet, constraints and limitations to our conventional perceptual systems actually mislead us to believe that we are separate. Not only do we perceive ourselves as separate from other human beings, but we also see ourselves as separate and distinct from all sentient life forms. As beings within a physical tangible reality, we feel that life's experience is a series of linear events. We have entrapped ourselves within the notion that space and time are the only coordinates within which we can define our existence. However, were it not for this optical illusion created by space and time, we might not be able to maintain a sense of self *(identity)* in a changing world.

This chapter, and indeed, all elements of this book, point towards a new Paradigm in Science. Within this new Paradigm the concept of *multi-dimensionality* takes a predominant role in beginning to explain apparent phenomena that we observe in our three dimensional world. The various scientific theories of our discussion in this and later chapters are also foundations that will help the reader better understand the principles that underlie the *EMF Balancing Technique®*.

We adopt the view that we, as human beings, are not only multi-dimensional beings, but that we actively _function_ as multi-dimensional beings in all our interactions, in particular, those pertaining to our essence as electromagnetic beings.

From this higher level perspective, we can open new vistas and possibilities in painting an expanding picture of reality. In painting this picture we contribute to a paradigm _shift_, i.e., a dramatic change in the way we view our world. We collectively create the _new_ Paradigm. In this new Paradigm, the bizarre, the mysterious, the paranormal, and the unsolvable become solvable. Here we have introduced major new concepts, central to our understanding of the material that follows. In the sections that follow, we will clarify and expand our definitions of the terms _Paradigm_ and _multi-dimensionality_.

A PARADIGM AS MODEL OF REALITY

Generally, the concept of Paradigm relates to a specific image, or model, of reality that prevails in Science, or a specific branch of Science. This image, or model, of reality, once established, carries with it certain patterns of perceiving, analyzing, and validating phenomena within the context of the _picture_ that is painted of reality. Paradigms exist not only in the field of Science, but in all aspects of our perception of our environment. Plausible explanations of phenomena that are perceived within reality become limited to the constraints imposed by the Paradigm itself. For example, during that time in earth's history where Science and religion contended that the earth was the center of the universe, it was believed that all objects in the heavens maintained certain orbits or movements relative to the earth remaining still.

To ensure that observations and beliefs conformed to the accepted paradigm of that time, i.e., the image that the earth was the center of the universe, very elaborate and colorful representations of the heavenly body movements were devised. Within the context of the existing paradigm of the time, these representations provided a _plausible_ explanation of observed phenomena. Of course, that paradigm was later shown to be incorrect. A major shift occurred in Science, and a new paradigm was born with the advent of Copernican astronomy in the sixteenth century.

A CALL FOR A SCIENCE OF CONSCIOUSNESS

Other instances of major shifts taking place in Science are seen with the advent of Einstein's theories of Relativity and advances in the theories of Quantum Physics. These theories have transformed forever, our perceptions of a purely mechanistic world...a world in which space and time are viewed as absolutes, and the view that everything can be explained on the basis of simple mechanical rules of behavior.

Not only are we unable to describe the quantum world by mechanical rules, but physicists now view the quantum world as one in which Consciousness participates and plays an active role in shaping our reality! *Now the challenge of defining the interactive role between Matter, Intent, and Consciousness stands before us!* Matter and Consciousness cannot be separated. Moreover, Consciousness interacts and influences the virtual realm of electromagnetic fields. Our ultimate challenge is to develop a Science of *inter-dimensional* physics that unifies Consciousness in the grand equation!

THE QUANTUM IS OUT OF THIS WORLD

From observations of the quantum world, it is now apparent that the reality of elementary particles has no respect for clocking time the way we do. In fact, within the quantum world of elementary particles a state of non-time and non-space is an accurate description of that virtual (*unseen*) reality.

Imagine that an elementary particle such as the electron is able to simultaneously share its existence with its own past, and its own future! We perceive that electron in our reality for only a fraction of its *time*, as it dances in and out of different time frames simultaneously. In doing so, the electron carries information of all its *time* experience --past and future-- within its very essence.

Keeping an appointment in this world would be a challenge! The street corner of your appointment could appear to be everywhere at once. All events would carry the property of connectivity, no matter what the extent of physical separation. This is that unusual property called *non-locality*. Events in the quantum world are instantly connected, even if they occur at separate ends of the universe! *What is this unseen hidden reality... this web or lattice that unifies and interconnects everything?*

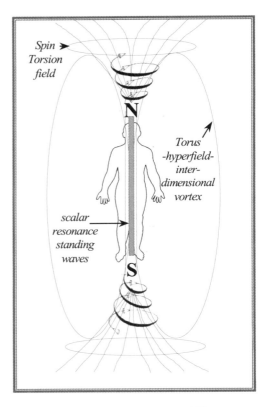

Figure 2.1 **Body Hyperfields**. *The physical body is surrounded by hyperfields-fields in higher dimensional space. The torus, an interdimensional vortex, is multi-layered like the skins of an onion. These energy fields carry the hyperspatial properties of torsion fields. Throughout the entire structures there is a flow, or flux, of energy. Bearden has calculated that the physical system is in constant open energy exchange with the vacuum (Cosmic Sea). The magnitude of this energy exchange is equivalent to the output of <u>one million</u> 1,000-megawatt power-generating stations! This is all 'free energy'[1].*

SOCIAL ETIQUETTE

Gone are the days when elementary particles are viewed as simple inanimate objects! Elementary particles have been observed to exhibit organic intelligence. Individually, and acting collectively within systems, these particles have shown us that they actually have an awareness of their outside environment. As we watched them, groupings of electrons have demonstrated that their *coordinated* movements can be influenced by information from the outside world. These particles are literally *in-formed* [3].These particles can tune-in, or resonate, and respond to received information- information that we are now understanding as being transferred through the vehicle of form!

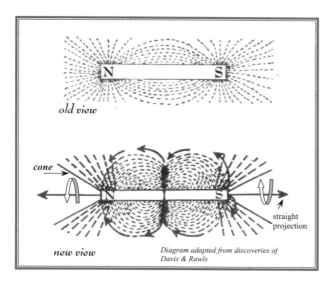

Figure 2.2 **Old & New View Of Magnetism.**
In the old view of magnetism, lines of force transmit from South to North pole-or in an alternate view, from North to South pole [2]. Davis & Rawls determined a new view of magnetism. Energy moves in both directions at the same time. The 'cables of forces' as defined by Davis & Rawls express a duality-each spins in an opposite direction as it leaves the pole travelling to the other. The pattern formed is a figure 8 loop! See Chapter Note #48.

We have witnessed these particles dance collectively in step- not missing a beat, not stepping on anyone's toes- as if following the conductor of a polished symphony orchestra! Visualize a region of organized influence that we call the *electromagnetic field.* Within this region you are witnessing a veritable light show. The photon of light, known by physicists to be the *messenger* of the electromagnetic field, cascades about delivering and exchanging information with electrons within the field. Physicists call light a reflection of the 5th dimension, because light originates from 'higher' dimensional space [5].

The human body emits photons- biophotons-from within the DNA! The more highly charged-up the electromagnetic field, the more active is this exchange of information! It is the information derived from our *evolving electromagnetic field structures* that provides us with our expanding awareness. Of course, it is the electromagnetic field that provides the organization-- the structure and form-- of the substance that we call matter. Without the electromagnetic field, there would be no materialization or manifestation of 'solid' objects. *Imagine that we will ultimately understand that light carries the patterns imprinted by Consciousness!*

Imagine that through the hyperfield structure of the multi-dimensional entity we call light, *we find that light is connected to the mind field of the human being!*

ROCK-LIKE WITH FEELING

But the display of intelligence is not all. Physicists are now modeling elementary particles as having *feeling*. These particles are being considered to have emotional, mental, and etheric aspects as part of their nature! As we observed from our earlier discussion, when inconsistencies or anomalies become unsolvable within a certain paradigm, eventually we are directed to alter the way we think, evaluate, perceive, and measure our assumptions of our reality.

As we integrate new knowledge and awareness into our expanding view of reality, we must ultimately transform the older theories that no longer serve us. Such older theories serve to confine us with unsolvable problems. We then enter into a new paradigm that allows us to look at these problems with a new perspective, one in which the unsolvable problems of the old paradigm become solvable. However, we have been shown through the work of Thomas Kuhn, that the old paradigms of Science are only overthrown with great difficulty. The introduction of a new paradigm is then associated with a "revolution" in Science. Perhaps some of the views presented here will find themselves as part of this new revolution that is already taking place in Science and in our understanding of reality.

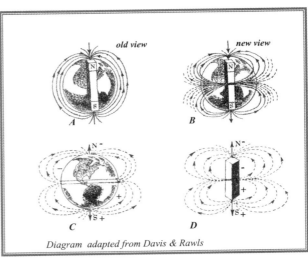

Diagram adapted from Davis & Rawls

Figure 2.3 **New View of Earth Magnetism.** *The old concept of the earth's magnetism (A) shows magnetic lines of force leaving the South pole and entering the North pole. In the new discoveries of Davis & Rawls, the earth's magnetic field (B) is similar to that of a bar magnet (D). Note the figure 8 loop pattern of the two distinct spiraling energies, as well as the opposite electrical polarities resulting from the flow. Both magnetic and electric properties exist simultaneously. In Figure C, Davis & Rawls present the magnetic measurement findings from space recordings and probes that confirm the pattern and polarity of earth's magnetic phenomena [4]. We find identical patterns within the human energy field. The principles of magnetism are universal.*

MULTI-DIMENSIONALITY IS MULTI-FACETED

The meaning of the term *multi-dimensional* is somewhat more of a challenge to define. From different perspectives, it carries different meanings. For example, the term is used in context to describe the possible existence of living multiple lives simultaneously, within different and separate space-time coordinate systems.

This is to say that if we view time- all of the past, present and future- as existing all at the same time, then our life experiences are all taking place in parallel realities at the same time. The separation of these lives is taking place only within our concept of time and our limits of conscious awareness. Separate 'life' experiences remain somehow connected through a common thread that links and connects us to the central core of our essence- that of a spiritual being.

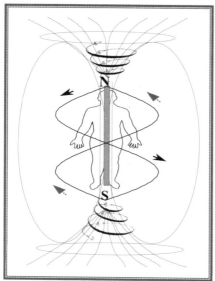

Figure 2.4 **Dual Flow.** *A major aspect of the human energy anatomy is that of human magnetism. According to the laws of magnetism discovered by Davis & Rawls, the primary energy flows are in two directions. These form the figure 8 loop pattern. Initiating flow in this circuit creates another "free energy generator". Note that this pattern establishes a resonance with the earth, as well as each biological cell! (See Chapter Notes #59).*

The notion that dimensions represent "layers" is a rather linear one. Consider, for example, a space in which you are able to tune into different radio stations on the "air waves". Each radio broadcast is found within the same "space". Turn the dial of the radio tuner, and you can select a different station. Add more radio broadcasting stations, and the signals simply get added to the existing space.

Theoretically, you could add a virtually infinite number of radio station broadcasts, and these would all occupy the same "space". Extend the tuning capacity of your radio set, and you could increase the dynamic range of your reception to include more "stations". Notice how the radio broadcast signals just pile up unto each other in "space". A characteristic of hyperspace is the ability to contain more than one thing in the same "space". Therefore, radio broadcast "space" is *hyperspace*! The radio signals are all in the same place, but they are separated by the characteristics of frequency, phase, or amplitude. Each differing characteristic is a new "dimension" for the existence of a vibrating pattern. Each signal requires specific tuning circuitry. The human senses function within limited vibratory ranges.

The only way to access the "dimension" is with the appropriate tuner. A limited tuner is totally unaware of the existence of other "dimension" around it, even when fully immersed within the same hyperspace. Human evolution is characterized by 'discovering' the existence of 'new' dimensions and tunable circuits within our energy dynamics.

For example, audible sound occurs within the approximate range of 20 Hz to 20 kHz (20 to 20,000 Hertz or "vibrations per second"). Sight occurs within the visible wavelengths of light. These tuning systems possess limitations, yet reality is much more than what is registered by the physical senses. In a sense, we could say that the physical senses limit our cognizance of the myriad of dimensions around us.These dimensions exist as elements of creation and are accessible from within our own multi-dimensional configuration. Expanding awareness encompasses the realization that we can consciously alter our internal architectural dynamics. In doing so, we expand our angular view outward to encompass a greater slice of this creation.

For example, it is not possible to see around corners, but from a viewpoint in hyperspace, we can transcend this limitation.

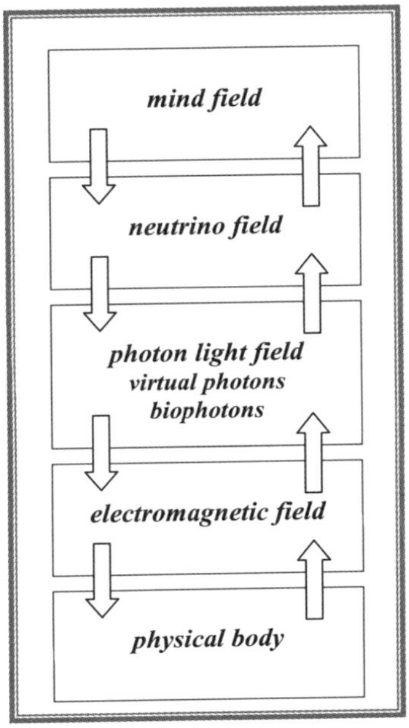

A DIMENSIONAL HIERARCHY OF INFLUENCE

However, the notion of multi-dimensionality that we wish to expand upon, relates to the existence of a *hierarchy of influence* that exists within the fabric or structure of reality. Reality is a broad term that includes both the universe that we perceive, and that which we do not perceive (*virtual reality*).

This hierarchy is structured as if there were a series of "layers", except that successively refined states of the layering process are not actually found on top (like a sandwich), but actually *within* courser layers of that reality. Imagine an onion with each of its layers fitting somehow *inside* the other. This is the idea of *nesting* or *embedding*. Unique layered states we refer to as *dimensions*. An interconnection exists forming threads that permeate the separate states, creating the cohesion that is characteristic of the wholeness.

Dimensional states are characterized by distinct properties- unique states of invisible vibrations. Although dimensions may simply differ by vibration or frequency, typically the distinctions are more complex. At the same time, the laws or rules that govern the characteristics or phenomena within a specific dimension, also vary according to the unique patterns of geometry that govern that specific aspect of reality.

Figure 2.5 **Life Consciousness Loop**. *The life-consciousness loop, as described by Bearden (Excalibur Briefing), connects the mind field to the physical body (tuner). The intermediary components of the loop are the neutrino field, photon/ bio-photon and electromagnetic fields. According to Bearden, the substructure of the loop can be engineered, patterned or structured in both directions.*

It is the unique expression of these patterns that underlie and differentiate possible experience that we may encounter as we journey beyond our familiar universe into these realms!

In our physical world, an example of layering is seen within the biological system itself: a biological organ consists of a collection of cells, cells are formed from a collection of molecules, molecules consists of grouping of atoms, and atoms consists of elementary particles. So then we ask, what do elementary particles consists of?

ENTER HYPERSPACE

Entering the virtual world takes us into *hyperspace* or the *vacuum* (to use terms coined by physicists) or the *Cosmic Lattice* (a term familiar to some readers). The vacuum is not empty; rather it is full... considered by physicists as a *plenum* of energy [47]. Although a region of non-time and non-space, the vacuum is the background fabric from which matter, time, and space emerge as dimensional properties. These properties give us a linear view of our reality. We continue the concept of layering, but within the virtual (*unseen*) world.

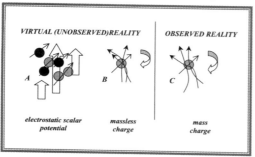

Figure 2.6 **Concept of Charge.** *Both particles of mass, and those without mass (massless) can possess charge- charge defined in the electric sense. The charged particle is visualized as a spherical spinning entity. The spin traps virtual particles-spin also traps light. For both mass & massless charge there is an ongoing flow or flux of virtual particles on and off the spinning sphere. (See Chapter Note #49)*

Elementary particles consist of further smaller illusive particles...each originating from their own respective layer or dimension of existence, far removed from of own. Yet as these particles or *energies* 'descend' into our existence that carry with them the knowledge of their remote homeland! *Imagine a virtual level of reality containing its own nested or embedded reality.* Imagine that light interacts with elementary particles and in doing so a little bit of *time* is taken away, and a little bit of *time* is added. This interaction of light and matter contributes to our linear perspective. Light consists of a multi-dimensional essence.

DEFINING THE LAWS OF NATURE

Physicists seek to understand the *laws* of nature. Contemporary theories are attempting to unify our understanding of how the known forces that we have discovered interrelate. The pursuit of finding a unifying theory stems from the belief that nature unfolds in a harmonious, elegant fashion. [We speak of gravity, electromagnetism, the strong and weak nuclear forces...how are these connected?] Physicists ask the questions "*is there a common origin or identity for these forces?*"...

"how do these forces become differentiated from a common origin?"

Plausible answers to these questions are found in modern day *string theory*. We learn that at some fundamental level of origin, a highly energetic entity called a *string*, provides the building block of matter. The string is indivisible. *Strings* combine to form specific and varied patterns of resonant vibration.

PARTICLE AS VIBRATING RESONANT STRINGS

A subatomic particle is simply the physical observable expression of one unique resonant vibration- an energy wave pattern in standing resonance. Matter can be understood as scalar wave resonance. The geometry of the patterns and the resonance of the vibration are what determine the nature, quality, and properties that manifests within our universe. All of physical reality can be modeled as groupings of strings, i.e., strings interconnected with strings at

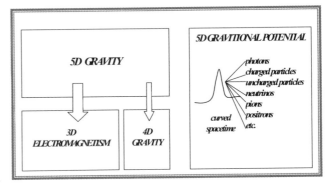

Figure 2.7 **Origin of Electromagnetism.** *According to 11D Kaluza-Klein theory, electromagnetism and gravity are unified in 5 dimensional spacetime-where 5D spacetime consist of a four space with one time. The 5D-gravity field is the fundamental source of producing both electromagnetism and the ordinary 4D gravity that we experience. (See Chapter Note #50.)*

every scale of observation. Note how DNA looks like many strings tied together in a series.

The grand unification of *string theory* takes place in a space of 10 dimensions. Superstring theory considers 26 dimensions. From here, the known laws of our universe take on an initial unified point of definition [6]. Although a 26 dimensional space is quite a complex notion for all of us to imagine, it is, paradoxically, from such a place that the laws of nature are simpler to define and explain. Mathematics can take us into an 11 or a 26 dimensional space, where the human intellect cannot readily follow. What can such theory tell us about the structure of reality? Perhaps our most sophisticated theory will not be complete until we factor and integrate Consciousness into the equation!

ADVANTAGE OF VIEWPOINT

Physicist Michio Kaku, author of *Hyperspace [A Scientific Odyssey Through Parallel Universes, Time Warps, and the 10th Dimension]* assures us that higher dimensional space is actually quite "simple and geometric". Perhaps so, and perhaps if we were not such masters at complicating our lives we could also see such space as uncomplicated!

The key to understanding higher dimensional space (never mind higher dimensional physics and mathematics) is to realize that "higher space" places us at a vantage point that provides us with a global, universal, or holistic perspective. From this vantage point the distinction between the observer and the observed disappears.

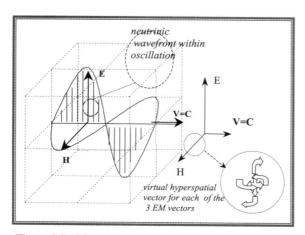

Figure 2.8 **Nature of Light (photon).** *In this diagram we expand on the nature of a photon (light). Each vector is not a simple entity. What lies beyond? Light is a bridge to higher dimensional space- and the bridge to the mind field of consciousness [7]. The cells of the human body communicate through the emission & absorption of bio-photons. DNA is a receiver, transmitter, translator, & storage center of photonic energy. Biophotons are emitted from the human hands! In William Tiller's view, light is a composite of electromagnetic radiation (in physical space), magnetoelectric radiation (in etheric space), and deltron radiation (from higher subtle realm). The photon exist beyond space-time. Arthur Young described the photon as consciousness itself! (See Chapter Note #51.)*

You become both the observer and the observed! From higher space one appreciates the grand viewpoint-the rhyme and reason of this experience we call life on earth in the 21st century. Is our grand purpose to remember and reconnect to our own individual multi-dimensional essence?

An analogy to vantage viewpoint is presented in the following. Consider the manner in which we may view a picture. In lower space you would be aware of the small details- you would view a piece of the picture. Whereas, from higher space you would view the whole image. The brain exhibits similar properties to this analogy. The brain can focus on the details (a lower space ability), or it can view the entire picture (a higher space, hyperspatial, multi-dimensional capability). Neither aspect is more desirable than the other. The key to optimum brain function is that both aspects function in harmony in order that we can consciously experience our greater potential. *What we observe as electromagnetic activity of the brain (such as the activity measured by an EEG, Electroencephalograph machine) is but a ripple and reflection of unseen higher-space brain function!* Electromagnetism is a reflection of activity in the 5th dimension. This unseen activity cannot be measured and quantified through conventional means.

CHANGE INITIATED IN HIGHER SPACE

From higher dimensional space we could observe how changes within the myriad of variables accessible there, result in change in lower dimensional reality. In fact we would understand that we need to access higher space in order to cause change of any kind in our reality system- one defined by 4 dimensions. Newton's apple can be defined by the geometry of three spatial dimensions. But indeed, an apple requires more than geometry in order to describe its essence. The apple possesses the additional qualities and properties of weight, fragrance, texture, color and hue, moisture content, etc. Each of these qualities adds 'dimension' to our description of the apple.

Let us define one specific individual apple and call this one *apple*. Let us also define one unique individual fragrance and call it *fragrance*. Suppose we would wish to alter the fragrance of this apple. Could we alter the innate quality of *fragrance* from our 3 dimensional space? Evidently... not. To affect this property, we must access some 'higher-space'. In this space, the individual design parameter called *fragrance* could be altered and then re-integrated into the whole energetic pattern called *apple*. It is the whole energetic pattern that expresses in our space, and it is the *wholeness* that gives it *unique identity*. In the realm of possibilities, *fragrance* takes on limitless possibilities. *Apple* is the expression of one unique combination, or wholeness, of all the ingredients that constitute its inner nature. Change any one of its internal ingredients, and to you it may continue to appear the same. However in its *wholeness*, it is different.

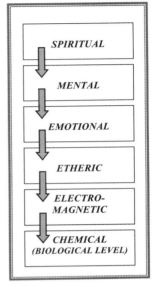

Figure 2.9 **Influence of Higher Levels of Reality.** *From William Tiller's perspective, imbalances must be corrected from an ordered hierarchy of influence. The subtle energy fields are necessary to effect change at the electromagnetic level. (See Chapter Notes #58)*

CITIZENS OF HYPERSPACE, OR RESIDENCE ABROAD

As multi-dimensional beings, there are elements of our essence that reside in this "higher space". These elements provide the guiding mechanisms that assist in altering our lives. As physical human beings we are equipped with electromagnetic access tools to higher space- *hyperspace*. In accessing these tools we more consciously function as multi-dimensional beings shaping our reality. This chapter will discuss aspects of our hyperspatial nature. *We have innate hyperspatial abilities.* These functions all occur typically within our unconscious awareness. *Intent* connects us consciously to our hyperspatial mechanisms.

Intent creates a ripple in time and space though which movement takes place. In stimulating the opening of the vortex of creation, Intent serves to guide and direct energies across inter-dimensional portals. Holding the Intent creates the tidal wave that alters space-time sending new events into the reality of our lives.

CONSCIOUSNESS IS MY PILOT

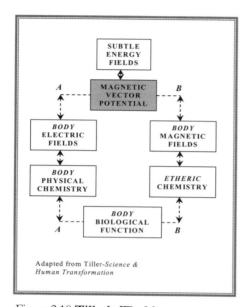

Figure 2.10 **Tiller's Working Hypothesis.** *William Tiller has formulated a model through an equation through which he encourages humanity to move forward with a new perspective[9]. This model connects the subtle energy fields to the human body's biological processes. Tiller sees the magnetic vector potential as the bridge between the subtle and physical realms. The human dynamic, understood from this perspective, becomes one in which we discover that we can exercise the greatest influence to physical biological function through the 'manipulation' of the subtle structures.(See Chapter Notes #55)*

Navigating through the inter-connected geometries within higher space becomes an *inter-dimensional* process. Imagine that distinct geometries or geometric patterns define the separate and distinct "layers" of our notion of complex space.

The key to connecting distinct dimensional elements is to find or establish the links, roadways, circuits, or portals that naturally link the geometries in harmony- in resonance. Consciousness navigates and permeates these geometric layers of all existence.

These roadways are the natural frequencies, life frequencies, magic windows, inter-dimensional nodal points, Einstein-Rosen bridge/wormholes, or geometric connectors. We understand the EMF Balancing Technique® as an inter-dimensional process creating integration within the geometric patterns across the full range of our multi-dimensional nature! An inter-dimensional process allows for the transfer or crossover of energy patterns between dimensions. These energy patterns connected to Spirit contain the element of mutability required within the physical realm of the human vibration. It is these patterns that create change and transformation! An evolutionary tool is one that stimulates personal growth and transformation.

INTERACTIONS ARE HIGHER SPACE CONCEPTS

To understand our interactions with others, as electromagnetic beings, we must direct our attention to hyperspace. We also require a basic conceptual language. Why? *Electromagnetic phenomena and human magnetism originate in higher space.* Electromagnetism, like light, is a ripple or vibration of the 5th dimension, connected with the warping of the geometry of higher space [5]. Today's physics is beginning to relate to this. Interactive phenomena take place through higher space. It is within the higher dimensions that *alchemy* takes place between Spirit and the myriad of co-operative elements at play to create nature *(All That Is)*, and change our lives.

LOOKING UP INTO SPACE

Consider the perspective that an aquatic life form may have from the confines of its dimension of *water*. This creature looks upward from the ocean depths to observe waves and ripples on the surface of its world called *ocean*. Perhaps our sea creature is curious and wonders what is the cause or origin of the waves and ripples that skim the surface of its world. If our aquatic friend is particularly astute, it may have already deduced that the source of the ripples is not from within its dimension, but from the one beyond called *air*.

But why is it that sometimes the waves are tumultuous, and at other times they may be calm? Why, it may wonder, is the surface of my world so chaotic, so disordered? {Have we considered how we inhabit this bi-dimensional planet- one with life forms so distinct and adapted to life experiences in two such differentiated physical states/dimensions: *air* and *water.* Yet consider how water contains the dimension of air (aquatic life extracts oxygen from the water), and how air contains the dimension of water (water vapor). *The ability of one dimension to contain another is a property of hyperspace.*}

Without a periscope our aquatic inhabitant is unable to peer into its neighboring dimension. If it did however, it still would not 'see' the cause of the waves rippling across the borders of these worlds. Even we do not 'see' the wind. We observe the effects of the wind. Perhaps through the periscope one of our fishy friends might catch the glimpse of a sailboat with sails outstretched, being propelled across the ocean by the force of the wind. From this observation, the understanding may develop that it is this wind, also, that causes the wave action on the water surface. But what *causes* the wind? We may say that the wind is caused by differential pressures that develop over the earth's surface (high's and low's). Yet what is the *cause* of these differential pressures? As we delve deeper and deeper into this line of questioning in pursuit of an ultimate cause, we discover a hierarchy of causative factors. This hierarchy can be equated to being layered, one within the other like an onion, or like the dimensions of space-- each distinct dimension allowing for the manifestation of distinct elements of *action* within the chain of these causative factors.

CAUSE ORIGINATES FROM ABOVE

Now, continuing with our analogy, we will say that what happens in a higher dimension will affect causative elements or action in that dimension below it.

For example:

1. Altering the temperature on the earth's surface may result in altered differential pressures;

2. Increasing the differential pressures (high's and low's) results in greater wind strength and velocity; and

3. Increasing the wind velocity or intensity, results in greater wave high.

In the meanwhile, our inquisitive dweller of the water world has just experienced an evolutionary leap of consciousness. In the quest for the ultimate causative factor, and from the depths of the ocean floor, our water bound brother has <u>seen the light</u>!

Within the causative chain of interconnected variables, the shining sun plays a role on the ripples that break the ocean's surface! But still, do we have the answer? What is the cause and nature of *Light*?

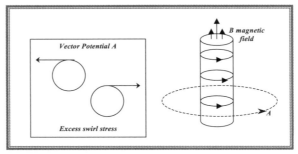

Figure 2.11 **Vector Potential.** *The excess swirling stress, clockwise or counterclockwise, in the vacuum, corresponds to the formation of the vector potential* **A.** *To form a magnetic field these potentials must exist, or form, in the vacuum state. The* **A** *field is the primary field(See Chapter Notes #56)*

HYPERFIELDS TRANSPORT PATTERNS FROM ABOVE

But isn't life like that too? Just at a time when you may feel that you are getting things figured out, and finding the answers, some new element of the puzzle enters-- moving you forward with the potential of even greater experience, discovery, and realization.

Each dimension beyond our known four (3 spatial dimensions and one time) can be called a distinct *hyperspace*. And each hyperspace manifest with its own unique expression of *hyperfields*. Hyperfields are energy patterns that carry the expression of specific action. We will understand that hyperfields supply and transport information. *Scalar waves, or scalar fields, carry, transport, and hold information as vibrational energy patterns in hyperspace.* Scalar waves are superluminal (faster then the speed of light).

At times we may get a glimpse of a hyperfield from the manner in which it interacts within our own reality. In most other instances, it may not be possible to detect because the hyperspace is not accessible for our direct observation- only through some secondary lens or filter that allows us to indirectly see consequences or effects from these hyperfields. Universal principle appears to follow the expression of 'fields within fields', 'vortices within vortices',... 'action within action'.

As we look inward from one level of reality into the next, we will find the expression of some organized field.

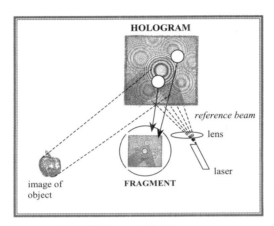

Figure 2.12 **Holographic Image Reconstruction.** *Projecting a coherent laser beam onto the surface of the hologram forms a 3-dimensional image of an object. The laser light 'exposes' or 'activates' the film. In the process, encoded patterns containing frequency information are translated into 3D form. The most significant aspect of the hologram is that any portion, piece, or fragment of it can be used to recreate an image of the original object. Any part contains or 'enfolds' the whole. In this sense, the hologram signifies the undivided nature of our universe.*

The organized field at the next higher level of reality will always carry the necessary patterns that serve for the expression within the "courser" layer of reality. An example of this is to consider physical matter. Physical matter is an organized expression of physical particles.

This organization is guided through the electromagnetic field. Without the electromagnetic field, there would be no plan or blueprint, and consequently no construction of three-dimensional reality. Altering the patterns within the electromagnetic field creates an altered expression of physical reality.

THE ELECTROMAGNETIC FIELD IS A HYPERFIELD

The electromagnetic field is, relative to our physical frame, the first hyperfield. *The electromagnetic field encodes within itself, the patterns and information of the hyperfields of yet higher dimensions.*

It is in this manner, that we say that light, and the electromagnetic fields are reflections and vibrations of the 5th dimension. Both these phenomena (of similar characteristics) are the carriers of encoding of higher dimensional information.

Both affect and influence the expression and organization of matter in physical reality. *Through our multi-dimensional nature, we are able to engineer our own reality through the conscious imprinting of patterns within the hyperfields of higher space.*

LENSES OF REALITY

Across the dimensional layers, there exist the potential of interjecting 'filters or lenses' that truly individualize the expression of individual life purpose. Perhaps such a filter may relate to imposing certain physical limitations and health issues relative to specific personal life objectives. Perhaps these filters may relate to enhancing specific attributes or capabilities that would be essential in fulfilling a certain life purpose. Perhaps such filters may relate to imposing certain restrictions to development of our optimum potential. In such a fashion, we may choose to face, and learn to overcome, certain challenges in our lives that would not otherwise be possible.

Today we are aware of the potential genetic evolutionary transformation that has been documented within today's children- and some of the adult population as well. A third strand within the DNA has now become a present evolutionary reality. Such a transformation is the result of Consciousness/Spirit choosing to alter the nature of the filters that have interceded in the manifestation of the individual as a physical being. The potential for expression of perfection always exists.

As the soul's purpose evolves and requires an enhanced vehicle for

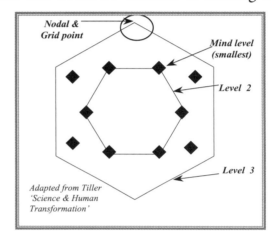

Figure 2.13 **Lattice Model of the Universe.** *Professor Tiller conceptualizes a 10-Dimensional lattice structure that connects the lattice of mind to physical reality (Level 3). Level 2 is the space of etheric substance[10]. Certain nodal points that are common to the multi-level lattice structure levels of the lattice structure are the connecting points that link and transfer energies and information between dimensions. According to Tiller, Consciousness & Intent guide this complete process! (See Chapter Notes #57)*

physical expression, this evolution becomes possible through the transmutation of matter. It is the willful cooperation of Conscious Spiritual elements that engineer the required energetic patterns to create change and transformation at our physical levels. This understanding empowers us to actively co-create a new tomorrow, and free ourselves from limitation.

A LATTICE STRUCTURE OF THE UNIVERSE PERMEATED BY SPIRIT

Consciousness navigates and permeates these geometric layers of all existence...

Here we wish to draw upon the scientific perspectives of a renowned scientist who has developed a unique view of the universe and the structure of the human dynamic within it. William Tiller, Ph.D., Professor Emeritus, Stanford University, Materials Science & Engineering Department, has created a bridge between Physics and Metaphysics. In his book *Science and Human Transformation: Subtle Energy, Intentionality and Consciousness*, Professor Tiller steps beyond classical thinking in Science. Tiller draws on his many years of research and experience in exploring subtle energy and unusual phenomena to provide us with a veritable resource of new insights. Included in his book are his research findings, theory, as well as a model from which we can begin to understand the multidimensional nature of our being.

All of Tiller's perspectives are founded on solid scientific thinking! Although we make reference to his work in our text, we are unable to do justice in presenting his ideas with the thoroughness covered in his own book. Tiller discusses a wealth of subject matter. These include topics on hyperspace, the energy radiations of biological systems, the effect of Intention on experimental equipment, and subtle energy devices. For anyone with an interest in subtle energy phenomena, Science and the new Consciousness, this is an indispensable resource [11].

UNIVERSE AS CRYSTAL LATTICE

An expert in crystal lattice structure, Prof. Tiller has formulated a unique model of the universe based on a *lattice framework*. Tiller intuits that this lattice matrix has the character of *hexagonal patterns*. [Perhaps evidence of this pattern can be seen from the hexagonal magnetic field patterns at the ends of a bar magnet, the simple hexagonal snowflake, or the hexagonal honeycomb.] These patterns create a geometry of harmonic grids that fill all of what we call *space*-- the *vacuum* and *hyperspace*. It is within the *vacuum* of space that Professor Tiller envisions subtle energies to exist.

VACUUM MODELED AS GEOMETRIC LATTICE

Physicists model the vacuum of space as some superfluid that is held in dynamic stability by a geometric lattice structure. For example, Erol Torun cites some experimental observations of quasicrystals that suggest that the vacuum may actually be modeled from an icosahedral structure [12]. In such a model, 3-dimensional space forms such as the icosahedron and the tetrahedron, actually represent projections of more complex original forms in higher space. This means that there are harmonic mathematical relationships that connect the geometries of complex space, and lower three-dimensional space.

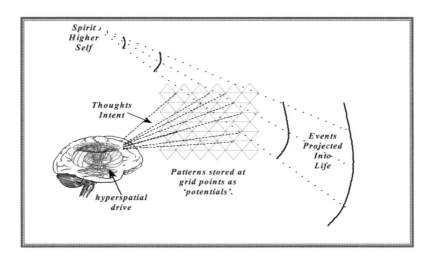

Figure 2.14 **Projection of Patterns of Events**. *In Tiller's view, thoughts and Intent cause "potentials" to be stored at the nodal points of the universal lattice structure. These potentials form as patterns that require "Spirit or Divine Self" to interact with the frequency patterns in order that they become events in our lives. The primary beam for projection originates with "Spirit" or Divine level of self. Tiller's view is that the primary beam from Spirit functions similar to a projection beam of a hologram- it interacts with the frequency patterns set by the mind level to project these into physical reality. Altering the patterns and potentials at the nodal junctions will change the events projected into our lives. In the illustration, Spirit provides the reference energy beam, similar to a holographic reconstruction process. The event in our life is a sort of holographic projection originating from a hyperspatial reality. The process is two fold: thoughts & Intent forms the patterns, with Spirit cooperating in the actualization process. The patterns & potentials at the nodal junctions* **can be programmed & changed by Intent!** *This alters the events projected into our lives. In our view, our thoughts and Intents establish patterns and potentials directly within the Universal Calibration Lattice ("UCL"). The UCL serves to amplify and project these patterns and establish a resonance with the external universe. The whole process is guided by Consciousness & Intent.*

The Tiller lattice is a multidimensional field structure. What is it? At the basis of this organization are light patterns that form the various geometric grid lines of space. These light-encoded grids define the patterns required for the unfolding of life, the galaxies and the stars.

> **This lattice grid structure exists outside of space-time, without the usual constraint of the cause and effect perspective. Time- all time past, present, and future- becomes connected through channels or connectors.**

Interdimensional nodal points (also called *magic windows* by Bearden) allow for energies and information to circulate between dimensions. The qualities required for accessing these channels of communication are tuning and coherence of the system as a whole. A unique and precise harmonic geometry exists between the lattice layers. The waves that travel through the latticework are information waves that relate to Consciousness. The lattice interconnects all of reality!

CONSCIOUSNESS & THOUGHT FOCUS ENERGY

According to Prof. Tiller's model, *potential* maps are stored at the nodal points. Here there is a conversion of consciousness into energies. These nodal points become the focus of our thoughts- our *intents*. They are in fact, the mind nodal network sites. Thought energy triggers the vast potential of energy stored within our Cosmic Sea.

From the potentials that are stored there, thought modulated patterns form. These patterns become projected as events into our lives, similar to the holographic principles! Through these energy patterns a communication is established for interacting with physical and subtle substance. A kind of feedback loop is now generated, because our response to these events is fed back to the grid where a new set of potentials and patterns form. New events unfold as a consequence.

THE HUMAN DYNAMIC IN 11-D

Tiller has also developed a model of the human dynamic. The picture of the human drama plays out on an 11 dimensional interactive set. As beings here to learn to apply *Intentionality* and *Love*, we function in cooperation with Spirit (the co-creative process) to set in motion the big drama. The extensive model developed by Tiller features significant points that are different from a conventional view in Physics. Key elements to be noted are the following:

1) The vacuum consists of a granular nature that is highly ordered and structured like a crystal lattice network. The overall lattice network is a superposition of varying layers that communicate through common junction points called nodes. It is through the nodal points that information waves filter down from 11-Dimensional to 4-Dimensional space.

2) HUMAN INTENTION is a fundamental precept. The model is built on the premise that the fundamental purpose of the physical body is to provide a vehicle for learning applied INTENTIONALY, and applied LOVE, for self-evolution.

3) Consciousness provides the information waves that travel the lattice network, affecting energy patterns and influencing particles that interact with physical and etheric substance.

4) The physical atom is surrounded by its etheric and subtle counterparts. It therefore is surrounded by emotional, intellectual and spiritual elements.

5) Light is a composite of electromagnetic radiation (in physical space), magnetoelectric radiation (from etheric space), and deltron radiation (from higher subtle realm).

THE ELEGANCE OF A PERSONAL WEB

In its elegance, the Universe unfolds in harmonious fashion [17]. The personal web that surrounds us is an energy structure of unique cellular design. Yet this cellular structure is similar to that of the outer universe. We call this personal web the Universal Calibration Lattice (UCL). We view the Universal Calibration Lattice (the UCL) as our primary connector to Tiller's universal lattice. The UCL serves to amplify and project the patterns that we place within it. These establish resonance with the external universe. Consciousness and INTENT guide the whole process.

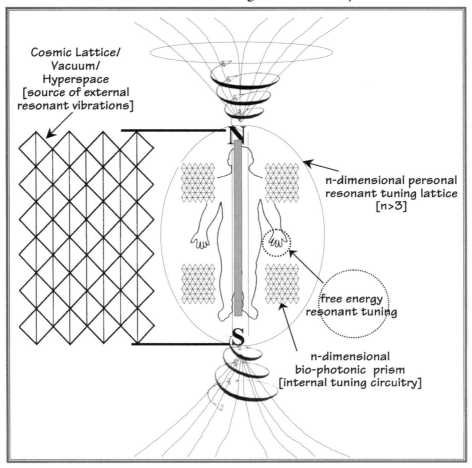

Figure 2.15 **A Resonant Personal Lattice.** *The Universal Calibration Lattice ("UCL") -- your personal energy structure, is interpreted as an n-dimensional (n>3) resonant tuning lattice. Here we have coined the term bio-photonic prism to denote a complex pattern within the human structure dynamic designed to interact with light. At the physical level this is a function of DNA, but similar helical structures exist in the subtle realm. Resonant structures interact. When the human energy systems are tuned to its natural vibrations, a resonance is established that allows for "charging" of the energy anatomy, & exchange of information. Establishing resonance between the UCL and the Cosmic Sea (vacuum) creates a "free energy generator".(See Chapter Notes #15).*

PSI, THE EXPLICATE ORDER, & THE NON-LOCAL UNIVERSE

GAZING AT CONSCIOUSNESS FROM A MICROSCOPE

As scientists penetrate the quantum world in the laboratory they have faced startling realizations....realizations that objective reality is a precept of the past. As Evan Walker aptly describes it in *The Physics of Consciousness: The Quantum Mind & Meaning of Life*:

> "We have discovered that the observer is a negotiable instrument of reality, and we have touched our own nature...We have found this consciousness standing there, looking back at us like an actor on the stage of reality, strangely playing the role of a writer writing the script we play" [18].

We see ourselves, with our minds, as active participants of the experiment. Imagine that physicists may not be discovering particles-- rather, they may be actually creating them! Brian Josephson, Nobel prizewinner in Physics, once remarked that in their diligent searches for strange new particles, the physicists might be creating their own reality [19]. For instance, a certain particle called the anomalon, has properties that vary from laboratory to laboratory. The suggestion is that the properties of this particle depend on who is *finding and creating it.*

NONLOCALITY IS OUT OF THIS WORLD

A startling discovery of Quantum Physics is the property that we call *nonlocality.* This property is described by the phenomenon that, when two particles interact, they continue to *influence each other and transfer information* between them instantly, no matter how far apart or separated they become! It does not matter if the particles or physical events are separated by billions of miles, or billions of light years, or the ends of the universe [21]! There continues to be an instant communication or transfer of influence or information between the systems! It all happens at some sub-quantum, unseen level of reality. As Nadeau and Kafatos remark:

> the Gisin experiment "obliged physicists to conclude that nonlocality or non-separability is a global or universal dynamic of the life of the cosmos" [20] .

The traditional concept of *locality* requires that all interactions be mediated by signals that are exchanged in space-time. These signals are limited to traveling no faster than the speed of light. Moreover, if the signals were local, then evidence of these signals would be observable in our space-time. Nonlocal phenomena are not constrained by these limitations. There is no speed barrier, and we do not observe the *signals* of interaction in our space!

Einstein referred to nonlocality as *'spooky action at a distance'*. The interaction occurs with no visible local signals. In other words, the discovery of nonlocality reveals that there is an unseen reality-- one that connects all physical events within the universe. This reality relates to an undivided wholeness existing at a fundamental level of physical reality. *In The Non-Local Universe: The New Physics & Matters of The Mind*, Nadeau and Kafatos see

"...mind, or human consciousness, as an emergent phenomenon in a seamlessly interconnected whole called the cosmos" [22] **. That unseen connecting reality is consciousness!**

Table 2.1 KEY CONCEPTS OF QUANTUM THEORY

NONLOCALITY

UNBROKEN WHOLENESS

CO-ORDINATED ORGANIZATION

INDEPENDENCE OF SPACE & TIME

INSEPARABILITY OF OBSERVER FROM EXPERIMENT

EXISTENCE OF A QUANTUM FIELD UNDERLYING ALL FORCES ON MATTER

A CONSCIOUSNESS THAT PERMEATES ALL LIVING & NON-LIVING THINGS

NONLOCAL PARTICLES INTERACT WITH ALL TIME

Strange ideas emerge as we consider the nonlocal properties of elementary particles. For example, Bearden discusses how the electron interacts with other hyperframes *(other space-time system)* while it graces us with its presence part of the "time" [23]. As we further understand these particles as kinks or warps in the fabric of space-time, it becomes even more bizarre! According to physicist Mark Hadley, the warp is so intense that space-time folds back upon itself forming a knot where time is looped into a closed curve *(visualize a figure 8 loop)*.

The past and future become all connected through this time loop. The loop enables the particles to interact not only with other particles in its own time, but also with particles that may *exist in its past or also in its future!* [24].

The observations of non-local phenomena are a very significant and momentous discovery in the history of science. The discovery that non-locality is a *fact* of nature, that our physical reality is non-local, carries dramatic implications that are only now emerging within the scientific community. The property of nonlocality extends beyond interacting particles and physical systems. *Consciousness*, the *mind-brain* system, and the *multi-dimensional aspects* of our beings are all nonlocal! All carry interactive ability with other systems irrespective of any distance that separates them.

MIND/BRAIN IS NONLOCAL SYSTEM

In his book *The Self-Aware Universe- How Consciousness Creates the Material World*, Amit Goswami discusses a recent experiment that confirms the nonlocality of interaction of the human to human mind-brain systems. Conducted by Mexican neurophysiologist Jacobo Gringerg-Zylberbaum, this experiment rates as the 'brain' equivalent of the landmark Aspect experiment that involved photon particles [25].

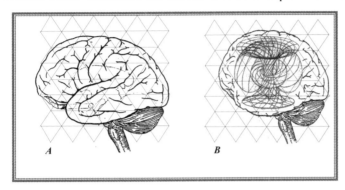

Figure 2.16 **Lattice Grid Network Within Brain.** *In Tiller's model, the 10-Dimensional universal lattice network permeates the brain (A)[13]. The nodal junctions have access to non-local information & patterns within the physical world, and 'know' what is going on elsewhere on the gridwork. That is, information **anywhere** in space-time is located **everywhere** at the nodal grid points of the lattice! In our view, the UCL (Universal Calibration Lattice) plays a role as primary connector to the external universe. The UCL establishes resonance with cosmic signals, as well as amplifies & projects the patterns & signals we place within it.(See Chapter Notes #61)*

In the experiment, two subjects were asked to interact for a period of time until they felt that a connection had been established between them. The two subjects were then placed in two separate Faraday cage. The Faraday cage ensures that there is shielding and blocking of all conventional electromagnetic signals.

The primary subject is now shown a flashing light (no knowledge of this event is available to the other subject). The flashing light immediately produces a measurable evoked potential as a signal on an EEG recording of the primary subject's brain. Amazingly, a signal of similar shape and strength (called a transfer potential) appears at the same time in the brain of the other subject! As Goswami explains:

> The two brain-minds act as a nonlocally correlated system. The correlation of the mind-brain systems is maintained through nonlocal consciousness and the quantum nature of our brains. Accomplishing such resonance is an inherent, and natural, ability of our nonlocal consciousness, and our quantum brain!

Goswami sees psychic phenomena such as remote viewing, as examples of the nonlocal operation of consciousness. Such paranormal phenomena "involve nonlocality--a jump out of your local space-time system"[26].

From this experiment we become aware that the human-to-human connection *will always* entail, unseen, but real, nonlocal correlations. In one regard, we can view the transfer of information or influence between the two human mind-brain systems as a form of *resonance.* This resonance has been accomplished through hyperspace!

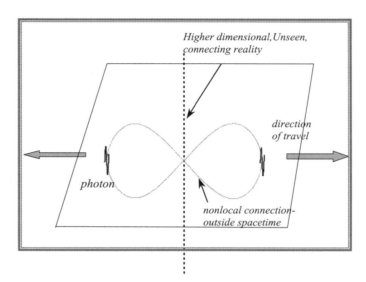

Figure 2.17 **Nonlocality- A Fact Of The Universe.** *In 1982, the Aspect experiment established a nonlocal connection between two photons of light that originated from a common event. These experiments obliged physicists to conclude that nonlocality is a universal dynamic of the life of the cosmos[20]. Human Consciousness, mind, brain, heart & emotion are all nonlocal! (See Chapter Notes #62)*

CONSCIOUSNESS AT HOME IN QUANTUM WORLD

How do local and nonlocal aspects of human consciousness connect? How does Consciousness interact with matter? These are not trivial questions! There is growing popularity amongst leading scientists that Consciousness is a player within the quantum world. More than this, however, is the notion that *there is actually no objective reality that is independent of Consciousness.*

This is precisely the discussion raised in *The Self Aware Universe,* by physicist Amit Goswami. Our universe as we see it is "*self-aware*" and it is Consciousness itself that creates what we call the material world [31]. *To appreciate this position is to fully experience the bridge between science and spirituality!*

Indeed, many a paradox and much quantum weirdness are dispelled when Consciousness is factored into material reality. On its own, the quantum world is an indeterminate place. Here it is not possible to speak about absolute properties. In fact the general description within this realm is with an equation called the *wave function.* The wave function is a description of probabilities or possibilities. Out of a multitude of probabilities, one choice becomes more likely than others. When this choice is made, there is a *collapse of the wave function,* and some unique physical event precipitates into the physical world.

The role of Consciousness in the quantum world is also discussed by Petersen in his book *The Quantum Tai Chi.* From Petersen's perspective, Consciousness plays a role in the selection of the phase angle of magnetization that acts to collapse the wave function creating our choice of reality [32].

In his paper *Physical Model of the Biofield*, physicist Andrej Detela makes the resounding comment that:

"There will be a great paradigmatic transformation in modern natural sciences...(and that) physicists will recognize, through intelligent quantum states, the mutual interplay of consciousness and matter"[33]!

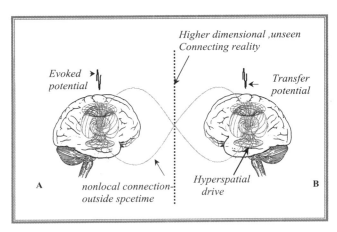

Higher dimensional ,unseen Connecting reality

Evoked potential

Transfer potential

A

nonlocal connection-outside spcetime

Hyperspatial drive

B

Figure 2.18 **Nonlocal Mind/Brain Connection.** *The experiment of Mexican neurophysiologist Gingerg-Zylberbaum established the nonlocal nature of the mind/ brain systems in the human to human connection[25]. The transfer of this information between subjects does not occur according to known conventional methods. The two brain/ mind systems act as a correlated nonlocal system that interact through a 'jump out of your local spacetime system'[26]. (See Chapter Note #52).*

Here we hear the echoes and reverberations of the late David Bohm. Perhaps no one individual has influenced and contributed more to our shifting paradigm in science than this great physicist of the 20th century! Here we find the concept of the holographic universe-- one in which mind and matter are inseparable!

AN UNDIVIDED WHOLE

For David Bohm, even the classic text that he wrote in quantum physics fell short of explaining the entire phenomenon that he encountered in his research in quantum physics. David Bohm's most significant contribution to science is his interpretation of the nature of physical reality. Bohm postulates that the ultimate nature of physical reality is not a collection of separate objects, but rather it is an *undivided whole* that is in perpetual dynamic flux. For Bohm, the insights he gained from quantum mechanics and relativity theory pointed towards a universe that is undivided and in which all parts *"merge and unite in one totality"* [34].

Bohm's undivided whole, like the ebb and flow of the tides, is not static. Out of the invisible aether all things arise and unfold. Into the aether all things eventually dissolve.

This constant flow of change in our reality Bohm called the *holomovement*. Within the holomovement, mind and matter are united [35].

"In this flow, mind and matter are not separate substances. Rather they are different aspects of one whole and unbroken movement".

Bohm also connected living and non-living things. "The ability of form to be active is the most characteristic feature of mind, and we have something that is mindlike already with the electron" [35]. Thus, matter does not exist independently from so-called empty space; matter and space are each part of the wholeness.

REALITY IS A HOLOMOVEMENT

To coin the term *holomovement*, Bohm reflected that reality is structured in a manner similar to that of the hologram. The visible reality that we know and experience is a holographic projection from a hologram formed in the invisible, hidden realm-- the *implicate order* of higher space.

Within the *implicate order* is the source of hidden order for all phenomenon, even those which appear to us as simple chance or randomness in our unfolded reality. The implicate order exteriorizes or unfolds to what we know as reality, and he calls this the *explicate order.*

The implicate order is understood as the fundamental and primary reality. Our exterior realities then become but a ripple on the vast Cosmic Sea, or explicate order as Bohm defined it. Everything that we know and experience is indeed the unfolded projections of the higher dimensional implicate order.

The implicate and explicate orders are interpenetrating in all regions of space-time, and each region enfolds all of existence, that is, everything is enfolded into everything. As Bohm (1980) explains,

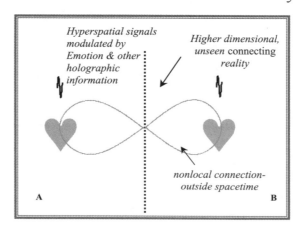

Figure 2.19 **Emotion Of The Heart Is Nonlocal.** *The mind/brain signals are modulated by the emotion of the heart, as well as other aspects of the human energy system. (See Chapter Note #53)*

"In the implicate order the totality of existence is enfolded within each region of space (and time). So, whatever part, element, or aspect we may abstract in thought, this still enfolds the whole and is therefore intrinsically related to the totality from which it has been abstracted. Thus, wholeness permeates all that is being discussed, from the very outset" [36].

HOLOGRAPHIC NATURE

Bohm believed that each part of physical reality contains information about the whole. In this light, every part of the universe contains the entire information of the whole universe. What is the web that interconnects subatomic particles? To explain the findings of quantum physics, Bohm proposed the existence of a whole new concept. He proposed the existence of a field that existed that interpenetrated and connected everything. This field he called the *quantum potential*. The quantum potential exists everywhere in space; its influence does not drop of with distance [like gravity], so its influence is equally strong everywhere.

The quantum potential becomes the organizing structure of the whole. For example, when individual electrons find themselves in a plasma [ionized gas], the collective activity is coordinated through the quantum potential field. How does it do this? *The quantum potential is a wave-like information field that provides the guidance to the electron.* Literally, the electrons access information from the quantum potential field, from which they *know* what is going on around them.

The quantum potential field provides the *information*, not the energy, to a system. This concept is analogous to a ship on the ocean that is under radio signal control from shore.

The ship is operating under its own energy, but its maneuvering instructions are being directed by radio waves. The radio waves do not carry the energy necessary for the ship to change course- they carry only the information! The same is the case for electron behavior. The quantum potential provides the course changing instructions required by the electron to interact with its environment. The electrons receive information instantly, anywhere in space, from the quantum potential. The intensity of the potential does not matter, *only its form*!

A JOURNEY BEYOND

Physicist Jack Sarfatti, as does William Tiller, takes us on another journey beyond conventional thinking. Sarfatti has developed a new discipline of thought that he calls *Post-Quantum* theory. The ideas are distinctive because they extend beyond conventional precepts in quantum theory. Simply stated it is this: *Sarfatti seeks to explain the interaction of mind and matter!* The interaction takes place in a realm beyond the quantum world.

Mind and matter interact through the intermediary *information waves* that both influence and organize matter. These information waves are guided by sentient Intent!

In Sarfatti model, Bohm's quantum potential becomes pilot q-bit information waves that actually originate from the mental wave fields ! *These waves are what are responsible for coordinating the complex and dynamic self-organization of matter.* Sarfatti provides the link between the mental wave field and the quantum potential field that provides the guiding information to the electron!

For Sarfatti, conscious awareness in the physical body is connected to nonlocal consciousness outside the physical body through an electron array within the brain. The electrons form *"a coherently phased array of tiny electric dipole nano-antennae"* [37]. *This array can be viewed as a form of coherently tuned lattice structure.* It is active in getting information into the *microtubules* of the brain. At the same time, the array connects the physical body to the mental wave fields.

INTENT DIRECTS PILOT WAVES

What is it that directs these pilot Q-bit information waves? Sarfatti explains: *"it is sentient INTENT"*[38]. The Quantum pilot waves are like information patterns. They are thought-like forms that organize matter. These waves operate outside space and time-they are nonlocal. They do not operate on the basis of intensity. Their thought-like forms guide the energy of the rocklike things. At the Quantum level the effects are very large, despite the small intensity of the information wave. Active information carries potential everywhere, but becomes active only where it has meaning. Active information <u>is</u> *form.*

BACK-ACTION IS SPIRIT'S INTERVENTION

The post Quantum theory of Sarfatti contains distinguishing features. A key

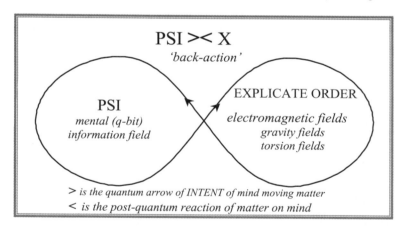

Figure 2.20 **Inseparability Of Mind & Matter.** *Sarfatti proposes that mind & matter interact through a principle of "back-action". Sarfatti explains that it is* **sentient Intent** *that directs "pilot q-bit information waves" that organize matter. Mental or thought energy can be converted into the electromagnetic field or light energy. According to Bearden, the effects of thought energy is to allow or perform the following: (1) Either wipe out the charge on a charged particle, or build up a charge in an object that previously had no electric charge; (2) Induce an electrostatic field on an external object; (3) Induce an electromagnetic field in space surrounding an object to interact with it; and (4) Condense subtle energies into the hyperfield flux of magnetic fields. Additionally, thought energy continuously condenses into electrical patterns that affect, shape, and modulate all vital process of the body. (See Chapter Notes #63).*

concept in his theory is what he calls *back-action*. Back action involves the interplay between mind on matter, and matter having interplay with mind. It is a two-way interactive process. The two-way process sets up an active feedback loop that connects mind and matter as an undivided whole! Sarfatti explains that the implication of back action is that the top-level control structure of the brain works moment to moment with its pilot information. There is an ongoing reconstruction process as the interactive process ensues. The interaction is *"pumped by external messages from the past, future and elsewhere outside of the momentary here-now light cone of the brain"*[39]. According to Sarfatti, back action *"breathes life into the equations of physics. It is the Holy Spirit"*[40].

There is still more to say about the back action process. The *INTENT* of mind acting on the quantum level of matter combines with the *back action* of matter on mind. This results in several phenomena:

- Spontaneously self-organizing systems
- Extraction of zero point energy from the vacuum
- A sentient intent-conscious experience
- Creation of "strange loops"

STRANGE LOOPS INTERCONNECT TIME

These ideas continue to be even more interesting. What are these "strange loops"?

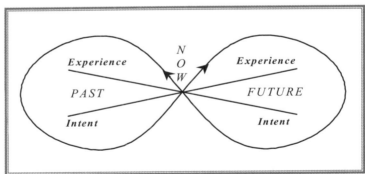

Figure 2.21 **Strange Loops of Consciousness.** *According to Jack Sarfatti, the mental field produces quantum pilot waves that are similar to information patterns. The quantum pilot waves are responsible for organizing matter. These operate outside space-time-- they are non-local! Mind & matter interactions are "pumped by external messages from the past, future, and elsewhere". These external messages set up a process, that Sarfatti describes as a dual form of strange loops, depicting: (1) Intent from the future loops with experience from the past; and (2) Intent from the past loops with experience from the future. Somewhere in the center of this looping process, we experience the NOW- moments of Consciousness. The mind & brain system involve interaction between a "classical" device"-- the brain anchored in space-time, and a "quantum device" -- the mind that is non-local. The non-local aspects of mind exist in hyperspace where the future & past are all present. Open communication in the mind/ brain, mind/ matter systems is communication with the external universe. This includes any part of it- at any distance in space or time!*

Sarfatti explains that they come in *dual forms*:

"Intent from the future loops with experience from the past, as in memories, together with the pre-sponse or backward causation " [41].
"*Intent from the past loops with experience from the future* as in precognitive remote-viewing [Jim Schnabel's book "*Remote Viewers*"] and in any kind of creative mental act" [42].

MENTAL FIELD INFLUENCES ALL CLASSICAL FIELDS

Here we introduce our first math equation. This equation Sarfatti describes as his most basic of post quantum theory:

$$PSI >< X$$

Psi = mental q-bit information field of thought
[Bohm's implicate order]
X = the explicate order's [Bohm's terminology]
material configuration of extended source particles,
in addition to the classical force fields.

The classical force fields include:

1. Electromagnetic fields (conventional Maxwell-Hertz type)
2. Torsion connection fields of various kinds
3. Chunks of three-dimensional space as in warps and wormholes
4. Einstein metric gravity field
5. Yang-Mills fields of the weak and strong interactions

> is the quantum arrow of INTENT of mind moving matter

< is the post-quantum reaction of matter on mind generating the indivisible moments of consciousness.

Sarfatti supports his theory with much more rigorous mathematical formulations than we see presented here. He suggests that there is now experimental evidence for post-quantum physics. He cites some recently declassified material on remote-viewing [54].

What can we summarize about Sarfatti's theory? Within its formulation we have *INTENT* acting on matter from the mental wave field. Matter reacts and a 'strange loop', indeed, results. The *past and future intents and experience* are all part of the equation at the same time. *All of this calls for the creation of major phase coherence!* We see that the mental field of thought, Psi, acts not only on matter particles, but also on the classical fields, *including conventional electromagnetic fields* (amongst others).

Thought Energy Is Convertible

This notion is well supported within the concepts of Bearden as well. Bearden sees thought energy as having the capacity of being converted *into* electromagnetic fields. Essentially, thought energy exists in a hyperspace frame that is removed from the electromagnetic field. But, by two successive *orthorotations*, this thought energy translates into another type of field- the conventional electromagnetic field.

Bearden discusses much of this at length in *Excalibur Briefing*. More generally, Bearden calls for a new calculus of higher dimensions that looks at the conversion of one kind of field into a different kind of field, with no barrier at all between physics and metaphysics. Moreover, Bearden sees that we require a new physics paradigm, one in which we

> **"must encompass both mind and physics within the same theoretical framework, if it is to succeed in explaining how mind affects matter"** [41].

The new physics paradigm must include *Intent*, or what Bearden also calls *Inception*, otherwise we continue to have unexplained mysteries in ordinary science.

According to Bearden, the effects of applying thought energy [*INTENT*] include the following electromagnetic effects:

- Either wipe out the charge on a charged particle, or build up a charge in an object that previously had no electric charge
- Induce an electrostatic field on an external object
- Induce an electromagnetic field in space surrounding an object to interact with it
- Condense subtle energies into the hyperfield flux of magnetic fields
- Condenses continually into electrical patterns that affect, shape, and modulate all vital process of the body

Making the Virtual Real

In *Excalibur Briefing*, Bearden discusses the nature of thought energy. Thought, or mental energy, can be viewed as virtual, or unobserved, *entities*. These entities exist as actual real objects within their own hyperspace frame, or *hyperframe*. If we could co-exist with these entities in the same hyperframe, they would be very tangible to us. However, our reality is a distinct hyperframe relative to thought or mental energy. Of course thoughts remain unobservable to us.

In *The Quantum Tai Chi- Gauge Theory: The Dance of Mind Over Matter*, Stephen Petersen suggests that the selection of neuronal patterning within the brain that formulate these thought forms is linked to mind, or consciousness. The actual dendritic (nerve ending) firing patterns within the brain are determined by consciousness. According to Petersen, the mind is constantly programming the brain in the selection of the best dendritic network to express itself[43].

The intensity or power that we can attribute to these thought entities is relative to the degree or level of neuronal noise that existed at the time of their creation. At levels of high background neuronal noise, or high levels of system incoherency, these thought entities carry little potential to participate in the physical manifestation process. Reducing internal system noise, along with improving system coherency, are means of increasing the magnetization power of thought energy. In fact, Petersen sees that

> **"Conscious thought and perceptions act as a polarizing magnet...the degree of consciousness of a possibility is represented by the degree of magnetic alignment of redundant cells in the brain or consciousness beyond"** [44].

But, just as Carl Jung recognized, a threshold exists that consciousness must exceed in order to pull events out of the 'personal or collective unconscious' and make them real.

THOUGHT ENTITIES COHERE TO LIGHT PHOTONS

According to Bearden, thought entities collect and cohere according to similar properties of frequency and form. Such coherence of thought energy creates the possibilities of magnetizing similar events in our conscious physical reality. Jung coined the term *synchronicity* to describe occurrences that defy the laws of probability-occurrences that obey a different law, the *law of similarity* [45]. Within the unconscious, all patterns of all time, both past and future exist. Any one of these patterns is subject to selection as experience in the NOW.

The process of connecting thought entities to physical reality occurs through the intermediary of the light photon.

> **The photon is the carrier of the patterns of the thought entity. Similar photons cohere, and collectively create an intensity that breaches the threshold that separates the Unobserved from Observed realities.**

We refer to this as the quantum threshold. Exceeding the quantum threshold creates activity at the level of the electromagnetic field.

CONNECTION TO OBSERVABLE CHANGE

The electromagnetic field connects us to observable physical change. Note how light is the carrier of the thought pattern to the electromagnetic field. In fact, in electromagnetic field theory, the photon [light], is the *messenger* that communicates information between particles of the field structure. If we were able to observe activity within an electromagnetic field, we would witness veritable light show- fireworks of various intensity, color and frequency.

These interactions are exchanges of *information*, to supply form, or *in-form*. Tiller adds that light is also comprised of magnetoelectric radiation from etheric space, as well as deltron radiation from the higher subtle realm. So the exchange of information from light includes the patterns and forms that originate from the unseen realities of the higher subtle realm! Light is a phenomenon outside of space-time. Arthur Young viewed light as Consciousness itself!

POWER THROUGH COHERENCE

Virtual or unobserved reality contains all possibilities, or probable events. However, in order to transform any pattern of possibility into our observed reality a process must be initiated. As Bearden states in *Gravitobiology: The New Biophysics,*

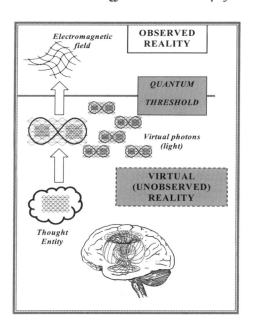

Figure 2.22 **Making The Virtual Real.** *From Bearden's discussion in* **Excalibur Briefing**, *we can view thought or mental energy as virtual (unobserved) entities. These entities carry patterns of probabilities, and cohere (gather or add up) according to their frequency & form. The patterns are added or transferred to virtual photons (light). Photons collect according to similarity of pattern coherence. The quantum change reaches the electromagnetic field frame and either creates or alters the electromagnetic field. Observed physical change ensues. Through tuning & resonance, internal patterns can affect external reality, and external patterns can affect internal reality through similar process. (See Chapter Notes #64)*

"As is well known in physics, a virtual entity can become real and observable if energy is added to it" [46].

Adding energy is a process of adding *charge, activation,* or *kindling* as described by Bearden. When sufficiently charged, virtual or ghost images ultimately emerge into the observable state. The key is to focus this energy through coherent internal states. As Petersen posits, this begins with the coherent magnetic alignment and activation of our brain cells.

Additionally we emphasize that we must maintain coherence, alignment, and integration of our own personal energy systems. In our view, it is within the Universal Calibration Lattice ("UCL") that we place and carry our patterns of possibilities. Strong connections to our personal lattice (*the UCL*) allow for the projection, or magnetic manifestation, of these patterns as events in our lives. Creating these energetic connections is a principle focus of the *EMF Balancing Technique®.*

A NEW ENERGY CONCEPT

As we leave this chapter, we would like to make a commentary about the concept of energy. In the old equation, we tend to think of energy as being a function of mass- i.e:

$$E = mc^2$$
[E=energy, m= mass, c= speed of light]

Note that this base equation can be more appropriately written as

$$m = E/c^2$$

– i.e. we can understand mass to be a manifestation of energy divided by (or slowed down by) the speed of light squared (c X c).

As we evolve in our thinking, we see from this chapter that Consciousness, the Mind or Mental field, interacts with matter at various levels. We see that Consciousness exercises a directing influence upon external systems that can contain large quantities of their own inherent energy. [The idea of radio waves from shore guiding the movements of a large ship at sea.] As we grow in Consciousness, our ability to interact with energy systems increases. So does our ability to organize and influence matter and energies.

Yet as we grow as energetic beings, we understand that it is not our own personal energies that we supply to accomplish this external influence. Our Conscious INTENT acts through the mental field of thought to produce the guiding *pilot waves* that actually influence the material world. This fact clearly and dramatically calls for a revision of the old energy equation. *How do we factor Consciousness (C-consciousness) into our new equation?*

THE ROLE OF CONSCIOUSNESS

We propose an equation for the new energy perspective. In this new perspective, we rewrite the equation and it becomes:

$$E = mc^2 \cdot C^2 \qquad (C=Consciousness)$$

In our new perspective, the manifestation of energy is *multiplied* exponentially by the power of Consciousness. And that reflects the power of Consciousness!

$$M \text{ (material world)} = E/(c^2 \cdot C^2)$$

From these equations, we can view the material world as a manifestation of energy, slowed down by the speed of light, with the intervention of Consciousness !

MULTIPLYIN G THE POTENTIAL

As we increase our level of conscious awareness, we *multiply* the potential, and the effect, that this creates in our lives! There are other Laws of the Universe that we are yet to recognize and put into common practice in our lives. The current laws established in today's Physics are significant scientific advances.

Yet, science is in its infancy in understanding the true dynamic and complex nature of our reality. Within this reality is the interplay of Consciousness and matter, and the role that focused *Intent* plays in manifesting our world. The Universe operates beyond the physical laws of which we are quite familiar.

In the law of Attraction, the Universe allows for *like to attract like*-- this is beyond our common conception that opposites attract.

> **Within Universal law, that upon which we place focused thought, with a determined resoluteness, will come to manifest in our lives. *This Intent flows from the Heart, and is most powerful when aligned with higher self!***

We need only allow for these Laws to operate in our lives, without imposing any restrictive *how* events will come about. The working of these Laws in our lives will bring with them their own contribution of balance as we attune ourselves to the universal flow of energies that are consistent with universal Law.

From this point of balance we can function with full open and awake awareness in our NOW-- the space-time from which we live moment to moment. Awareness gives us knowledge from which wisdom is gained from life experience. In applying Universal Law, we establish not only a resonance with the Universe, but also a resonance with our own Divine purpose.

"We are hyperspatial objects of some sort
that cast a shadow into matter.
The shadow is our physical organism."

Terence McKenna, *The Archaic Revival*

CHAPTER THREE

INTRODUCING
THE
UNIVERSAL CALIBRATION LATTICE

An Inter-Dimensional
Web

We as human beings consist of a geometric collection of
harmonic waveforms of light- guided by intelligence.
Bruce Cathie, The Energy Grid
The more light your body can hold, the higher your vibration
and the greater your ability to transform the energy around you into a higher order.
Sanaya Roman / Orin, Spiritual Growth

Today's science has established the chemical-electrical nature of our physical biological systems . However, in a larger sense, we are much more than carbon, chemicals and electrical potentials! Our nature is also electromagnetic. We know electromagnetism to be an inter-dimensional phenomenon.

WE ARE LIGHT BEINGS!

As electromagnetic beings we are part of the electromagnetic spectrum that contains both visible and invisible light. We know from the branch of science called "quantum physics" that light is the foundation of the electromagnetic field. The photon of light is the smallest quanta of this field, and it is also the messenger that provides the communication between particles of the electromagnetic field. Therefore, it is very clear that we are light beings - carbon-chemical-electrical-light beings [I].

As such, we can alter our vibrational frequencies! We possess actual circuitry that can be altered through resonant processes.

The idea of "light-being" or "light body" takes on a valid scientific application when we realize that an electromagnetic field would provide a veritable light show, if we had the capacity to perceive it with our physical eyes [2].

In the 1800s, physicians experimented with using electrical energy for healing. The results of these experiments were far less than satisfactory. The electrodes used to conduct the electricity often burned the skin. Healthy organs within the body were unintentionally zapped because the electrical charges were difficult to direct. I believe these electrical treatments misfired because in the evolutionary scheme we were not ready for that type of healing; instead, we were required to continue to focus on the chemical aspect of our being.

We have evolved greatly along that path, and developed medications to help the body in many ways. Without a doubt, there are numerous medical miracles readily available to us today. However, as creatures of evolution, we are moving more towards the electrical nature of our being, and seeking sources of healing which reflect this evolution: homeopathy, herbs, natural medicines, live vibrational essences, and new supplements that affect the cellular structure and the DNA [3].

Those educated in modern medicine have been forming unique alliances with practitioners of complementary therapies. I often meet and work with highly educated people who have chosen to end their traditional ways of practicing, or to add alternative approaches to their existing practice. Interestingly, I have also worked with those offering alternative work that now desire some mainstream education. How fortunate we are to have such individuals who can offer us the best of both worlds!

Even as we embrace ourselves as light beings, we must still honor our chemical heritage, and choose with wisdom and discernment all the substances we put into our bodies as we evolve. As we elevate our awareness, we will often naturally make decisions to stop the unconscious inclusion of chemicals into our bodies through medications and diet. In the late 1970s, I managed a health food store. To most people (except the Californians!) those of us promoting health food and a natural approach to nutrition were strange people with strange ideas. The notion of eating healthy foods without chemical additives, pesticides, preservatives, synthetic hormones, antibiotics, and so on, was not a mainstream concept at that time. I'll never forget how elated I was the first time I saw brown rice in the supermarket. What was once considered a weird concept was now normal!

We are developing a greater ability to access and express more of our spiritual electrical nature. As we integrate the chemical and electrical facets of our being, we will learn to use electrical/energy methods to heal our bodies. Doctors are beginning to work with electricity and electromagnetism to treat neurological imbalances and other conditions. But understanding our own role in the healing process remains a powerful piece of the puzzle.

As we become aware of how to use the Universal Calibration Lattice to hold the full electrical charge of our being, we can change our DNA energetically and electro-magnetically. This increases our capacity to access innate wisdom for accelerated healing and learning in what may seem to be miraculous ways.

Just how miraculous can it be? I experienced accelerated healing of asthma in myself and with my daughter. In my mid-thirties I developed asthma. When I resisted taking medicine three times a day, the doctor told me in no uncertain terms that I was an asthmatic and would probably die an asthmatic. So, I took the medication as I needed it, while affirming that some day I would not need it. For now I was grateful that it helped me to breathe. I also used homeopathic remedies and with the help of my homeopathic physician, began to uncover the issues that were the source of the asthma. Soon after that my daughter Shana developed asthma too. Somehow, it was okay for me to gasp for air, but watching my little six-year-old struggling for breath was very distressing. Both of our conditions persisted for over a year.

One day, my daughter Shana had a very bad asthma attack. The remedies and the medication gave her no relief. I did a personal meditation where I felt myself at the center of the universe and I asked with all my heart, "What am I missing?" I then experienced a sensation of energy moving throughout and around my entire body for more than an hour. Then, in the area of my thymus, I felt warm, flowing golden light beginning to radiate down my arms and out my hands. I went upstairs and placed my hands on Shana; in moments her breathing went from short gasps to one long, deep breath. She has not had asthma since.

The next day I decided that I did not want asthma anymore, so I focused in my high heart/thymus and requested this area to generate the light and energy once again. My chest filled with the warmth of golden liquid light. In five days, after requesting and receiving the energy five times, my asthma was gone. That was fifteen years ago and I have remained asthma free ever since.

Would it be possible to generate enough energy so that when we hurt ourselves the energy could produce instant regeneration? Could we regenerate and heal instantly any wound or disease that tried to manifest itself within our field? A few years later, in early summer, I had a big-time learning event. You know the type . . . where you do everything wrong and learn an everlasting lesson? A friend of mine accidentally started a fire in my kitchen. By the time I discovered it, it was almost out of control. On my stove was a pot enveloped with flames shooting up to the ceiling. The microwave was melting, the cabinets over the stove were on fire, and the whole kitchen was filled with a heavy cloud of black smoke. Without thinking, (and I mean without thinking!), I grabbed the pot of fire, ran to the back door and threw it outside. This was not a good thing to do.

The fire burned my hands and arms, turning them a deep purple-red. The veins in my hands were swollen and very painful. I was traumatized and emotionally upset. I remember thinking, "Where is all that energy I work with?" I called three other friends and asked them to come to the house to help me. One of them suggested that we go to the hospital and I agreed. As we prepared to leave, I started to feel a tingling sensation in my arms and hands. The feeling was very strong and I was clearly aware that it originated in my thymus/high heart area. The tingling intensified and I told my friends what I was feeling. Then right before our eyes, my hands changed from purple-red with swollen veins, to a normal color and texture in less than three minutes. Not even a blister remained as evidence of the event. The intense emotional upset changed into feelings of complete peace and I could laugh about the drama of the lesson.

I suggest a balanced approach to this possibility, however. Our bodies are clearly capable of healing themselves, but can we always expect accelerated healing? The wonderful challenge each of us now faces is to create and maintain a strong energy anatomy, one that is capable of holding and using all of this energy! Intense emotions can cause chemical and hormonal changes within the physical body. You need not pick up a pot of fire to create intense emotion. That is not an activity I recommend! The Masters have consistently asked us to express ourselves with love. I believe we are just beginning to be able to express this love, this high-voltage energy, and we have just begun to experience what that really means. We do heal and we do regenerate, some of us quite well, but it still takes time.

The idea of accelerated healing and regeneration does not lessen the beauty or sacredness of our present reality. The possibility of accelerated healing is offered in the spirit of support, as the next goal for us to reach for in our evolutionary process, without feeling guilty about where we now stand. I have noticed that as we have accepted greater responsibility for ourselves, we have created a kind of new age guilt! "How did I create that? Why did I create that?" These questions to self are necessary and good as long as we understand the ultimate importance of all of our manifestations. Everything we create is for a reason.

YOUR PERSONAL CONNECTION TO THE COSMIC LATTICE

The Universal Calibration Lattice is our personal connection to the Cosmic Lattice, the unlimited or universal energy source. It permits us to make use of the unlimited energy of the Cosmic Lattice much like an electrical transformer, transferring energy from one circuit to another.

This is why we often refer to this process as the "rewiring for the new energy." It allows us to receive and use the energy we are learning to release from the Cosmic Lattice and from within ourselves. An important note - the Cosmic Lattice does not exist only in some far away or exotic place. It permeates our very existence, right down to the cellular level, and beyond, into our subatomic energy field.

I had the honor of contributing a chapter about the *The Universal Calibration Lattice* ("UCL") to Kryon Book VII, *Letters From Home.* People from around the world have responded to this chapter with reports of powerful experiences of recognition. As you read the information here, and study the illustration, be aware that you may feel or sense an electrical "charge," or buzzing. This is a vibrational energy moving through you as you resonate with the information. Perhaps you may simply have a strong intuitive feeling that you somehow "recognize" the UCL, and know that it makes perfect sense to you on a cellular level. Even if you feel nothing, the pure intellectual concept may stimulate new understanding, and that too is energy movement. Consider this material as assisting you to hold an energetic posture, one that contributes to a reality of elegant empowerment.

There are many wonderful abilities to develop as you strengthen your connection to an unlimited source of energy. The *Celestine Prophecy* showed us that strengthening our own connection to unlimited source means that you no longer need anyone else's energy. What a relief! Think of all the games you no longer need to play. Think of all the energy that becomes available because you simply choose to no longer play the game. What would you do with all that energy? Be assured that a deep sense of personal freedom is being developed in our new paradigm.

The energy pattern of the UCL is universal; its form and structure are basically the same for each individual human. Its primary purpose is to hold the greater electrical charge available to us as evolving humans. The UCL enhances and celebrates the evolution of the individual. The beautiful paradox here is that this structure also enhances the connection to the Oneness of *being here now*. The new reality we are creating celebrates the strength of the individual and the beauty of the connection of all, regardless of culture. This will not be an easy concept for everyone to accept. It is up to those of us who understand this oneness to practice living its consciousness. For example, no matter where I am on the planet -- at the airport, in the malls, and especially before I begin to teach -- I love to look at people. I see the oneness as an expression of the divine, and my first thought is always, "There you are!" to honor the individuals present. My second thought is, "How many here know we are all connected?" I am delighted when even one individual looks up and smiles. It brings me great joy to find meaningful ways to celebrate our diversity and our oneness everyday.

If you want to excel at communicating on a universal level, become familiar with this part of yourself. When you gain a basic understanding of how this wiring system works, you realize you are communicating with the universe and with one another all the time. We have all heard bits of wisdom such as, "thoughts are things," or "you are what you think," or "say what you mean and mean what you say." These adages are all the more important when you realize just how far these messages are traveling, and what an integral part they play in the creation of everyday reality. Learning how to say what you mean and mean what you say is not a mystery. You can develop this skill through practicing clear communication with yourself and others every day, even if you never say a word! You are a part of the Cosmic Lattice, simply by virtue of your existence. You can always strengthen your connection to it through prayer, meditation, energy work or intent. Now, by working with awareness of the UCL, you have an additional means to strengthen this connection. The connection becomes stronger the more you use it, in much the same way you strengthen the muscles of your physical body with repeated exercise.

It is important first to understand the concept of the human energy anatomy itself. Its existence can be predicted or implied by the electromagnetic laws of physics. Just as the physical anatomy is composed of many systems - muscular, skeletal, and endocrine, among others - we now know that the energy anatomy is also composed of many systems. One of these is the chakra system, well known in ancient spiritual and metaphysical texts. The mental, etheric and emotional bodies are also systems in the human energy anatomy, well documented by many modern day spiritual thinkers. In this book, I present to you some of the knowledge and experience I have gained through years of intense work and documentation concerning the system in the human energy anatomy known as *The Universal Calibration Lattice*. I have had over 12 years of hands-on experience with working directly with this energy field. This knowledge I am sharing is a combination of research, personal and intuitive exploration and direct hands-on experimentation with this field and its intimate connection with our energetic bodies.

> **The outer strands of the UCL are like an extension of the sympathetic nervous system. When you learn how to express feeling and intent through these strands, you clarify and amplify your communication with the Cosmic Lattice.**

The UCL creates a personal resonance with the Cosmic Lattice to fully empower your co-creative process. The resulting vibration within the Cosmic Lattice can now respond profoundly and intimately to you. Don't limit your relationship with the universe; make it as deep and loving as you want. Don't stop until every cell of your being is full. We are invited to participate in the cosmic scheme of things in a way that only the Masters before us have accomplished. We honor these Masters when we roll up our sleeves and say, "me too." Each one of us is a master in the making; we are learning in our lives here on Earth how to be in our mastery. Each one of us is also soul, and we are learning how to embody that aspect of Self as well. In our oneness with the all, we are co-creating our mastery.

Until now, the general path of the spiritual seeker has been vertical; we have reached upward to our Higher Self, the God Self. And recently, a resurgence in the indigenous teachings directs us to reconnect with the very ground beneath our feet, to honor the life-giving force of Mother Earth. These vertical energy movements were appropriate in the old energy dynamic. However, now is the time for us to mature into more powerful spiritual enablement. This evolution involves a horizontal spiritual movement - honoring and recognizing the sacred nature of the here and now which exists in every direction around us - not just above us or below us! We are able to use and practice that maturity within the horizontal existence of duality. I believe the existence of duality can even be fun. As you look at the illustration of the UCL you will observe the horizontal fibers forming figure eight patterns that connect the chakras to

the long informational fibers of the Universal Calibration Lattice. As you exercise and strengthen these horizontal fibers, you will increase your co-creative ability. This is our spiritual path in the new energy. Now, we come to realize that home is right where we are. We can create heaven on earth, enabled with the opportunity to build the framework with joy.

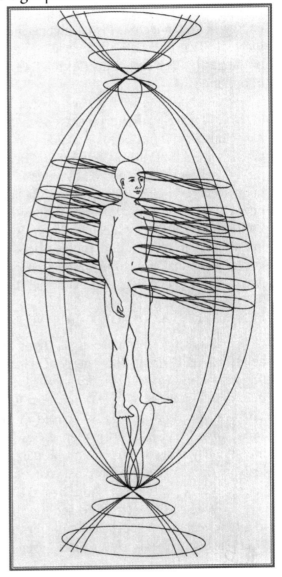

There is much more to this structure, but for now let us master the basic understanding. Keeping company with "new thinking" individuals has been a real joy in my life. It is very inspiring to be with those who are able to see a bigger picture. However, one of our greatest challenges is to be willing to patiently learn about parts of the smaller picture - the microcosm of our own lives. When we do this, we soon realize that the smaller picture really is a reflection of the bigger picture; the microcosm and the macrocosm are equally significant. This chapter will discuss parts of the lattice that relate to the interconnectedness of all things. When we touch one part of the UCL, we affect every other part of the UCL. Touch one system within the energy anatomy and you affect every other, and so on.

Illustration 3.1 **Long Fibers**

Illustration 3.1 shows some of the long, vertical informational fibers of light/energy that surround the individual. The long fibers behind us contain information about our history, those on either side of us process the information energy we give to and receive from the world, and the long fibers in front contain information relating to our potential or future. Note also the figure eight horizontal fibers that appear to connect from the body to the long informational fibers through the chakras. These are called self-balancing loops. They carry information to and from the long fibers. The illustration also shows the core energy that radiates vertically through the center of the body. This core energy represents the present, the now. The top of the column of core energy is the Center Above, located about 24 inches above the crown of the head. This is where the body's energy field connects with the higher energies of self. The Center Below, located 24 inches (60 cm) beneath the feet, connects the individual's energy field with the energy of the Earth. Each component of the UCL performs a specific function, and we will look into that next.

Perhaps the UCL always existed, and we just didn't have vibrational access to it. Now, because of the recent energy changes of the planet and our evolution of consciousness, it has become available to us. My personal experience of "watching" the Universal Calibration Lattice form and begin to activate in the human energy field leads me to believe it was not always there. Nevertheless, it is now a system within the human energy field. Many of you are already aware that we are more than just our physical bodies. We are also composed of several ethereal bodies. The Universal Calibration Lattice permeates all of our bodies in all dimensions. This seemingly infinite system of light and energy fibers is the sum total of the entire electromagnetic energy field that holds our various energy bodies, our crystalline memory structures, and our DNA encoding. Ultimately all these together form a singular "body."

FIGURE-EIGHT LOOPS OF LIGHT AND ENERGY

Studying the figure-eight loops of the UCL provides some insight into our ability to redistribute the energetic charges in our system, and the reason for this redistribution. The specific location of electrical charges within the UCL significantly determines how we co-create our realities. The greatest freedom is available to us when our personal energy is focused in the central column or core of our being, our "*now time.*" All transformation takes place in this "*now time.*" The ability to intentionally move energy from one part of our anatomy to another is an evolutionary leap in the co-creative process. We are learning how to rearrange these electrical energy charges within our entire being.

When I first started to see the figure-eight loops, I wondered what they were. In all my years of metaphysical and spiritual studies, I had never seen or heard of them. I was hesitant to talk about them, even with other energy workers. I often observed variations in the loops within individuals. While some of the loops were strong, balanced and flowing, others were constricted or distended. For several years I did not understand the nature of the loops in the front area of the lattice; they did not appear to be complete. I later realized that this area of the lattice is still evolving.

The figure-eight loops are conduits through which the electrical charges travel. These conduits contain pre-encoded information in the form of circular patterns. The circular patterns regulate the flow of energy through the loops according to the individual's inner wisdom. These loops contribute to the self-balancing and self-regulating nature of the UCL. The charges randomly rearrange themselves depending on our actions and thoughts. A more direct way to affect the charges of energy is through receiving and/or practicing the EMF Balancing Technique®, an energy method specifically designed to work with the UCL.

In the beginning of my work, I observed the loops delivering information to the core energy in the form of electrical charges. When I later observed the core energy sending information back out through the loops, I was intrigued, and eager to understand the implications of such movement. The core energy has a profound effect on the physical body, and this effect will increase significantly with our evolution. I watched as the loops in front of the body became more complete. I realized we had taken a grand evolutionary leap with the activation of this part of the UCL. This horizontal movement of energy is a substantial part of co-creating the most enlightened life we can.

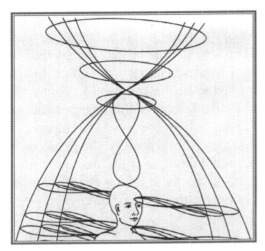

Illustration 3.2 **Self-Balancing Loop Above**

From an esoteric point of view, the figure eight is an infinity symbol, representing the personal connection between you and Creator, and the infinite partnership with the universe. There is a self-balancing loop above the head that regulates the higher or inspirational energies as they flow downward and through the entire structure of the UCL. (How many of you often feel the tingles or goose bumps of truth?) This downward energy movement reinforces the circuitry necessary to create your heaven on earth. When we feel this downward flow of energy, we often call it divine inspiration. Consider what is possible as the energy flows in both directions, from above to below, and from below to above. (Tingles of truth should flow both ways!) Therefore, an important part of the equation as we reach for partnership with Creator is for the energy of the human spirit to move in both directions. What happens when it does? Reinforcing the flow of energy in both directions helps us to hold the full electrical charge of our being. This creates a sacred union between the "as above" or divine energies, and the "so

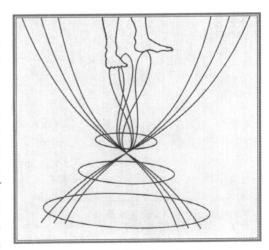

Illustration 3.3 **Self-Balancing Loops Below Feet**

below" or human energies.

A balanced relationship between these two energies is desirable. A deep personal connection to the source of unlimited energy creates an energetic posture of freedom within many levels of our being. The UCL enhances that connection, and the stronger the vertical energy movement, the stronger our connection becomes.

There are self-balancing loops beneath the feet that regulate the earth energies as they flow upward and through the entire structure of the UCL. I made an important discovery about these loops beneath the feet. When I started to work with energy, most of my clients believed that "negative" energy was released into the earth or someplace else. Sometimes clients would worry about leaving negative energy in my office. I knew they were not leaving this negative energy, but nevertheless I asked them to visualize a golden dustpan at the bottom of each foot that would take care of this negative energy. A few years later, as my sight improved, I was finally able to see more of the process. One day I watched as the energy flowed from the client's feet, through the figure eight beneath the feet, and back up through the UCL, calibrating into the next pattern of balance. So the release of "negative" energy is now a recycling of the energy. We are taking greater responsibility for our energy and ourselves than ever before.

THE INFORMATIONAL FIBERS OF THE UCL

THE BACK FIBERS: YOUR PRISM OF PERSONAL EMPOWERMENT

There are 12 long, vertical fibers of light and energy called the *"Long Informational Fibers"* that form the outer perimeter of the UCL. These long fibers are arranged in four groups, each group containing three fibers. These fibers carry the energetic information of your entire existence (see Ilustration 3.4). The long fibers are represented by the twelve dots, as viewed looking straight down from above the head.

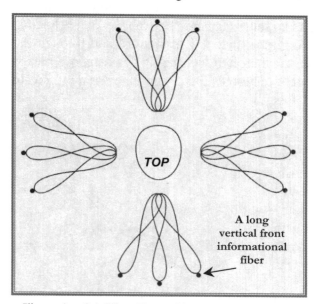

A long vertical front informational fiber

Illustration 3.4 **View From Above**

The back fibers are the three fibers behind you, and the area that radiates from the chakras and connects with these back fibers is called the *"Prism of Personal Empowerment."* These back fibers contain the information relating to your personal history, including past life events and all of the events you have experienced in your current life. They also contain your patterns of genetic tendencies, such as physical appearance, health and well being.

The information is held within the back fibers of the UCL within very small, geometrically patterned disks of light. As we accept greater responsibility in the co-creative process of our own lives, historical information relevant to our evolutionary growth becomes more readily available.

These disks hold the information in place electromagnetically, similar to how information is held on computer disks. When a larger than usual energy charge surrounds one of these light disks, it will often manifest as a reality that repeats itself again and again in what we call *the present* or *now time*. If that reality is one we desire, then the repetition contributes to our self-empowerment. Too often however, our energy history creates a pattern that is not desired, and it becomes an anchor of energy that holds us back from forward movement. When this happens, we find ourselves creating the same unwanted situations repeatedly.

You may have had an unsuccessful relationship with a certain kind of partner, yet you continue to attract the same type of person even when you are aware that this is not healthy for you. Or, you may attract similar kinds of friends or events knowing they do not serve your best interests. Energy from the past that you may not be consciously aware of, including past-life events, may still be creating a charge that affects the present. If you have not sufficiently resolved such events, they divert your energy and affect everything you do. Residual energies from past experiences that have remained unbalanced can, and do, cause a variety of unwanted effects in our daily lives. Many traditional therapeutic approaches do not reach deep enough into our energetic anatomy to bring about a balancing and release of old unwanted energy patterns. Some therapies do bring about beneficial changes, but often only after lengthy processes. It is far more desirable to work directly with this energy, through energetically balancing these back fibers so your energy body can release and recycle the extra charges of energy. When this release occurs, it can expedite traditional therapies, or in some cases, bypass them altogether.

The ability to rearrange these energy charges creates an opportunity for release, often known as a karmic release, from restrictions of the past. I like to refer to this opportunity as a "state of grace," one that we have earned and continue to earn as we learn our lessons in life.

When I first started teaching, many students were afraid because they had read or heard about predictions of an epic earth cleanse involving great catastrophes. One of the first profound realizations I had in my early twenties revealed that there was no need for any such catastrophic events. We already had the means to destroy ourselves and certainly didn't need a natural cataclysm to accomplish that. However, it had become clear to me (and many of you) that because of large-scale changes in mass consciousness over the previous 25 years, the potential reality of our future had changed. I told these students that I did not foresee those calamities. In fact, what I saw was a time in which we could access and use the golden energy that is a part of us all in a way that we never could before. I felt we were at least on an individual level reaching a golden age, one that we have dreamed of for a long time. When I realized we were attaining this state of grace and opportunity, I wanted to know how would we, as responsible human beings, manifest that grace in our daily reality?

Balancing the energy charges within the Personal Empowerment Prism transmutes the energy history or the past into a column of golden wisdom and support. The more we work to balance these charges, the stronger we become. Using the UCL to release and recycle excess energy surrounding old events frees this energy for more beneficial investments. In effect, we reclaim the energy we have overly devoted to our history, particularly to highly charged emotional attachments to past events. We can then use that energy in the now, without reliving the pain of the events that caused the overload. When we gracefully release these charges and reclaim the energy, the record of the event remains, creating a state of "lesson learned, wisdom gained." We transform the anchor holding us back into a golden column of wisdom and support that empowers us in our co-creative efforts.

When we clear and balance this area, we heal and empower ourselves. In some cases we are able to neutralize the electrical charges of genetic, physical and psychological patterns that are no longer helpful to us. As you strengthen and balance your Personal Empowerment Prism, you may spontaneously release a condition if you no longer need to experience that pattern as part of your evolution.

> **The energetic fibers are composed of conscious elements of light. They respond to our intention. Consciously directing an energy flow or expressing a preference for an outcome is called giving intent.**

When you give intent to clear your old karmic agreements, you will free up the energy that was attached to past events. Wisdom and higher spiritual understanding is available to you right now, right here on Earth. You have already created the foundations of an enlightened life. As soon as you recognize that, you can then assume more of the responsibility to bring your life to the next level. The UCL holds the higher charge of energy that assists you in claiming this personal state of empowerment.

CORE ENERGY - UNIFICATION OF THE CHAKRA SYSTEM

Once we have freed up our energy from the past, where exactly does it go? The energy charges release into the core energy and become available in the *now*. Observe the column of pure light and energy through the center of the body (see Illustation 3.5). The core energy is the primary open circuit of the Universal Calibration Lattice that connects us to the energy of the Universal Energy Source or Cosmic Lattice. Universal energy circulates throughout the UCL. Secondary connections are made through the fibers themselves as the disks of light transmit and receive information and energy.

An exciting and beautiful challenge of the new age is to learn how to function with empowerment while merging spirit and biology. The core represents the now, and this is where you will find and learn to use the energy you have reclaimed from your past. You will also discover that the UCL allows you to access energy from the future to use in the core energy of *now time*. As you bring in and focus your energies within the core of your being, slowly and one step at a time (sometimes big steps, sometimes small steps!), this merger occurs. When you confidently radiate your core energy in daily life, it is as if the chakra system unifies into a single glowing beacon of golden light, signifying the true nature of the human as a being of light. The next step of this dance with the Universe is to radiate energy throughout the Cosmic Lattice and express the infinite Self. Become clear and strong inwardly and of course you become clear and strong outwardly.

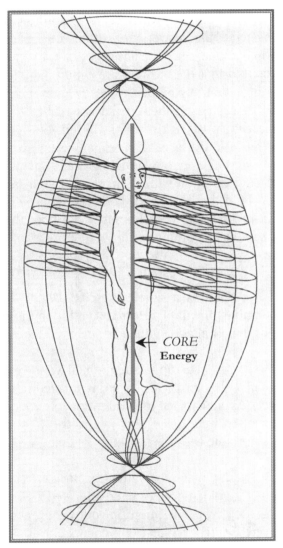

Illustration 3.5 **Unifying The Chakras**

The major chakras are the energy centers of the body that correspond to the endocrine system. As the chakras work more harmoniously with each other, they can bring about hormonal changes in the endocrine system that help reawaken a more efficient communication between our crystalline memory structures and our DNA instruction codes. This process creates an expanded communication with the Universe, and an energetic re-wiring and strengthening of the UCL, allowing it to hold a greater charge. The UCL is similar to an electrical transformer that allows 220 volts to run through a 110-volt system. This effectively enables us to use the highly refined energies available interdimensionally. Holding the full charge of our being requires the ability to make effective use of available energy!

The core is the place of transformation that encourages us to increase our vibration and enjoy balance, health, regeneration, and longer lives. It's exciting to think that we can access this core energy simply through the intent to do so, anytime, anywhere. And the more we use our core energy, the stronger it gets. When we radiate our core energy, we unlock and activate deeper levels of our innate intelligence, which I like to refer to as our spiritual intelligence. The stronger the flow of energy within the core, the greater the access to the innate wisdom or spiritual knowledge within.

During my many years of spiritual seeking, I was repeatedly told by spiritual teachers, "the answers are within you." Encouraged, I would go and live life, and life would happen, but the answers did not come often or easily. There came a time when I was told that the answers are within me once again, and I said to myself, I don't want to hear that any more! I want to know exactly where inside of me these answers are, and how I get to them. I did not realize that I would reach these answers through an energetic posture. So now I will tell you - please be patient here - the answers truly are within you! But now I can tell you exactly where and how to look for them!

The core of your being holds unlimited potential. Through your intent you can place a question within the core of your being, and an answer will reveal itself when you hold the posture of core energy. You will find many answers are easily accessed from within the core because it is here that you are deeply united with the energy, wisdom and truth of Spirit.

THE POSTURE OF CORE ENERGY - A MARTIAL ART OF THE HEART

Here is a simple exercise called, "Radiating Core Energy" to use in everyday situations. It will be referred to often in the remainder of this chapter. You can think of it as a martial art of the heart.

1. Focus your attention in your center below. Sense, feel, imagine, or think about a golden pool of energy, located about 24 inches (60 centimeters) below your feet. As you focus your attention on your center below, direct your energy to flow downward and give the intent for a strong connection. Take a moment to be comfortable with the sensation of being well grounded.

2. Focus your attention in your center above. Sense, feel, imagine, or think about a golden pool of energy located 24 inches (60 centimeters) above your head. As you focus your attention on your center above, direct your energy to flow upward and give the intent for a strong connection. Enjoy the sensation of opening to your higher energies.

3. Now, give the intent to radiate your core energy in all directions, like a brilliant, fluorescent beacon. Once again you will sense, imagine, feel, or think about the sensation of radiating your core energy. When you hold your energy in this posture, spiritual intelligence (and much more) becomes available to you. You need

only briefly focus on these energy centers, and then silently or aloud state the intention to radiate core energy. You will find that it becomes automatic and very easy to think to yourself *"center below, center above, radiate core energy."* Practice this posture so that you may live in it daily.

A primary characteristic of radiating and strengthening the core energy is a feeling of profound peace, no matter what may be happening in your life. When you balance and radiate your core energy, you are radiating peace. You can do this in the quiet of your own home, on the top of a mountain, or in line at the supermarket. You can ask a question while in this posture, or simply experience what you feel without asking anything. You will notice that very often a coincidence or synchronicity may occur that is beneficial to you and the situation you are in. Could it be that holding the posture of core energy contributes to producing these coincidences? Can radiating core energy produce beneficial synchronicities elsewhere in your life?

THE VERY SIMPLE SECRET OF MASTERY

Think of the attributes of mastery. What does mastery mean to you? Unconditional love, peace, wisdom, humor? When I ask this question in class, the list can grow very long, as people describe their thoughts on what characterizes a "master." Whatever attributes are meaningful to you, you will find increased ability and strength to stand in your own mastery when you hold the posture of Radiating Core Energy.

I love to tell people the secret of mastery. I tell students of all the initiations I have had, of the marks on my body -- and I've done things I wouldn't even tell them about-- all in the name of knowing my own mastery. It all comes down to this. . . are you ready? In all my years of seeking, the secret of mastery, in one simple word, is PRACTICE! Practice your compassion, practice your love, and practice your wisdom. Practice anything that means mastery to you. Practice patience, with yourself, your family, your friends, and with every human being you come into contact with. The more you practice something, the better you become.

The opportunity to practice mastery exists abundantly in daily life. What are we to become masters of, if not our own lives? Your life, exactly as it is right now, provides you with all the appropriate situations you need to practice mastery. There are those who say, "We are masters and we just need to remember that." Or, "I am a master and I know it." And there are also those who say, "What? Me, a master? You must be kidding!" No matter what your understanding, mastery, like enlightenment, is not some distant destination. It is a way of living life right here and right now, and a true master is constantly growing in the ability to co-create the most enlightened life they can. (Do you notice a theme?)

Shift happens in life, and you may find in some situations you hold your mastery very well. You will conduct yourself according to your highest standards. Then there will be situations where you will not hold your mastery very well. You will not conduct yourself according to your highest understanding and the expression of your mastery was lost. When this happens, think of how you would have preferred to respond to the situation. Then, just like in the song, pick yourself up, dust yourself off, and start all over again. I promise you, the Universe will give you a chance to practice again! (and again and again!)

THE SIDE FIBERS -THE BALANCE OF GIVING AND RECEIVING

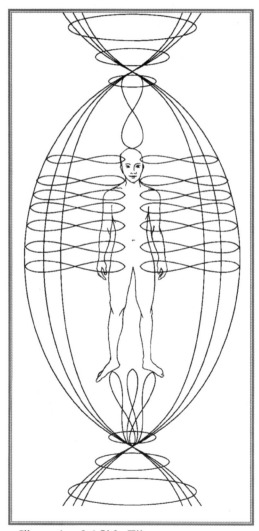

Illustration 3.6 **Side Fibers**

There are three long informational fibers to the right of your body (see Illustration 3.6). The area that radiates from the chakras and connects with these side fibers is called the Prism of Benevolence. Within these long fibers are small geometric disks of light that transmit the energy you give to the world. You connect energetically to people, groups, places, and things through these fibers. You invest your personal energy through your thoughts and actions. Making these connections with conscious intent contributes to a balance in giving and receiving.

Take some time and think about all the relationships in your life. What or who are you supporting? Are you happy about where your energy is going? Are you sending energy where you want it to go? As you assess where you send your energy you may find some connections that are no longer appropriate for you. You now possess a greater capacity to choose where you invest your energy out in the world.

Suppose you have a connection that you no longer wish to support or fuel with your energy?

Here is an exercise that will help you reclaim the energy you have sent out into the world.

EXERCISE: RECLAIMING YOUR ENERGY

Hold the posture of Radiating Core Energy.
Focus your attention on the Prism of Benevolence [side fibers on your right].
Express gratitude to the person or place where you are connected and give intent to bring your energy back to you.

Why gratitude? There have been many volumes written about the magic of gratitude, and it remains an important foundational truth. So simple and powerful, "Thank you for all we have learned together. I now choose to bring my energy back." Magic words? I like to think of this kind of statement as a magic attitude. This attitude can consistently co-create freedom and enlightenment within all your life experiences.

Think of how you would like to support this world, how you wish to invest your energy with your family, friends, community or associations. Again, focus your attention on the Prism Of Benevolence. Consciously give the intent to send your energy into the world. Then observe how you feel as you offer the energy of your personal support.

There are also three long fibers on the left side of your body. The area that radiates from the chakras and connects with these side fibers is called the Prism of Inclusiveness. These fibers on the left side contain disks of light that receive energy from the world. In many cases these energy disks are not activated enough to ensure that you are receiving supportive energy. You may hold the posture of Radiating Core Energy. Then, focus on the Prism of Inclusiveness, and ask yourself, "Am I receiving the desired support from people, groups, places, or things?"

Are you receiving energy from places that you would prefer not to? As you answer these questions, hold an energetic posture of gratitude for all of the support you are receiving. This will help to transmute the energy charges into a more usable form.

EXERCISE: HOLDING THE ENERGETIC POSTURE OF GRATITUDE

Hold the posture of Radiating Core Energy.
Then radiate the intent for gratitude throughout all four prisms of the UCL.

You can hold an energetic posture for almost anything - strength, peace, wellness, etc. The steps of the exercise are still the same: first Radiate Core Energy, and then radiate the specific intent throughout the UCL.

When the long information fibers on both sides of the body are in a relative state of balance, it is easier to disconnect from unwanted relationships. You also can avoid sliding back into unhealthy patterns due to energy input from people, groups, places and things in your sphere of reality that previously drained energy from you. Your discernment increases as you consciously accept or decline new life connections and relationships. Practice, practice, practice! (smile)

THE FRONT FIBERS - YOUR PERSONAL POTENTIAL PRISM

As I travel and teach, I meet many different people who are naturally at different points along their journey. Some will say, "I have been doing and accomplishing my whole life, and I don't want to do another thing. All I want right now is peace." I urge them to build their peace as deeply and powerfully as they desire within the energetic core of their being. If this is where you are on your path, I remind you that we are all beings of infinite potential and you may choose to activate any one of those potentials. There is no formula for choosing, no right or wrong choice, no need to do anything specific. You may even choose to do nothing, to just be still and know. And of course even doing nothing is doing something! No matter how you choose to build your peace you are still creating the magic of momentum. Because you are a creator, I gently suggest that sooner or later you will once again actively want to create!

HOPES, DREAMS, WISHES, INTENTS

There are three more long informational fibers in front of you. The area that radiates from the chakras and connects with these front fibers is called the Personal Potential Prism, a field of abundant potential and possibilities. In linear time, we would call this the future.

> The disks of light in these fibers hold information regarding your hopes, dreams, wishes, and intents, and function as transmitters, which attract "like" energy unto themselves. With conscious intent you can selectively activate or insert new hopes, dreams, and wishes into these long information fibers. These fibers are a very important aspect of the mechanism for tapping into the energy of the Cosmic Lattice.

WORRIES AND FEARS

In addition to hopes, dreams, wishes, and intents, the energy charges of worries and fears are held in the front fibers as well. The information from these charges is communicated to the Universe, and the Universe faithfully responds. You may be familiar with the old idea that you will often attract to you what you fear most. So what do we do with the knowledge that the Universe responds to all of our signals - especially those signals that we may not want a response to? There are ways to lessen the charge. While holding the posture of Radiating Core Energy, you may give the intent to release excess electromagnetic energy surrounding a worry or fear-filled charge. Once you intent is expressed, take whatever practical action you can in your life to continue to neutralize the charge of the worry or fear.

Sometimes, seemingly out of nowhere, a worry or fear will present itself. A very simple and effective technique comes from the Silva Mind Method®. Mentally place a "Cancel, Cancel" stamp on the fear. Do this as you hold the posture of Radiating Core Energy, and it works even better!

WORTHINESS

Many volumes have been written about the importance of self worth. In a few words, here's how I feel: Self worth is a key element in the co-creative process. Many of us feel deep down that we are unworthy of Creator's bounty. When we don't feel our self-worth, we diminish our ability to co-create. We are each a "part" of Creator, an individual part of the whole, and therefore we are, by definition, worthy. It is essential to our co-creative ability that we recognize our innate worthiness. You might wonder why such a magnificent Creator would allow us to feel unworthy. Here is the true measure of the magnificence: Creator allows us free will, and waits patiently for us to recognize that the miracle we are waiting for has already happened. We are the miracle. It is time to understand and appreciate what we already are, and do the necessary work to uphold our part in the cosmic scheme of things.

THE BIG IF

What does it mean when we feel we've become pretty good at co-creating, yet a particular idea or desire does not manifest? It may mean that the particular intent is not the one to advance your growth at this time. As you practice co-creation, your discernment will improve. This allows you to recognize more easily which of your goals are in alignment with your Soul's progress. Something I have found to be particularly helpful in the co-creative process is to qualify any intent I wish to manifest - " ... IF it is in accordance with soul's growth, or soul's next step."

What does this big IF really mean? It means that we are giving the intent to move forward in our quest for wholeness, to take our rightful place as a fully functioning harmonic force in the universe. When we do this, we accept the responsibility of ourselves as co-creator, and we contribute our utmost for the harmonic of the universe, or for the "good of the whole." If you truly wish to act on behalf of the good of the whole, you must first embrace the importance of developing your own wholeness. If you want to change the world, the best place to begin is with yourself.

DYNAMIC OF AN IDEA

When you have a new idea, inspiration, or desire, you may feel your excitement starting to build, stirring your passion, and bringing in the energy of your heart. Quite often before you even get to the next step of co-creating, though, you start to remember when you were told you couldn't, or when you tried something similar and it didn't work. And before you know it, the energy of the idea starts to dissipate before you even do anything with it. The next time you have a new idea that excites you, try this:

EXERCISE: ENVISIONING THE DYNAMIC OF AN IDEA

Hold the posture of Radiating Core Energy.
Envision the idea encoded in a disk of light.
Consciously place the disk of light in the information fibers in front of you.

The energy of the idea is now in a place where it can be amplified and transmitted throughout the entire cosmic lattice.

JOYFUL TENSION

Once you place your idea or intent in the fibers in front of you, a healthy tension is established. Yes, tension. Think of it as a tension of joy, between your "*now*" experience and the reality you wish to manifest. Energetic tension between you and the Universe can be an exquisite state. Create the appropriate tension with your magnificent partner and you have established a co-creative flow. Be attentive to your surroundings, for the Universe always provides you with the raw material you need to evolve. The indications may not be immediately evident, but once you have discerned them, the next step in the manifestation process requires action on your part. Take the appropriate steps to fully realize your intent. Remember that old saying - Don't wait for your ship to come in - row out and meet it!

Learning how to calibrate the long fibers in front of you is essential to successful co-creating. When you place your desire into the fibers of the Personal Potential Prism, the message beams out into the Universe as if amplified by loud speakers. The Universe answers by adding energy to whatever it is you wish to co-create. As we evolve in this manner, we develop the ability to send our energy out more gracefully and purposefully.

CO-CREATIVE CYCLE

To facilitate and ensure successful manifestation with your partner the Universe, trust in your newly developed skills and send clear, uncluttered messages through your front fibers. This is not magic; there is still work involved, and joyfully so. State your goals and intents to the Universe and remember that the Universe always gives you everything you need to move forward. There is a saying, "When life gives you lemons, make lemonade." Life has given us all consciousness, and what we do with that consciousness is our individual choice. If you can look at the lemons with a sense of gratitude and find the meaning in them, you may discover the coincidences or synchronous events that propel you forward, sometimes one small step at a time, sometimes in giant leaps. These synchronicities come in the form of new connections and resources, fresh ideas, skills and talents to develop, and increased focus. As we polish our co-creative abilities in our daily lives, we produce more synchronicities. We continue to make one connection after another and our communication link with the Universe continues to grow, becoming an unlimited source of energy. In this cycle we co-create for ourselves the work, relationships, creative expressions, and abundance that nourishes our evolution.

What we are really doing when we co-create is bypassing three-dimensional reality and opening our energy circuits to communication with larger aspects of Self. By trusting the part of ourselves that is our potential being, we develop a working relationship with that potential. Opening up our energy circuits is like blazing a new path through the woods. Each time we walk that path, it becomes more familiar, and easier to get to our center of peace, calm, and strength. This is how we move our goals into harmony with Spirit and discover our true life contract or contracts (there can be many). The more skilled we are at putting the appropriate energy charges into the long information fibers in front of us, the greater the charge available to us as we create our present reality from the future. Deepak Chopra reminds us of this when he says the wizard creates his reality backwards, allowing energy from the future to create the present. Finally, when we co-create through the Personal Potential Prism, we are not asking Spirit to hand us the end result of our desires, we are asking for the tools to create them ourselves.

EXERCISE: CREATING A GREATER CO-CREATIVE CHARGE IN THE *Now*

Hold the posture of Radiating Core Energy.

Place your attention behind you in the area of the Personal Empowerment Prism, and honor your history by acknowledging that everything you have learned or experienced has been appropriate. Then, firmly center in the now by giving the intent to increase the radiating of core energy.

In this energetic posture you may now effectively co-create through the long vertical information fibers located in front of you. This is the posture of energetic accomplishment that helps us to maximize our potentials as we align with our magnificent, infinite partner, the Universe. In this front portion of the UCL, you can focus your co-creative energy in a laser like manner.

CIRCULAR TIME

Linear time is the perception that time happens in consecutive moments, one after the other. Linear time is our traditional way of thinking about time and it is a convenient way to understand the facet of our experience we call human. *Circular time,* on the other hand, is the perception of time as a multiplicity of events occurring

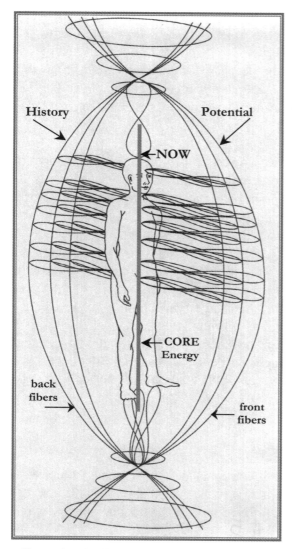

Illustration 3.7 **Circular Time**

simultaneously, separated by our interpretation of those events. In circular time, the terms "past," "present," and "future" are understood in a more fluid and universal way. Circular time is a convenient way to understand the facet of our experience we call spiritual. Ultimately, there is only the ever-present *now*.

Take a look at Illustration 3.7. Notice how the back fibers and the front fibers are connected to the core energy by figure-eight loops. Information in the form of energy charges circulates from the back fibers, our history, through the loops and into our core energy, or *now time*. Energy charges from *now time* also circulate through the loops back to our history.

Likewise, energy charges from the *now* circulate through the loops to the fibers in front, our potential, and this energy of potential then returns to the core or *now time*. When you combine these two patterns, the net result is that the energy circulates completely through from the front to the back and vice versa. The essence of these simple patterns helps to explain statements such as "there is no such thing as time," or "there is no past or future, everything is happening in the *now*."

Thus our *now* experience is created by a flow of energy from our history and potential. The ancients have taught us that the only moment we truly have is now, and all transformation takes place in *now time*. As we learn how to live in the *now*, we are carrying the greater charge of our being. The greater the charge you hold in *now time*, the greater your transformation.

NEVER-ENDING STORY

The UCL is still evolving. Recently, twelve more strands have become activated. In Illustration 3.8 , these newer strands are represented by the 12 dots which form the innermost circle. Also shown in this illustration are four large, non-symmetrical figure 8's surrounding each individual group of three long fibers.

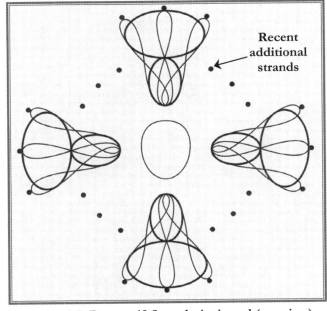

Illustration 3.8 **Recent 12 Strands Activated (top view)**

In Illustration 3.9 , a familiar pattern emerges when an outline is drawn around each of the four groups. Variations of this pattern have been depicted throughout human history. This pattern exists above our heads and beneath our feet. Connect them and you have the framework of the Universal Calibration Lattice!

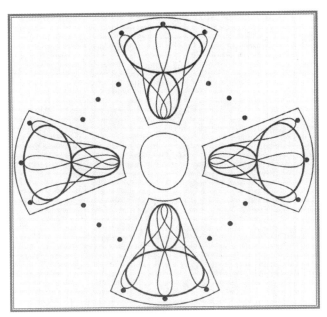

Illustration 3.9 **Familiar Pattern (top view)**

When we work with intent and energy exercises, the UCL will continue to form. As we exercise and strengthen the UCL, we increase our capacity to hold the new energy and to manifest our multidimensional selves completely. Even as you read these words and study the illustrations, you are stimulating the energy of the UCL within your being. From the point of view of our infinite Self, the journey is never ending and the joy is indescribable. What a great plan!

... and then it is right to give what you have found ..."
Richard Bach, *Jonathan Livingston Seagull*

CHAPTER FOUR

MULTI-DIMENSIONAL CIRCUITS

Your Portal to Hyperspace

Reality is merely an illusion, albeit, a very persistent one.
Albert Einstein

The greatest illusion is that we have limitations.
Robert A. Monroe

Is there a Cosmic Internet? How do we send messages to a distant receiver? What is the mechanism for sending 'energy' over the airways? Is there a mechanism associated with known paranormal phenomena?

Beyond the visible electromagnetic activity of the brain is a realm of *scalar wave* activity and *hyperfunction* processes. Throughout these structures are mechanisms for establishing *awareness* beyond the physical systems- outside our space-time. These processes provide the mechanism for *nonlocal* phenomena. The brain is a quantum non-local processor.

The mind/brain system carries innate ability to communicate outside of local space-time through unseen dimensions. Patterns of information travel through hyperchannels, and these carry influence on the subtle fields of matter at distant locations.

A HOLOGRAPHIC PROCESSOR

From the work of scientist such as Pribram, we have discovered that the brain operates under holographic principles. For example, memory and vision are functions that are not specific to any one localized area. Different parts of the brain share access to the whole information. Amazingly, in instances where an area of the brain had been surgically removed, some brain functions continued unhampered.

It was discovered that the brain was actually far more of a *frequency* analyzer, than simply an analyzer of voltages, or potentials. The brain does not function as a simple analogue processor. Rather, the brain functions as an analyzer of electromagnetic wave patterns. Along, with the heart, the brain is a large producer of electromagnetic activity, energy patterns, and radiation.

A FLUID INTERFACE

In *Gravitobiology: The New Biophysics*, Bearden discusses a baffling medical phenomenon, a condition of the brain called *hydranencephaly*. In *hydranencephaly* the individual has as little as 5% of brain material within the skull cavity. The balance of the space, 95%, is filled with fluid. Yet the person with this condition functions as does any normal person. What does this tell us about the hidden functions of the brain?

As a way station between the internal and external worlds, the brain continues to function as an interface, even in the case of *hydranencephaly*.

> **Part of the mystery lies within hidden nonlocal scalar wave activity and scalar potentials.**

Other aspects of this mystery are to be unraveled through understanding the properties of the structure of water. The hidden structures provide the energy channels of communication that allow 'fluid' to function as a substitute brain. Such phenomena cannot be understood on the basis of simple electromagnetic theory. Moreover, the brain serves as an interface between inter-dimensional realities! Our notion of holographic encompasses higher dimensional reality. As such, in its wholeness, we refer to *All That Is*. All is connected. Ultimately all is one!

HYPERSPATIAL CONNECTOR

Bearden introduces us to another aspect of the brain's processing capability. The brain is a producer and detector of *scalar waves*. The scalar wave is the connector to higher dimensional space-- the vacuum of hyperspace. It is the scalar wave that navigates through channels between dimensions. It is through such channels or portals that we connect to the primary vortex of creation. In connecting to the vortex, the energies of spirit enter the physical realm of our human vibration.

> **The key to connecting distinct dimensional elements is to find or establish the links, roadways, circuits, or portals [natural frequencies, life frequencies, magic windows, inter-dimensional nodal points, Einstein-Rosen bridge/wormholes] that naturally link the geometries in harmony- in resonance.**

As its name suggests, the scalar wave is defined by a scalar, magnitude, or 'quantity' value. Hence, a scalar wave transmits or holds information.

The scalar wave is a hyperspatial wave. It exists outside the usual constraints of space and time. It travels at superluminal speeds (faster than light) as a type of pressure disturbance in the vacuum of space. In the same way that a sound wave travels in air, the scalar wave travels as a *hypersonic* disturbance in the vacuum.

Scalar waves may form elaborate and complex stationary interference patterns. In such a case we call them scalar *fields*. Such structures then exist in the vacuum of space-hyperspace. The interference patterns form a unique lattice structure. Bearden describes this as "an ordered lattice of spacetime/vacuum" (*see figure 4.2*). It communicates across both space and time!

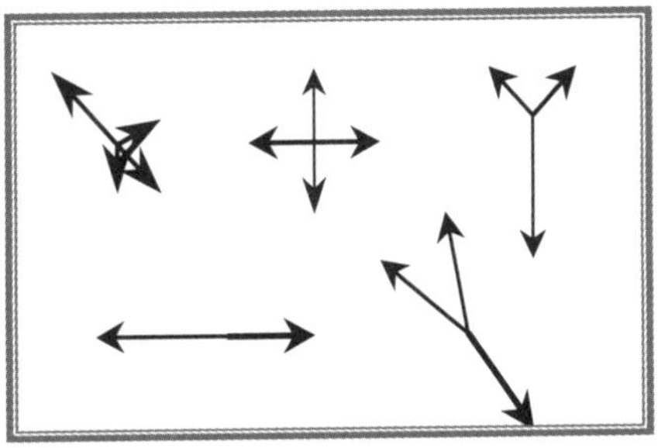

Figure 4.1 **Patterns of Scalar Substructure.** *Outward appearances can be deceptive because each of the systems has its own unique patterned substructure. Scalar waves exhibit such distinct patterned substructures. The scalar wave transports information as patterned electromagnetic substructures. An example is to create a scalar healing pattern that will cure a disease, and then expose the biological system to this scalar 'radiation' or immunization. The brain produces scalar waves. It is implicit that these scalar waves from the brain are patterned according to the intent of the individual. The electromagnetic substructure of "thought" appears in the scalar wave.(See Chapter Notes #22)*

AN ARTISTIC VIBRATING FABRIC

The vacuum is like the background fabric that provides the canvas on which to build our space-time reality. Out of the vacuum we find the ingredients (i.e. energy and blueprints/morphogenetic fields) to construct a three dimensional physical reality. The morphic fields described by Sheldrake can be understood as scalar fields. Physical matter can be viewed as standing waveform patterns. This is a form of scalar resonance.

A scalar wave is not like a conventional electromagnetic wave. Although a relationship may be established between both waves, the scalar wave is not detectable by conventional means.

RESONANCE WITH TIME

Such waves stress or vary space-time. They are free to move in four or more dimensions. The scalar wave can move *in time only*, i.e., it can sit in one place and fluctuate the flow of time (or other properties). It can also move *in space only*, i.e., with time standing still. It can move in varying combinations of these two instances. Such modes of behavior are described as *resonant* phenomena. As we see, resonance can manifest itself in different ways. Here, the concept of resonance can be expressed as an association uniquely with *space,* or with *time. To live in the NOW is to be tuned to resonate with this space-time!*

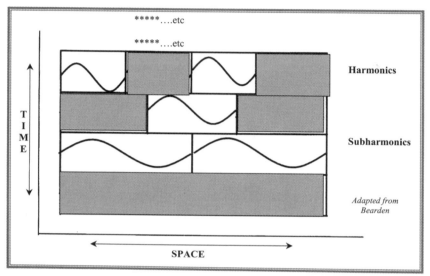

Figure. **4.2 Space-time Lattice.** *The spacetime lattice is ordered in frequency, energy, space, and time. The n-dimensional (n>3) lattice, represent the hidden order, as well as the holographic interconnectedness of all things across time & space. It is our interpretation that the **UCL** represents such a spacetime lattice structure with all associated hyperspatial attributes. Such a lattice can be tuned because ordered internal structures relate harmonically across spacetime. The internal non-local structure responds through resonance effects. A tuned lattice relates harmonically to both past & future spacetime coordinates & events. Space-time coordinates connect through hyperchannels.*

PROGRAMMABLE PATTERNS

At the basis of the scalar wave is the scalar potential. One such potential is the electrostatic scalar potential (*see Figure 2.6*). This potential is at the basis of the electromagnetic wave. These are highly ordered internally.

Internally, the scalar potential *connects to both local, and non-local, space!* The scalar wave transports these patterns as information through hyperspace. The most significant characteristic of the scalar potential is that it contains a *substructure.* Encoded or patterned within the potential are very specific electromagnetic patterns. These patterns are able to communicate energy across the harmonics of the frequencies found within the scalar potential.

These patterns can be programmed or engineered to have specific interactive effects with matter, and their subtle fields [1]. The ordered lattice of space-time/vacuum formed by the scalar potential is an n-dimensional (n>3) structure. *It communicates across both space and time!* It is impossible to visualize or illustrate what such a lattice would look like. Within the lattice is an ordering in frequency, energy, space, and time. The lattice represents the hidden order, as well as the holographic interconnectedness of all things across time and space.

It is our interpretation that the Universal Calibration Lattice (UCL) represents such a space-time lattice with all associated hyperspatial attributes. *Such a lattice can be tuned because the ordered internal structures relate harmonically across space-time, and respond through resonance effects.* A tuned space-time lattice relates harmonically to past, present, and future. Our multi-dimensional *human* dynamic structure relates through a harmonically tuned space-time lattice.

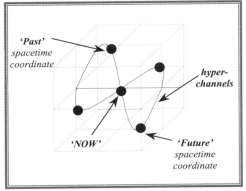

Figure **4.3 A Space-Time Connector.**
An n-dimensional (n>3) spacetime lattice recognizes spacetime as a continuum. A tuned lattice establishes a harmonic relationship between spacetime coordinates such that resonance exist between the internal structures. Connections between distant spacetime events become established through hyperchannels that are frequency dependent ('the magic window' or interdimensional nodal point concept of Bearden & Tiller). Hyperchannels are naturally tunable.

THE HUMAN BRAIN AS SCALAR TRANSLATOR/INTERFEROMETER

A system that can convert scalar waves into electromagnetic waves, and from electromagnetic energy to scalar waves, is called a *translator*. The Earth is one giant scalar wave *generator/translator*. The Earth has multiple resonant scalar modes [3]. The earth, moon, and sun form a unique scalar system. *The earth is, therefore, a multi-dimensional structure.*

On a smaller scale, other translator systems include -stressed crystals, some semi-conductive materials, dielectric capacitors, plasmas, and *scalar interferometers*- to give a few. The *human brain* is also a translator of scalar waves, i.e., the brain can convert electromagnetic energy into scalar waves, and scalar waves into electromagnetic energy. The electromagnetic activity of the brain is the visible measurable component. The scalar activity of the brain is not detectable by ordinary means.

Scalar waves can be combined to create interference patterns. When the interference pattern is focused appropriately, it will manifest, or produce, energy at a distance. Such a device is called a scalar interferometer. According to Bearden, scalar technology exists that can transmit energy through hyperspace [4]. This technology can cause energy to manifest within three-dimensional space at some distant point and have impact on physical systems at that location. At distant locations, patterns can be programmed or engineered within scalar waves to have specific interactive effects with matter, and their subtle fields.

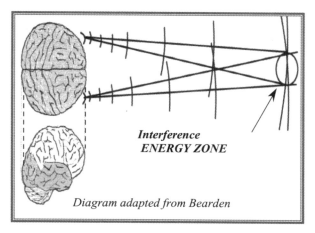

Interference
ENERGY ZONE

Diagram adapted from Bearden

Figure 4.4 **Brain As Scalar Interferometer.**
According to Bearden, the brain is an emitter & receiver of scalar waves. The two hemispheres combine their functions to form a scalar interferometer- they can create interference patterns from interference beams that focus energy, or electromagnetic waves, at a distance. According to Bearden, scalar technology uses the principles of the interferometer to transmit information and energy around space through **'hyperchannels'.** *We do not perceive these hyperchannels in 3D space. But they exist. The effects of the scalar interference beams materialize & become visible in 3D space. The sophistication of the brain opens these* **'hyperchannels',** *and actually, hyperchannels are constantly open. These are the communication mechanisms of the* **'hyperfunctions'** *of the brain. When 'healers'* **channel** *energy, the process would more accurately be described as* **hyperchanneling!** *(See Chapter Notes #24)*

HEMISPHERIC INTERFEROMETRY

Within the human brain the two hemispheres of the cerebral cortex function together as a scalar interferometer. Such a notion is shared by Ervin Lazslo [5]. According to Lazslo, the activity within the neuronal networks of the brain-within the action potentials that govern dendrite firing-may be significantly affected by the scalar topology of the vacuum.

Variations of this topology can cause a shift in neuronal activity from one complex activity pattern to another. This may happen even under extremely fine variations to the scalar potentials.

Within the brain there is amplification of vacuum level fluctuations, and these produce observable effects on the brain's information processing systems. The two cerebral hemispheres have the ability to produce scalar waves and scalar beams that form interference patterns at a distance.

Within the interference zone, the frequency patterns of the scalar beams interact with physical system to produce either ordering or disordering effects. As a scalar interferometer, the brain transmits energy and information around 3D space, through what Bearden calls *hyperchannels*, in hyperspace.

The scalar waves interact with the subtle fields. When reference is made to healers channeling energy, in context to our above discussion, it may be more accurate to describe the process as hyperchanneling!

A ParaNormal Connection

Invisible aspects of the brain's scalar functioning relate to paranormal phenomena [6]. According to Bearden, remote viewing, telepathy, precognition, psychokinesis, etc. indeed all the phenomena of classical parapsychology, are explicable with the properties of scalar waves. Scalar waves, operating in hyperspace or the vacuum of virtual space, find themselves linked to the same domain as the subtle realm! The neural synaptic network of the brain is ideal for scalar wave generation. The brain and nervous system combine to form a tuned resonant system, i.e., a true detector/emitter of scalar waves!

Hyperspatial Drive Mechanism

Further developments of the hyperspatial aspects of brain function are presented in the publication *Ancient Wisdom & Modern Physics*. In this book, researchers report the mapping of three-dimensional configuration of the magnetic fields produced by the brain.

What is unique about these magnetic field structures? They represent hyperspatial structures! Through these structures are mechanisms for establishing *awareness* beyond the physical systems-outside our space-time.

To produce these magnetic mappings of the brain, very high precision instrumentation is required. The SQUID (Superconducting Quantum Interference Device), along with other specialized devices, were utilized for this purpose. The sensitivity of their equipment was able to detect field strength as small as a nanogauss (a billionth of a Gauss- 10^{-9}). This is extremely small field strength to measure.

When plotted on a three-dimensional map, the 3D magnetic measurement formed unique pictures of *hyperspatial field structures* . The researchers describe the following profile:

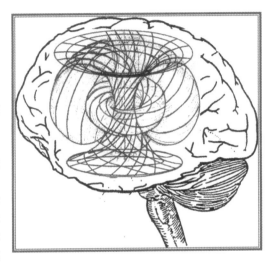

Figure **4.5 Hyperfields Of The Brain.**
The illustration was synthesized from research findings reported in Ancient Wisdom & Modern Physics. The two principle shapes are hyperspatial forms: they connect to hyperspace. The donut shape is called the torus. The double-ended trumpet shape is known as the Einstein-Rosen bridge. Within this complex there exist spinning & spiraling light & energies that are both trapped & emitted. This hyperspatial system is responsible for connecting & anchoring us to our particular space-time-our notion of time. As well, herein we find the mechanism for inter-dimensional communication, conversion, & storage of both energies and information. The key aspect to this electromagnetic system is that it is the result of collective or synergistic contributions of six components of the brain (see text). (See Chapter Notes #25)

"The overall geometry is an ellipsoidal prolate spheroidal cavity containing a sub space of a toroid traversed by a hyperbolic, non-linear Einstein-Rosen bridge......(in American lingo) an egg shaped cavity containing a doughnut crossed by a sausage" [7].

No illustrations are provided in the original publication *Ancient Wisdom & Modern Physics,* so we have improvised our own figures in this text. It is worth noting that the following are visual representations only, since there was no direct access to the researcher's data.

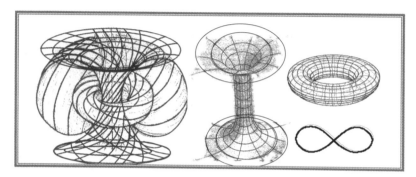

Figure **4.6 Hyperspace Connectors.** *The torus (donut shape) is an inter-dimensional vortex. It is layered like an onion, with other torii nested inside. The torus stores & translates energy & information. Note that the torus is the **halo** that is envisaged spiritually or metaphysically! The cross section of the torus is the **figure 8 loop**- universal characteristic of magnetism! The Einstein-Rosen bridge is the connector to hyperspace & parallel realities of space & time.*

HYPERSPATIAL FORMS

The cylindrical form with trumpet-like ends is known as the Einstein-Rosen bridge. *This is your connector to hyperspace and parallel realities!* The donut shape figure is called a toroid or torus. The torus is a hyperdimensional shape connected to the formation of space-time. Within this hyperspatial complex there exist spinning and spiraling light and energies that are being both trapped and emitted. These inter-dimensional figures create a system that is responsible for connecting and anchoring us to our particular notion of *time.* Herein is the mechanism for inter-dimensional communication, as well as the conversion and storage of both energies and information. Within the midbrain

"is a relativistic spatiotemporal cavity with local enfolded hyperspatial bridges that undergoes harmonic resonances to magnetic and acoustical stimuli. The implications are almost astronomical"[8].

SYNERGISTIC GEOMETRY

This magnetic field configuration within the brain represents an inter-dimensional vortex that connects our external universe to unseen, virtual dimensions that are far removed from our normal conscious awareness and physical senses. The geometry of these magnetic hyperspatial structures are the result of the combined magnetic field contributions of six components of the brain structure. This is important to realize!

The overall three-dimensional fields result from the active and total contributions of the *thalamus, hypothalamus, hypocampus, amygdala, pituitary,* and *pineal* functions *collectively* .

> All of these components must work together, synergistically, to produce this ideal magnetic field profile. If any one of the six components is inactive, or if the contribution of any single component is removed (*through under-functioning or dormancy*), then the brain does not fulfill its maximum *potential magnetic hyperspatial functioning.*

This means that *training with activities and exercises* that can directly influence these brain areas are necessary if an individual is to evolve towards their potential hyperspatial abilities. However, *it is our potential to awaken all our brain areas, and we can achieve it!*

STIMULI TO BRAIN

According to researchers, Tai Chi masters exhibit magnetic fields that were *elongated* in the vertical axis, i.e. the length of the cylindrical tube of the Einstein-Rosen Bridge. This elongation of the vertical axis indicates a greater degree of potential variance to space-time effects. So Tai Chi masters could conceivable influence (*if not reverse*) the aging process. Along with proper Tai Chi form, the researchers suggest that the study of Sacred Geometry is a powerful stimulus to the brain. A wide range of movements broadly classified as *Qigong,* or *Chi Kung,* and *Falun Gong* also qualify [9].

> When you work with geometry the "angles and diagrams have their space-time analogues in the Mind, Soul and Spirit" [10].

All geometry has its correlate in "frequency domain", the domain in which the brain functions electromagnetically. Electromagnetic activity inherently relates to scalar potentials and hyperfields. Of course, *all visualizations* directed towards conscious activation of brain centers are *direct stimulus* to the brain's electromagnetic activity! *Consciousness and Intent direct the activity of the hyperfields of the brain.*

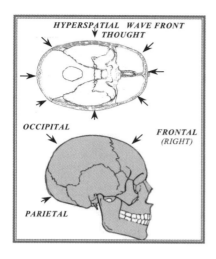

Figure 4.7 **Thought As A Multidimensional Wavefront.** *(Diagram adapted from Matrix III). Information & thought enter the brain as a hyperspatial, multi-dimensional wavefront. The brain has multiple systems that are designed to resonate to a variety of magnetic & acoustical stimuli. As a crystalline resonating organic structure, the brain translates the universal frequency spectrum into electrical impulses. The bones of the cranium, along with the internal liquid crystal structures, establish harmonic resonance to frequencies from higher dimensional space. These higher frequencies become converted & connected to 3D electromagnetic fields through channels of complex vibrating patterns within the crystalline structures.*

A Living Crystal

The brain can be described as a *"crystalline resonating organic structure that grounds the mind. As the mind interpenetrates the brain, different anatomical structures resonate with, and ground particular aspects of the mind's functioning"* [11]. Four systems within the human skull are designed to resonate to separate functions. These are:

- the two hemispheres (functioning as one system)
- the sensory cortex
- the 3rd and lateral ventricles
- and the skull itself

Each system of the brain functions separately to receive, process, and amplify, varying aspects of the universal frequency spectrum. The skull, or cranium, is made up of a crystalline structure. The crystalline ionic structures are compounds of calcium carbonates and phosphates.

This material is able to undergo very complex vibrations that form a 12-dimensional hyperspatial field structure or lattice. The lattice connects 3 dimensional fields to the hyperspatial dimensions.

Thought Resonator

The cranium is made up of five bones that share in the formation of resonant patterns within the cranial cavity. These patterns are, collectively, responsible for translating a hyperdimensional thought waveform into a signal that is registered in the brain . In Figure 4.8 we see a five-fold resonant pattern set up between the five cranial bones of the skull. The internal structures within the cranial cavity-the brain itself- is also formed from crystalline material.

The mind-brain complex interrelates through antenna-like structures in the brain that form *energy templates* at microscopic levels. The process involves the Fourier translation of holographic patterns from hyperspatial coded information into electrical outputs within the brain. We see the brain as a masterpiece of Sacred Geometry. The bone structures of the cranium form a cavity that is capable of enfolding a unified field [13].

Hameroff and Penrose have been studying the microtubule structure of brain cells and propose that these are involved in aspects of intelligence as well as being the locus of consciousness. The microtubule, or cytoskeleton of the cell, exhibits properties that allow them to function at the quantum level for information exchange [13]. The water within the microtubules can become highly structured and ordered through quantum coherence by the simple action of *focus or intent.*

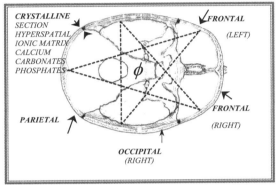

Figure 4.8 **The Brain As A Masterpiece Of Sacred Geometry.** *(Diagram adapted from Matrix III). The five sections of the cranial bones establish a resonant pattern within the internal liquid crystalline structures of the brain. The connecting fissures of the 5 major bones of the cranium allow for a range of linear & non-linear motions & complex vibrations to take place. The natural resonant frequency of the cranium falls in the range of 840-890 MHz [also a DNA resonant frequency] (cellular telephone frequency). The crystalline structures of the cranium allow for the formation of a 12 dimensional hyperspatial field structure (lattice). The resonant pattern that we see in the figure is the 5-point star. This Pentangle is the symbol of the ancient Greek school of Mathematics that was founded by Pythogorus. The golden mean ratio, PHI (ϕ) (1.618) is expressed through various ratios in the figure. Geometric structure is resonant to higher dimensions, light & sound.*

RESONANCE REQUIRES CHARGE

The resonant systems of the brain depend on the ability of the biological cells to hold an electrical ionizing charge. Through this electrical ionizing charge, *Consciousness can express itself through matter!*

High electrical potentials are required in the brain-nervous system network for all this to work at optimum levels. It takes a lot of electricity to fuel the system. As we carry a higher capacity of *charge,* we enable the expression of Consciousness through matter- for Spirit to express itself in the biology. This capacity can be enhanced through the EMF Balancing Technique®.

MUTLI-DIMENSIONAL CIRCUIT CONNECTIONS

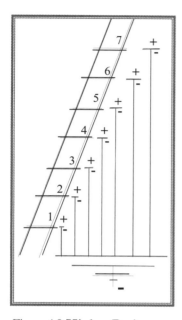

Figure 4.9 **Higher Brain Circuits Require Higher Charge.** *This illustration conceptualizes the requirement of higher 'charge' in order to activate higher brain circuit functions. The charge or potential is derived from the activation and contribution of successively more and more cells of the white and grey matter of both brain & spinal cord. Higher charge is equivalent to higher capacitance or storage of electric potential. The brain circuits relate to frequencies of light. Frequencies of light vary in energy level according to color. Cellular awareness rises accordingly, and consciousness can more clearly express itself through the body! Increasing the energy flow and activating brain cells are the keys to expanding awareness & achieving dialogue with Spirit.(See Chapter Notes #26)*

THE LAW OF OCTAVES

We have introduced the idea that the brain has been designed with innate hyperfunction abilities. These hyperfunctions hold the key to unraveling the mysteries of our innate paranormal potential, and our ability to influence matter and field structure from higher levels of the virtual reality.

Not too surprisingly, therefore, there is wiring and circuitry dedicated to various specialized process relating to both our normal, as well as, our multi-dimensional, functions.

The brain circuits discovered by Timothy Leary were found to be consistent with the *law of octaves*. There are eight brain circuits [14]. There are many examples of the octave playing a significant role in our world. For example, we find the I Ching consists of 64 hexagrams (a base 8). As well, modern geneticists have found that the DNA-RNA dialogue --- the molecular information system governing life and evolution -- it transmitted by 64 (8x8) codons [16].

CIRCUITS RELATE TO COLOR & CHARGE

Each of the first seven circuits of the brain is said to resonate with a particular vibrational frequency of the color spectrum: in ascending order these are- red, orange, yellow, green, blue, indigo, and violet . Generally the first four circuits could be equated to left-brain operation, and the last four (5-8) are associated with right brain functioning. As such, the left-brain circuits are concerned with terrestrial affairs, while the right brain circuits are dedicated to extraterrestrial or evolutionary purposes.

Our consciousness is viewed as being related to the same seven frequencies and colors. Therefore our awareness is shaped by the mixed qualities of the vibrational frequencies that are active in these circuits.

For each person this mix is different. As consciousness expands, higher levels of brain circuitry kick-in. In this sense, the thresholds of the circuitry already pre-exist in the brain. As we engage in actively regulating the secretion of brain hormones, we create chemical changes in the brain that allow for enhanced aspects of consciousness to unfold.

The work of Dr.Timothy Leary, as well as that of others researchers, have correlated the individual brain circuits with certain areas of the brain. Each of the seven brain areas contributes successively to jacking up the electricity, or potential charge, between the alternating grey and white matter of the brain. This applies to the brain/spinal cord system as an integrated whole. The white and grey matter contribute alternate negative and positive electric charge that work jointly as a capacitor (as in electronics) to store increasing amounts of *charge.*

As the capacitance effect increases (*see figure 4.9*), the tuning of the brain circuitry is affected as a whole. This alters the frequency of the overall brain rhythm. The brain cells become tuned to higher frequencies, so they will now respond to receiving and storing more subtle energies. The cells can now hold a higher level of awareness.

The primary purpose of the body is to hold an ionizing charge so that consciousness can express through it [16]. The whole system functions on the basis of chemical activity, ionizing fluids, potentials, storing of charge, and electricity.

Altering our brain frequency is equivalent to altering the operational states of the individual circuits.

CHEMICAL CONNECTORS

The nervous system is an essential component of the brain circuitry. As an extension to the brain, it serves to *amplify the brain signals*! *A fine tuned, healthy, energized nervous system enhances brain operation!*

The nervous system is a self-contained network that floats within the physical body. The body of the nervous system is separated from the physical body- i.e. the nerves and the body do not make contact. The only connection between the two separate bodies is through chemical reactions-- *the chemical hormone transmitters.*

The hormones function as broadcasters of frequency patterns.

The brain-nervous system complex functions at one *level of consciousness.* The physical body functions at another distinct *level of consciousness.* These two levels of consciousness communicate through chemical *hormone transmitters.*

We interpret our feelings from these chemicals!

That is, we interpret our feelings through the action of one level of consciousness relating/communicating to another through chemical activity. When this system is not *fine tuned*, when this communication does not function at optimum levels, *our sense of reality can be distorted indeed*! Our emotional balance is directly linked to good communication between two separate levels of consciousness. This communication system is linked through chemical hormone transmitters/broadcasters.

	CIRCUIT	BRAIN AREAS	COLOR FREQUENCY	GEOMETRY
8	NON-LOCAL QUANTUM	Outside body		Multi-dimensional
7	META-PROGRAMMING	Frontal lobes	violet	Multi-dimensional
6	NEURO-GENETIC	Right hemisphere 3left lobes, 3 right lobes	indigo	Multi-dimensional
5	NEURO-SOMATIC	Right cortex Inner brain	blue	Multi-dimensional
4	SOCIO-SEXUAL	Left neo-cortex	green	Euclidean
3	TIME-BINDING SEMANTIC	Left cortex	yellow	Euclidean
2	EMOTIONAL	Thalamus, pons & 4th ventricle	orange	Euclidean
1	BIO-SURIVAL	Brain stem	red	Euclidean

Table 4.1 Brain Circuit Characteristics

PREFERRED PATHWAYS ALTERED BY CONSCIOUSNESS

Brain signals habitually follow certain preferred pathways. The pathways that are followed are selected from literally thousands of possible paths. The overall brain activity plays a role in 'tuning' and modulating the signals. The electrical potentials in the brain pathways can be altered by an act of consciousness, i.e. *Intent*. Therefore, *there is no habitual though pattern that we cannot change.* The secretion of brain chemicals, the hormones, can be controlled by an act of consciousness. The secretion of hormones alters the electrical potentials in the pathways.

Accordingly, there is no emotional response that cannot be changed. New choices of signal pathways are established as stored patterns of potential energy within the cells.

Millions of brain cells can be activated and made to contribute higher electrical potential states to the brain *by an act of consciousness.* As this happens, tuning of the brain circuits takes place. As higher levels of electricity are stored, thinking capacity increases. For many people, brain cells remain switched off, unused, for perhaps their entire lifetime. This need not be, as we can consciously participate in awakening these cells that can contribute to accelerating our evolutionary development.

SPECIALIZED PROCESSORS

It has become evident that certain components of the brain are engaged in the processing of uniquely specialized tasks. Within each of the designated brain areas are the established habitual pathways that processing follows. These pathways are simply one of thousands of other possible options that could be established. A significant discovery established that the formation of brain pathways is highly influenced by a process called *imprinting.*

The imprinting process is very active during certain stages of our growth and development, such as in early childhood and our early teen years. At these times certain habitual patterns of response are created and stored in the brain. These are stored as actual electrical potential maps within the cells. These stored patterns serve as *templates* for all later processing.

The idea of being "stuck in a pattern" is a very literal description of neural activity in the brain following the same pathway repeatedly, over and over again and arriving consistently at the same programmed "response action". However, there is no response action that cannot be changed!

CHILDHOOD DEVELOPMENT OF PATHWAYS

During our critical periods of neurological development, the imprints that are formed establish delimiting constraints upon our learning ability. We become conditioned, and we can learn only according to the extent that our imprinted circuitry permits. If the "software" of the brain circuitry develops to higher degrees of sophistication and complexity, this impacts on the learning process.

The overall development of an individual is enhanced when each successive imprint pattern adds to the existing software complexity of the operating system. This results in added complexity and power to the brain's information processing system. The tuning of the overall brain frequency and rhythm is raised. Brain capacity increases. Brain cells tune to higher frequencies and connect to higher levels of awareness. Establishing more sophisticated brain "software" is what we wish to help establish early in life for our children. Specific educational approaches equip young children with more capable "operating software" [21].

> There exist a limited number of *windows in time* during the child's neurological development in which the benefits of the positive imprinting and stimulation are established [20]. With the optimum early imprinting and stimulation during these *windows of time*, the child becomes equipped with sophisticated *templates* for more complex brain functions. These are the tools that the child subsequently carries for life!

As we increase our ability to process information, we raise our brain capacity. We also increase our awareness and raise our level of consciousness. We engage in kicking-in our evolutionary brain circuits that connect us with our multi-dimensional reality. We can assist our young children for this to occur earlier in their lives.

ROLE & CONNECTION OF THE CIRCUITS

All areas of the brain play an active role in contributing to brain circuitry. There are no redundant parts. All circuits fulfill important functions. However, certain components may be underactive or dormant. This leads to certain brain circuits being dormant, or underactive. Circuits 6 and 7 require the bridging of the two halves of the brain and getting both hemispheres to work in unison.

Moreover, the harmony and resonance between the circuitry becomes a function of proper chemical secretions from the glands-- notably the pituitary and pineal glands-- as well as the presence of ionizing potentials (charge) at the cellular membranes. Highest overall capacity is derived when the circuits can become integrated and work as a whole. However, circuit one can contribute to "freezing" the brain's function at this level because of the effect of *fear* on the network.

The greatest handicap to our own evolution is fear. Because of this emotion we prevent ourselves from functioning in the higher circuits of the *right brain* which are related to our evolutionary, and multidimensional, destiny. Because of imprinting and socio-economic conditions, the majority of people find themselves *unable to rise above circuit levels 1 and 2*. Many people remain preoccupied with the basic issues of security and survival.

Circuit 4 is central to the overall system. It has the capacity to supply power to the higher centers, *or shut them down*. Within the structure of the 4th circuit, we find a close correlation between consciousness and the physical matter body. Here, chemical secretion of hormones results in our emotions.

We relate to these secretions as a measure of who we are. Accordingly, hormone exchange and balance can alter our very character. From this 4th center there is a regulation of life-energy that can only be expressed in the chakras if they are open. All our feelings are polarized and controlled in this area of the brain. We feel this area as the center of our being.

Table 4.2   Brain Circuit Function

	CIRCUIT	FUNCTION	KEY PRECEPT
8	NON-LOCAL QUANTUM	Outside body	
7	META-PROGRAMMING	Control Lower Circuits	Perception Of Infinite Realities
6	NEURO-GENETIC	Collective DNA DNA-RNA Dialogue Intuition	Synchronicity DNA Collective
5	NEURO-SOMATIC	Integrative-The Whole Thought	Process Emotional Patterns
4	SOCIO-SEXUAL	Supply Power To Higher Levels	Emotional Center Of Being
3	TIME-BINDING SEMANTIC	Linked With Voice	Intellectual Center Sense Of Time
2	EMOTIONAL	Connected To Voluntary Nervous System	Ego
1	BIO-SURIVAL	Endocrine & Life support Fear shuts Access To Higher circuits	What Is Safe

Circuit 5 plays an integrative function working with concepts and patterns coming from our higher emotions. The *pituitary gland*, when triggered to release hormones, *activates the function of the 6th level circuit*. Our inner vision stems from here. This is what we also know as *intuition*. Circuit 6 is connected to perception of the future. The future is being constructed at level 7, and both level 6 and 7 are closely linked. The 6th circuit has been called the *Collective DNA Circuit*.

AN EVOLUTIONARY CIRCUIT

The term collective means that this circuit has access to the entire evolutionary script-- what we call past and future.

Imprinting of this circuit is through *bio-electrical stresses* [17]. This circuit is involved in the processing of the DNA-RNA feedback loop or dialogue. To understand this process we review the relationship between these two molecular structures.

The DNA holds the information or blueprints, but this information must be "extracted" in order to be useful. The role of RNA is key, because it "reads and copies" the DNA. At this stage another element enters the picture-- the histones. Histones are simple proteins that combine with nucleic acids to form nucleoproteins. Histones function to block the transfer of genetic information that is not used in the development of new cells [18]. Cell differentiation, an important biological function, is the result of this action by the histones. However, because the histones coat the DNA, there may be indiscriminate blocking of information that would contribute to our evolutionary process. Does the creation of new anti-histone proteins lie within the realm of this circuit?

DIALOGUE WITH SPIRIT

Circuits 6 and 7 are called the *universal translator*. When the nervous system is able to receive signals from the RNA-DNA dialogue, then these higher circuits trigger [19].

Activation of these circuits is the means of opening the book of knowledge within the DNA. These circuits are called the universal translators.

What becomes evident from this discussion is the connectedness between DNA, the brain's processing circuitry, and the Mind/(subtle information fields). All three must interrelate in some *strange loop* of their own for evolutionary steps to move forward.

In this chapter we have seen how the brain is designed as a magnetic and acoustic resonance chamber. Because of its structure, the brain is also a bio-crystalline *prism*, receiving and amplifying cosmic signals. As a prism, the brain separates light into its 7-frequency/color components. These light energies are present in varying degrees in the 7 circuits of the brain. As we become able to raise the intensity of light in these circuits, then the functions and capabilities of the higher circuits will come within our conscious awareness. As we connect more strongly with our multi-dimensional nature through these circuits, we connect with *Spirit*.

Studies have shown that the brain can be 'entrained' (*made to vibrate or resonate*) with a variety of outside source frequencies. [A good example of this is the effect of cellular telephone frequency has on *the brain or DNA structure itself!*] All brain pathway patterns have correlations in what we have referred to as the scalar or subtle realm. It is through this realm that we exercise the greatest influence to the organizing scalar potentials that are the patterns stored within the cells. It is also through the subtle realm that we can affect the tuning of the brain's circuitry.

When the brain circuitry is tuned, it can better process and amplify the light frequencies through the nervous system. This will have a powerful **effect** on the operating levels of individual circuits because we are raising the **electrical** potentials within the individual cells. As the electrical potentials are raised, all **circuits** trigger into expanded operation.

TUNING THROUGH INTERACTION

Dialogue with Spirit develops through conscious use of these higher circuits, and is accelerated through integrating and tuning the DNA/Brain-Heart/Mind complex. We can affect this tuning directly through the human energy field. Balancing the human energy field affects the tuning of the brain-nervous system complex. At the same time, pathways are opened and formed for more *light* energy to enter the systems and activate these brain circuits. This is but one of the processes that takes place with the *EMF Balancing Technique®*. As the brain and nervous system awaken to the dialogue between DNA-RNA, and, as this information is collected and processed by this higher brain circuit- *the book of knowledge will open to reveal its most inner secrets.*

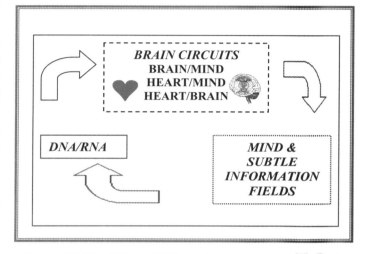

Figure 4.10 **The Triune Of Evolutionary Process.** *The Brain, Mind field, and DNA form a triune that must be integrated, tuned, and activated if accelerated evolutionary processes are to take place. The subtle information fields carry the original blueprints of DNA. The RNA 'reads' the encoding from the subtle fields in a similar fashion that a foreman of a construction site will 'read' a blueprint from a drafting table. Both RNA & the foreman require light! The requirement is that the full light spectrum of colors be available to fully translate and transfer encoded information from the subtle fields to RNA. The higher frequencies of light are higher energy electromagnetic waves. These require highly charged electromagnetic fields in which to operate. The DNA/RNA process is connected to the higher brain circuit functions that collect information for processing. For optimum efficiency, the DNA/Brain/Mind complex is tuned & balanced with the full spectrum of light frequencies, and supplied with optimal levels of electrical charge or potentials. The central role of the Heart suggests that the master control ultimately lies within the interfaces of Heart/Mind & Heart/Brain systems. Evolution is connected to this triune circuitry!*

"The human form is a conglomerate of energy fields...
those energy fields have been bent and contorted
by a lifetime of habits and misuse."
Carlos Castaneda, "The Second Ring of Power,"

CHAPTER FIVE

GROWING
IN AWARENESS

Aligning With The Axis Of Consciousness

*People like us, who believe in physics, know that the distinction between
past, present, and future is only a stubbornly persistent illusion.*

Albert Einstein

There is an increasing focus around the ideas of *expanding
consciousness, increasing awareness,* and bringing *more of Spirit* into
the body-- into the biology. How can one relate these notions to
something tangible? How do you expand Consciousness? These are big questions that
can preoccupy many learned scholars in the field of cognitive sciences and related
disciplines.

Here we will approach the subject from a rather pragmatic perspective. We will
define Consciousness, as used in this section, as *awareness of self.* To expand
consciousness is to expand the knowing of who you are. To know who you are is to
reconnect with your multi-dimensional essence! Is this the key purpose to our
existence? *Imagine looking outward at your greater Consciousness through a physical
construct of yourself made by Consciousness!*

EVOLUTION RELATES TO EXPANDING CONSCIOUSNESS

We can intuitively connect the concept of expanding consciousness and
increasing awareness to some internal process of evolution. In Professor's Tiller's view,
*"human evolution is characterized by, and limited by, the penetration of spirit into
dense matter"*[1]. In the evolutionary process, greater degrees of consciousness can be
associated with achieving more complexity within the systems.

In his thesis of parallel universes, Everett demonstrates that complexity can
essentially be measured using information theory. The greater the number of
interactions with the outside universe, the more you know. The more information that
you can extract from the external universe, the greater is the internal complexity.

Tiller sees these as organizational structures that may be neural at one level, but of a subtle nature at other levels. By necessity, these organizational structures are needed to provide a "skeletal template for the spirit substance" [1].

As we look at ourselves as multi-dimensional beings, we can understand that evolutionary process will affect all structural layers of our essence simultaneously. Somehow, the ultimate impact on us, as self-aware beings, will be dependent upon the degree of interconnectedness, balance, and coherency that exists within our system's organization.

Human evolution is characterized by 'discovering' the existence of 'new' dimensions and tunable circuits within our energy dynamics. These dimensions exist as elements of creation and are accessible from within our own multi-dimensional configuration. Expanding awareness encompasses the realization that we can consciously alter our internal architectural dynamics. In doing so, we expand our angular view outward, to encompass a greater slice of this creation.

CRITERIA FOR EVOLUTIONARY PROCESS

So we look at the question "what is the main requirement for evolutionary processes"? In his paper *A Physical Model of the Biofield (see Appendix C)*, Detela provides the general direction to the answer- the main requirement of evolutionary processes is *information*. However, structures must be in place, or develop, in order for these processes to take place.

- An informational base
- An evolutionary component

In particular, Detela states that there must be a capability of storing an enormous amount of information *(bits of information)*.

The evolutionary aspect is connected to the self-organizing ability of the field structure.

The two processes are inseparably linked. Detela describes this as a symbiosis of both. There must be a source of primary information for evolution to take place. At whatever level of the living organism structure we chose to look at, the principles remain the same. More complexity within the organism develops through the evolutionary process. This contributes to greater levels of information handling ability, enhanced communication systems, and a higher degree and efficiency at which energies are utilized for various processes. The principles of evolutionary process extend beyond the biofield to all subtle energy structures.

Table 5.1 CRITERIA FOR EVOLUTIONARY PROCESS
INTERACTION WITH THE SOURCE OF INFORMATION
FLOW OF INFORMATION
ENERGETIC STRUCTURES--*wiring & subtle "skeletal" structures*
ATTUNEMENT BETWEEN SOURCE AND RECEIVER---*coherence & resonance requiring tuning*
ABILITY OF RECEIVER TO DERIVE MEANING OF INFORMATION--- *as in the idea of active information* requires tuning, balance, & coherence within system
ABILITY OF RECEIVER TO HANDLE THE INTENSITY AND THE FORMAT IN WHICH INFORMATION IS DELIVERED ---*requires tuning, balance, & coherence within system*

Evolutionary process is not limited to changes within the biofield. All subtle aspects of our energy anatomy play a role as an interactive *whole*. As we have seen from Sarfatti's interactive loops, mind and matter play a dance in self-referencing each other on an ongoing basis.

Information comes in and information goes out in a self-referencing loop. Under the *back action* principle the ongoing interaction produces a solution that is "self-consistently changing its generating equation"[2]. Communication is at the basis of evolutionary processes.

Therefore, expanding consciousness is related to communication, information and information processing ability. We must also consider processing the flow of energies that are associated and required for the process to take place. Accordingly, we can now establish some basic criteria necessary for evolution to take place. These are summarized in Table 5.1.

CONSCIOUSNESS OF A SYSTEM DEFINED BY AN EQUATION

Of course we cannot define or describe Consciousness by an equation. However, the principles of information theory can be helpful in establishing a measure of the internal complexity within a system. We connect complexity to greater abilities to interact and exchange information with the outside universe. Greater complexity becomes synonymous with higher degrees of consciousness.

Professor Tiller has proposed a formula, or equation, that can be used to characterize the consciousness of a system. This equation is related to information theory. Tiller relates level of consciousness to the channel capacity, or measure of a living system's ability to handle and process information. The general form of the Consciousness equation is:

$$\text{Consciousness} = A \cdot \Delta\gamma \cdot \ln_2 (1 + P/N) \text{ [3]}$$

where the parameters of this equation are defined in Table 5.2. The equation is based on a formula in engineering communication theory.

TABLE 5.2   EQUATION OF CONSCIOUSNESS
$\text{Consciousness} = A \cdot \Delta\gamma \cdot \ln_2 (1 + P/N)$
(adapted from William Tiller)

TERM	DEFINITION
Consciousness	channel capacity quantity of information processed
A	a constant
$\Delta\gamma$	bandwidth of the system -effective frequency range, related to γ & γ_0 - a function of γ_0
γ γ_0	frequency natural resonant frequency [personal tone]
$\ln_2$	log to the base 2
P	signal power of the system intensity level
N	noise level of the system

MATHEMATICAL PERSPECTIVE

It is not necessary that you completely comprehend the mathematical concepts presented here in order to understand the importance of energy anatomy.   The mathematical portion is presented here to enhance the depth of your understanding if you choose to view it from a math perspective. However, if you wish to skip the math, simply jump to the section below entitled *Solutions to the Human Equation.*

In our equation the term A is simply a constant, so we can ignore this for our discussion. The term $\ln_2$ means $2^{(n)}$,which is 2 raised to the power of whatever is contained in the brackets. For purposes of our discussion this also can be ignored.

From a mathematical perspective, what are significant to us are the terms $\Delta\gamma$, γ, P, and N. To grow in Consciousness, we are looking for those factors that will give greater mathematical solutions to this equation. How can these variables be modified to result in a greater solution to the equation? We have solved this equation below. In order to raise or increase the value of the solutions to our consciousness equation, any combinations of the following conditions may apply:

- increase $\Delta\gamma$
- increase P
- decrease N

How can we relate to this equation as a human being? Let's look at the solution in terms of the human perspective.

SOLUTIONS TO THE HUMAN EQUATION

INCREASE RESONANT FREQUENCY

Increase $\Delta\gamma$ This is bandwidth, or effective frequency range or response (sensitivity) of our energy anatomy. This is a measure of the frequencies, or patterns, that one can receive or perceive. It is therefore directly related to the information handling capacity of the individual. In general, bandwidth is a function of the complexity of a life form.

For an individual, $\Delta\gamma$ becomes a function of the person's base vibration or frequency- i.e. one's resonant frequency γ_o. The higher the resonant frequency of an individual, the greater is their bandwidth or ability to communicate (two-way) information. In this equation, in order to increase consciousness you must *increase your resonant frequency* γ_o. Your resonant frequency is a <u>system's</u> property. It is related to the degree of tuning, balance, internal integration, connectedness and coherence that exists throughout the entire organizational energy complex.

As structures evolve in balance, the resonant frequency is raised. System bandwidth increases with a greater response to outside vibrations. One's personal tone experiences an adjustment upward. There is a rise in internal rhythm as a whole. This is equivalent to a raise in Consciousness level. We have seen in an earlier chapter how the brain's overall rhythm responds in a similar fashion. As the brain functions more as an integrated whole, its frequency is raised. It becomes more capable as a processor of multi-dimensional information as it carries more charge.

INCREASE FLOW

Increase P. P is signal power. For an individual, this represents the ability to carry, handle, and process higher levels of *energy*. If a person is to increase in Consciousness, one must *increase the ability to flow more energy* through their anatomy. This is equivalent to increasing your charge.

Increased energy flow requires the opening and balancing of existing channels within the 'skeletal' fabric of the energy anatomy. Increased energy flow also requires the evolutionary process of developing new wiring, or new energy channels, within this fabric. This wiring is necessary to accommodate the higher levels of subtle energy flow in and out of the individual's energy anatomy.

The wiring also contributes to increased internal complexity or intelligence of the processing hardware. This complexity can then accommodate the presence of more of Spirit in all levels of matter. It allows for more exchange of information. A greater communication with the external universe ensues. Furthermore, we must become more coherent in every aspect of our being. Coherence results in high amplification of our power levels, and greater system capacity. Evolution is linked to increasing the flow of information, and energy, through our subtle energy anatomy.

ESTABLISH COHERENCE

<u>Decrease **N**</u>. N represents the noise in the system. This term has the ability to adversely affect our equation. For a human being, this translates into what can we consider to be the "noise" that clogs up the equation and minimizes our lives. We need look only at all those factors that we allow to "hold us back". These include, but are not limited to, our fears, our run-away emotions, our apprehensions, our clinging to the past, hanging on to patterns that no longer serve us. This list goes on and on. It's all those things for which we seek the empowerment to change about ourselves, and our lives!

To increase our Consciousness, we need to *decrease the noise in our lives*. We also need to establish internal integration and coherence. We must develop an evolutionary energy anatomy that supports and amplifies our *INTENTS*, and communicates these to the external universe. We need to increase our "charge", or "energy flow" of our whole energy anatomy-- our whole being. We must actively participate in co-creating our lives.

GEOMETRICAL ARCHITECTURE OF CONSCIOUSNESS

We can understand that to become more conscious beings, we somehow become more complex. This complexity enables us to become better communicators -- receivers and transmitters-- with the outside universe. As we get to know more, a greater amount of information will become available to us. We will then transmit more information about ourselves outwardly.

But what do we look like as more conscious beings? How do we become different? How do we change?

Are we more conscious because we have become more intelligent? Are we more aware because our brain interface begins to function at a superior level? Do we know more because our DNA has evolved-that more strands and chromosomes have come on-line? Do we communicate better because the DNA-RNA dialogue improves and our associated brain circuits function in a superior multi-dimensional fashion? Are we more conscious and aware because our energy fields have evolved?

Of course, the answer to each of the above questions is a resounding YES! Yet, we are looking for a fundamental way in which to characterize *how* we are different.

> **As we become more conscious and aware, as we hold more of Spirit in matter, our fundamental and underlying multi-dimensional architecture changes. Because consciousness expresses itself through a grid, lattice or web of life. Alignment of geometry is alignment of the pathways of Spirit.**

Consciousness functions through the pathways and the interconnections of the architecture of geometry. Our multi-dimensional architecture is fundamental to manifesting our 3-dimensinal reality. To raise our consciousness in 3-D reality, we must improve, or *complexify* (to coin a word), the geometric grids and patterns within our personal architectural designs. We must also align our personal grids to those external ones (*Cosmic Lattice, Earth Consciousness Grid*) upon which we depend for both physical and spiritual nourishment.

As we become more complex beings we build more wiring, more circuits, more pathways, more connections to our existing ones. More complex and elaborate geometry sets into our energy fields.

> **We activate more energy templates, and our personal lattice structure evolves to become more integrated.**

We ourselves become more integrated in the spiritual, mental and emotional aspects of our being. An internal resonance becomes a measure of our alignment within all aspects of our multi-dimensional nature. Our resonance to the Whole becomes a measure of our alignment to the external universe in which we are all ONE.

AN INTER-DIMENSIONAL TOOL FOR EVOLUTION

As we decrease the noise in our lives, increase our energy channel capacity, and increase our resonant frequency, we become a more coherent and integrated being. We increase our consciousness, expand our awareness, and find ourselves in *higher communication with Spirit.* The *EMF Balancing Technique®* is an evolutionary tool. It enables the underlying processes of rewiring, internal balance, tuning, integration and coherence to take place and develop. These processes are essential for evolution. Ultimately we connect evolution to personal transformation.

The Universal Calibration Lattice (*the UCL- your personal connection*) and the EMF Balancing Technique© both enable and facilitate our connection to the external universe. As we take an evolutionary step forward to balance and rewire our internal energy systems, we raise our personal charge. In doing so, we unlock the potential of connecting with more of the Spiritual essence of our whole being!

We _are_ growing in consciousness. Consciousness can be related to communication and to our information processing ability. Increasing consciousness is directly related to building more complex geometric structures within our energy fields. Activating *energy templates,* and creating new pathways and wiring is the key to accelerating this process.

> By increasing our resonant frequency, increasing our power levels *(charge),* and reducing the noise in our lives, we can accelerate our growing in consciousness. Higher communication is the link to *more Spirit,* as we develop evolutionary subtle *skeletal* wiring that enables more of Spirit to be present in all levels of our being.

CHAPTER SIX

RAINBOW
HANDS

Your Pot Of Gold

The most beautiful thing we can experience is the mysterious.
It is the source of all true art and science.

Albert Einstein

Many significant ideas, concepts, discoveries, as well as much contemporary scientific thought will be introduced in this chapter and the one that follows. Any one of these ideas could be pursued in much greater depth. All are elements of a new paradigm that is required to better understand our nature as electromagnetic beings. In this, and the following chapter, our overall goal in this brief layman's thesis is to attempt to present and demystify a multi-faceted, multi-disciplined, and complex subject. It is from the perspective of the *collective* concepts that we begin to get a feel for the immense scope of our higher dimensional electromagnetic nature. The answers and understanding that we seek truly reside within the rediscovery and remembering of our multi-dimensional essence.

We open with this relevant statement by Brian Greene from *The Elegant Universe*:

"...If you sweep your hand in a large arc, you are moving not only through the three extended dimensions, but also through these curled-up dimensions" [1].

So you see, not only do we possess a multi-dimensional nature, *we move through a multi-dimensional space!* What lies within these curled up dimensions?

RETURNING TO THE 5ᵀᴴ DIMENSION & THE MIND FIELD

In Chapter 2 we introduced the concept that electromagnetic and magnetic fields have their own multi-dimensional nature and origin-- the 5ᵗʰ dimension and beyond. What lies beyond? These fields have within them, hidden, nested unobserved realities. The hyperfields of other spaces-- higher dimensions-- show their presence in magnetism, and they show their presence at the hand.

The hyperfields, like scalar waves, are the inter-dimensional connectors. Hyperfields cannot be ignored. Bearden stresses that the hyperfields are the fundamental fields rather than electromagnetic fields;

"The hyperfields collect coherently and kindle into electromagnetic fields, creating or destroying it" [2]! **Ultimately, the hyperfields connect to, and are influenced by the mind field.**

All electromagnetic activity is connected to fluctuations that occur within the *vacuum of hyperspace*. The mind field produces the pilot information waves that direct and organize the electromagnetic fields through the intermediaries of the hyperfields. The mind interacts with matter through the hyperfields. Light is the intermediary carrier of the encoded patterned life energy!

In our next chapter, we will see that the torsion field is always associated with electromagnetic fields, and is a connector to it. This is the primary hyperspatial interactive link to the subtle energies. It is at the basis of the *human-to-human connection* whenever you assist another with the *Rainbow in Your Hands*. On this note we commemorate the pioneering contributions of Davis & Rawls to our ongoing advancement in the understanding of human magnetism. Davis & Rawls *encouraged everyone* to explore their natural energies, not only for themselves, but also for the benefit of others.

MANIFESTING ENERGY IS NATURAL

We all exhibit natural energies, this is our nature! This is the message to us from Davis and Rawls [3]. We need not do anything "special" to manifest this energy, it just is!

Our energies originate from outside space-time! Matter is but an alternate expression of light, and light exists outside of space-time.

Light is in constant communication with each particle in existence. It is literally the messenger of the electromagnetic field. Light continues to flow through us. It is within the essence of our cells, and the DNA. The DNA is tuned and corrected by this flow of light!

We are energized by light. <u>This flow must not be impeded!</u> Impeding this flow results in a multitude of disorders that we experience as human beings. Many factors may contribute to impeding the flow. Correcting the flow restores and enables the natural, normal, healthy processes within our systems. Increasing the flow results in evolution of our innate potentials! *Our innate systems operate on the basis of superconductivity, i.e., flow without resistance.*

Unified Source

At their origin these energies are unified. From the whole of this primordial energy, we derive all subsequent electromagnetic potentials within our being. As living matter bodies we are in open energetic exchange with the background *fabric* of all existence--the *vacuum of hyperspace,* also known to others as the *Cosmic Lattice.*

This background fabric exhibits the properties of fluidity [a superfluid], elasticity [like a rubber band], a variety of possible vibrational modes, and a grid structure throughout all of space, from the microcosmic to macroscopic scale.

From this fabric of pure potential, this energy is molded, formed, and patterned to create this unique moment in time and space. Moment to moment, a reconstructive process takes place. We experience these as *moments* of our lives. Within each moment, a *new* reality is reconstructed in accordance with the data and *Intent of Consciousness* at that time.

This is the holographic constructive process-- moment to moment-- the *holomovement.* The hidden inner order unfolds into the outer observed reality. This is the action of Spirit and Consciousness that permeates the *lattice of the cosmos.*

The various scientific elements of our discussion in this chapter are principles that underlie the *EMF Balancing Technique®.* We encourage the reader to explore how the power & principles of the *Science of Intent* and the *Geometry of Balance* can be both *harnessed and applied, to alter and create for you,* a new reality!

Multi-dimensional Mirrors

The hands are the mirrors of the biology, the human energy systems, and the subtle energy layers. They provide multidimensional holographic type information.

The hands map out a complete acupuncture system.

The acupuncture points and meridians in the hands relate to all aspects of one's physiology and state of health. This means that the body's physiology and energy states can be affected by 'treating' the hands. All physiological processes, biological states, electromagnetic polarity of the organs, balance and function of endocrine system, etc… could, theoretically, be detected at the hands.

The hands [*along with the feet*] contain the largest concentration of energy exchange ports of the body. The acupoints [acupuncture points] are hyperfield connectors to virtual (*unseen*) sources. Each acupoint has an associated torsion field offering potential hyperspatial interaction (*spin-spin interaction*). The meridian network collects the flow of *scalar currents*. In proximity to another human being, the hand presents possibilities of rich resonant interactive effects. As a multidimensional instrument, the hand connects to our higher potential states of perfection.

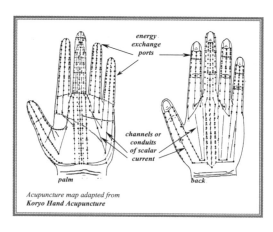

Figure 6.1 **Multi-Dimensional Mirrors.** *The hands are the mirrors of the biology, the human energy systems, and the subtle energy layers. They provide multidimensional holographic type information. The acupuncture points and meridians in the hands relate to all aspects of one's physiology and state of health. These acupoints are hyperfield connectors to virtual sources. Each acupoint has an associated torsion field offering potential hyperspatial interaction (spin-spin interaction). The meridian network collects the flow of scalar currents. In proximity to another human being, the hand presents possibilities of rich resonant interactive effects.*

A Multiplicity Of Energies

Varied energies have been detected at the hand. These include magnetic, electrostatic, infrasonic, microwave, infrared, ultraviolet, and pulsed magnetic. These are the fields detectable with conventional equipment. Other fields include the vortex polarity detected by Dr. Yao and the spiral spinning fields detected by Davis & Rawls. Evidence of chi or qi emission from the hands is now well established. The hyperfield phenomena (*chi, scalar, spin/torsion*) bypasses ordinary detection devices.

Although unobserved, the hyperfields are the primary causes of all electromagnetic phenomena. It is the total combined fields of the hand that present unconventional, hyperspatial influence to the biology and the subtle energy bodies. Resonance occurs through hyperspatial nonlocal phenomenon. Field interactions occur in the virtual state. Torsion interactions are unusual phenomena [see next chapter]. The hand is a *multidimensional instrument*.

CENTERED ON THE HEART

Within the approximate center of each palm is *laogong* point . This point is also known as Pericardium 8. It is point number eight on the Pericardium meridian energy channel. The Pericardium meridian flows outward from the *heart* area, then along the inner arm to the palm and tip of the middle index finger *(see Miracle Healing from China)*[4]. The laogong point area is the site of measurement of much rich and varied energy. These include the magnetic, electrostatic, infrasonic, microwave, infrared, ultraviolet, and pulsed magnetic mentioned above. Additionally, there are energy patterns surrounding this area that follow vortex circulating patterns [*Dr. George Yao and Davis & Rawls*]. The circulating vortex fields are indications of primary higher dimensional energy systems.

Emission of energy from this area is related to both healing & demonstrations of unusual 'feats'. This energy is most popularly called *chi* or *qi*. But this energy is also known by dozens of other names and references across various cultures and groups. *Chi* or *qi* is not subject to detection by usual devices.

Chi may be understood as a *derivative* of scalar wave phenomenon. Human magnetism can be felt & experienced about this area when both hands are moved from side to side across this point. *The energy and fields at the hand are related to the emotion and expression of the heart. The brain/heart system interrelate to pattern the fields at the hands.* These are nonlocal phenomena.

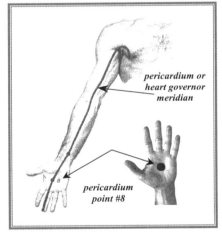

Figure 6.2 **The Laogong Point.** *The laogong point is located at approximately the center of each palm (see dark circle). This point is also known as Pericardium 8, because it is point number eight on the Pericardium meridian energy channel. The Pericardium meridian flows outward from the* **heart** *area, then along the inner arm to the palm and tip of the middle index finger. The laogong point area is the site of measurement of much rich and varied energy. These include magnetic, electrostatic, infrasonic, microwave, infrared, ultraviolet, and pulsed magnetic. (See Chapter Notes #31)*

pericardium or heart governor meridian

pericardium point #8

PRIMAL VORTEX POLARITY SYSTEM

Dr. George Yao detected what he termed the *primal energy vortex polarity system*. According to Dr. Yao, *the primal energy system*

"... determines and controls the orientation of all other energy systems of the human anatomy" [5]. **This master system organizes and influences the natural flow of all self-healing forces built into the human energy system.**

The vortex polarity system relates to motions of particles or forces in twirling spiraling fashion. These are of the twirling clockwise, positive, centripetal, compressive manner; or in a twirling spiraling counterclockwise, negative, centrifugal, expansive manner.

Vortex polarity has been established as follows:

- the right hand palm carries a counterclockwise negative vortex polarity
- the left-hand palm carries a clockwise positive vortex polarity

The reference to negative or positive here, is not the same as conventional electrical polarity. These are two different things, with different characteristics. The vortex polarity centers of the hands (as well as the body) described by Dr. Yao can be understood as *spin/torsion/scalar fields* that are *hyperspatial*, having higher dimensional origin. They are primary causal fields with the characteristic of influencing all systems 'dimensionally' below them. They play a role in the manifestation of electromagnetic energy at the hands. It is through the agent of the mind field that we are able to influence the hyperfields that form the electromagnetic fields. It is through the spiraling vortex field that connection and communication is established to the *primary vortex field of creation.*

MASTER INFLUENCE TO ALL ENERGY SYSTEMS

The human energy anatomy is organized according to a hierarchical level of control and influences. Dr. George Yao has detected, described, and mapped such a system that is of *hyperspatial origin*. Dr. Yao refers to a *primal energy vortex polarity*

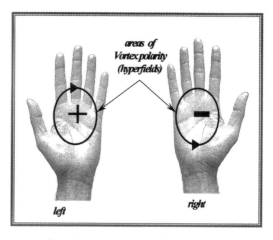

Figure 6.3 **Vortex Polarity.** *Dr. George Yao detected what he termed the* primal energy vortex polarity system. *The vortex polarity centers of the hands (as well as the body) described by Dr. Yao can be understood as spin/torsion/scalar fields that are hyperspatial, having higher dimensional origin. They are primary causal fields with the characteristic of affecting all systems 'dimensionally' below them. Electromagnetic fields are effects of such unobserved hyperfields.*

system that determines and controls the orientation of all other energy systems of the human anatomy. As such, the primal vortex polarity system directs the natural flow of all self-healing forces built into the human energy system.

According to Dr. Yao, the electrical, magnetic, vibrational, blood circulatory, nervous system, acupuncture meridians, reflex points, and proportional systems' are all adversely affected when the primary vortex system is out of balance.

In mapping out this primal energy system, Dr. Yao's work corroborates the presence of hyperspatial fields at the hands. Within Dr. Yao's description, each hand exhibits a distinct *vortex polarity*. The vortex polarity field consists of twirling and spiraling motions. They are further evidence of hyperfields at the hands.

Table 6. I Elements of the Primal Energy Vortex System
Based on research of Dr. George Yao

	RIGHT HAND Palm	LEFT HAND Palm
MASTER CONTROL SYSTEM	*Controls and orients **all** energy systems of energy anatomy Controls the natural flow of **all** self-healing forces Influences the electrical, magnetic, vibrational, blood circulatory, nervous system, acupuncture meridians, reflex points, and proportional systems*	
OUR COMMENTS	*A primary higher dimensional field of Consciousness -Scalar/torsion/spin field hyperfield exercising influence over electromagnetic fields -influenced by Emotion of the Heart & Intent - programmed through the mental field*	
VORTEX POLARITY	*Negative Centrifugal Expansive*	*Positive Centripetal Compressive*
DIRECTION	*Counterclockwise*	*Clockwise*
OUR COMMENTS	*Hyperspatial spin/torsion/scalar fields at the hands -Influenced by Emotion of the Heart & Intent -programmed through the mental field*	

Magnetic Polarity Discoveries Of Davis & Rawls

After several decades of research on magnetism, its nature, and the effect of magnetism on biological systems, Davis and Rawls published their book *Rainbow in Your Hands*. The description on the front jacket of this book reads:

"The first book ever written that scientifically supports and instructs the Science of the Laying on of Hands" [6].

We wish to place emphasis on their statement: the first book ever written that scientifically supports .... Perhaps very little is known about the work and contribution of these two researchers. In this chapter, we commemorate their achievements.

In The Flow

Davis and Rawls observed that there is a constant flow of energies in and out of the human system from our electromagnetic environment. From observation, they formulated the view that the brain functions as a receiving and transmitting station of energies that are intermixed or modulated with *thousands of body frequencies*. All these energies are generated and detectable at the hands [7]. These energies have a profound effect on another human being.

According to David and Rawls, human electricity, magnetism, and electromagnetism consist of thousands of alternating currents and voltages of many different frequencies of energy. These they called a *complex* of energies. Some of these energies, they believed, were still unknown and not yet understood [1976].

Colors represent specific vibrations of light energy. Your hands generate all the colors of the rainbow, all frequencies of light. This is the message of *Rainbow in Your Hands*. Davis and Rawls expressed their belief that the energy of the hands can be tapped for one's own benefit, as well as for others. They encourage everyone to explore their natural potential:

"Everyone has the natural energies for the Rainbow in Your Hands"[8]. **In this regard, Davis and Rawls state that we are all equal, we all exhibit the natural fields, and we all carry the potential to assist another in some way with these natural energies!**

Human Magnetism

What are some of the principle observations of this energy? In one experiment, a subject's hands were placed near the sides of a sealed glass chamber. Inside the chamber charged particles created a flow of positive and negative ions. When the subjects hands were placed near the sides of the glass chamber the charged particles danced to wave motions of the hands. *As the hands moved, the wave patterns of the charged particles followed the direction of the hands.* The hands produced the same action as the effect of a bar magnet.

From many observations, measurements, and experiments, it was apparent to Davis and Rawls that one of the basic energies found in the hands is similar to that found in an ordinary magnet. It is *human magnetism.* When the hands are clasped together as in 'prayer position', Davis and Rawls found human magnetism to cause energy to flow in the closed loop that is formed– the energy flows from right palm to left palm.

MAGNIFICENT MAGNETICS

What are the magnetic properties in the human hands? The palms of both hands exhibit different and opposite energies. Moreover, each hand has *both* kinds of energies– *magnetic* and *electric.* Davis and Rawls call this the *Law of Nature,* an expression of the principle of duality. Positive and negative energies exist together and cannot be separated. Similarly, North and South magnetic poles exist together and cannot be separated. *On the palm side of the hand there is a magnetic and electric polarity that is opposite to what is found on the reverse side of the hand (backhand).* The characteristics of each hand, as determined by Davis and Rawls are summarized in Table 6.2. The magnetism of the right *palm* is similar to a *South* pole of a magnet. The *back* of the right hand is similar to a magnet's *North* pole. It exhibits a negative polarity. The magnetism of the left *palm* is similar to the *North* pole of a magnet. The *back* of the left hand is similar to a magnet's *South* pole. It exhibits a positive polarity.

Table 6.2 Key Electromagnetic Properties Of Hands *Based on research of Davis & Rawls*				
	RIGHT HAND		LEFT HAND	
	Palm	Back	Palm	Back
MAGNETIC POLARITY	*South*	*North*	*North*	*South*
ELECTRIC POLARITY	*Positive +*	*Negative -*	*Negative -*	*Positive +*
SPIN CONE SHAPED VORTEX	*Clockwise*	*Counter-Clockwise*	*Counter-Clockwise*	*Clockwise*
QUALITY	*Strength Expansion*	*Reduces Pain*	*Reduces Pain*	*Strength Expansion*

DISCOVERING THE MAGNETISM

The magnetic center of each hand can be felt and detected with a little practice. It is located in the approximate area known as the laogong point in the palm of each hand. Anyone can find this zone-with a bit of practice. Here is a simple exercise and method of locating it. Begin with this warm-up exercise to increase your sensitivity. Place both palms together as in the prayer position (*see Figure 6.4*).

Figure 6.4 **Step 1 of exercise.** *Begin the exercise by placing the hands in the prayer position. Apply pressure evenly for 2-3 seconds. Release pressure abruptly. Keep elbows raised. Repeat 3 times. This opens the energy channels leading to the hands. Proceed with the side to side motion.*

Align fingers and thumbs evenly, and apply pressure by pushing inward evenly over the entire surface of the hands. Raise elbows up to the sides so that they are parallel to the ground. Hold this posture while applying pressure for two to three seconds. Now release pressure abruptly. Repeat a few times. This action primes and opens the energy channels to the hands.

Return to the prayer position, but now keep the palms about ½ to 1 inch (1-2 cm) apart to start. Move the hands very close together without touching, and then smoothly apart. Repeat several times for a minute or two. Next, move your hands from side to side across the center of each palm. The center of each zone of the hand will begin to feel like it contains a small circular magnet.

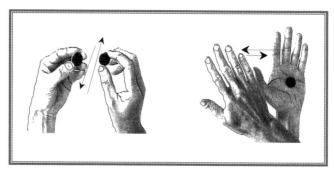

Figure 6.5 **Step 2 of exercise.** *Human magnetism effects can be perceived by moving the laogong areas in proximity from side to side with both hands. Hold the hands 25-50mm apart. Allow time for the energy to build. Then move from side to side. Using two ceramic disc magnets can simulate this feeling. Hold two 25mm diameter ceramic magnets about 25mm apart. Move them from side to side. Try with both poles opposing and both poles attracting. As you increase sensitivity at the hands you will discover the similarity of the feeling at the laogong area without the magnets. (25mm equals approximately 1 inch)*

PLAYING IN HYPERSPACE

Using two circular disc magnets can simulate the human magnetism that you will experience in this exercise. Obtain two ceramic disc magnets, 25mm X 6 mm.

Hold these between your fingers and slide the magnets past each other. Maintain a separation of 1-2 inches (25-50mm) between the magnets.

What you are actually experiencing when you slide the magnets back and forth the repelling or attractive forces-involves *the distortion/curving of space-time.* This is also playing with gravity! There is actually a distortion and movement from within the vacuum/aether superfluid! *We are playing in hyperspace* !

As your practice the exercise and become attentive to the feeling, you will detect two little doughnut (*torus*) areas of the palm that interact. Each doughnut area represents its own zone of pressure gradients where virtual forces are set up *(see Figure 6.6).*

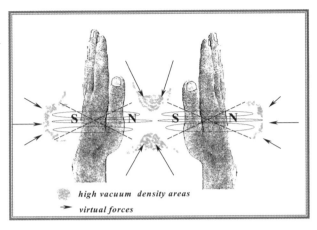

Figure 6.6 **Vacuum Density Fluctuations.** *The electromagnetic fields of the hands affect the local state of the vacuum density (indicated as gray areas) or Zero Point Energy state. This creates local curvatures in the spacetime stress. The region between the hands becomes a high stressed zone where the opposing magnetic poles & vortex centers collide (Bloch wall area). New fields and virtual forces appear. These are perceived at the hands as apparent forces (shown by arrows) when the hands are moved from side to side across the laogong point area. Each singular magnetic pole disturbs the ambient density of the vacuum. This is also shown on the reverse side of the hands. Any disturbance to the balance of the vacuum state can induce the flow of scalar currents.*

The sensations that you feel between the magnets is the feeling of magnetism that you'll come to experience by sliding your hands across each other. They are that similar.

As you slide the palms across each other you may sense an area that feels like the top of a hill or balancing point. A little bit off to one side or another, and you may feel like you've fallen off. Pressure gradients exist throughout the palm area, and are a reflection of interaction with the vacuum-aether superfluid! As you play with this exercise and become more and more attuned to your own human magnetism, you'll convince yourself that *there is a rainbow in your hands!*

What does the magnetic field look like? In their book *Magnetism and Its Effect on the Living System,* Davis and Rawls revealed some new discoveries about the nature of magnetic fields. These discoveries changed the way we view the properties of the magnetic field. The old and new views of magnetism are shown in Figures 2.2 and 2.3. In these figures we see that as the magnetic flow proceeds in two directions from

South to North pole, and from the North pole to the South pole, it forms a *figure 8 loop*. This figure 8-loop pattern exists for a bar magnet, as well as for the magnetic field of the earth. It is a law of magnetism. *It is also a property of the human magnetic field* (see Figure 2.4).

MAGNETIC FREQUENCY IN RESONANCE

In their research, Davis and Rawls discovered that the South pole of a magnet is a positive polarity with respect to the North pole, which is a negative polarity. By convention, if a bar magnet is suspended on a string, the South pole of a magnet is the end that points to the earth's magnetic North Pole. The energies of a magnet flow in *two* directions simultaneously- from the South pole to the North pole, and energy leaves the North pole and travels to the South pole.

The North pole energy spins in a counterclockwise direction (to the left looking at the end of a bar magnet North pole), whereas the South pole energy spins in a clockwise direction (to the right looking at the end of a bar magnet South pole). The energy of each pole forms a cone shaped vortex (*see Figure 2.2*), moving outward from a point from the tip of the bar magnet, and expands as it moves away through space. Within this expanding outward vortex is an inner, or 'reverse' vortex, that is a secondary expression of power and energy.

These two energies complement each other, and exist together. *Magnetic energy is dynamic* – it has a *frequency*. The frequency stems from the vibration of particles within the field structure that are in constant spinning, spiraling motion.

> **Magnetic energy is dynamic-- it has a frequency. The frequency of the magnetism is a resonance established with the vacuum.**

Figure 6.7 **Bloch Wall Zone.** *At the center of a bar magnet an area of zero magnetism exists called the Bloch wall. Within this zone the energies change course (phase) by 180° forming the figure 8 loop pattern within the zero magnetism zone. Interestingly, the Bloch wall phenomenon is associated with observations of forces of antigravity, levitation or diamagnetism. Where these energies focus, local stresses are placed on space-time itself. The Bloch wall effect is therefore a hyperspatial or n-dimensional facet of magnetism.(See Chapter Notes #32)*

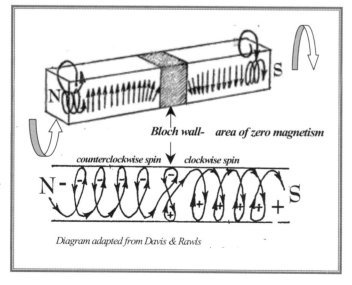

Bloch wall- area of zero magnetism

counterclockwise spin ⬇ clockwise spin

Diagram adapted from Davis & Rawls

A CENTER MAGNETIC VOID

The center of a magnet is *a point of zero magnetism*. This equator of zero magnetism is known as the *Bloch wall*. The earth also exhibits *areas* of *Bloch wall* characteristics.

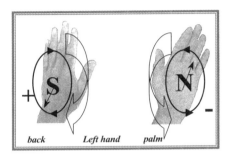

Figure 6.8 **Magnetic Properties Of Left Hand.** *Davis & Rawls established the left hand to have magnetic and electrical properties. The palm of the right hand is a magnetic North pole with a negative electrical polarity. Spin is counterclockwise for the palm. The back of the right hand carries symmetrical opposing fields. Here is a magnetic South pole, with positive electrical polarity. The spin is clockwise on the back of the right hand. The two magnetic poles have distinctly different characteristics and effects. The spin fields are hyperfields (hyperspatial & higher dimensional) having effects outside of normal 3D space. The magnetic field is associated with a hyperspatial torsion field.*

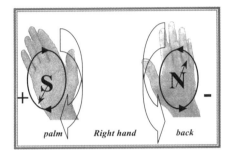

Figure 6.9 **Magnetic Properties Of Right Hand.** *Davis & Rawls established the right hand to have both magnetic and electrical properties. The palm of the right hand is a magnetic South pole with a positive electrical polarity. Spin is clockwise for the palm. The back of the right hand carries symmetrical opposing fields. Here is a magnetic North pole, with negative electrical polarity. The spin is counterclockwise on the back of the right hand. Where magnetic fields exists, there are also the unobserved causal potentials of magnetic phenomenon (the vector potential/magnetostatic scalar potential). The potentials have hyperspatial origin & inter-dimensional influence.*

At the center of the magnet, at the Bloch wall, the energy flow undergoes a 180-degree phase change, *making another figure 8 loop at its center.*

Davis and Rawls conducted tests on weighing substance that was placed at the center of two opposing magnetic poles. When a North and a South pole are brought in proximity to each other, clockwise and counterclockwise vortex patterns meet forming the *Bloch wall* of neutral magnetism at the center. When a substance was placed at the center of this zone, there was a measurable change of the weight. The opposing vortex fields created a new phenomenon. According to Davis and Rawls, the change in weight results from *a change in gravity* that is created by the two opposing vortex magnetic fields.

"We believe we have established the relationship between magnetism, electricity, gravitation and atomic energy structure, therefore demonstrating a basis for the unification of these energies" [9].

DISTINCT BIOLOGICAL EFFECTS

In 1936, Albert Roy Davis made the discovery that the two poles of a magnet affect biological systems in two completely different ways. Over successive decades, thousands of experiments were conducted to determine the affects of each magnetic

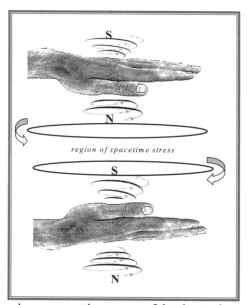

Figure 6.10 **Spin Interactions Of Vortex Centers.** *Where North & South magnetic poles meet, the clockwise and counterclockwise circulations do not simply cancel and disappear-they form stresses on the curvature of spacetime itself. New field effects appear The hand encounters magnetic/vortex polarity areas throughout the human energy fields These include the energy exchange ports of the skin (acupuncture points), and all other minor & major vortex areas such as the chakras. Interactions occur between hand and vortex centers at the hyperfield level. Hyperfields engage high energy, sub-elementary particles. A virtual (unobserved) reality contains further substructure. Field interactions defy conventional explanation. Torsion field properties, & their interactions, underlie these phenomena.*

pole on a wide range of biological systems-- from investigating plant growth to the healing of bones and tissue. Davis' work earned him the recognition of being known as the founder of the Science of Biomagnetics.

Davis and Rawls observed that the two poles exhibit differing energies, and these create two distinct results on living things. The research of Davis and Rawls conclude the following: *the right hand palm promotes strength, expansion, and encouragement; the left palm has the ability to arrest and reduce the condition of pain.* Both hands used together combine these effects. When the hands are used together on a subject, Davis and Rawls observed a flow of energy through the individual, or over the *surface* of the individual. The magnetic field is able to penetrate the body. But there is a dual action. The energy flows in two directions:

"When you apply the laying of the hands, or <u>thought energies</u>, what you are sending will return, and could give you far greater strength than you expressed...this is a scientific fact" [10].

These words continue to reverberate the convictions and integrity of these two great contributing scientific researchers of the 20th century.

HUMAN ELECTROMAGNETIC EMISSIONS

The hands provide a vast array of natural electromagnetic fields. In this text we look at these fields as being a source of *active information* to the subtle energy body-- that is, the fields of the hands do not supply the source of energy required to affect changes to what are inherently *self-organizing* system. As we discuss later in this text, the torsion field of the hand transmits information without the transfer of energy. *This is an important scientific concept.* Even at *subtle levels* of magnitude (i.e. average person output level), the interactive effects of this energy on information *field structure are very powerful.* Later discussions in this chapter will punctuate the full depth of this statement.

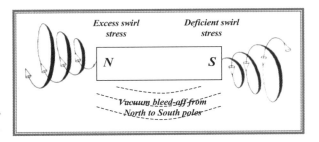

Figure 6.11 **Formation Of Magnetic Field.**
Magnetic poles are formed by stress or potentials that form in the vacuum. The excess clockwise or counterclockwise stresses result in the spiraling vortex type observations at the poles. Within the vacuum, the excess stress bleeds-off from the North to South pole, forming the observed magnetic field. (See Chapter Notes#34)

CHI EMISSION

The study of the energies that are emitted from the hands has been a major focus of research in Qigong (pronounced chi gung, also spelled Chi Gong). In China, chi from practitioners is harnessed for healing within hospital institutions. China has known for millennia that an energy called *qi* or *chi* can be cultivated, or accumulated, and emitted form the hands.

This energy has been the subject of extensive study and research in China. Emitted from the hands, this *chi* is used to influence biological systems for healing. The properties of this energy are very relevant to our discussion because we all produce and supply this *chi*. The energy flows from a point in the hand centered about the laogong energy point, but also from the fingertips as well. Even at subtle levels, this chi carries influential impact, because in hyperspace it is the information content that is the catalyst to change.

The various forms of energies that emanate from the hands that have been measured with instrumentation include *magnetic* fields, *electrostatic* fields, *microwave* emission, *infrasonic* emission (sound frequencies below 20 cycles per second), and *ultraviolet* spectra [11]. Other observations include pulsed magnetic energy and infrared (color red frequency) emission from fingertips. The benefits of this healing energy projected unto patients have become extensively documented. So too are the actual health benefits of performing various Qigong exercises by the patients themselves.

Various individuals have developed, from years of practice, very high levels of *chi* emission. These are referred to as Qigong Masters. The energy fields that they are able to produce are documented at many times higher than average people. Sometimes the emissions measure off-scale on the detecting equipment. These *Masters* have been the subjects of many amazing research tests and demonstrations of what this *chi* energy can do.

CHI ALTERS REALITY

For example, in one instance a Qigong Master was asked to influence a laser light that was located several kilometers away. Under his influence, the intensity of the laser was fluctuated by as much as ten percent.

In other demonstrations it has been possible to :
- Alter molecular composition of liquid crystals
- Alter the *time* of a crystal based timepiece
- Alter chemical compositions of various liquid solutions
- Alter the composition of gases in an infrared cell
- Alter the structure and characteristics of DNA & RNA
- Alter the structure of water

All these feats, and many more not mentioned in this list, defy the conventional laws of Physics [12]. As we are coming to understand, the total emissions from the hands, although having measured magnetic characteristics, is even more complex in its nature. In an article on scientific research in Qigong, Dr. Yan Xin makes the following conclusions about *Qi* [13] :
- *qi* can be observed and measured
- *qi* demonstrates properties of both matter and energy
- *qi* can convey information
- *qi* can be influenced by human thought and emotions

Qi is described as being related to all living and non-living things-- that is all things possess qi. As well, qi is related to our four know fundamental forces- the electromagnetic, gravitational, strong, and weak nuclear forces [14]. However, qi is also associated with energies and phenomena that are not explainable by these four fundamental forces. An example of this is an experiment where individuals used Qi to shake pills out of a sealed bottle-i.e. the pills passed through the solid wall of the bottle. Clearly, there is a quality associated with Qi that goes beyond the four known forces. As such, it is not possible to measure all of its characteristics with conventional instrumentation. It is quite evident that there are hyperspatial abilities of the human multi-dimensional complex at play!

EARTH RESONANT EMISSION

The study of emissions of the hands of "healers" has been a focus of the research of Zimmerman. Using a high sensitivity magnetic field measuring device called a SQUID ("Superconducting Quantum Interference Device"), Zimmerman was able to measure pulsed magnetic fields emanating from the hands of 'healers' [15].

> Low frequency sound waves, in the range 8 to 12 Hz (cycles per second), are very predominant in the energy spectrum of hand emissions [16]. This is the alpha frequency pattern of the brain's neural network, and also corresponds to the earth's natural resonant frequency-- the Schumann frequency. Measurements of the magnitude of the biomagnetic field during 'healing' are as much as 1000 times higher than the normal biomagnetic field.

The increase of the biomagnetic field strength in these cases is not associated with an increase in the flow of current in the biology [17]. A correspondence between field strength and current would be expected if the biomagnetic field was generated by simple biological cellular origin. The observation suggests that there is another source of energy that one can tap. This energy flow may be the result of tapping into the Earth's magnetic field through resonance.

The attunement of the biological system to the earth's frequency provides for the ideal transport of information into the biology. Various wave patterns can "piggy back" on the carrier signal-- the Schumann resonance frequency. A variety of higher frequency signals can modulate the 8-Hertz carrier, in the same manner as radio broadcast stations modulate a base carrier frequency to transmit their information. The human brain/nervous system complex tunes into the scalar wave emissions of the earth. As a scalar translator, the earth collects the varied cosmic energies and broadcasts these into a frequency language that all life on the planet recognizes. All life on the planet requires these emissions. Life, along with the planet earth, forms a relationship in symbiosis. *It is no mistake that we see the earth's natural frequencies in the human energy fields!*

Table 6.3 Principle Emissions Detected At The Hands.

EMISSION TYPE	Magnetic Electrostatic Infrasonic (below audible sound) 8-12 Cycles/second)	Pulsed magnetic Infrared Ultraviolet Microwave
UNCONVENTIONAL	Bio-photons- light emitted from biological systems Light is multi-dimensional/hyperspatial scalar Chi / scalar waves Vortex spiraling energies -hyperfields	
COMMENTS	Unconventional energies are not detectable with conventional equipment & techniques Scientific research has demonstrated that the fields at the hands are influenced and modified by Intent	

The attunement of the biological system to the earth's frequency provides for the ideal transport of information into the biology. Various wave patterns can "piggy back" on the carrier signal-- the Schumann resonance frequency. A variety of higher frequency signals can modulate the 8-Hertz carrier, in the same manner as radio broadcast stations modulate a base carrier frequency to transmit their information. The human brain/nervous system complex tunes into the scalar wave emissions of the earth. As a scalar translator, the earth collects the varied cosmic energies and broadcasts these into a frequency language that all life on the planet recognizes. All life on the planet requires these emissions. Life, along with the planet earth, forms a relationship in symbiosis. *It is no mistake that we see the earth's natural frequencies in the human energy fields!*

BIO-PHOTONS IN BIOLOGICAL SYSTEMS

The role of light in biological process was rediscovered by Fritz Popp in 1976 [18] . This German researcher discovered that all living cells emit photons of light. These are called biophotons. This light emitted is observed in the wavelength band of 200 to 800nm (nanometers). Since their discovery, we have learned that the Biophotons are stored and released from within the helix of the DNA molecule. The helix serves as an antenna to both receive and emit light. Popp determined that the biophotons emitted were coherent. The implication is that the DNA is not only a carrier of the blueprints, but that it also plays a significant role in the conduction of light and electricity. When electrical conduction operates as a coherent process (all electrons in step together) without resistance, this is called superconductivity. The DNA is a superconductor of light energy!

> *Biophotons are believed to be involved in the triggering of all biochemical reactions within living cells. Biophoton emission carry the encoded patterns required for communicating changes to the physiological states of living systems.*

Light is stored as a source of energy within the helix of the DNA. Cells communicate through light emissions of specific frequencies. Light is the carrier of information. The DNA molecule is not the only molecule in the human body that is photoactive, i.e., sensitive to light. The receptor of light in the retina of the eye, the flavin molecule, can be found almost everywhere in the body. The heme family of molecules, from which the blood hemoglobin is formed, as well as melanin, carotene, and many other metalloenzymes are all photoactive [19].

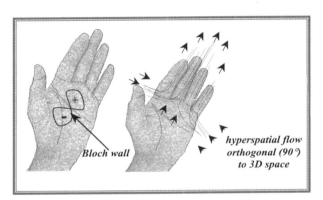

Figure 6.12 **Hyperspatial Flow At Hand.** *The observations of the properties of magnetism indicate that a* Bloch wall, *or zone of zero magnetism, exists within the palm of the hand. A hyperspatial flux, or flow, of 'free' energy enters here. Intensifying the figure 8 pattern affects the associated field structures-with the consequence of increasing flow. This principle applies throughout the energy anatomy where* **the figure 8 pattern** *exists at both micro & macro scales. (See chapter Notes#35)*

RESONANCE CAUSES EMISSIONS

Dr. George Yao describes a cell as being alive with "bioelectric plasma resonating between two poles" [20]. Bioplasma is a term developed by early Russian researchers who have done much pioneering work in studying the biofield of living things. *Plasma* is a state of highly ionized or charged particles. *The resonance of a cell causes the emission of light photons.* Dr. Yao describes the colors as follows:

> The principle color is *yellowish-golden*. But at the poles of the cell the colors are different. The positive pole of the cell is *reddish*, whereas the negative pole is *bluish*. Overall, the entire spectrum of seven colors is produced in a single cell [21].

The biophoton emissions of the hands contain the full spectrum of these colors. Biological light emissions encode a complete and detailed information patterning about the organism!

LIGHT ILLUMINATES SUBTLE REALM

What is light? Our most advanced theories explain light as a reflection of the 5th dimension. Light is conventionally thought of as having simply an electromagnetic nature, constrained to three-dimensional space. However, modern physics recognizes light as some multi-dimensional entity (*see Figure 2.8*).

> **Tiller has added that light possesses the qualities of magnetoelectric radiation [from etheric realm], and deltron radiation [from higher subtle realm]. Light is a connector to the subtle realm, the quantum world, and the mind field!**

CELLULAR BIO-PHOTONIC COMMUNICATION SYSTEM

Imagine playing a particular note, chord, or music score to a living cell, and then being able to observe a specific chemical reaction in a biological cell. Imagine turning on the switch of a chemical function by providing a cell with a simple radio broadcast. Imagine sending a signal over the Internet, receiving this signal at a distant location, and then using this signal to trigger one of a thousand different enzyme reactions within a cell.

The work of Dr. Jacques Benveniste has confirmed the role of electromagnetic signals in communication between molecular cells. Using simple electronic methods, Benveniste has recorded specific molecular signals. In 1995 Benveniste recorded and replayed molecular signals using the simple sound card interface of a computer. When a recorded signal was 'played' back to related biological systems, the cells responded as if it was in the presence of the original substance!

According to Benveniste, any molecular signal can be efficiently represented by a spectrum of frequencies that fall in the range *between 20 and 20,00Hz*- the same range of frequency as the human voice   [22]! This research can shed new light on the merits of *talking to your cells*. Sound carries great and amazing potential. *Fundamentally, sound, light, and geometry are all harmonically related!*

BIOLOGICAL WALKIE-TALKIES

The biological systems communicate like radio sets, through <u>co-resonance</u>. Communication becomes very molecule specific, and each interaction occurs at the speed of light, at a very unique *frequency pattern*. Water plays a significant role, as it is the mediator of the communication. The water is believed to amplify and relay the transmitted signals. Water has memory. Water can store patterns of information for extended periods of time. It has been referred to as a liquid crystal. The ability of water to retain a pattern of information comes from the capability of transforming the geometry of the molecular bonding of the water molecule. Many different structural forms are possible [23].

Frequency information patterns are stored within the lattice structure of water. The capacity of information storage within water is virtually infinite. Electromagnetic fields can imprint a pattern in water. However, if water is imprinted by a pattern from scalar (*non-Hertzian*) waves, it is retained for longer periods. Rein reports that scalar *non-Hertzian* patterns in water could be stored, and successfully 'played' back, even after three weeks. More generally, water is beginning to be accepted as the mediator between the material and subtle energy worlds [24]. This is based on water's ability to accumulate, store, and transmit energy and scalar information patterns.

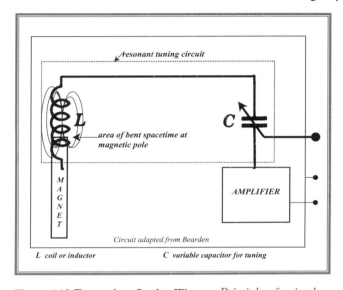

Figure 6.13 **Detecting Scalar Waves.** *Principles of a simple scalar wave detector are shown in the diagram. The circuit is placed in a shielded enclosure to isolate it from normal electromagnetic radiation. The enclosure does not shield against scalar waves. A scalar wave entering the enclosure will cause an oscillation within the area of bent spacetime at the magnetic pole. (See Chapter Notes #36)*

A SCALAR BIOPHOTON

Light is in communication with the subtle energy bodies! As Bearden explains it, there are actually two types of biophotons. One of the biophoton types is actually a *scalar photon.* These are not detectable by conventional means. The scalar photon is a subtle phenomenon. The *scalar photons* travel in *hyperspace,* or the vacuum, which of course, is also the home of the *subtle energy bodies!* Along with the patterns of information, biophotons are *colored,* and more specifically can be *colored* through the programming of the mind field. A scalar photon provides *active information.* As such, the scalar photon is a syntropic stimulus to the self-organizing and reordering activities of the cell *(negative entropy, reversing disorder, see Appendix B).*

Light is a measurable emission from the hands of Qigong healers [*in the form of infrared and ultraviolet*]. But we have also heard that the *qi* complex exhibits qualities that are not explainable by ordinary electromagnetic waves. In fact, some of the characteristics of qi relate to scalar waves.

A scalar wave can be generated from the oscillations that result from the contraction and relaxation of spinning electrons. The propagation of scalar waves curve local space-time. When this occurs, the balance of the vacuum potential is disturbed, and the energy stored there can be tapped. [This is sometimes referred to zero point energy. When the balance state is disturbed, virtual particles from the physical vacuum of space are turned into observable elementary particles. These can be harnessed in electrical circuits producing *free energy*.]

Interestingly, one method of generating scalar waves is with the use of a caduceus coil. Such a coil is made from two interwoven conductors, wrapped like a helix. Current is driven in opposing directions, resulting in a cancellation of the visible components of the electromagnetic energy, leaving the scalar component as a potential in the vacuum. Of course the *DNA molecule is a helix, just like a caduceus coil*, and DNA has active scalar wave properties.

SCALAR WAVES DEFY LINEAR TIME

The scalar wave consists of two superimposed components, each of which interacts differently with matter. One component -*the positive time/* positive energy wave- interacts with negatively charged electrons. The other -*a negative time*/negative energy wave- interacts with the positively charged protons in the nucleus. According to Bearden, each biological cell is composed of subatomic biopotentials. These biopotentials are found within the nucleus of the atoms and may form disordered and unstructured patterns of scalar energy. *These patterns also form mirror substructures in the vacuum.*

SCALAR CHARGE

Natural scalar energy abounds around us. Our systems are in constant flux, or flow, of absorbing and releasing this energy. It is possible to *increase this flow*, or exchange the rate of flow with the outside environment.

Scalar energy is absorbed by the cells, resulting in a *charging and organizing* of the biopotentials. This is something that conventional fields cannot do. Ordinary electromagnetic fields do not supply an *organizing* potential; they can only affect the magnitude to the biopotentials.

> Once the cells are charged up, they can release the stored potential as two differing types of light photons- one is the conventional photon, the other is a structured scalar photon that contains a complete information pattern of the cell.

If this pattern emanates from a diseased cell, then this disease pattern is broadcast and communicated to all cells in the body. The nucleus of the cell can charge up like a capacitor. As the nucleus accumulates this scalar energy, it can repeatedly undergo the *charge-discharge cycle* supplying energy and electricity for a variety of processes *at the biological and non-biological level* .

At the cellular level, the scalar waves charge the biopotentials that are the basis of cellular function. The cell responds with stronger magnetic and electrical alignments and a *higher charge*. It is now more capable of **converting** and processing food energies into light energies and storing them in the cell as ultraviolet light. The minimum potential, or charge, for activating DNA for cellular division is more easily reached. The higher potential provides the electricity that RNA requires to read the DNA. As RNA scans the DNA with the *complete light spectrum of frequencies (our evolution)*, it creates a holographic projection of DNA. As RNA topologically matches this projection, a copy of DNA results for reproduction. What incredibly complex & intelligent processing occurring within this micro-universe!

Scalar wave technology holds great and amazing potential to our ideas of healing. The medicine of tomorrow will truly be one of vibrational medicine [25]. As Bearden explains, this new approach to healing is to create a *scalar wave containing a healing pattern*, and then supply this information to the cells [26]. [*This has been already accomplished through research (Rife, Priore)-this technology already exists* [27] ! Also see the work of Hulda Clark.]

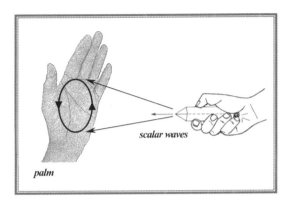

Figure 6.14 **Sensing Scalar Waves.** *The palm of the hand is sensitive to scalar waves. Use a quartz crystal and have the end point trace around the laogong area of your palm. Practice to become sensitive to the energy emission of the crystal. The quartz focuses & amplifies the scalar waves of the hand holding it. The palm's acupoints are receptive to scalar waves. These enter the nervous system. The nervous system conducts scalar waves and 'feels' the effects of the scalar waves that are translated into electromagnetic radiation. The nervous system/brain network provides the resonant circuit for detection. The spacetime curvatures at the palm, due to non-linear effects, cause some scattering of scalar waves-these reduce into its electromagnetic substructure. This detection system makes the hand a sensitive detector of subtle energy.*

This healing pattern will result in reversing the disease in addition to supplying a permanent scalar immunization to the body's own biofield.

A SCALAR MATRIX

Scalar energy originates from a sub-nuclear level of the atom. Puharich has proposed that scalar waves originate within the elementary particles of the proton: from the monopoles and anti-monopoles within the proton. In the body, Puharich suggests that the non-Hertzian scalar fields *emitted from the hands originate from the hydrogen bonds that connect the DNA strand together.*

Glen Rein has proposed that communication exist between protons and neutrons within a nucleus, as well as between nuclei of the same molecule. The molecules all interconnect through a quantum information *network or matrix*. This information matrix stores all the characteristics of the molecular structure at the intersection points of this network. Rein calls this the Intramolecular Matrix Theory. Stimulating the matrix with the appropriate scalar (*non-Hertzian*) frequency allows access to this information [27].

HAND HELD SUBTLE RESONANT DETECTOR

The hand is a sophisticated scalar wave detector. This sophistication is due to by brain/nervous system complex, and the multi-dimensional aspects of our being!

In Figure 6.13 we illustrate principle of detecting scalar waves using a bar magnet. The key element is to understand that a magnetic pole represents *an area of curvature of space-time.* Incoming scalar waves are influenced by the curvature of space-time. Within the region of the magnetic pole, the scalar waves will be scattered. The oscillation of the space-time curvature at the magnetic pole will translate as observed current in the associated simple circuit. Scalar wave detection is possible through a number of unorthodox techniques. However, this technology exists.

The hand also produces a zone of curvature of space-time, because an equivalent magnetic pole exists here as well. The idea is much the same as we discussed in the circuit above. However, the hand is supported by very sophisticated and complex *resonant tuning circuitry.* The nervous system behaves as a waveguide for scalar waves, and is an extension of the brain's processing circuitry. The brain is supported by the mind field. This we can understand to be some nonlocal quantum supercomputer. We are speaking of a multi-dimensional, nonlocal, hyperspatial level of sophistication!

Scalar waves are scattered at the palm. Some of the scattering will result in scalar waves being reduced to normal electromagnetic waves that may be felt by the biology. This may be equated to the manner that the biology is sensitive to microwave activity. Other scalar waves will enter the meridian channels and interact with the nervous system. Of course, the brain is a scalar wave translator (emitter-detector), and together with the nervous system, detection of scalar waves at the hand becomes a whole body/being, hyperspatial phenomena. This point is key to understanding the overall process. We cannot simply isolate the hand as a detection device, because we function as integrated, whole multi-dimensional beings in the process!

As sources of electromagnetic potential, the hands will both create, as well as respond to, gradients in the vacuum. [Gradients are due to *differences* in parameters, or values, at two separate points. In the vacuum, the potential can be understood as a local fluctuation in the energy density at that point. Magnetic fields vary the local density in the vacuum. They alter the local symmetry that normally exists at that point. When this symmetry is disturbed, a flow takes place from a *high to low* energy zone (*see Figures 7.2 & 7.3*). These flows can be called scalar currents. Local fluctuations are actually fluctuations to space-time itself.]

Gradients within the subtle fields are what we *read* with the hand, along with the associated resonant tuning circuitry. As we evolve within our energy systems, we become more perceptive of these gradients. We resond through co-resonance . [We are using the hand as a pointer only...the whole human electromagnetic system is active in the read process.] Anywhere gradients exist, there will always be some form of scalar current flow. Two hands together can initiate this scalar current flow (*see figure 7.3*). The magnetic potentials that exist at the hand disturb the natural balance or equilibrium state of vacuum density. When this occurs, natural currents flow within the vacuum. In this manner, the hands provide the source of disturbance only- not the source of the 'flowing' current. [In resonant circuits only a source of *voltage* or potential is required.] We return to this in the next chapter.

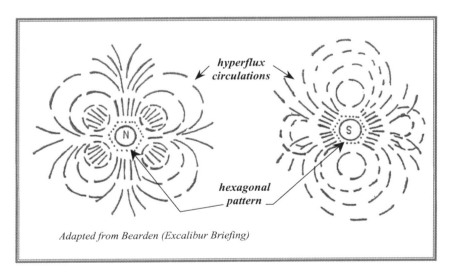

Adapted from Bearden (Excalibur Briefing)

Figure 6.15 **Magnetic Hyperflux Circulations.** *This figure demonstrates the rich hyperfield patterns associated with magnetism. The North and South pole hyperflux patterns are taken from Bearden's Excalibur Briefing. Note that each pattern has a central geometric form- the hexagon. The field patterns are distinctly different at each pole. The North pole has four primary vortices-the South pole has two primary vortices. These circulating patterns are hyperspatial and engage high-energy threads of sub-elementary particles. They have interactive field effects in our virtual (unobservable) realities. These vorticular patterns are traces of substructures that exist within magnetism. Magnetism transcends many levels of virtual existence.*

Magnetic Hyperfields From Hyperspace

To begin to understand what is occurring at the hand, and in particular, what is at the basis of the interaction between the hand and subtle energy fields, we must continue to speak from hyperspace. A hyperspace is removed from our time and space. We generally think of a hyperspace as being of a higher dimension. Within hyperspace are the *hyperfields* that operates within that frame of reality. Yet the hyperfields may make some visible presence known in our reality. For example, the electromagnetic field is a hyperfield of the 5th dimension. This field produces the effects of electric and magnetic force fields in our 3D space. Yet we say that there is a substructure, or nested virtual reality, to the electromagnetic field itself. Removed from the frame of the electromagnetic field is the hyperspace frame of the neutrinic field (*see glossary*). So we have mentioned two levels of hyperspaces removed from physical reality- the electromagnetic field, the neutrinic field, and, according to Bearden, the next level is the mind field (*see Figure 2.5*).

Hyperfields Kindle Into Electromagnetic Fields

What is important to our discussions is to realize that hyperspaces, and their hyperfields, are responsible for the phenomena we experience in our simple 3 dimensional Euclidean spaces. Magnetism is a phenomenon connected to hyperspace- i.e. *the causes or potentials that create our magnetic field exist within other spaces- within higher dimensions.* The mental field acts on the hyperfields. Bearden has proposed that:

> **Thought patterns can be impressed into the magnetic hyperfields. Thought energy can "Induce an electromagnetic field in space surrounding an object to interact with it, or Condense subtle energies into the hyperfield flux of magnetic fields"** [29].

Figure 6.16 **Asymmetrical Hyperflux Patterns.** *Bearden has identified these as 'hyperfield flux' associated with the magnetic field. Note in the diagram that the circulations are not symmetrical at each pole. Also note the strong hexagonal pattern at each pole. These are the fields that occupy other than 3D space, and therefore have an effect on the virtual (unobserved) realities that they encounter. Where magnetism is detected, these hyperfields exists outside of our conscious awareness. Hyperfields interact with subtle energies.*

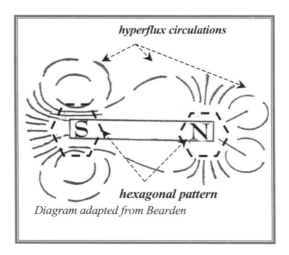

hyperflux circulations

hexagonal pattern

Diagram adapted from Bearden

HYPERFLUX DETECTION

Hyperfields associated with magnetism have been detected! In his book *Excalibur Briefing,* Bearden documents the detection of the hyperflux circulations associated with a bar magnet. We illustrate these in Figures 6-15 & 6-17. Note from these illustrations that each magnetic pole exhibits a distinct vortex pattern. The vortex pattern at each pole is different. Each pole exhibits different properties. The discovery that opposing magnetic poles have separate, distinct effects on biological life [as discovered by Davis & Rawls] is connected to this distinction. These effects can be understood through the energetic interactive processes that are taking at each magnetic pole. A magnetic pole is the source that stimulates the addition, or removal, of energy from a region in hyperspace. This addition or subtraction of energy may have significant effects on biological systems!

Also note the strong hexagonal patterns that surround the magnetic poles. *Are these indications of a lattice structure of higher space?* We can use these hyperflux circulating patterns to enrichen our view of magnetism at the hand. The laws of magnetism are universal.

HYPERFLUX AT HAND

In Figure 6.17 we have created an overlay of Bearden's patterns onto the human hands. Here we have used the magnetic polarities of the hand as discovered by

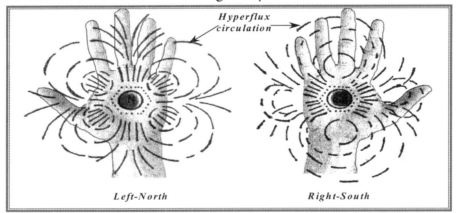

Figure 6.17 **Hand Hyperflux Circulations.** *This figure demonstrates the rich hyperfield patterns associated with human magnetism. The North and South pole hyperflux pattern are taken from Bearden's Excalibur Briefing. We have overlaid these upon the human hands! The composite is derived from the Davis-Rawls magnetic discoveries of the hand, added to Bearden's general hyperfield patterns for magnetic poles. Note that each pattern has a central geometric form- the hexagon. The field patterns are different at each hand. The North pole (left palm) has four primary vortices-the South pole (right palm) has two primary vortices. These circulating patterns are hyperspatial and engage high-energy threads of sub-elementary particles. They have interactive field effects in our virtual (unobservable) realities. These vorticular patterns are aspects of the virtual substructures of magnetism. Human magnetism transcends many levels of virtual existence.*

Davis & Rawls. What is dramatic to realize about this illustration is that *these multiple vortex patterns originate and are happening in hyperspace-a higher dimension. Within that space they are interactive with other field structures!*

Universal Flow Of Similar Free Energy Generators

Our diagram of Figure 6.18 illustrates the equivalency of magnetic principles of a permanent bar magnet & the human hand. The bar magnet is characterized by a figure 8 flow pattern from S to N, and from N to S. The figure 8 pattern also appears at the magnet's Bloch wall zone of zero magnetism. *Similar patterns are shown at the hand.*

A bar magnet exhibits two types of polarity: magnetic & electric. These polarities form dipoles. It is the dipoles that establish the mechanism for creating *vacuum engines* that extract *free energy* from the vacuum (here also called the *universal energy source*). A permanent magnet derives its 'permanency' form an ongoing, continuous, flow & exchange of energy with the vacuum. Any depletion to a magnet is automatically *re-charged* by the resonant circuit that a magnet has established with its limitless energy source. A permanent bar magnet is a free energy generator .

One magnetic pole is a *deficient* potential energy zone. The other is an *excess* potential energy. zone. Here we have shown the South pole as a deficient zone . At the South pole, energy is pushed-in from the vacuum, or viewed conversely, pulled-in by the magnet. At the North pole, energy is pushed-out of the magnet, or viewed conversely, pulled-out by the vacuum. The push-pull action can be equated to a form of vacuum pump or engine.

Magnetic circuits are in resonance with the fabric of space-time. There is an ongoing replenishment of *universal energy* to the magnet's resonant circuit.

The magnetic poles each have a separate effect on biological systems. One pole will deplete *(discharge)* a zone of bioenergy. The other will concentrate & deliver excess bioenergy. Because of these significant real biological effects *that will occur*, it is of outmost importance that 'magnet therapy' be undertaken only with a thorough understanding of the magnetic principles & conventions- in particular the convention used in designating the magnetic pole.

The principles of magnetism apply at the hand. For either hand, one side is a South, the other side a North. Universal energy is extracted, or pulled-in, on one side of the hand, whereas energy is expelled on the opposite side. This flow is established in resonance with the universal energy of the vacuum. The energy that has been expelled has been modulated & patterned by the frequencies of the human energy

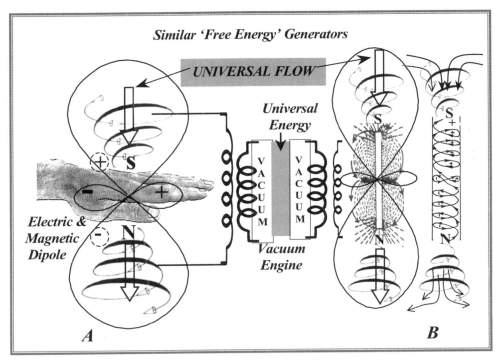

Figure 6.18 **Universal Flow Of Similar Free Energy Generators.**

system. Note how this discussion is consistent with the Davis/Rawls' discoveries that electromagnetic energies are constantly *flowing through* the human energy system.

EXPANSIVE HOLOGRAPHIC MULTI-DIMENSIONAL VIEW

It is a given throughout this text that we function as multi-dimensional beings, and that we carry the *gifts* of hyperspatial functioning. Electromagnetism originates in the fifth dimension, and light is a reflection of the 5th dimension. The 5th dimension connects to higher space.

> Our electromagnetic nature originates in higher spaces of complex geometries. Light is a reflection of the 5th dimension.

We are not necessarily conscious of the hyperspatial aspects that underlie our biological processes-for example the scalar/quantum biophoton communication system. But it is there, working away quietly in the background.

The brain functions to keep us *locked* into this notion of space-time [and not some other], without our conscious awareness that other realities exist parallel to our own. We cannot succeed in understanding our hyperspatial nature and abilities if we limit our view of reality to that which we perceive with our senses in a 3 dimensional space. When we say that the universe is a holographic projection we do not mean that what we see is not real- it is a real projection that originates from higher dimensional space (*albeit a stubbornly persistent illusion as Einstein would say*). From this higher space of complex geometry, our 4D space [include time] is but one slice through it. From a view from 8D space, everything in 4D is connected.

Non-locality-the perplexing problem of instant communication in our space- is easily understood from an 8D space that sees our space as one whole connected slice amongst other possible worlds [30].

All of this to say that *it is natural* for our systems to deal with hyperspatial waves and signals.

Our higher *selves* reside in these complex spaces. Our *selves*, and our systems, keep in touch through signals that travel the hyperspace Internet. Of course, a lot of signal processing-modulation, demodulation- takes place along the way. The understanding of our interactive effects in the human-to-human connection must begin from the vantage point of higher space.

The hand is not an isolated multi-dimensional instrument. We are beings with holographic interconnected systems. We function always from within the essence of the whole.

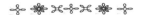

CHAPTER SEVEN

COLORFUL
INTERACTIVE PHENOMENA

Touching The Web Of Life

Imagination is more important than knowledge.

Albert Einstein

The discussion of the torsion field that follows may appear a little too fantastic to be real. Below we allude to the existence of external torsion field technology. We do so with the express intent that the *external* serve as a pointer to our own *internal* technology. As we discover and awaken our own internal mechanisms, we will better understand that it is the potential of this internal technology that is too fantastic to be real! We are transceivers (emitter-receivers) of torsion fields. Consider that our best science fiction of the 20th Century has been based on the far-reaching ideas of theoretical physics.

A MENTAL FIELD CONNECTOR

Modern day theorists suggest that the mental field of consciousness interacts with the torsion field [1]. The torsion field then becomes a connector to physical reality through the electromagnetic field. Once we begin to fully appreciate the interactive effects of torsion fields, we will open the doors to much further research and far greater acceptance. We know about the classical fields of electromagnetism and gravity. However, we know little about the connection between these two fields. The torsion field has become a more recent topic of focus within physics. It has been referred to as the *Unified Field* sought after by Einstein.

There are suggestions that torsion field technology has been explored for more than a decade in Russia. In the western world, Bearden speaks of scalar wave

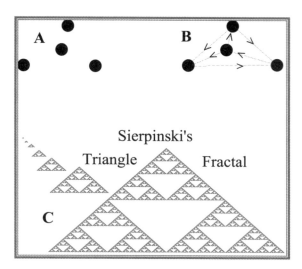

technology. *Torsion* and *scalar* appear to be synonymous terms, yet originating from separate planetary hemispheres. Current publications use the term torsion widely. Other references also include the terms *axion* and *spin* fields. Perhaps in the near future we will have some defining guidelines that can unify all these concepts.

SPINS & SPIRALS CREATE FIELDS

It appears that torsion fields are the result of the characteristic of spin. Rotation, or spin, is characteristic of all objects- from atoms, to stars, to galaxies. Spinning objects create disturbances within the vacuum of space- the fabric of space-time itself. These disturbances travel at superluminal speeds carrying information.

For an object, the collective spin patterns of all the individual particles superpose, or add-up. The collective disturbances create unique interference patterns around that object.

Figure 7.1 **Scalar Tetrahedral Structures.** *Each of the four points of **A** represents a distinct fluctuation within the symmetry/balance of the vacuum. These fluctuations can be understood as disturbances to the energy density at the points. From these fluctuations are created the scalar potentials. Collectively the points represent a pattern (**B**). Here it is the stable and fundamental form of the tetrahedron. The relative differences of values, or energy densities, between the 4 points result in gradients being established in this medium. The gradients result in scalar current flow (high to low)- vibrating stationary waves. The scalar flow creates the connecting channels between the points. These channels serve as conduits of light & electromagnetic sound waves. (See Chapter Notes #24).*

These patterns are actually extremely detailed information fields that contain everything about the whole object. Any portion of the field could be used to reveal information about the whole object. The field is holographic-- any part of it contains information about the whole.

Connected to spin or rotation are vortices-- spinning spiraling patterns- that would be seen within the background fabric that we call the vacuum. For example, the earth is sitting in a spinning spiraling vortex of its own. At the same time, the earth's vortex is swept along by the larger vortex created by the sun. The planetary system is directed and maintained by the sun's vortex pattern. From such a concept we have something new to learn about the nature and origin of *gravity and magnetism*! More than one perspective exists in explaining *reality*.

INFORMATION INTERACTION

Information or torsion fields are subject to interaction. Interacting with this field may alter the physical characteristics of the object.

The aura surrounding the human body is called a torsion field by Russian researchers. Bearden calls the human aura a scalar aura, because it is actually created by the interference patterns of scalar waves.

Torsion fields are known to interact, i.e., to exchange information. The intriguing thing is that the interaction takes place hyperspatially-- outside our common notion of space-time. A new view of brain function is that it is a transceiver (receiver-emitter) of torsion waves. [This is similar to the concept of translator of scalar waves.] These are all further expanding notions of our multi-dimensional capabilities.

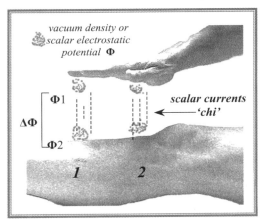

The torsion field is known to transmit information patterns without the transfer of energy. It is becoming quite apparent that the torsion field will play a role in helping us to understand how we interact in the human-to-human connection. The torsion field will also help us to understand how we can alter our physical reality for the benefit of ourselves, and for all of mankind.

Within the *Rainbow in Your Hand* are the magnetic hyperfields and, we add, the hyperspatial *torsion fields*. Already, science has begun to document unusual and amazing properties of the torsion field. We can no longer ignore the existence of our own hyperspatial electromagnetic nature. The torsion field is the primary hyperspatial interactive link to the subtle energies. It is at the basis of the *human-to-human*

Figure 7.2 **Hand Detection of Scalar Waves**. *Variations of potential* ($\Phi\Delta$) *exist between* $\Phi 1$ *and* $\Phi 2$. *This is the case for the zones 1 or 2 shown above. These differences cause scalar currents to flow in the virtual reality. The hand and nervous system form a sophisticated scalar wave detector. As the hand moves throughout the subtle energy field, the interactions lead to physical sensations (detection) at the hand. The nervous system and brain are an integrated translator (detector - emitter) of scalar waves.*

connection whenever you assist another with the *Rainbow in Your Hands.*

HAND HELD SUBTLE ENERGY DETECTORS

In Figure 7.1 we illustrate the concept of scalar potentials and gradients. In the tetrahedral figure, each of the four vertex points (endpoints) represent local disturbances to a background state of equilibrium within the vacuum or cosmic lattice.

These four points are unique areas of energy fluctuations that have been established within the medium. Collectively they create *form*. The geometry of this form will translate as specific properties, characteristics, or function in our space. The differences in energy densities that define the points of this form, will enable scalar flow to take place between the vertex points. The differences, higher or lower, are what create the gradients in energy densities that enable this flow to take place.

The tetrahedral form of Figure 7.1 is found within this self-similar structure-- a fractal. The scale of this structure can be extrapolated from microscopic to macroscopic. Resonance within this structure equates to alignment of the inter-dimensional geometry. By creating the perfect internal symmetry, this enables communication & information exchange between cells. Within the vacuum, such a similar structure represents stability, symmetry, and balance. Within the human energy field, such a structure also represents balance.

The lattice that is formed can be described as a "geometric collection of harmonic wave-forms of light guided by intelligence"[29]. Tuning is the process of creating resonance between geometry, and the geometric cells. Light, & sound permeate the lattice. Geometry, light, & sound are all harmonically related!

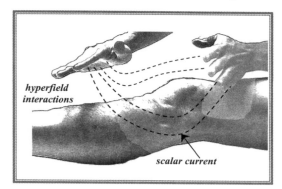

Figure 7.3 **Inducing Scalar Flow.** *The two hands supply the potentials to induce the flow of scalar currents. These currents can be set up naturally in the medium. The scalar waves are electromagnetic sound waves with a rich patterned frequency substructure. These are cleansing to the meridian channels that open under a kind of high potential ultrasonic action. As well, hyperfield effects to the subtle energies cleanse the field of lifeless obstructions. These are torsion field effects.*

In the previous chapter we introduced the idea that the hands will both create, as well as respond to, gradients in the vacuum. We mentioned that gradients are due to *differences* in parameters, or values, at two separate points, and that in the vacuum, the scalar potential can be understood as a local fluctuation in the energy density at that point (*see Figure 6.6*). Anywhere gradients exist, there will always be some form of scalar current flow. Two hands together can initiate this scalar current flow. Standing scalar waves will oscillate between the hands, in the subtle (hyperspatial) realm. These waves carry a rich substructure of frequency and patterns programmed from the originator. When these waves enter the meridian system, a form of *hypersonic* (*ultrasonic*) action clears the channels of stagnant substance. The scalar wave is an electromagnetic sound wave. [These concepts are illustrated in Figures 7.2, 7.3, and 7.4.] *Fundamentally, sound, light, and geometry are all harmonically related!*

The process is similar when we consider the human hands, because magnetic fields vary the local density in the vacuum. In altering the local symmetry that normally exists at that point, a flow takes place from a *high to low* energy zone. These flows can be called scalar currents. Again we mention that local fluctuations within the vacuum are actually fluctuations to space-time itself.

Figure 7.4 **Hyperfield Interaction of Hands**. *Conventional energy from the hand interacts with biological matter in conventional ways. Underlying the biology are the information fields (biofields) and the subtle energies. These are subject to interaction with the unconventional fields- the hyperfields. High-energy threads of virtual sub-elementary particles form primary and secondary vorticular fields that impact on the subtle energies. The spin/torsion fields are hyperspatial. Their effect on altering the information fields ultimately results in change at the biological level.*

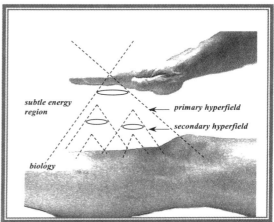

Gradients within the subtle fields are what we read with the hand, along with the associated resonant tuning circuitry. Our multi-dimensional nature enables us to respond through co-resonance.

The hand is a pointer only…the whole human electromagnetic system is active in the read process.

A MOST UNUSUAL SCIENTIFIC ENTITY
THE TORSION FIELD

How can it be that two laser beams of light can either attract or repel each other? How can light beams behave as if they were magnets, attracting or repelling each other? Ordinary concepts of forces do not allow an explanation of these phenomena. The answer is found within our discussion that follows.

REVIVING A THEORETICAL CONCEPT

To appreciate the unseen hyperspatial interaction that is at the basis of the human-to-human interaction, and at the hand, we continue our discussion with that unusual entity known as the torsion field. The torsion field has been discussed in theoretical literature since the early 1900's. Yet this field has been largely ignored in classical physics. Einstein's mechanics does not take into consideration the existence of torsion field interaction. This significance cannot be overlooked, because the torsion field has today been referred to as Einstein's unified field.

Extensive research under the heading of "torsion field" has been the focus of several research groups in Russia for several decades. Akimov reports that today's world periodicals total about 10,000 references to the torsion field research. Original research papers on the topic originate from about 100 authors. Half of these torsion field theorists work in Russia. Akimov also discloses that the world's first torsion field generator was built in Russia in the 1980's. The development of the torsion generator led Russian scientists towards extensive research opportunities that presented both experimental and practical results. According to some Russian scientists, the torsion generators were able to simulate the unusual feats performed by psychics-- as well they were found to be able to produce new phenomena not exhibited by these same psychics [2]. Today, torsion fields can be detected by a variety of methods [3].

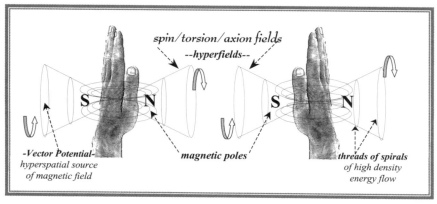

Figure 7.5 **Torsion Fields Of The Hands**. *Spin/torsion/axion fields exist at the hands. Where electromagnetic fields exist, it is fundamental that torsion fields **always** accompany these fields (Akimov, Tarascenko, & Nachalov). Although outside our conscious awareness, these torsion fields are nonetheless an aspect of our multidimensional reality. They exhibit influence in regions or dimensions where aspects of our own energy anatomy resides. Interactions take place at unconscious levels, yet these fields are directed by conscious thought & focused intent. All electromagnetic phenomena are the secondary effects of invisible, virtual hyperfields-of 5D+ origin. Our entire multidimensional nature is reflected in the rich structures of the hand. Indeed, the hand is a holographic instrument of our whole being. (See Chapter Notes #25).*

OMNI-PRESENT FIELD

Why is the torsion field tantamount to our discussion? *Because torsion fields are associated with all electromagnetic phenomena!* As we continue, it will become evident that the torsion field is a most unusual entity. Torsion fields are directly equated to subtle energy fields.

We are electromagnetic beings of multidimensional character and hyperspatial origin! As such, we produce (*amongst others*) electrostatic, magnetic, and electromagnetic fields. These have been conclusively detected at the hands, the heart and the brain. As we have stated repeatedly, electromagnetism has its origin in 5th dimensional space. As electromagnetic beings, we are also expressions of higher dimensional, hyperspatial characteristics. Inherent to our hyperspatial nature is what researchers refer to as the *torsion field*. All objects and living things possess and produce torsion fields. *These torsion fields are subject to interaction* .

The following statements are perhaps *the most central to our scientific discussion, and carry major implication to our understanding to subtle phenomena and information fields*. We should be clear on the following <u>important fact</u> that has been emphasized by Nachalov in his paper *Theoretical Basis of Experimental Phenomena*:

"In the framework of the theory of electro-torsion interactions, it is shown that if electrostatic or electromagnetic fields exist in some region of space, then there always exist torsion fields in that region of space. Electrostatic or electromagnetic fields without a torsion component do not exist"[3].

Akimov & Tarascenko present a similar statement:

"In the conceptual plan, the deduction that torsion fields always accompany the appearance of electromagnetics is extremely important for a large number of fundamental & applied problems"[4].

THEORETICAL BASIS OF ORIGIN

Spin, or angular momentum, and the interference of wave patterns, generates the torsion field. Every particle spins or rotates on an axis. Spiraling action is observed on every scale from the microscopic to the macroscopic. It is the spin of the elementary particle that traps light. The two primary fields, gravity and electromagnetism, are well known, and produce long-range effects. A third field, the torsion field, is also a long-range field- but its properties are much 'richer' than the former two. Some of the unusual properties of torsion fields are [5]:

- The torsion field exhibits a minimum propagation speed not less than 10^9 X c (1,000,000,000 times the speed of light, c, in vacuum).
- The torsion field propagates into the future as well as the past.
- The torsion field transmits information across great distance without the transfer of energy.
- Torsion fields interact with laser beams, altering frequency, and can affect quartz crystals.

ASTRONOMICALLY SPEAKING

Scientific confirmation of the above two unusual properties is found in the research of the Russian scientist Kozyrev, reported to us by Nachalov & Sokolov. Kozyrev's intriguing discoveries are the result of his many observations using telescopes. Kozyrev noted that his telescope was able to record incoming signals from stars *even when a metal screen shielded the telescope.* A metal screen blocks normal electromagnetic waves, but is unable to block scalar or torsion waves.

> **This clearly indicated that light, an electromagnetic wave, had some component that could not be shielded by metal screens, i.e. light has hyperspatial components within its substructure that do not propagate in 3D space.**

The hyperspatial components cannot be blocked, or shielded, by a metal screen. Ordinary electromagnetic wave components can be. Further telescopic observation investigated the incoming light from a particular star while directing the telescope in three different positions [3,4,5,6]:

- The visible position of incoming light –this is the light that originates from the past and has taken physical time to travel the distance
- The "true" position of the star as defined in astronomy. Here the recorded signal was much stronger then in #1. The very existence of a recorded signal from the same star at this position was interpreted as receiving radiation of the star at velocities *billions of times greater than the speed of light.* This meant that the light signal did not take time to reach the telescope-- it arrived in the NOW!
- A position symmetrical to the visible position of the star, relative to its true position. This fact was interpreted as *a detection of an incoming signal from the future position of the star!*

The very same results were also obtained with the telescope shielded with a metal screen. The signals at the telescope had hyperspatial counterparts. All these observations were interpreted as the registration of <u>*torsion waves*</u>.

PARANORMAL PHENOMENA CONNECTED TO TORSION FIELDS

According to Sokolov & Nachalov, there exist both theoretical and experimental reasons to conclude that various paranormal phenomena are connected with certain manifestations of torsion fields. Moreover, Nachalov states that:

> **"It has been established that torsion generators allow us to not only replicate all phenomena demonstrated by so called psychics, but they**

also are able to demonstrate effects that were never demonstrated by any psychic"[6].

Nachalov & Sokolov report that what we observe visually by Kirlian photography are torsion fields. These are the same fields observed by psychics, usually interpreted as the aura. Because torsion fields have been considered as unified fields, the 'aura', or subtle energy fields, can be considered as unified fields [7]. As such, we can consider a state within the subtle field, in which, ideally, the electric, magnetic, gravitational, and spin fields are in a state of equilibrium- a balanced state.

When external torsion fields interact with the unified field of subtle energy, the internal balanced forces become disconnected, creating polarization effects.

Figure 7.6 **Body Torsion Fields.** *As major producers of detectable electromagnetic fields, the heart and brain are generators of torsion fields and scalar waves. The whole body produces its unique torsion field (also called the scalar aura by Bearden) that, holographically, contains every minute detail about the entire living organism. Torsion fields carry detailed information maps as patterns within their substructure. A torsion field imparts its spatial configuration onto other torsion fields. The torsion field at the hand is modified by the patterns of the heart and brain (emotion & intent). Torsion fields are hyperspatial phenomena of unusual properties.(See Chapter Notes #29)*

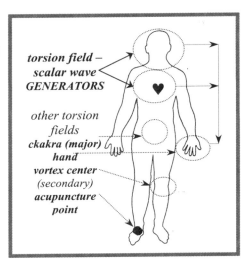

torsion field –
scalar wave
GENERATORS

other torsion
fields
ckakra (major)
hand
vortex center
(secondary)
acupuncture
point

So, to speak of a unified field, or state of equilibrium, within the subtle energy fields of man, is to literally speak about a geometry of *balance*. Working with the geometry of the subtle field serves to return the internal forces to its unified state of equilibrium and balance.

Thus we eliminate areas of polarization, or charge, within the field that have been maintaining the substructure of the field in its unbalanced state. The overall process is an inter-dimensional activity of geometric alignments.

TORSION FIELD CHARACTERISTIC OF ALL OBJECTS

All substance, living and non-living, possess its own characteristic torsion field. The spins of atomic and subatomic particles all superpose, or add up, a total collective field, which determines the intensity and nature of the torsion field in the space surrounding each molecule. This is also true in the space surrounding the substance /object) as a whole, and a superposition of all spin fields results.

So each object or substance has a torsion field with a unique spatial configuration based on its geometry. Alter an object's torsion field, and the object's geometry can literally be altered!

> The structure of the torsion field can be *charged* (altered, influenced, imprinted, polarized) by an external torsion field, i.e. there is spin-spin interaction. The object's torsion field takes on a new configuration (as a polarized state), and this configuration will remain intact even after removing the source of the external torsion field.

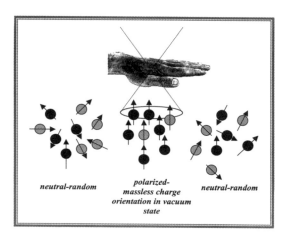

neutral-random   polarized-massless charge orientation in vacuum state   neutral-random

Figure 7.7 **Vacuum Polarization.** *The spin/torsion hyperfields of the hand disturb the neutral balanced state of the vacuum. The polarization is more than simple preferred orientation of massless charge. A complete pattern of information is transferred to the vacuum state-mirroring that of the hand. It is a pattern of resonance. It interacts with the subtle energies transferring information. There can be non-local effects. (See chapter Note #30)*

DNA PHANTOM - A TORSION EFFECT

An example of this phenomenon is the DNA phantom effect [8]. In this experiment the DNA is removed from a test chamber, but light continues to interact with the region of space previously occupied by the DNA sample- as if the DNA were still present! Here the torsion field of the DNA creates a polarization within the vacuum state.

The polarization of the vacuum is actually a *complete detailed pattern* of the DNA structure. This pattern is "left behind" (as a metastable state) in the physical vacuum and remains for a period of time. The polarized pattern, the torsion field, is, *subsequently interactive with light.*

> What we understand is that physical reality has a complete copy of itself in the vacuum. A good discussion on the principles of waveform patterns being established in the physical vacuum is found in the work of Alex Kaivarainen. Kaivarainen presents a comprehensive model of the physical vacuum, matter and fields, and this model explains all paranormal phenomena, non-local information fields, as well as the principles of wholeness and self-organization [9].

What this means is that a field of certain spatial configuration, or pattern, *can be recorded on any physical or biological object*, as well as to the physical vacuum state where a record also exists. *Changes to the spin state of a substance can alter its electrical properties, its magnetizability, thermal conduction, and other properties* [10].

Figure 7.8 **Torsion Fields of Objects.** *Every object possesses its own torsion field. The spatial configuration of the torsion field is related to the geometry of the object. The figure illustrates the field configuration of different geometries. Note that there are Left and Right torsion fields. Torsion fields can be generated as a result of distortion to the physical vacuum. (See Chapter Notes #26).*

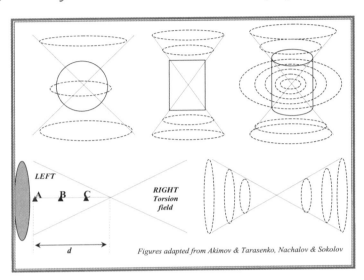

TRANSFER OF CONFIGURATION

A dramatic example of the interactive effect of an external torsion field in altering physical structure is proposed by Nachalov & Sokolov in the following experiment [11]. These two Russian researchers propose that a torsion generator developed by Yu V. Tszyan Kanchzhen can be used to alter the characteristics of living things. We are unable to verify if such a generator actually exists, or if such an experiment has actually taken place. However, we wish to point out that the concepts and ideas are intriguing. It is the principles of the process that are relevant to our understanding.

Consider a torsion field generator, designed with both transmitter and receiver chambers. Now, in our proposed experiment, we place a duck in the transmitter chamber, and then place a hen in the receiver chamber. In such an arrangement, the hen becomes the receiver of the torsion field of the duck. Over a period of a few days of exposure to the transmitted torsion field, the hen would begin to take on duck characteristics. The hen may physically gain web feet, a duck bill, etc..

Here we are talking about the potential engineering of the physical state using applied torsion fields (*Bearden calls it scalar wave technology*). Accordingly, physical reality can be molded, altered, and modified through the interactions of the torsion field! In the above example, the information field that defines the pattern of the hen would become "charged up" with the patterning of a duck. Given sufficient time and exposure to the influence of the external torsion field of the duck, the hen's information field becomes repatterned. As a consequence, the hen's physical structure takes on new features. As the hen's information/torsion field would charge up with the duck's pattern, and the physical biology of the hen would re-organize itself over time, to conform to the modifications within its information field.

REALITY IS A PROJECTION OF PRIMARY SUBTLE FIELDS

From this discussion it cannot be overly emphasized that physical reality is truly the projection of the primary subtle information fields. *It is these field structures that are subject to interaction, influence, and change.* Ultimately these subtle fields provide the patterns, or information base, that guide elementary particles in forming physical reality. In the same manner that a radio signal can guide and control a ship at sea, the "subtle" information fields, and subtle energies, guide the patterns of expression of physical matter as we see it! For physical change to take effect, the torsion field must alter the patterning of the subtle information fields that are the actual blueprints of matter! This is obviously what occurs in the case in our example above.

However, *torsion fields always interact, even if there are no immediate or obvious effects!* No dramatic change to physical reality is necessary. Subtle interactive effects occur within the subtle energy fields, and at the quantum level. Virtual (unobserved) patterns placed within the subtle fields, can, according to Bearden, be kindled, or charged up. Once the individual has added sufficient energy to the pattern, the quantum threshold is breached, and the virtual pattern now becomes real in physicality.

TORSION FIELDS YIELD RESONANCE INTERACTION

Although the torsion field does not change the energy of any system, it can act on the phase of the wave function, and in doing so *imparts information to the system.* For example, biological cells and biological processes are known to be sensitive to infinitesimally small electromagnetic fields and fluctuations in the earth's geomagnetic field.

Conventional electromagnetic theory cannot explain these low order electromagnetic fields effects to biological effects. However, consider that the biological electromagnetic fields have torsion field counterparts. It is the <u>torsion field interactions</u> that can explain the small-scale interactions that impart information. This was observed with an ion (charged like particle) in a protein molecule that was subjected to an external torsion field. The ion responded to the external field in a *resonance-like* manner [12]. The biological effect on the protein ion occurs from torsion interference effects at the quantum level.

RESONANCE TO FORM

Resonance interactions can also occur from passive torsion field generators.

Russian researchers have determined that some objects, particularly those following certain geometric properties and special shapes, produce resonance interaction with biological objects [13]. The shapes investigated include pyramids, cones, cylinders, triangles, spires and domes. The findings were that any object with geometrical proportions that follow the rule of the golden ratio (I: 0.618) could be considered as passive torsion generators.

Passive torsion generators create polarized disturbances within the physical vacuum. The patterns of polarization result in the virtual forces from the vacuum that are interactive with biological systems. The property of a substance open to influence by torsion fields is spin. Spin is associated with virtual vortices set up in the vacuum state. The torsion field is able to change the rate of any physical process. For example, it has been experimentally determined that a torsion field can *significantly alter the oscillation frequency of quartz crystals* [14].

adapted from Nachalov & Sokolov

Figure 7.9 **Torsion Field of Magnet.** *Shown in the figure is the shape of the torsion field for a permanent magnet. Note that there exists both a Right and a Left torsion field (magnetic North is a Right torsion field). Every physical object has a torsion field. Because of this fact, the torsion field of a permanent magnet is able to interact with any substance-even those that are not magnetizeable or are diamagnetic. (See Chapter Notes #27).*

MAGNETICS PRODUCE TORSION FIELD

A natural object that is able to affect any physical substance is a permanent magnet. A magnet can affect an object, even if that object cannot be magnetized- any object, living or non-living. How? Every permanent magnet possesses its own torsion field. This discovery was experimentally established by Russian researcher A.I. Veinik [9].

A permanent magnet possesses not only oriented magnetic moments, but also classical spin orientation that yield the torsion field. The torsion field, and its effects, is separate and distinct from what we know and see as magnetic lines of force. The torsion field can affect any substance, even those that are not magnetizable. For example a magnet can have an effect on the properties of water. Water is *diamagnetic*, meaning it cannot be magnetized. However the *structure* of water will respond to the torsion field of the magnet. Of course, any magnetic field is associated with a torsion field. As sources of detectable magnetic phenomena, *the hands are sources of torsion fields* (*see Figure 7.5*).

MAGNETICS CONNECTED TO SPIN

A magnet is formed from the coherent alignment of the small charged particles (magnetic domains) that are at the basis of material substance of the magnet. Each particle is a small spinning sphere with a North and South pole. Under the influence of an outside force, such as the presence of the magnetic field during crystallization of the substance, or the presence of a flowing current, a uniform orientation of the spinning spheres will result. The substance becomes magnetized.

The uniform and coherent collective spins of the charged particles set up a spin/torsion field. The spin field forms two cones, outwardly from the center of the magnet (*see Figure 2.2*). Within one cone the collective spins contribute to counterclockwise vortex force potential action. In the other cone, the collective spins contribute to a clockwise vortex force potential. These spin fields cause the circular movement of threads of particle energy to circulate in the vacuum.

A MAGNETIC FLOW

The magnetic poles set up gradients in the vacuum that result in the magnetic lines of force, i.e., a flow. The influence of the spin field contributes an interesting effect. As particles flow along magnetic threads they are caused to deflect either clockwise, or counterclockwise, along their path, that is the particles follow a spiral path. Each magnetic pole disturbs the density of particles in the vacuum. This creates gradients that disturb the natural balance of the vacuum. The pressure gradients are directed either toward, or away, from the magnetic pole.

The gradient will always manifest as a flow. Even if it is unobserved, a scalar current or movement always results. Drawing from the unlimited energy source of the vacuum, the magnet initiates a flow into the South pole. With the spiraling vortex action of the spin field, the threads of particles appear to be pulled into the South pole as they are pushed by the gradients set up in the surrounding area. The clockwise spinning vortex is the centripetal, compressive, condensing action, pulling energy into the pole (*see Figure 6.11*).

CENTRIFUGAL & CENTRIPETAL ACTION

The spinning vortex condenses, concentrates and focuses the flow from the vacuum into the South pole. The opposite occurs at the North pole. The flow leaving the North pole follows the counterclockwise spiraling vortexes. This is the centrifugal, expanding motion, the combined action of the two poles is to produce a push-pull type of pump mechanism that draws energy from the vacuum at the South pole and directs it out the North pole. Here we have the principles for harnessing zero point energy, 'free energy' by the engineering of potential gradients within the physical vacuum.

A permanent magnet is a *vacuum engine* that maintains its permanency by continuously drawing upon the unlimited energy source of the vacuum (also called the Dirac Sea, or Cosmic Sea) [16].

MAGNETICS IN RESONANCE WITH SOURCE

The bar magnet sets up a *resonance,* i.e., a closed circuit in tune with the source of vacuum energy- in which its electromagnetic fields receive and maintain a continuous permanent charge. The permanency of a magnet comes from this closed circuit that makes a magnet a *free energy generator* [16].

Similar principles would apply to the magnetic fields at the hands establishing a resonance with the energies of the vacuum (*see Figure 6.18*). In such an instance, the human magnetic field is continuously charged by the electromagnetic energy of resonant frequencies of the vacuum environment. One example is the Schumann frequency that is also the natural frequency of the human system. Such a resonance would translate as receiving free energy, or 'channeling'.

POLARITY A PROPERTY OF SPIN

At each magnetic pole there exists threads of charged particle flow [18]. These follow opposing patterns. One flow is a clockwise movement of charged particles, which manifests as a negative electrical polarity. The other pattern is a counterclockwise flow of charged particles, which manifests as a positive electrical polarity.

The direction of the vortex spin is what establishes electrical polarity. The spin density of the vortex-- the density of threads off particles spinning in the vortex-- establishes the gradient or strength of the electrical polarity. Here we have described how electrical polarity is the effect, and not a cause, of potential gradients that are established in virtual reality.

Electrical polarity can be strengthened. Various approaches to do so are:

- Balance and charge or strengthen the gradients (*trap more light*)
- Balance and adjust vortex spin directions
- Increase spin density by drawing more energy threads into the vortex

The above actions will effectively alter the electromagnetic properties of a spinning vortex such as a chakra. The above discussion may also very well describe the action of the chakra. This is a critical reason why a chakra must always be adjusted and balanced to its correct spin orientation, and not left in a static, or non-spinning state. The vortex or spin of the chakra will take on a higher electrical charge. [A chakra can be viewed as a mini Einstein-Rosen bridge- an inter-dimensional connector.]

Such a principal was demonstrated in an experiment by Pat Flanagan in 1976. Flanagan spun water in a vortex and discovered that spinning water developed an electromagnetic field. At a vortex spin rate off 1000 RPM (revolutions per minute), a 4-inch (approximately 10 cm.) vortex of water developed 10,000 volts! The vortex was allowed to collapse, with the electromagnetic energy being absorbed by the water molecules. The water became charged magnetically! Magnetically charged water has a positive influence on ion exchange in cell membranes. Charging water enhances the crystalline properties of the liquid. It was the life work of the famed Viktor Schauberger to study and harness the power of a spiraling water vortex [19].

OMNI-PRESENT AGAIN

If a bar magnet is placed in a closed container, the magnetic lines of force will be trapped. Effectively, this squashes the magnetic field, as we know it. However the spin field of the magnet cannot, and is not, shielded by the enclosure. This is because the torsion field of the magnet exists in the physical vacuum – which is different from our 3D space. We refer to the vector potential that exists in the absence of an observable magnetic field (*see Figure 2.11*). The famed experiment, known as the Bohm-Aharonov effect, established that the vector potential has a far-reaching effect even when no magnetic fields exist in normal space. According to Tiller, *the vector potential is the link to the subtle realm.* The vector potentials exist for a bar magnet. A vector potential establishes the magnetic fields at the hands.

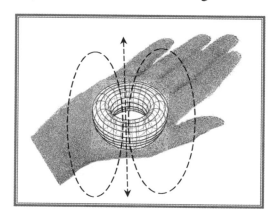

Figure 7.10 **Halo in Hand**. *The toroidal (donut) shape is a principle characteristic of the magnetic field. The North South magnetic axis is centered at the midpoint of the hole in the middle of the torus. This form is one aspect of the spinning spiraling vortex motion that both captures and emits light and energies. The torus is a hyperspatial inter-dimensional connector of virtual realities. It is an interdimensional vortex.*

THE HAND AS LIVING ANTENNA

Returning to the magnetism of the hand, we discover some interesting similarities to a bar magnet, but we also discover some extraordinary differences. You see, as carbon electrical light beings, we are endowed with the ability to modify or modulate frequency – unlike silicone-based matter.

Emotion and intent temper the vibrations in the human energy field. The holographic nature of the human body, and the human energy field, places all of these vibrations in the palm of your hand!

This is well documented in the work of Valerie Hunt, the HeartMath Institute, Davis and Rawls, and many others. The effect of emotions can also be can be seen in the records of Kirlian photography along with other aura photographing technologies.

The hand couples to the heart, as well as to the *Intent* and scalar action of the brain. The human body is a living antenna and as such is both receiver and transmitter of an incredible range off frequencies. The palms of both hands carry opposing magnetic polarity. The reverse side of each hand also carries opposing magnetic poles. A *spin/torsion* field extends conically in both directions from the center of the palm (*see Figure 7.5*). A *torus* is centered about the magnetic equator and protrudes equally on both sides of the hand.

The vortex spiraling field of the hand is most likely connected to the shape of spiraling energy within the DNA. The spiraling vortex is multiplied many orders of magnitude as the energy expands outward collectively from within the DNA template.

TORSION FIELD - SPIN/SPIN INTERACTION :THE FINAL ANSWER ...

There are no final answers, but we can continue to speculate on the possibilities. What are other interactions that can result from the fields of the hands?

Let us consider the impact of the spin-spin interactions of the torsion fields from the hands with biological and subtle matter. Torsion fields interact with other torsion fields. This is a scientific fact . There is also instance where there may occur interactive effects between the torsion field's energetic substructure and the electromagnetic field directly.

This is explained by Alexander Shpilman, who designed a unique generator of the torsion field. He also discusses the physical properties of torsion fields. Shpilman uses the terms *spin* and *axion* to be synonymous with *torsion*. So spin/axion/torsion fields relate to the same entity- and we use this terminology interchangeably. According to Shpilman, the spin/axion field consists of complex forms of interlacing spiral structures. In particular,

> "along threads of spirals there is a flow of energy of large density having a pseudo charge, creating a magnetic field". The threads and spirals are "very sensitive to size and direction of the vector potential" [20].

Shpilman describes the spin/axion/torsion field as the birthplace or source of virtual particles. Within the spaces of the *"threads of spirals"*, particles similar to neutrinos are generated, and these carry a variety of characteristics including *a spectrum of resonant frequencies*. From his several years of experimentation and study of the effects of torsion fields on biological matter, Shpilman has observed that the impact of an applied external spin/torsion served to:

- Increase the bioenergy flow to plants
- Increase an animal's immune system
- Have a long-term (several weeks) residual influence, even after removal of the external field.

Shpilman also discusses the use of passive torsion generators by an individual, and remarks that the activity within the field structure is largely dependent on the *thoughts of the experimenter* [20].

INTERACTIVE POTENTIAL

The human hand provides natural spin/torsion/axion field. We *are* generators of spin fields. The interactive possibilities of this field with other spin fields include the acupuncture points (acupoints or energy exchange ports), chakras, and all other primary/secondary or minor/major vortex energy centers of the human body and energy anatomy.

We may also entertain an interactive process that takes place between the hands' torsion field and the information field that surrounds the biology. Consider the information field to be a vibrating web of electromagnetic energy, yet dynamic, alive, and evolving. We can call this the biofield.

The biofield is one specific type of *information field*. Other subtle energy structures can also be called *information fields*. So the term information field is used broadly.

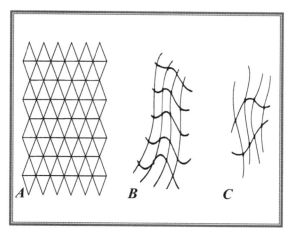

Figure 7.11 **Crystalline Field Structure.** *We can conceptualize an information field, or subtle energy 'layer' to consist of an n-dimensional (n>3 with hyperspatial characteristics) crystalline lattice structure [A]. The electric and magnetic vectors each have virtual substructures that connect & relate to higher spaces. The* geometry *of this lattice structure establishes a* resonance *to more complex space. Nodal junctions, where multiple vectors interconnect, share information, and, when tuned, have interdimensional access to information and energy flow. Normal patterns [B] within the lattice can become deformed [C] by influence of outside 'noise'. Patterns [C] represent input to the crystalline lattice that is not harmonically stored.*

All these subtle structures possess some form of electromagnetic nature, and this means that torsion fields are always associated- *in fact these information fields are torsion fields* [21]. We must keep in mind that there is a hierarchical structure within both physical and subtle matter.

Subtle energy fields, or information fields, are organized by their respective higher dimensional origins. Torsion fields interact with other torsion fields.

Is it possible to remove noise from the subtle fields? Is it possible to repattern the biofield for normal good health? Is it possible to disturb, scramble and destroy the biofields of parasites that clog up man's biofield, and propagate disease? Is it possible to eliminate the noisy patterns that have become embedded in the subtle fields, originating from the emotions?

Emotions create scalar electromagnetic activity from the brain/nervous system and endocrine glands. *The scalar activity produces patterns of disturbance* and these become embedded within the subtle field structures.

Technologically, these things have been happening for some time. The work of Priore, Rife, Hulda Clark.... amongst others relate to these ideas. Moreover, Bearden contends that current scalar technology provides 'information patterning' potential, and that it is being exploited. As well, the experimental results of Russians torsion field research has demonstrated the ability to alter the physical properties of living thing. All these considerations point to one resounding conclusion:

> Physical reality is subject to alteration-patterned information can be transferred- physical changes can be time-reversed- disease patterns can be eliminated and health restored...all through simple access to, and alteration of, <u>the information fields</u> that organize matter (both living and non-living).

Such feats have already been the product of the technologies of the 20th Century!

A CONNECTING FIELD

All living cells, and every molecule that form them, are connected to this invisible lace-like biofield structure (*see Appendices A & C*). The web, or biofield, provides not only the invisible interconnectedness of the cells, *but also the platform upon which the cells plan the required work.*

This information field is like a drafting table upon which cellular functioning is first drawn out- in a virtual sense. From this work-plan, there is subsequent implementation by the physical processes. The work of DNA is first processed within the biofield structure. Within the biofield, the cell finds the required patterns and structures that have been encoded for the living organism. But at the same time, the field is receiving inputs from the cells that updates the global web structure itself.

> For evolution to take place physically, the new evolved states must be planted into the field structure in order for the cells to have access to this updated information.

Herein we have the principles of cellular evolution.

> New information for the cells must appear in this web/biofield/information field in order for physical change to occur.

According to Bearden and Russian researchers, the structure and information content of this field can be engineered and altered with existing technology. Physical changes may manifest according to the altered patterns that can be implanted into the information field.

Biologists recognize that cellular repair is guided by an invisible influence- whether we call it the biofield or morphic field. It these invisible fields that provide a holographic projection into 3D space that are the necessary and required patterns for the formation of the biological repair. The physical elements of the cells rebuild by following a detailed blueprint sent in from higher space. The biofield, as an information field, *follows the holographic principle-* any part of the field contains the information of the whole.

CONSCIOUSNESS LINKS TO TORSION FIELD

As multi-dimensional beings, we carry the technology to alter, influence, and change our physical reality?

Consciousness and Intent guide the torsion field.

Herein, we have a mechanism for connecting the mind field to subtle structures through the torsion field!

The formulation of torsion field theory is not layman's subject. Nor is the subject matter of most scientists. The mathematics used is an extraterrestrial language of its own. As such we are dependent on the real experts and specialists to interpret the physical ideas related to mathematical theory. One such expert is Jack Sarfatti of the Advanced Intelligence Agency.

Earlier in our text we introduced Sarfatti as the innovator of 'post quantum' theory- a discipline that seeks to explain the interaction of mind with matter. Sarfatti has reviewed a primary text of a Russian author on torsion field theory [23]. What we discover is that Shipov connects the mental field of consciousness to the torsion field. This is evident in the following two statements cited by Sarfatti [22]:

From pg. 74 of Shipov's text:

At this level of reality a decisive role is played by 'superconsciousness'. Which appears as the active origin of the ideal that acts within the framework of the universal principle of relativity [22].

And in a second instance, from pg. 75 of Shipov's text:

Transition from the first level of reality to the second one (the level of the primary torsion field) occurs...under the action of an external torsion field whish is shown by experiments to be, apparently, the vehicle of 'the field of consciousness' [22].

In layman's terms, it is declared that Consciousness is the key player within the implicate order of reality. The ordering influence of Consciousness is active through the interconnecting link of the torsion field!

CONSCIOUSNESS, INTENT & FIELD STRUCTURE

Studies of 'healers' have shown that the bio-electromagnetic fields at the hands can be modified & strengthened by the Conscious Intent of the practitioner. The torsion field is *always* associated with the appearance of an electrostatic, magnetic, or electromagnetic field.

Modifying & strengthening the bio-electromagnetic fields at the hands also modifies and strengthens the torsion fields in the region of space surrounding the hands. The torsion field acts on the vacuum to impart its information structure through pattern polarization of the medium. *Therefore the region of space surrounding the hands is patterned by conscious Intent.*

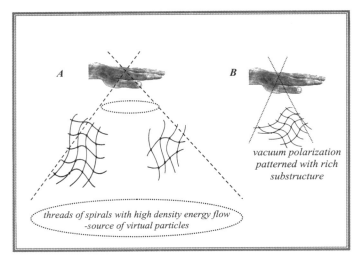

Figure 7.12 **Torsion/Crystalline Field Interaction.** *The spin/torsion field consists of threads of spirals with high-density energy flow. As well, the torsion field is a source of virtual particles that interact with the subtle fields. The interactions with a subtle energy field (A) result in a disorganization of the information field structure. With this disorganization, the distorted, noise patterns are, effectively, eliminated. The subtle field will rebuild, reorganize (rewire itself) harmonically, in resonance. This restructuring is guided by a higher virtual reality. Additionally, the vacuum environment remains polarized with the torsion field/scalar wave patterning (B) even after removing the hand. The bio-electromagnetic fields of the hand are modified by Conscious Intent. The torsion field is directly connected to these bio-electromagnetic fields. Therefore the patterning of the vacuum by the torsion field contains information **programmed by conscious intent.** The polarized patterning of the vacuum continues to have an influence, through information transfer, on the restructuring of the subtle fields.*

Removing the hand *does not dissolve the patterned information field structure* within the vacuum. The torsion field has <u>*activated*</u> the medium surrounding the subtle fields with *information wave patterns* that appear as *templates of organization, geometry, structure and form* . These influence the restructuring of the subtle fields. Torsion fields transfer information without the transfer of energy.

The subtle field responds to information wave patterns according to where the patterns carry *meaning* to the subtle field structure. This is like seeking sympathetic vibration and harmonic resonance. Throughout this text the term <u>*vacuum*</u> refers to

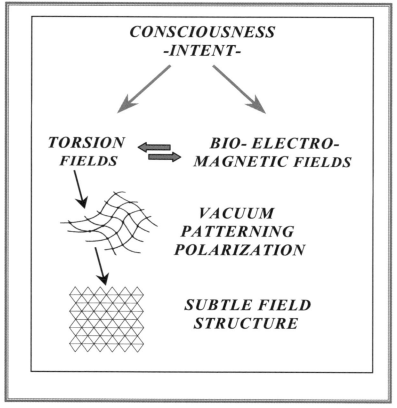

Figure **7.13 Consciousness, Intent & Field Structure**. *Studies of 'healers' have shown that the bio-electromagnetic fields at the hands can be modified & strengthened by the conscious intent of the practitioner. The torsion field is* always *associated with the appearance of an electrostatic, magnetic, or electromagnetic field. Modifying & strengthening the bio-electromagnetic fields at the hands also modifies and strengthens the torsion fields in the region of space surrounding the hands. The torsion field acts on the vacuum to impart its information structure through polarization of the medium.* Therefore the region of space surrounding the hands is **patterned by conscious INTENT**. *The torsion field has* <u>**activated**</u> *the medium surrounding the subtle fields with* information wave patterns *that appear as* **templates of organization, geometry, structure and form**. *These influence the restructuring of the subtle fields. Torsion fields transfer information without the transfer of energy.*

something 'physical'. The vacuum is a plenum-an ocean of energy at the basis of material physicality. It is considered to be a form of superfluid, gaseous medium that offers no resistance to flow.

Disturbances within the vacuum cause & generate the various observed forces-gravity, electromagnetism, and torsion fields. Engineering or structuring the vacuum state results in the engineering of the observed forces. This gives the possibility of extracting energy directly from the vacuum ('free' zero point energy).

Polarization of the vacuum refers to the preferred alignment or orientation of the random unobserved particles that form the actual substructure of the vacuum. *Patterning* within the vacuum is the results of standing wave forms that are established as a result of various types of deformations of the vacuum medium [9].

> These standing waves represent an ordering and structuring within the vacuum leading to higher organization, or *negative entropy*, within the medium. According to Kaivarainen, the standing wave forms are at the basis of *non-local information fields* and the principles of wholeness and self-organization.

REWIRING THE SUBTLE FIELDS

An information field, like the biofield or other subtle field, is an n-dimensional (n>3) structure. Other virtual realities exist within, and beyond, the immediate visible active elements of the field. This principle applies to all other subtle structure fields. Subtle fields are holographic-- any part of the subtle field contains complete elements of the whole.

> The restructuring of a subtle field is best described as an
>
> n-dimensional holographic projection. From this perspective, the mystery of self-organization is completely solved. The holographic projection from a higher space always guides the outcome in lower space!

The holographic image contained within the subtle field structure is the *potential* information available to reconstruct a field. New potential information can be added! *This follows the principles of torsion field interaction!* Consciousness guides the process.

In the evolutionary process, the subtle web rebuilds. As it rebuilds, it is new and *it is rewired better than before.* The predominating influencing factors at reconstruction include:

- The inter-dimensional flow or flux of higher energies & the bio-energy transfer from light
- The holographic nature of the field that has been modified with information patterns from the torsion field programmed by Intent
- The patterns that remain in the vacuum (surrounding medium) programmed by Consciousness and Intent.

The rewiring results in a superior structure with a greater potential for evolution than the previous one. A greater degree of function within the information field is equivalent to *greater intelligence*. Signals become strong, clear, *coherent* & amplified. Communication and energy channels expand and open.

A NEW PARADIGM OF INTERACTION

Our paradigm of interaction consists of several bold new elements. Consider that:

- The brain is a scalar translator/interferometer and torsion field generator driven by Intent.
- The brain couples to the heart - an electromagnetic power plant/torsion field generator driven by emotion.
- The hand is a torsion field/scalar-wave multi-dimensional instrument. This collective hardware is supported by hyperspatial aspects of our higher being.
- Consider that this hardware is infinitely programmable, and tunable to function in co-resonance.
- *Consciousness* & the mind field are at the very basis of setting the patterns that organize the substance of both virtual and observed physical reality.

Such is a model of the 21st century for understanding subtle field interaction within our new paradigm of co-creating our reality.

CHAPTER EIGHT

THE
MASTER SWITCH

The Heart Of It All

Love is a canvas furnished by nature and
Embroidered by imagination.

Voltaire

Throughout our discussions it has been a fundamental precept that the brain, Intent, heart, and emotions are governing factors to the fields at the hands...and to our human-to-human interactive processes.

The brain is no passive player. Bearden has proposed that the two hemispheres of the brain function as a large producer and translator of scalar waves. The brain is constantly forming electromagnetic patterns.

These patterns are created with a grouping of synapses that fire in unison. The grouping of synapses is determined by consciousness.

The conditions of firing at the synaptic gaps are favorable to the production of scalar waves, and each pattern of synaptic firing is associated with a scalar wave pattern that enters hyperspace. Theoretically, this pattern lives on forever. The change from one firing pattern to another represents the actual thought that becomes encoded as patterning within the scalar wave. So the scalar wave is the mechanism for transporting *thought information* across time and space. When this scalar wave is intercepted and translated by an individual, a telepathic incident has occurred. Scalar technology could also, theoretically, accomplish a similar result, i.e. appropriate scalar technology that reads scalar waves could "read" a thought. Likewise, appropriate scalar technology could "send you" a thought. One facet of the thought process, therefore, is the creation of scalar waves with a programmed intelligent patterned substructure. It is this wave that interacts in virtual reality to structure matter/substance at the quantum level.

> **Focus Produces Emotion Based Patterns. With focused intent, specific frequency patterns, i.e. Color & information (*thoughts produce unique scalar patterns*)- are produced by the brain and are transmitted through the nervous system.**

The nervous system acts as a waveguide for scalar waves. These frequency patterns from the brain also produce resonant response in the cells throughout the whole body. Collectively this scalar energy in the form of *scalar biophotons* is directed to the hands by willful intent. As Davis and Rawls have discovered, all the energies from the brain are found at the hands [1].

The HeartMath Institute reports that ongoing research is looking at measuring and detecting the subtle energy fields around the body. They are adapting very sensitive and specialized equipment to measure the various electromagnetic components that could reveal properties of the subtle field. The researchers of the Institute believe that one's internal emotional and mental states can affect the qualities of the photons emitted from the body. They suggest that these internal states can modify the frequency (color) and the flow of the biophoton emissions. They anticipate that this will be verified through their research [2].

POWER GENERATING STATION

The hyperfunction and scalar abilities of the brain truly enable incredible possibilities. Our thoughts, intents, and emotions direct and influence these biological faculties. They are the mechanisms behind paranormal abilities. The brain, along with the whole biological system, is designed with innate ability to transmute energies from outside sources. Energy is collected, transmuted, and processed for various biological and non-biological needs. The electromagnetic fields of the brain play a role in the altering of energy form one form into another.

We also see the DNA of each cell as a converter and storage place of light energy. When the brain is brought into higher functioning through activation of all its components, and when the cells of the whole body are tuned in resonance, the biological system has the capacity to become one huge *focused and coherent power generating station*. Bearden makes an in-depth calculation of the actual amount of energy our biological systems dissipate as energy flow from the vacuum and through virtual flux exchange: *it is the awesome equivalent of 1,000,000 powerplants, each producing 1,000 megawatts of energy!*[13]

CHARGE = FLOW

The *rate of flow of energy* in and out of our energy anatomy is equated to one's charge. This *charge* is the relative difference in the flow or flux intensity of a particle (or system), as compared to the flux intensity of the ambient vacuum background (*see Figure 2.6*). This difference we also call the *potential.* <u>Charge</u> is not a fixed quantity, it is a variable. The flow of energy through one's anatomy, or charge, can be altered through conscious intervention. However, in order to increase the flow of energy there must be circuitry in place to handle the additional "load". <u>*Opening existing energy channels*</u> *and conduits is the basis requisite.*

IN HARMONY WITH THE FLOW

Because the energy anatomy channels are inter-related and inter-connected, the next requirement is to <u>*establish balance and harmony*</u> between the circuits. This requisite ensures that all potential conduits participate in the energy distribution without *overload.*

> *Overload could create possible imbalance symptoms to nervous system, brain, physical and subtle bodies* [3]. *Once existing energy circuits have reached their flow capacity, it would appear that the potential 'charge' has reached its potential limit. However the next step is an evolutionary leap! —Create and establish new circuitry for the energy and information handling purposes.*

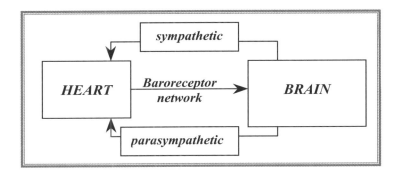

Figure 8.1 **Head Heart Connection.** *The heart and brain are connected through distinct communication and feedback systems: the barareceptor network directs information about the heart's physiological state to the brain- the sympathetic and parasympathetic channels relay communication from the brain to the heart. Synchronization of heart-brain function, and balance within the communication systems has been found to be influenced by the emotional state of the heart (source Heartmath Institute).*

MASTER IGNITION

What is the real key to turning on this power plant? Of course *tuning* and *coherence* of the whole system is a prerequisite. Once this is done how do you turn the power on? There is increasing experimental evidence, notably from the HeartMath Institute, that the emotion of the heart may be the ultimate *master switch* of the power plant.

Expression of the feelings of appreciation, caring, and unconditional love, focused at the heart, trigger measurable beneficial physiological effects in the human body [4]. The heart's radiated energy spectrum increases. Various physiological functions including brain waves, respiration, and heart rate can be affected in dramatic ways by the emotions.

> **"Every thought we think and emotion we feel is reflected in the heart's electrical systems which affects the whole body"** [5].

The heart is intimately connected with brain function. The heart and brain are linked through the sympathetic, parasympathetic, and baroreceptor systems. The two-way communication can result in emotion of the heart either enhancing higher brain function, or shutting it down.

EARTH & HEART RESONANCE

Dan Winter presents some revealing results about the interaction between the human emotion of love, and the earth's environment. In the experiment, a subject was asked to establish a state of deep, focused, feeling of appreciation and love. The heart signals were monitored and sensing equipment was also placed within the surrounding environment, and also at a nearby tree field. What amazed the researchers was that the magnetic field of the earth in that local environment 'tuned-in' to the heart signal! The coherent heart signal and the earth's magnetic fields established a *resonant* alignment.

According to Dan Winter "the Earth grid 'frequency locks' with the human heart at the lowest frequency or at the longest wave length of biology's most intense resonator. The Heart, the Brain, and the Earth all had their key information broadcasting on the same channel" [6]! Dan Winter feels that the heart energy is the focus to aligning and empowering all other centers. The heart is capable of producing coherent frequency radiation, and the key to this coherence is the heart emotions of love and appreciation.

The experiment above shows us that all life is connected to the scalar pulse of the planet. The scalar heartbeat of the earth provides a vital source of bioenergy and information to all living things. The core of the planet receives the incoming scalar waves from the sun and moon, translates these waves, then modulates and rebroadcast to surface life [7]. All life shares common resonant circuitry with the earth, and all life share common resonant circuitry. Through the earth's core, we share in the scalar emissions of the sun, galaxy, and the universe. All is united-- all is connected.

Figure 8.2 **Earth & Heart Resonance.**
Resonance to the emotion of the heart was demonstrated with the earth's environment 'tuning in' to the heart signal of a meditator focusing on love and appreciation. Dan Winter reports local variations to the earth's magnetic field, as well as variations to electromagnetic signals from a nearby tree. According to Winter, the local environment 'frequency locked' to the central power spectrum of the human heart. All life is connected to the scalar pulse of the earth, and all life shares common resonant circuitry with the planet.

GAUGING THE POTENTIAL

That hyperspatial fields exist at the hands-- of this we can be sure . We have clear evidence that these fields exist. We also have evidence that there is still more to be discovered and understood. Einstein first used the term *subtle energy* in reference to energy phenomena that could not be measured by ordinary means. The energy may be subtle, but some extraordinary observations of the effects of 'Qi' energy are very demonstrable and evident.

Dr. Gerber reports another example of an amazing feat demonstrated by a Doctor of Acupuncture [8]. This individual had trained himself to build up energy by focusing attention within his abdominal region, known as the *Hara*, a place where physical and subtle bodies are thought to strongly connect. Once the intensity of energy had achieved a sufficiently high level, the doctor could project this energy through his hands across a room to a patient. [This is a similar feat demonstrated by many Qigong masters.]

When individuals placed their hands on the abdomen of the doctor while he was projecting energy they received electric shocks and were forced to withdraw their hands. The same doctor was able to cause a balled up piece of newspaper to ignite in flames by simply placing his hands around the outside of the newspaper ball. The flame ignited from the <u>inside</u> of the paper ball.

INNATE ABILITY TO ACCUMULATE CHARGE

What is evident from these demonstrations is that there is an *inherent and natural* ability amongst everyone to accumulate and store energy. The feats of energy emission above (common amongst Qigong masters) tell us that the potential also exists to store very large amounts of chi-- albeit with the requirement of long term dedicated practice. Where and how is this energy storage taking place?

It takes place *somewhere within our <u>multidimensional energy anatomy</u>*. When storage of energy takes place within the energy anatomy, the *potential*, or *charge*, of the system is raised. Changing the potential of the field refers to a *gauge*, or *regauge*, to the system.

A *gauge* to the field can take place with no outward detectable change to the magnetic and electric force fields. It is a process of providing *free excess energy* through successive cycles of the charge-discharge process [9]. Raising the *charge* or *potential* of an electromagnetic field increases and elevates the photonic (light) interactions that are taking place within that field. This is significant because light is the conductor of neutrinic waves-- the hyperspatial carrier of bioenergy information [10]. More light interactions result in greater information and energy transfer-- a greater *flow* and *exchange* with the outside environment.

This flow and exchange is a requisite for all evolutionary processes to take place. Bruce Cathie has remarked that:

"We as human beings must consist of a geometric collection of the harmonic wave-forms of light-guided by intelligence" [11].

Cathie believes that the body's bio-energy system is tuned to react to the *harmonics of light*. This includes the body's acupuncture meridian system.

VECTOR POTENTIAL: A GAUGE FIELD

Researchers refer to the vector potential field as a gauge field. Physicists generally consider a 'field' as a region to store energy. Vector potential generators have been found to exert biomedical influences to the skin, heart, and autonomous nervous system. As well, the vector potential field has shown that it can influence the nuclear magnetic resonance spectra of liquids.

Researchers Takashi, *et al*, identify a *vector potential field* from the human body [12]. They suggest that this vector potential field is the result of the presence of electric currents in the body. Accordingly, *they contend that the human body with its vector potential field would exert biomedical influence to another human being.* [No doubt, *the vector potential field* is connected to subtle interactions in the human-to-human connection (Tiller)].

STORING THE POTENTIAL WITHIN THE LATTICE

How can this energy be stored? One method of storing personal energy is through the mechanism of standing waves and the scalar potentials. The UCL (Universal Calibration Lattice) is interpreted as an appropriate 'cavity'-a resonant cavity- within which standing waves can form. The standing waves form *scalar resonance* within the resonant cavity. These standing waves form according to the geometric properties of the UCL, and are, therefore, unique to each individual. Tuning is specific for each person.

The scalar waves are hyperspatial, so they are not constrained to our concept of time. These waves can resonate across time. The uniqueness of each personal lattice implies that a tuning takes place that is unique to each individual.

> **Sound and light are harmonically related, and the internal harmonics of the standing waves create an n-dimensional lattice (n>3) of chords that are tuned to the individual's unique personal 'tone'.**
>
> **Thus, the lattice structure would consist of a geometric collection of harmonic wave-forms of light-guided by intelligence. [Cathie's remark seems so appropriate here.]**

The scalar waves are electrogravitational waves, or electromagnetic sound waves. The standing waves represent variations of the flux or flow of virtual particles that set up the *potentials*. Establishing resonance within the UCL *charges up* the potentials. This is an interpretation of one the processes that occurs through the EMF Balancing Technique®.

SCALING THE GATES

A second observation from our "chi emissions" feat described above, is that this phenomenon may not simply be demonstration of *stored-up energy*. It may be a "complex" of factors. Qigong masters appear to be connected to the "flow" of energy from its source. A source from which the potential draw is, seemingly, without limit. The build up of charge (in the above case in the abdominal area) may be construed as the minimum threshold "voltage" level required to open the energy gate to the Cosmic Sea.

We see that various brain circuits require a minimum threshold of biological charge in order to be activated. The cell must reach a minimum charge in order to enable DNA activity for cell division. Light itself is quantized, and electrons must absorb light of a minimum energy in order to be propelled into a higher energy state. Thresholds exist even at the quantum state. All these *gates* have minimum entry requirements.

> **We see that various brain circuits require a minimum threshold of biological charge in order to be activated. In order to reach minimum threshold levels of charge we must strive to open up our own basic energy channels.**

And, literally, _these channels must be balanced_. Accordingly, we can then become <u>charged-up</u> to our minimum 'voltage' threshold levels. Once these minimum threshold levels are met, the internal multi-dimensional controls will trigger, and enable, the opening of our own floodgates to higher energies. *What lies beyond these gates ?*

But first, -we must be _rewired_ for the task.

"Elements, chemicals, cells, atoms and molecules—
these partially compose your living sculpture,
but you are the one who directs their activity through your
conscious beliefs, which then initiate all of these
great creative powers that give our body its life,
and insure its constant reflection of the self that you believe you are."

Jane Roberts, Seth "The Nature of Personal Reality"

CHAPTER NINE

EVOLUTIONARY
SYSTEM
OF LOVE

EMF Balancing Technique®

Subtle matter…is very magnetic.

R. Leichman, Einstein Returns

Steve Bhaerman, known to many as the new-age humorist Swami Beyondananda, introduced many distinguished speakers at a Science and Consciousness conference in Albuquerque, New Mexico. He commented during his presentation that, "... the imaginary barrier between science and spirituality dissolved a bit more today. It seems strange to need scientific proof that love, compassion and joy are good for us ... it works in practice, but does it work in theory?"

Those who work with subtle energies know that these techniques are gaining greater and greater acceptance in mainstream thinking each day. An article in the Journal of the American Medical Association (JAMA 11/11/99) declared that alternative therapies should no longer be considered outside the sanctions of traditional medical therapies, but rather as complementary to those therapies. If alternative approaches work, then they belong. It is my personal vision that a new level of professionalism is being born for these complementary therapies.

As described earlier in this book the Universal Calibration Lattice ("UCL") is our personal energetic doorway to linking with the vast energies of the Cosmic Lattice. The term "calibration" means to gauge or to strengthen. To be an effective link, our personal lattice (our UCL) should be balanced, calibrated and thereby strengthened. The most potent way to achieve this work with the Universal Calibration Lattice is through the EMF Balancing Technique® .

The EMF Balancing Technique® is both a procedure and a process. The basic intent of an EMF Balancing Technique® session is to balance the human electromagnetic field, allowing the individual's energy to open as many circuits as possible to the Cosmic Lattice.

The EMF technique was born of love. Since then it has developed a strong foundation built on experience and scientific knowledge. At first, when I was asked by others why it worked, I was not afraid to say, "I don't know." Then I gave the intent to know *why*, and the universe started to bring answers, often right from the students in my classes! Thousands of people the world over, with quite diverse backgrounds, have become EMF Balancing Technique® Practitioners. Among these are a growing number of scientists, engineers and medical doctors. They have often reported back to me, "I can tell you why you say this works this way, or that works that way!" I have always used my heart to feel and my sight to see the movement of energy. It is rewarding to have a scientist support my more intuitive process, and confirm the precise mechanics of the technique. I am deeply grateful to those who have offered their understanding and knowledge for what I have always simply accepted as true.

Teaching a systematic procedure was very unfamiliar to me as I am more of a "go with the flow and do what you feel" kind of person. My astrology chart stereotypically supports this. When I mention my personal astrological chart aspects to those in my EMF classes, I always get a good laugh from those who know what such alignments usually characterize.

The universe has a delicious and wise sense of humor. How else could I explain the irony of my job? A go-with-the-flow gal like me teaching an exacting and precise procedure primarily to those who seek freedom from the restrictions of form! A lot of people who do energy work have done so to escape those traditional restrictions and I deeply understand this desire. However, I must tell you that mastering procedure and form can lead you to an even greater freedom and effectiveness of expression.

In my years of teaching I have met many beautiful healers engaged in a variety of energy modalities. The EMF Balancing Technique® technique does not lessen the value of any other type of energy work, including free-form work. In fact, quite the opposite is true: I have found that understanding the UCL and the fundamental principles of the EMF technique enhances the performance of other modalities. The essence of the EMF Balancing Technique® is to honor one's innate wisdom, so I honor the wisdom of all in this field. Do we as energy workers need to divide exclusively into either free-form energy processes or into processes that follow a procedure? Of course not. We can enjoy the best of both worlds, my friends...

Many of you consciously work with energy. Some of you were taught to do this by another person. Some of you are so sensitive you simply follow what you feel and that is very appropriate. Can you still become one with the energy if you use a technique or follow a form? Absolutely. Think of the powerful demonstration of oneness exhibited by a martial artist who follows a distinct procedure in order to merge and become one with "chi" or "ki" energies. The EMF Balancing Technique® is like a martial art of the energy of the heart. Following its form releases tremendous amounts of love energy.

A Call to Universal Calibration   - The Human -to-Human Interaction

The Universal Energy Source, or the Cosmic Lattice as it is referred to in this book, has been described as the most powerful form of energy in the universe. Whatever your belief system, it is easy enough to accept that the universe is full of energy. A major premise of this book is that as evolving humans, we are capable of tapping into this energy source consciously. Physicists study the energy of the universe hoping to discover an unlimited, free and clean source of power for our planet. As individuals we can move into a vibrational frequency that allows us to use this universal energy for our own growth. While we may have to wait for our scientists to make these discoveries on a global scale, as individuals, nothing prevents us right now from strengthening and balancing our own energy anatomy in order to utilize more of the energy of the Cosmic Lattice in our daily lives.

The Universal Calibration Lattice is our personal interface with the Cosmic Lattice. The calibration process enables the UCL to hold, and the human to use, more of the abundant energy charge available in the universe. I call this calibration process a "rewiring for the new energy." Electrical charge is the Divine spark or power that resides in all of us. When we develop and strengthen the ability to create a resonance between our charge and the electrical charge of the cosmos, we gain a new form of empowerment. The goal of the call to Universal Calibration is for individual humans to consciously create a stronger non-denominational, ongoing and interactive union with one another and with the Infinite. Continued calibration of the UCL strengthens our "energetic muscles" in much the same way that working out in a gym strengthens our physical muscles. This process of energetic evolution sets the stage for karmic release, co-creation and personal empowerment. The UCL is <u>alive</u>. It is capable of completely resonating with Unconditional Love. It can bring about, within our physical bodies, a complete expression of the golden energy beings that we truly we are as we integrate our Spirit and our Biology .

Our daily lives provide us with all the material we need to evolve spiritually and materially. We can grow more efficiently and effectively when we have more energy. Could it be that spiritual growth and the material world are this closely linked? Many of us have noticed increasing synchronicities or beneficial "coincidences" in our lives. In his book, *The Celestine Prophecy*, James Redfield introduced this concept beautifully on a mass scale. This was just the beginning! Today, an increasing number of us are already living the reality that home is right where we are, and all of us have the same opportunity to create a personal heaven on Earth.

The changes many of you are feeling began in the late 1980s, as the magnetic grids of the earth began to shift. It has been documented that airport runways were renumbered because the alignment with magnetic north began to change significantly.

Greg Braden, in *Awakening to Zero Point* documents changes in the Schumann Resonance, the measure of the base pulse frequency of the Earth, or her "heartbeat." These earth changes continued throughout the 1990s, and many believe they will intensify at least until 2012, a date familiar to many as the ending year of the ancient Mayan calendar. We have also witnessed this century some of the largest solar emf events that have ever been recorded. These changes are not limited to natural phenomena, however. They are also compounded by the proliferation of electrical gadgets and appliances and the subsequent electromagnetic frequencies they generate. Today, we are surrounded by more "man-made" electromagnetic fields in our day-to-day lives than ever before. Every electrical, electronic, computer, telephone or radio type device generates electromagnetic fields. Electrical wiring in our homes and businesses generate electromagnetic fields even when appliances are turned off. Automobiles (through their generators and alternators) create massive electromagnetic fields. Our bioelectromagnetic fields, our energy fields of the body, are constantly bombarded with external forces that can push our personal fields out of balance. Technology brings us many benefits, but we must also remember that we are part of this energetic "soup." The spirit is vastly more powerful than the material. However, balance and calibration with universal energies is our doorway to continued growth and harmony. Energy work, specifically calibration of the UCL, is very important during this time if we are to successfully evolve and keep pace with all the electromagnetic changes around us.

When I asked my friend Lee Carroll what the UCL looked like to him, I felt the familiar warmth in my heart that I know to be Kryon, and I heard Lee respond, "I don't know what this answer means, but it is "crocheted." Yes, what a wonderful way to describe the UCL! As mentioned previously, fibers of light and energy radiate horizontally from the chakras. These fibers form figure-eight shaped loops that connect to the long vertical fibers of energy. When the fibers are stretched in one part of the UCL, other fibers may respond in another part. Like the Cosmic Lattice, the Universal Calibration Lattice is pliable and interconnected. Our personal energy lattice is truly a microcosm of the macrocosm!

At the quantum level, calibration of the fibers of the human energy anatomy is highly complex. Each person's calibration has a unique mathematical formula underlying the relationship between one's personal vibrational frequency and the Cosmic Lattice. On a conscious level, intent plays an important role. The basic intent of an EMF Balancing Technique® session is to balance the human electromagnetic field, allowing the individual's energy to open as many circuits as possible to the Cosmic Lattice. The person receiving the session may give a specific intent for almost anything, from healing, to Self-knowledge, to simple stress reduction. The primary focus, however, is balance. As fibers of the UCL are activated through calibration, a rewiring occurs, and a new electromagnetic order is created within the individual's energy field. This new order produces a stronger structure to receive energy from the Cosmic Lattice. After the connections have been strengthened, there is often a dramatic increase in the success of co-creating process.

It had been some time in my own teaching since I had spoken of love. For a long time, I felt the word was misused. The energy of human beings and the Earth is finally ready for a constant flow of Love, and we are going to be able to handle it. We can do this graciously, lovingly, and joyfully using the UCL.

All the love we have poured into God, masters such as Jesus or Buddha, other spiritual leaders, families, and our relationships, is a potential reflection of the love we have for ourselves. When we claim that love, self-esteem grows. This love of our whole Self is vast, and the vessel must be strong enough to hold it. This is one of the reasons we strengthen the UCL. Holding that love in ourselves first, we become whole, or wholehearted. We then share our love with others from a different perspective than we have ever before known. Activation of the Universal Calibration Lattice is an integral part of the preparation to receive the energy of Self Love as it rises like the Phoenix within us.

RESONANT TUNING OF THE LATTICE AND ELECTROMAGNETIC FIELD BALANCING

Resonance equals 24/7 Initiation

Initiations and alignments are very powerful and resonant events. However, we don't need to be in the Great Pyramid to experience initiation; all of our sensory interactions create a resonance within our being, and we are continuously resonating with our environment. Everything you see from the moment you look in the mirror in the morning, to all the things you observe throughout the day, creates a resonance. Everything you hear -- sounds, voices, music -- creates a resonance within you. Everything you touch or feel, and everything you smell creates a resonance. Witness the widespread use of aromatherapy. Tastes create resonance; we love our favorite foods and restaurants. When we use our intuition, what we intuit creates a resonance within us. Because everything and everyone we interact with produces resonance, it is easy for me to accept that all of our experiences can be considered as initiations or alignments. This understanding has enabled me to appreciate in a practical way that everything is spiritual.

THE BLESSINGS OF RESONANCE - CREATING ENERGETIC HARMONY...

There are initiations or resonant experiences we choose by association with people we consider to be wise or holy, those we know as gurus, spiritual teachers, religious leaders or channelers. These people carry a specific resonance, and we feel drawn to them to experience that resonance. When you spend time in their presence, their wholeness speaks directly to your wholeness, and in this way your life becomes enriched. When you experience increased insight or other blessings as a consequence of your encounter with this person, many attribute that gift to the guru or teacher. In an empowered state, however, we take responsibility for our own lives. From this perspective, we can see that the apparent blessings of the guru or teacher are actually the results of you experiencing a more expanded and resonant state of your own being. When you accept the responsibility as co-creator of these results, you honor not only yourself, but also pay the ultimate tribute to the facilitator of the resonance. And remember -- your resonance affects others, and so on, and so on . . .

Deepak Chopra is a human being with a resonance of wholeness that is felt and recognized by many. In a mainstream national magazine, he is referred to as a living national treasure. This is quite a title, but Chopra carries it with casual elegance. What happens when we meet someone like this? Several years ago, my husband Stephen and I went to Rhode Island to hear him lecture to an audience of about 1500 people. During the break, he sat on stage to autograph his books. Stephen and I waited patiently in the line. As we moved forward, I chatted with a young girl behind me. She was clearly in exuberant anticipation of her face-to-face meeting with this great man. She said to me, "I want a hug from him!" Out of the corner of my eye, I could see him autograph book after book in an apparently meditative state from which he did not look up. Remembering my experience with my own Indian guru, Swami Muktananda, I knew it was important to approach a teacher with no expectation. Instinctively my inner mother arose, and I offered this young girl some unsolicited advice so that she might not be disappointed in her meeting. I reminded her that earlier in his lecture he had stated that we were all sharing molecules just by being in the same room together. I assured her the hug wasn't necessary and encouraged her to simply enjoy the meeting and the molecule sharing.

Much to my surprise, when Stephen presented his book to be autographed, Deepak looked up and the two became engaged in a conversation. After a few moments, Stephen introduced me, " ... and this is my wife, Peggy Phoenix Dubro," and I intended to simply say, "Hello, a pleasure to meet you." Instead, I heard myself say, "Earlier you talked about 'no beginning and no end.' I experienced that myself, first in my early twenties, and again a few years ago. It completely changed my life." He looked deeply into my eyes, and I let him look, for I was standing in truth. The next thing I knew, this great man reached forward and gave me a hug. I vaguely remember my husband escorting me away, and I have no idea how the young girl behind me reacted! My husband and I continued to enjoy the rest of the evening. The next day when I woke up, I felt very different inside, and I realized that my second experience of "no beginning and no end" was not meant for me only. I now recognized a responsibility to share it with others. And at that time I had no idea how many "others" that would be.

TEMPLATES OF LIGHT AND RESONANCE

How does this resonance occur human to human? Everyone has his or her own sacred templates of light and energy. In seeking to know ourselves, we begin to activate or give life to these templates, causing them to vibrate in a unique way. These templates hold the key to communicating inter-dimensionally in the quest to achieve our unique purpose in life. They are also the way each of us holds and communicates our piece of the greater cosmic puzzle to ourselves and to others. This is all accomplished through the phenomenon of *resonance*. The term "resonance" here means to vibrate energetically in phase or harmony with something. The templates are like tuning forks, and we all affect one another with our resonance. There are very specific templates within each individual that hold the key to greater knowledge in the form of access to higher dimensional templates.

When we consciously understand this relationship, we begin to take responsibility for the resonance we create. My job is to see the Divine in everyone, and these sacred templates assist me in doing that in a deeper way than ever. I cannot tell anyone what knowledge his or her own templates will reveal to them; it is up to each individual to discover and activate their own sacred templates. What a worthy endeavor! My personal templates held the key to those of the UCL and the EMF Balancing Technique®.

My experience of receiving or channeling the energy templates of the EMF technique was to "become" them energetically. To date, I hold five of these templates. They are three-dimensional, diamond shaped patterns of light and energy. They look like two four-sided pyramids joined at the base, forming the geometric shape known as an octahedron. These templates hold a resonance specific to the EMF Balancing Technique®. A trained EMF teacher transmits this resonance in a very specific manner, allowing the student to begin to resonate with the templates. The immediate nature of this energetic alignment with the work allows the technique to be taught quickly. In turn, the resonance transferred to the new practitioner helps to awaken, or clarify, the information within the UCL of each individual receiving a session from the EMF practitioner. Each template is associated with a particular phase of the technique, and I shall describe them in more detail when we discuss these phases.

The EMF Balancing Technique® is performed entirely within the parameters of the UCL, which extends approximately two feet out in every direction from the physical body. The practitioner traces precise patterns through the UCL with a series of graceful, Tai Chi-like movements. For the majority of the session, the practitioner works above or around the body; and for some of the balancing work, the hands are placed gently and respectfully, directly on the client's body.

Initially as I was interpreting and learning the correct patterns, three tall Beings of golden light were always present, standing to my left. I lovingly called them the "Three Wise Guys". I was generally able to follow the patterns correctly, but when I would occasionally fail to do a particular movement the right way, I was always corrected in a loving and patient manner. At these times, I would feel as though my arms and hands were not my own as they were gently moved in the preferred sequence.

One day, it became clear that it was time for what I was doing to have a name.

Since I had worked so diligently to learn all these specific patterns and put them together in a systematic procedure, I assumed that I would be the one to create the name for that procedure. My creative juices flowed as I thought of some really catchy and flashy titles -- my favorite was StarGate. But just as I felt myself feeling satisfied with that decision, there came a strong direction from the Three Wise Guys. "No StarGate," I heard. "It must be called the EMF Balancing Technique®." What? I thought incredulously. That's not catchy or flashy. It's dull! I was embarrassed at my thoughts, but that's what they were. "No!" these beings responded emphatically, and then proceeded to graciously explain that EMF stood for electromagnetic field, and in the near future, people would become very aware of EMFs and this name would have meaning for many people. Today we know the electromagnetic field of the human body holds many keys to our evolution. So, here we are in 2001, and what follows is a report on the current status of the EMF Balancing Technique® at this stage of its unfolding.

✳   At this point, the EMF Balancing Technique consists of four different phases. In each phase, the practitioner traces a unique series of energy patterns within the client's UCL. While the patterns that are traced are the same each time the client receives a particular phase, the calibration that results from that session is unique. This unique calibration is determined by the client's innate wisdom relative to their current life situation. I am still amazed at how personal the Universe is with each of us!

The EMF practitioner traces specific patterns through the energy field in a precise and thorough procedure. Moving from the feet to the head, front to the back, and from the head back down to the feet, the practitioner interacts with all portions of the client's UCL. The energy is Self-directing and Self-regulating, flowing and filling in exactly where it is needed in the field according to the client's innate wisdom. Thus, no guesswork, analysis or judgment is needed on the practitioner's part. By simply following the procedure, the most beneficial outcome for the client is co-created.

Many people can feel the energy moving through their bodies during a session, but even those who don't feel it receive the same benefits. In time, most begin to feel some sensations, ranging from subtle to startling, that are associated with the session. These sensations are often described as temperature changes, pulsing, tingling or buzzing. Some have even commented on getting the impression of being touched, even when the practitioner is working a foot or more away from the client's physical body.

Each EMF Balancing session takes about 45 minutes. Initially, the four phases are received sequentially, over a period of time that typically ranges from four weeks to four months. Each session begins with a simple blessing, given silently or aloud by the practitioner, "From the Creator within me, to the Creator within you, and the Company we keep, let us begin." I like this opening ceremony because it serves as a mutual acknowledgment and honoring of inner wisdom from one co-creator to another. We don't need to ask for the energy to become available; we declare that we are going to use it, and then we do.

After stating the opening ceremony, the practitioner begins the session with the energetic body preparation. This preparation involves series of movements and intents offered by the practitioner, and begins a grand circulation of energy through the UCL. In a sense, the practitioner sets up a resonance with the movements of the procedure, and the client responds accordingly on an electromagnetic level. With the energy now moving more freely through the UCL, the practitioner continues with the session.

Each session follows a prescribed sequence of steps consisting of preparing, opening, clearing, balancing and closing. The work is thorough, addressing all the major and minor energy centers of the body. It is interesting to note the rings of light and energy that surround the head horizontally and vertically. At a certain point during each phase, the practitioner gently cradles the client's head, directing the rings to adjust themselves into an evenly spaced and healthy pattern, according to the client's own wisdom. Some practitioners have reported seeing, sensing or even hearing these rings align during this portion of the calibration.

As each phase comes to a close, the practitioner performs the profound high heart alignment, placing one hand on the client's thymus area in front, and one in back, and then directing the energy to flow between them. In effect, this also aligns the heart with the universal heartbeat, the vibration of love. The practitioner reminds the client to be aware of their own light and energy as it radiates throughout the body, going exactly where it is needed for their highest good. The closing blessing, offered silently or aloud, states, "I honor you and the Creator within you."

Each session calibrates the entire UCL, which stretches, releases, and reorganizes itself into the next highest pattern of balance. The calibration of each phase builds on the one that came before. We've just looked at some of the elements common to all four phases. Now, let's take a closer look at each phase individually.

EMF BALANCING TECHNIQUE PHASE I - WISDOM AND EMOTION

The intent of a Phase I session is to balance the head and the heart. A person who thinks too much without the ability to feel is out of balance. And conversely, someone who reacts mainly through emotion, without reasoning or wisdom, is also out of balance. Traditional thinking has often held mental capacities in higher esteem than the emotional aspects of our personality. We are now beginning to understand that emotion is an important part of a broader, more well-rounded definition of intelligence. The Phase I EMF session helps to create a balance between the intelligence of the mind and that of the heart. Through this balance we will express greater levels of spiritual intelligence. It is desirable to make our life decisions from the perspective of this more integrated Self, and I enjoy encouraging students to explore the idea of "thinking with your heart and feeling with your mind."

During the clearing part of the session, the practitioner gracefully clears several of the primary energy centers by directing energy to the center with one hand, while simultaneously clearing with the other hand. Clients often describe this clearing as a feeling of gentle tugging on strings of energy within their field.

After the prescribed areas are cleared, the practitioner moves into the balancing portion of the session. Placing one hand beneath the body and the other on or above each center, the practitioner shares with the client an important characteristic of the energy, "This is universal energy, not my personal energy, and you may have as much as you choose." This statement generally invokes feelings of nurturing and unconditional love for the client, creating a sense of fullness and peace. You may feel some of this too!

The practitioner then works with the rings of light around the head, and activates the energetic template associated with Phase I. The practitioner asks the client to visualize a column of golden energy extending through the entire body, from the feet to the head. A simple hand movement draws the golden light all the way up through the body and to the top of the head. The work around the head is concluded by inviting additional energy adjustments to take place; this completes the energetic alignment and ensures stability to the new patterns. Phase I concludes with an emphasis on anchoring the client's energy in the here and now. The client leaves this session with feelings of peace, calm and balance. For some, their first experience with the EMF Balancing Technique can foster a spiritual awakening.

EMF Balancing Technique Phase II - Self-direction and Self-support

The intent of a Phase II session is to promote Self-direction and Self-support. Phase II builds on Phase I by allowing us to reclaim the excess energy we have invested in our past. This is accomplished primarily by working with the Personal Empowerment Prism. The three long, vertical informational fibers of light and energy at the back of the UCL, along with the figure-eight or infinity loops that emanate from the back chakras, and the template from Phase II, come together to create a prism-like structure. The long informational fibers carry our personal history -- hereditary or ancestral patterns, past-life information, and all the events that have happened in our current lifetime. As we work within this Prism, we calibrate the energy that has been holding us back and that energy transmutes into support.

Many of us are still searching for the "state of grace" that has been promised to us from a variety of sources. Others have forgotten even the possibility of such a pristine and glorious state, trudging along in the muddy and tar-like conditions of old energy dynamics. When we take responsibility for ourselves however, and do the work to open our energy pathways, we can earn this state of grace or karmic release.

(Perhaps this is where the "work" in lightworker comes from!) By directing gold light to balance the long information fibers behind us, we are able to gracefully release some of our karma and the hereditary tendencies that are no longer helpful to us.

The goal in Phase II is to retain the wisdom of the experiences and events from our past, moving into a state of gratitude for all we have learned. This transforms the energy of our history into a golden column of wisdom and Self-support. To encourage the calibration process, we express several intents. First, we give the intent to release any excess electromagnetic energy surrounding old events that no longer serve us. Second, we give the intent to activate those tendencies in us that will encourage our forward movement and create the posture of Self-direction and Self-support. Our third intent is associated with the spine, where our vital and kundalini energies are located. This intent is to encourage a strong personal resolve and spiritual backbone. We were born with and hold energetic restrictions within the spine. These restrictions were designed to help us learn by providing us with appropriate lessons. So our intent here is to release the need to recreate these karmic events, and simply retain the wisdom of the lesson. In addition to working with the long fibers, self-balancing loops, and spine, we also clear and balance several of the major energy centers. In a series of unique, fluid and graceful movements, all this work is accomplished through working with the back section of the UCL.

As we finish, once again we work with the energy around the head, and activate the energetic template associated with Phase II. The closing continues to encourage the individual to be well anchored in this reality.

EMF BALANCING TECHNIQUE PHASE III - RADIATING CORE ENERGY

The Phase III session intensifies our core energy, the vertical column of light and energy fibers throughout the center of the entire being. This session strengthens our ability to radiate the light we hold and encourages the unification of the chakra system. In Phase III, we first focus our intent on clearing the smaller energy centers throughout the body. These lesser known centers have a profound effect on the major chakras and are a vital component of one's overall energy flow. Phase III can be characterized by the idea that it's not the mountain that will wear you out, but the grain of sand in your shoe.

In Phase III, we work with two diamond-shaped light templates. The first template pattern begins at the Center Above and ends in the sixth chakra, the area known as the third eye. The second template pattern begins at the knees and ends at Center Below. These templates increase awareness of the Center Above, the Center Below, and the Core Energy, so that the Core becomes the spiritual strength of the being. Using these templates, we give our intent to radiate our core energy throughout our entire physical being. This process connects and radiates the energy of our individual UCL with universal energy, or the cosmic lattice.

In Phase III, the highly refined frequency of platinum energy is introduced.

The platinum energy feels different from the gold, slightly cool with a quality of strengthening. It represents the merging of the female and male aspects of universal energy according to our present understanding. In this phase, the platinum energy joins with the gold for increased balance; this union within our energy anatomy creates an alignment of the chakra system with our core energy, producing another vibrational shift. This alignment encourages us to express more of our spiritual intelligence as we take a greater role in the universal scheme of things.

After the Phase III energetic body preparation, the practitioner clears the energy centers located at the shoulders, inner elbows, wrists and palms, hips, knees and ankles. Clearing these areas helps to open and clear many other parts of the body. Those who tend to carry tension in the neck and shoulders, for example, may feel some relief after this session. The practitioner also clears the jaw and the third eye, promoting an increase in intuitive awareness.

After clearing the front of the body, the client gently rolls over so that the practitioner can address the back of the body. The practitioner clears several more centers, including the energy center under the ribs that holds the last vestiges of old energy dynamics. Then the practitioner clears the back of the neck, a very sacred area of our energy anatomy. At this time in human evolution, a concentrated amount of refined energy enters the human energy field through this center.

After the clearing is finished, the client once again rolls over onto their back. The next series of movements encourages the energetic posture of radiating core energy, which often produces a deeply satisfying feeling of peace. The client may also feel stretched or elongated as their core energy is strengthened. The practitioner balances the core energy by tracing an infinity pattern over the entire length of the client's body. The two templates of Phase III are then activated, strengthening the link from the core energy to the center below and the center above. The session concludes with the alignments around the head and anchoring the client in the now. Client and practitioner have accomplished a great deal at this point; the entire energy field is cleared, allowing the client to live more powerfully in "now time."

EMF BALANCING TECHNIQUE PHASE IV –
ENERGETIC ACCOMPLISHMENT & FUTURE POTENTIAL

In Phase IV, we focus our intent on energetic accomplishment. Here, the practitioner calibrates the long informational fibers in the front of the UCL so that we may joyfully co-create our potential. In my many years of private practice, I observed that the figure-eight loops connecting to the long fibers in the front of most people are not complete; rather they are still in a state of formation. I also observed that after a Phase IV session, these loops became not only much stronger, they were also more completely formed.

I frequently see people with good hearts and energy fields full of potential.

The "ripeness" of their fields is hard to miss! But I find these wonderful souls are often frustrated because even though they are well aware of their potential, they are unable to manifest it. Phase IV encourages the individual to manifest their potential by completing and strengthening the figure-eight loops in their UCL. No matter how accomplished you may consider yourself at this stage in your life, consider what it might be like to have even more effective manifestation skills. We are each the source of our own metamorphosis; learning how to use the energy of the lattice enhances the outcome of our actions and intentions. Activating our UCL through these sessions establishes the groundwork for holding the full charge of our being.

The diamond shaped Phase IV template extends throughout the entire energy anatomy, encompassing the templates from the three preceding phases. The Phase IV template activates the entire EMF template system at this stage in its development, and includes all of the energy of the Personal Empowerment Prism, the Core Energy and the Personal Potential Prism. Combining intent and action with the Personal Potential Prism is a powerful way to tap into the energy of the future, allowing it to play a significant role in the creation of our now. Phase IV shifts our energy to a present moment awareness which is balanced by the wisdom of the past and the potential of the future.

As in the first three sessions, the practitioner begins the Phase IV session with the energetic body preparation. Directly after the UCL is prepared, the client turns over on their stomach, and the Personal Empowerment Prism is addressed. The client and practitioner then give intent to honor the client's history, calibrating the long informational fibers, the self-balancing loops and the spine. Calibrating the Personal Empowerment Prism encourages the client to express appreciation for the wisdom they have gained through their experience. After honoring the history, the client rolls over once again, ready to center in the now and radiate core energy. The intent to center one's awareness in the now moment serves as the foundation to begin working with the Personal Potential Prism. This phase is comprised of especially beautiful movements that are rich with symbolism.

The practitioner then directs golden energy through the fibers of the UCL in the front, allowing the client to become more aware of the field of potential possibilities that is directly in front of them. Excess electromagnetic energy surrounding any worry or fear-filled events or potentials is then released and the client's unique potential is activated.

One of my favorite parts of the session comes next. The practitioner activates the self-balancing infinity loops that connect the core to the Personal Potential Prism. This simple movement is exquisitely sacred and beautiful -- if you want to bless another human being, this is the embodiment of that blessing. Encouraging the empowerment of another human being is a privilege, and also a gift. When you empower another, you empower yourself.

The opening of the energy centers in this session is quite distinctive. The graceful and elegant hand movements resemble the opening of an inner door, facilitating the client's ability to reach deep within to open fully to their potential. Think about what it would mean to consistently connect with your potential self in confidence and love. The practitioner continues with more movements through the UCL, and the resulting energy patterns represent the opening to potential self through wisdom and love, the great tools of co-creation. At this point in the session, the client may experience new sensations, ideas, or intuitions. The balancing in Phase IV is performed slowly and deliberately as the client continues to bask in the energy of love. The practitioner then works briefly with energy around the head, and concludes the session.

The EMF Balancing Technique helps to open the energy circuits so that you may co-create the most enlightened life you can, but it is the individual who must choose to take the responsibility that comes with co-creation. This responsibility is a partnership with the universe, and is a great privilege. We practice our mastery every day as we continue to polish our skills of co-creation.

COMBINATION, DISTANCE AND SELF-SESSIONS

Practitioners also learn how to use the EMF sessions in combination form. This means combining certain phases together. Phases are merged at specific points creating what we call double sessions. When you consider that each session with its multiple movements and patterns was conceived independently, it is remarkable to see how appropriately they fit together -- as if it were all planned in advance!

From our own experiences and from the research in quantum theory we know that time and space are not necessarily limiting factors. We also know from experience that "hands off" sessions are a powerful form of energy work. There are several forms of EMF distance sessions that EMF Practitioners are qualified to perform. These sessions may be facilitated by the practitioner talking to the client over the phone as the client receives the session. Alternatively, the practitioner and client may simply agree upon a time to "meet" and the session is performed without verbal contact, perhaps with a phone call afterwards to follow up. Hands off sessions may also be accomplished with the client and practitioner in the same room. This is a useful option in the case of a bedridden client, one who cannot move on the table, or a client who simply prefers a completely hands off session. While distance work does not replace the primary use of the technique -- the human-to-human, face-to-face, mutual honoring -- it is nonetheless a viable form of utilizing the energy, and many people are drawn to it.

During the training, the practitioner also learns how to give a Self-session. It should be noted that the practitioner also receives great benefits each time he or she performs the sessions for another. As the practitioner stands in the energy and intends balance for another human being, the practitioner's field also responds. Facilitating balance for another individual creates the harmonics of balance within you. In addition, one insightful doctor in France commented to me on the physical benefits that the practitioner receives simply by performing the movements!

The practitioner training for the EMF Balancing Technique is six full days. By some standards, this may be considered brief considering the amount of material to be learned in such a complex and thorough system. However, the learning does not stop at the end of those six days. I characterize this work as a martial art of the heart, with "martial" referring to the strong and active intelligence that is inherent in spiritual well being. I like the analogy of the martial artist -- the more practiced and precise the practitioner's movements, the stronger the calibration of balance for both the client and the practitioner. During a recent radio interview with a distinguished Hawaiian healer, I was delighted when he commented how awesome it would be if energy workers put the same amount of commitment and practice into our work as those who practice the martial arts!

BALANCE, AND A FEW WORDS ABOUT HEALING

The primary purpose of the EMF Balancing Technique is to balance and strengthen the UCL, which contributes to the overall well being of the individual. As one continues to embody more advanced levels of balance, one's understanding of spiritual well being grows and new levels of empowerment are attained. This well being can contribute to one's ability to "heal" others or to be "healed" themselves. The EMF Balancing Technique practitioner facilitates healing by working with the UCL.

Throughout history, volumes have been written on the subject of healing, and even now we continue to evolve our definition of what healing is. When we have a disease or injury, the body can often heal itself, but sometimes outside assistance is needed to facilitate the healing. There are many important factors to consider when choosing the appropriate medical and/or holistic methods of facilitation. In any system of thought, all healing is ultimately self-healing.

The primary role of the physician, the acupuncturist, the shaman, or any other person representing a healing modality, is to facilitate the patient's natural ability to heal. Whatever the choice, each individual has the right to claim his role in this process we call healing. The role of self-empowerment may be one of the most important factors in the healing process!

Even though one may be experiencing dis-ease, they may also be in a state of well being and empowerment. I have known this to be true in my own life and in the lives of the clients and students I have worked with. To energetically stand in the golden posture of balance, and then take action from that place of balance, contributes to co-creating the most enlightened life one can, regardless of the outer circumstances. In the EMF work, we focus first on the strength of the individual and then build from there. The dis-ease may be physical, mental, situational, or of another nature. Some people have even had EMF sessions to assist them with embracing their own physical death. I do not view death as a failure, but as a transition. As stated in my forward to this book, I am absolutely passionate about every human being having the right to experience and know their self-empowerment in any given moment -- no matter what the circumstances are in their life!

These experiences, my own and those of the teachers and practitioners of the EMF Balancing Technique will be presented in the next book, "Restoring the Electromagnetic Laws of Love."

"... a gift to the world for those will accept it."

Richard Bach, *Jonathan Livingston Seagull*

CHAPTER TEN

THE
NEW HORIZON

A Call To Universal Calibration

A POWERFUL AWAKENING

The night of September 11th, 2001, I awoke to a light glowing throughout the room. At first I thought someone was shining headlights into our second story window. As I became more alert, I realized I was looking directly at the Cosmic Lattice. At that moment, the lattice looked very different than it had at any other time I had seen it. I observed unique patterns in the Lattice for some time, drawing no conclusions and making no judgments. Then I went back to sleep, wondering "what was this difference"? Not until midmorning of the next day did I realize that the portion of Lattice presenting itself to humanity was stronger than ever before.

The Lattice that connects all of us had been strengthened by the events of the previous day. The worldwide community of humankind has experienced a resounding emergency wake up call for unity. As planetary citizens we know we must move beyond hate, expand our scope of tolerance, and open to new levels of compassion and acceptance of one another. Now we each have a golden opportunity to learn to go beyond our limited understanding of love. Collective consciousness has created a new opening. Understanding the *energy* of love is the next step - the heart of humanity has now been prepared to hold this new energy dynamic. The new expression of love is different and you will know it when you experience it. We are forever changed by the events of September 11th, 2001 and what we do with that change is in our hands.

UNITED IN SPIRIT

On September 29th, 2001, at 9:00 p.m. in the evening, starting in New Zealand and progressing around the globe, through each of the time zones – (Australia, Malaysia, Hong Kong, Singapore, India, Israel, Turkey, Italy, Switzerland, Germany, France, Great Britain, The USA, Mexico, Hawaii, and many more countries) - EMF Practitioners and Teachers around the world joined together to give a Phase I EMF session to a very special client, the consciousness of humanity. This group also agreed to provide this same special client the remaining phases of the technique on October 10th, November 11th, and December 12th, 2001. Teachers and Practitioners have also pledged to continue with this sequence as long as it is appropriate to do so.

To understand this call to Universal Calibration, let us look at one of the fundamental properties allowing the calibration to occur, changes which begin within our very own physical bodies.

HORMONES AND OUR PHYSICAL EVOLUTION - THE CHEMICAL-BIOLOGICAL LINK

The chemical composition of the human body plays an important role in the evolutionary process. Diet, specialized supplements, physical exercise, even the air we breathe and our state of mind - all contribute to this chemical makeup. One of the chemical-biological systems that plays a role in our evolution is the human Endocrine System. The endocrine system is one of the physical counterparts to the subtle energy structures that form our energy bodies. The endocrine glands provide highly specialized chemicals which they release into the body's chemistry at precise times and for specific reasons. These secretions are called hormones. Hormonal secretions play a key role. Could it be possible that a minute shift in hormonal secretions will open new areas within the brain, and trigger the mind's ability, or consciousness, to perceive a greater reality? In the 1960's, there was a mass movement to expand consciousness through the use of chemicals. This drive was a demand by collective consciousness to push back the limits of normalcy. Can this be done in a simple way, as a part of everyday, ordinary life, without drugs, and without losing one's mind, or going "crazy"? In the new millennium, we are learning to reach even more deeply inside of our selves to find the key that unlocks the riches of our own chemical "factory". The following exercise is designed to stimulate the endocrine system so that it may produce a hormonal balance conducive to an evolutionary leap in consciousness.

EMF BALANCING TECHNIQUE® SPIRAL SWEEP EXERCISE

The Spiral Sweep is a small, but important, part of the information contained in the complete EMF Balancing Technique® system. A lifelong metaphysical scholar, Hadassah Roberts, first wrote the fundamental pattern of this exercise. Hadassah was a beautiful and wise old woman I hardly knew but one who commanded respect by her very presence. The first time I read this exercise in 1987, I recognized how important it was. Hadassah seemed almost amused that I found the exercise so profound, stating she was "happy someone thought it to be useful". I received permission from Hadassah to use the exercise in any way I felt was appropriate. It was the energetic tool that opened and prepared my field for what was to come! When Hadassah transitioned in 1996, she was one hundred years old. I gratefully honor her wisdom.

The final portion of the exercise, was "suggested" by Little Hawk, a Native American friend and Lakota pipe carrier. "Star person!" she lovingly demanded of me one day, " what are you doing to connect people back with the earth?" Over the years, the exercise has evolved even more, while still retaining the fundamental pattern.

The Spiral Sweep in its present form helps to prepare the energy body for the greater charge we are now capable of holding and using in everyday life. As many of us are realizing, the sacred event we have been searching for has already occurred, and it is us, the very reality of our existence! When we honor ourselves and all life in this way, we honor the source or creator of our existence, no matter how we envision the Creator.

This exercise may be read slowly if you choose. Once you are familiar with it, you may go as fast as you like. You may simply visualize the energy patterns while reciting the numbers one through twelve.

1 - GOLDEN SKELETON

Feel, sense, imagine or think about golden energy spinning around your feet in a clockwise motion. Allow this energy to permeate the soles of your feet. The mineral composition of your bones makes the skeleton a good conductor of this refined energy. Now, bone by bone, direct this golden energy through your skeletal system. Direct the energy through the bones in your toes, all the bones in your feet, your ankles, up to your knees, your kneecaps, and through the bones in your thighs. Direct this energy through your hip bone, down to your coccyx or tailbone, up the sacrum, and now up through your spine. Bathe each of the vertebrae with this golden energy. Direct the energy to flow through the bones in the shoulders and shoulder blades, down the breastbone and around the ribs. Direct the golden energy down through the bones in your arms to your wrists and to all the little bones in your hands and fingers. Now direct your attention and the energy up to the bones in your neck, around your jaw, through your teeth and your entire skull. You have just bathed your entire skeletal system with golden energy. Allow the feeling, or the sensation, or the image of radiating a golden glow throughout the bones in your body. Breathe deeply and relax.

2 - GOLDEN BRAIN

Place your attention within your sacred brain and give the intent for your brain to absorb this energy. Begin with the cortex, the gray matter covering the top of the brain. Directly beneath the gray matter is the white matter, the largest portion of your brain. Allow the white matter of your brain to absorb this golden energy like a sponge. Your consciousness will balance the "feel" of this golden energy through both sides of your brain. One of the functions of the white matter is to assist with all extrasensory perceptions. Focus your attention between your eyebrows, a little higher, and about an inch into your brain. Here you will locate the pituitary; a small pear shaped gland. Direct the golden energy to completely surround this little gland, and then give the intent for this energy to be completely absorbed. As you channel the energy through this gland, give the intent to activate the hormonal changes in your body that are appropriate for you as you take your next evolutionary step. The pituitary is the first point of contact energetically connected to the pineal gland.

Now place your attention in the center of your brain. This area is sometimes referred to as the sacred chamber. Here you will find the pineal gland. It is a small, kidney bean shaped gland. Direct the energy to surround your pineal gland, and then give the intent for this gland to absorb all the golden energy it can. You will also find in this area of the brain the hypothalamus and thalamus. Your thalamus is a fan shaped organ composed of gray matter marbled with white matter. The two sections of your thalamus are located in the two hemispheres of your brain. The thalamus is responsible for the power of visualization you are using right now. Visualize or imagine a golden butterfly as your thalamus radiates a golden glow! Give the intent to intensify the expression of your sacred nature.

Bring your attention to the back of your head; place your focus within the base of your brain. Located here is an egg shaped organ called the pons. Imagine this egg shaped organ, your pons, to be completely glowing gold. Finally, and with strong intent, direct this golden energy all the way down your spinal cord. You have just energized your brain. Breathe deep and relax.

3 - THE ENDOCRINE SYSTEM

Now, refocus your attention, and begin to guide the golden energy downward, through your endocrine system. First, focus the golden energy within your parathyroid and thyroid gland in your lower throat area. Give the intent for the golden energy to be completely absorbed and infused into these glands.

Above your heart center, beneath the breastbone, is the thymus gland. The energy center associated with your thymus gland is called the high heart center. This gland and the energy of this area are an important point of origin for the radiating of the golden energy within our physical body. The intensification of the energy radiating from the high heart center is one of the keys to the powerful expression of our electrical spiritual nature. As we increase our ability to express this electrical energy, we can then accelerate the healing process when the body has gone out of balance. It is in our best interest that we stimulate this area. Direct the golden energy to circle your thymus and be completely absorbed. Intensify your intention and as the thymus fills with golden energy it will reach a point of fullness and then radiate that golden energy throughout the cells of the entire heart area. Visualize your entire heart area radiating a golden glow!

Place your attention on the heart muscle. The heart is not part of the endocrine system. However, the pericardium, a sac that surrounds the heart, may fill with a few precious drops of hormonal fluid. This fluid will contribute to the increased radiating of the heart energy. Give the intent to fill the heart with the golden energy of evolution and love.

To the left of the navel is the pancreas and as we stimulate this organ with golden energy, give the intent to strengthen your ability to continue to digest and assimilate the energetic changes that are taking place within your entire being.

Now place your attention in the lower back on the adrenal glands. The adrenals sit atop the kidneys. Use the golden light and give the intent to completely regenerate the adrenal glands.

A little further down, bring your attention to the sexual glands, the ovaries or testes, and hold the golden energy within this part of your body. Enlightenment is for every cell of your body including those cells beneath the waist. Direct the energy down through your hips, thighs, calves, and soles of your feet. The physical body has now been energized. Breathe deeply and relax.

4 - ENERGY AROUND THE FEET

The energy now swirls clockwise around your feet and creates a strong grounding effect. Strengthen the grounding effect with the understanding of how important it is to have a deep relationship with the energy of the earth. This sacred grounding contributes to our ability to hold the higher energies that are now available to us. The vibrational frequency of the energy changes and it begins to gently rise up through the energy field as a concentrated golden ray of light and energy. We will direct this golden ray through each of the energy vortexes associated with the glandular system. The change in the energy can sometimes be noted as a change in temperature or a tingling sensation as you begin to direct the energy up through the energy vortex of the feet, through the energy of the legs, to the base of the spine.

5 - FOUNDATION CENTER

Place your attention at the base of your spine and feel, sense, think about, or imagine a glowing sphere of red, vital energy. As the golden ray gently enters this sphere, a beautiful pattern like a golden starburst begins to form and radiates in all directions. Give the intent to bless, strengthen, and balance the energy center at the base of your spine. As you do this you create the sacred foundations within your being that are needed as you continue to integrate the energy of your divine nature. The ray of golden light rises to the next energy center, the sexual /creative center.

6 - CREATIVE / SEXUAL CENTER

As the ray of golden energy rises upward towards the sexual/creative center, focus you attention within your orange sphere of creativity. The golden light radiates throughout this orange sphere once again in a starburst pattern. Give the intent to be mindful of how you express your sexual energy. Your sexual energy is part of your vital force and can be directed to facilitate your evolution. This area is also your seat of creativity. Encourage the flow of energy from here to enhance your co-creative efforts in life. Give the intent to bless, strengthen and balance this center. Breathe.

7 - SOLAR PLEXUS CENTER

Now the golden ray of energy moves upward. Direct the golden energy to enter the yellow sphere of the solar plexus. As the golden energy resonates within this area you may feel, sense, think about, or imagine a pattern that looks like a sunflower. Remember that the solar plexus is also known as the seat of the subconscious, and all the facets of the sparkling sunflower image are a reminder of all the facets of you.

Breathe deeply, and give yourself permission to be!

8 - HEART CENTER AND HIGH HEART

Now direct your attention and the golden ray of energy higher, into the beautiful emerald green of the heart center. Sense the energy bursting into a beautiful kaleidoscope of gold and green energy, pulsing into complex patterns. Each one of us holds an original piece of the Creator in our heart, and together we create the One. Place your attention above the heart in the area of the thymus, this area we refer to as the high heart area. Here you will find a concentration of the golden light; give the intent for this golden light to intensify. You may feel the warmth and fullness of your heart as the unique light pattern of your heart energy unfolds. As you feel or sense the balance within your heart, first nurture yourself with this love and then radiate the love outwards.

9 - THROAT CENTER

As the energy of love continues to radiate outward, direct the golden ray upward and into the blue of your throat center. This center is a special gateway, it is the place where the "as above, so below" energy merges and translates into usable power. This is the center for the expression of your piece of the truth. Remember the power of the spoken word. Strive to speak words of truth only, in even the smallest of matters. Allow the energy to polish how you express yourself to the world. You may turn your head slowly from side to side as you work the energy through your throat area. You are almost finished with this exercise, take a deep breath and refocus your attention.

10 - THIRD EYE

Now concentrate and direct the ray of golden energy up through to the center of your brain. From the pineal within the center of the brain to the pituitary near the center of the forehead is the area known as the third eye. Here the energy is indigo in color. As the golden ray gently pierces and radiates through this majestic indigo center, the light patterns resemble a multi-faceted jewel. Give the intent to deepen your wisdom and increase your understanding. You may contemplate what does it mean to "think with your heart, and to feel with your mind." This area is also associated with telepathy, the 6th sense we are now developing at an accelerated pace.

11 - CROWN CENTER

Refocus and increase your attention as you direct the golden light up through your crown center. As the golden energy gently swirls around the top of your head your unique pattern of light-- a halo -- forms. This is an energy pattern of union. The golden energy of your human nature merges with the purity of your divine nature.

12 - HOLD AND RELEASE

Now, breathe in deeply through your nose and hold your breath for a moment, let the energy build. With strong intent breathe out through your mouth. As you breathe out, visualize a fountain of colorful energy rising up out of your head and spiraling down, around, and throughout your entire being. This movement strengthens your lattice and deepens your connection with the energy of the earth. Take a few moments to enjoy. You may even feel a sense of being home.

Namaste, dear friend ... This completes the exercise.

A suggestion – read the exercise into a recorder and then listen to your own voice guiding you through the Spiral Sweep.

Where do we go from here?

As we continue to evolve, so too does the lattice. As mentioned earlier, there are twelve more informational fibers forming, or becoming accessible at this time within the UCL. The EMF work also continues to evolve. The first four phases of the EMF Balancing Technique are foundational for the new resonance of our time. The light templates for the next four phases (phases five through eight) of the technique are already present within my energy field. The templates are becoming very active, and I am ready to interpret them. These four phases will focus on the multi-dimensional aspects of our selves as we change and mature in our creative abilities and in our personal power. Of course, our personal resonance will have an effect upon the earth.

By the year 2012, there will be a total of twelve phases to the work. The final four phases (phases nine through twelve) will focus on a new resonance of brotherhood and sisterhood, a living awareness of world family. At that time we may have the opportunity to secure and define a consciousness of genuine service to one another.

I often say in class how grateful and honored I am to be the representative for this work. I've been shown each step of the way only when I have been able to accept the responsibility for it. This work represents one of the understandings that will help us actualize the potential reality of peace filled empowerment. However, the broader vision of this work is still astounding to me – I watch strangers from many places come together in a single class. EMF Practitioners from ten different countries participated in a recent Teacher's training in France. They worked together and quickly bridged the differences of their cultures. As evolving human beings they honored one another in their union and in their individuality as they worked with this energy. This is the universal energy of love in action, and it works! We all believe this resonance profoundly contributes to planetary healing at this very special time in human history.

THE ENERGY OF LOVE

As you might expect, EMF trainings are always filled with the palpable energy of love. As a result people often share the words "I love you" with one another. I feel a great love for my students when we work together with this energy, and I too enjoy sharing these feelings of love. However, I often wondered, how I could say the words "I love you", to people I had just met and have it resonate with the truth and freedom I was actually feeling? To find an answer to this question, I went to a special place of consciousness and "met" with several of my favorite light beings. (You may call them angels if you wish, or you may even say I imagined them.) In any case, dear reader, I would like to share my experience with you as a closing to this book.

I have always felt that the lessons of self-empowerment are present and continue on all levels, so I was not surprised when the answer to my question came in the form of another question ... "What else do you think you might say?" ... I thought for a moment and then answered: I could say "In the light, I love you". With a smile of approval, one of the light beings embraced me, and said, "that is very good." Then the energy of this special place intensified, surrounding and permeating our beings. The warmth of the light flooded through my body and I felt a state of profound peace ...

"That is very good ... but we see it just a little differently" ... then the words were gently spoken ... "In the light we are Love!"

(... and for those of you who know me, TA DA!)

End Of Book

APPENDIX A

THE BIOFIELD

Connecting Web Between
Physical And Subtle Realm

The biofield is the link between the physical body and the subtle energy fields [1]. Other links do exist, such as the chakras and the acupuncture points. The biofield connects to the physical body at the quantum level [1], and is active in the regulation of biological processes. We can understand the biofield to be the etheric body as known in eastern philosophy [1]. According to Andrej Detela, the concept of the biofield is attracting support across a now greater interdisciplinary realm in science- physics, biology, and cognitive science. The associated paper *Physical Model of the Biofield* [2] (*see Appendix C*) is written by a physicist, and, of course, from the viewpoint of a physicist. This paper is a major step forward in recognizing the first level of "subtle" matter beyond the physical organism.

NEW REALM FOR PHYSICS

Very little is known about the physics of the biofield. Establishing some basic laws at this level would eventually assist us in extending our understanding of the physics of the more subtle levels. We will briefly discuss some of the salient features of Detela's hypothesis of the structure of the biofield. We feel fortunate to have the opportunity to reprint this paper in our appendix. Publications on this subject from the perspective of a physicist are rare, even today. We express our gratitude to Andrej Detela for sharing his views and ideas, and providing our readers with access to this publication. Much scientific thought is required to formulate the hypothesis set out in his paper.

REALITY AS INTER-DIMENSIONAL CONNECTEDNESS

Throughout our text we have presented the view that reality has a fundamental interconnectedness through a holographic or a hierarchical structure. We have seen how this perspective is shared by Bohm, Tiller, Bearden, Kaivarainen, Sheldrake (below), and Detela [1,8,9]. There is a virtual reality nested within each order, level, or layer that we choose to look at. For example, electromagnetic fields are generated by sources or "disturbances" in higher dimensional space [7,8,9]. The mental and emotional aspects of our being affect the etheric and the physical. Fundamentally, this perspective tells us that the part reflects the whole, and that the whole is reflected in the part.

A phenomenon in the biofield has some "counterpart" reflected in higher dimensional space.

As an electromagnetic web structure, the biofield consists of scalar or torsion field derivatives that we can view as more subtle states. Changes to the structure of the biofield are, essentially, reflections of changes in higher dimensional space. Patterns within the web of the biofield have some correlation within scalar potentials that carry these patterns in higher dimensional space. So, although we cannot see or measure the subtle states directly, we can at this time *infer* that modifications to the biofield web structure *are* associated with modifications to the higher subtle levels of our multidimensional being.

SUBTLE INFLUENCE

Information enters the biofield from higher dimensional space. An evolution to the structure of the biofield is also reflected as an evolution of more complexity within the higher subtle levels. Detela suggests that the biofield is capable of repairing small defects to the web structure-- that *the biofield contains mechanisms for cleansing undesired forms within its field structure.* [These ideas are supported with theoretical foundation.] Certainly, these are features that we hypothesize are characteristic of the higher subtle states. Repairs within the biofield imply repairs within the more subtle levels. A cleansing within the biofield implies a cleansing within the subtle levels. Information storage within the biofield has some analogous form or pattern in higher dimensional space. These are the perspectives that are useful to consider as we look into the scientifically intangible subtle realms. Consider that some individuals have explored subtle regions without the aid of scientific equipment [3]!

BIOLOGIST HYPOTHESIZE FIELD STRUCTURE

Many phenomena such as the storage and exchange of information in biological systems cannot be understood in terms of biomolecular processes only. As early as the 1920's, biologists realized the necessity of hypothesizing the existence of a 'field' structure to explain various biological processes. A modern day biologist, Rupert

Sheldrake, has done much to promote public education on the concept of a *morphic field.* "Morphic" comes from the Greek "*morphe*," meaning *form.* Sheldrake further defines the term for us: 'Morphic' comes from the Greek work for form, *morphe.*

"A *morphic field* is a field of form, a field or pattern or order or structure"[4].

Sheldrake believes that such fields organize not only all living organisms, but also the forms of crystals as well as molecules. Morphic fields come in a variety of types. If the field is active in bringing "form" into existence it is termed a *morphogenetic* field. These fields serve to interconnect matter and energy. Sheldrake declares that the concept of morphogenetic fields is widely adopted by developmental biologists. But there are also other kinds of field morphic fields- there are cultural, mental, social, and behavioral types as well.

All these fields contain a cumulative memory of experience. Any one of these fields is sustained through the morphic resonance of 'morphic units' that have been influenced by the field at some time. Morphic resonance is a phenomenon whereby the past field structures will influence the current organization of the morphic field. *The characteristics of the field can be transported across boundaries of space and time-* i.e. they are hyperspatial (existing outside space and time).

The fields interpenetrate and extend through the space-time continuum. A morphic field exists for every level of existence. These are referred to as morphic units. They may be subatomic particles, atoms, molecules, cells, whole organism (plant, animal, human being), planet, galaxy etc. The field for each morphic unit contains the genetic blueprints of how that unit should develop in physical reality. We can perceive the field as containing the potential patterns of organization specific to every kind of living or non-living form. The morphic fields are nested (layered within each other) according to hierarchies required by the morphic unit. For example, a morphic field at the cellular level, which contains molecular level fields, followed by atomic level fields, and so on, down to the smallest particle, organizes a biological cell.

A 3-D WEB WOVEN FROM SUNLIGHT

In our discussion that follows, we will adopt Detela's definition of the biofield as a three-dimensional web, analogous to tiny threads in a three-dimensional textile, woven from vibrating electric and magnetic fields. The biofield is woven from sunlight. Structures within the biofield trap photons. This is similar to the fashion in which the chiral structures of the proteins in plants are optically active and trap sunlight.

> The three-dimensional web structure consists of definite *patterns of threads* in space. This web interacts with atoms and molecules in living cells. Within living cells, these atoms and molecules are most likely the protein and nucleotide structures of the microtubules and DNA helices. A similarity of helical structures exists at both levels, the physical as well as the subtle biofield.

In earlier discussions we have seen how the biofield provides the mechanism for self-organization in living organisms. The biofield is capable of syntropic self-organization-- reversing entropy to create more highly developed web structures. As an animate structure, the biofield consists of a stable *informational* component. This stable component exists in symbiosis with an *evolutionary* component. It is the *evolutionary* component of the biofield that enables repairs of small defects to the web structure.

Detela suggests that the biofield contains mechanisms for cleansing undesired forms within its field structure.

A HELICAL WEB

The biofield web is constructed of field lines that intertwine like a twisted rope-- *like a helix*. One field line twists to the left, the other to the right (*see Figure I of Detela's paper*). Such a structure can

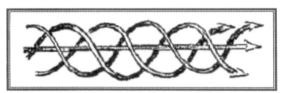

Fig. 1 (*Detela*)

intertwine and integrate easily into similar biological structures. In order to create stable structures in time, the helical field lines actually form *closed loops* (*see Figure 2 of Detela's paper*). These closed-loop structures are identical to threads of toroidal knots. A torus can be visualized as the space occupied by a sphere travelling in a circular orbit. The torus looks like a magnetic field, or the magnetic field looks like a torus because it is pumped by Vortices [6]. The torus

Fig. 2 (*Detela*)

manifests a primordial field. All primordial fields are fractal, cumulative and holographic [1]. The hierarchic complexity is repetitive on many levels.

Holography is a wave phenomenon that relates to dynamic paths [5,6]. As a vibrating light structure, the biofield is a holographic projection from a higher dimensional reality. In 3-dimensional space, light is the mechanism that interacts to reconstruct a hologram.

The biofield results from the holographic projection of a different mechanism. This mechanism is thought, or consciousness, operating from a dimension of no space and no time. *There is no linear time-- only a perception of such as consciousness moves through a whole different reality field.*

A KNOTTED STRUCTURE

Imagine a torus (a donut form) with threads wrapped around it to form a simple knot. The most simple of these knots is shown in Figures 3a and 3b of Detela's paper. There are two because these two knots are not mirror images of each other. There is a left-handed and a right-handed knot- they are chiral, like the chiral structure of the DNA helix. Consequently the helical knots of the biofield integrate easily into the similar helical structure of DNA and microtubules. The knot is an anchor in the space-time continuum-[5] a four-dimensional anchor. It is an informational thread. The magnetic field of this knot can vary according to the size of the knot. It also can vary according to the density of the fluxons (*magnetic flux quanta*) that flow through the noose.

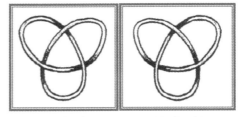

Fig. 3a *(Detela)*   Fig. 3b *(Detela)*

EVOLUTION OF KNOTS

Under certain conditions, the web structure can evolve. Evolution results in the transformations of simple knots into more complex forms. These can be any one of a wide array of possible patterns (*see Figure 4 of Detela's paper for one example*). As well, groupings or clusters of knots that form patterns can evolve into more complex internal structures. As more complex knots and patterns develop, more information is added to the web structure. At each evolutionary step, the web develops a greater capacity for developing even more complex forms and patterns within itself. Internal stable patterns of the biofield result in self-organizing within its structure.

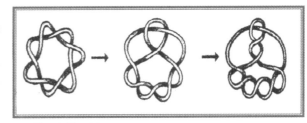

Fig. 4 *(Detela)*

MAGNETIC THRESHOLDS

What conditions trigger the evolution of the knot structure? The stability of the knot is dependent upon the magnetic field strength. As the magnetic field increases, at certain critical levels of magnitude the knot can become unstable. It can change form abruptly. An additional pattern is introduced as the knot is transformed into a structurally more complex form. The added complexity represents the information added – the evolution. This process also applies to groupings or clusters of knots that form spatial patterns. Certain syntropic conditions can trigger the evolution of the web structure. One of these is adequate amplitude of the magnetic field density. Another condition is the presence of an electric charge with high mobility. Detela refers to an electrically charged particle with a very small rest mass that escapes normal detection. Ultralight charged particles form, and co-exist with, the web of the biofield.

But our story does not end here. It is only the beginning! In Detela's closing remarks

"Life is at the very basis of space-time structures."

What are the meaning and the consequence of evolution to the biofield web structure? Further, we would like to generalize this question to address not only the evolution of the biofield, but also the higher subtle fields. What is the purpose of the evolutionary structure? What story does it tell? How does this story integrate with the living organism?

UNLOCKING THE POTENTIAL

Newly formed web structures have a vibration that must be synchronized with the existing web. A tuning and integration of additional complex structures must take place. A resonance is established. The new structures must become 'hardwired' to existing circuits in order to be effective and contribute to information gained and intelligence added. New structures add more complex vibratory patterns. The rhythm of the vibrations of the biofield as a whole must change to integrate the new rhythm of the evolved structures. This rhythm is raised. To evolve, the system re-tunes and re-balances itself. What story does an evolved biofield tell? As more and more information is added to the biofield, the added complexity now points towards the potential *future prospective*. Templates are formed that carry the potential of creating change in living cells.

> **For example, the hidden potential of DNA can be unlocked through resonance with newly formed (or activated) templates within the biofield- templates that reflect the evolutionary process!**

It is these templates that *guide* the biological process as well as the evolution of living cells. The key is to unlock this potential, and integrate the future into the physical living organism.

On this note, we find it most appropriate to end this section with the poetic words of Andrej Detela: the tune of the newly formed webs is

> **"A story-teller and a dreamer, it is the carrier of evolution, it is the self-sensitive *life purpose* that impregnates the pores of all living organisms".**

SELF-ORGANIZING SYSTEMS

Active Information In the Human-to-Human Connection

D
o we dare speak of a topic that breaks a classical Law of Physics- the second Law of Thermodynamics? On the questions of Law we consult the views of two scientists:

"I prefer to drop the metaphor of 'law' altogether, with its outmoded image of God as a kind of law-giving emperor, as well as an omnipotent and universal law-enforcement agency" [1].

In this instance we have Rupert Sheldrake's general commentary on the notion of laws and absolutes in his paper *The Variability of the "Fundamental Constants", Do physical constants fluctuate?*
And in another instance:

" Some complex quantum particles may already be too clever for obeying a law which was meant and formulated to deal only with very simple, inanimate bodies" [2].

Such is the comment of Andrej Detela, physicist of the J. Stefan Institute, and author of the two papers featured in the Appendix of this text. One of these papers (*Self-Organization Within Complex Quantum States*) is the theme subject of this section- as we look at the notion of self-organization.

REDEFINING AN OLD LAW

There is a branch of Physics that is concerned with the storage, transformation and dissipation of energy. This branch is called Thermodynamics. The first law of thermodynamics states that energy can neither be created nor destroyed. The second law, also known as the law of entropy, goes on to state that in all processes some of the energy involved loses not only its 'ability to do work', but that it is degraded in quality. According to this law, entropy always increases, i.e. there is always increasing 'disorder', and the process is irreversible. It's an ongoing process- and it is all downhill!

THIS LAW HAS BEEN RED EFINED !

Of course we do not share the view that life, and human destiny, is a process that is all downhill, nor is it irreversibly headed downhill! Human life and human experience cannot be understood in terms of a "classical" system in physics. Life is a process that acquires higher degrees of complexity, along with knowledge, information, and understanding gained as major aspects of our evolutionary process. Our destiny is an evolutionary one, certainly one that presents its occasional "uphill" challenges that contribute to the internal evolution of the human being, and collectively for the human species. These challenges contribute to our "lessons learned".

COMPLEXITY REVERSES DISORDER

As multidimensional beings, with spiritual essence, we are creating more and more connections through rewiring processes that are actually increasing our potential for internal order, coherence, complexity, and yes, intelligence. We are acquiring more information, and more information is flowing through us. In the last 50 years, Science has recognized that information gained by a system actually represents negative entropy-- a reversal of the process of increasing disorder [3].

By growing in complexity as we process information, we become more capable beings, better able to tap into the potential of the universe. As dynamic multidimensional living "energy systems", we are in constant and open exchange of information, and energy, with our external environment. As we evolve, we further this exchange, and we also alter the very internal architecture that allows us to relate to our external universe.

INTELLIGENCE & ORDER AT THE QUANTUM STATE

David Bohm discovered some curious phenomena at the level of quantum physics. For example, his observations of the behavior of electrons in plasmas and in metals indicated that electrons possessed qualities of 'organic intelligence'. We have introduced the case of two light particles, that, when in quantum terms, are entangled-are able to instantly communicate irrespective of their distance of separation.

Both of these observations beg for a "non-classical" way of looking at reality. In 1977 a Nobel Prize in chemistry was awarded to Russian born scientist Ilya Prigogine for his discoveries that also begged for a new way of interpreting nature. Prigogine observed that, contrary to the second law of Thermodynamics, certain mixtures of chemicals could actually spontaneously produce higher degrees of internal order and internal arrangement.

ENERGY REVERSES ENTROPY

Essentially, Prigogine's work demonstrated "that when energy was introduced into any field, its complexity increased…it did not disintegrate rapidly by entropy" [4]. Spontaneous ordering within systems does occur. Out of unrestrained disorder there can, and does, arise order, contrary to the old view of thermodynamics.

A system can indeed demonstrate negative entropy. According to Bearden's remarks, "…the more chaotic the disorder, the greater the stability of the ordered patterns that emerge" [5]. Although it is popular to speak about Prigogine's self-organizing structures, it should be noted that "quantum self-organization exists on a much deeper level, and is not powered by irreversible thermodynamical differences" [6]. Whereas physical phenomena are active dynamic process interpreted in time, quantum states display a different concept of time: instantaneous temporal interconnectedness. *Totally different concepts of time and space are valid within quantum states, the biofield, as well as other subtle energy states.*

CONSCIOUSNESS COLLAPSES THE WAVE FUNCTION

When we speak of quantum states we are referring to the level of reality beyond subatomic particles. Quantum physics will speak in terms of "probability wave functions" due to the inability to specify all the classical information of subatomic particles at the same time. The quantum state is a reality distinct from the macro world that we observe. However, it is also the closest "reality" that we can observe that is somehow associated to the subtle realm.

Bohm defined a new quantum feature- the *quantum potential*. This is an information realm connecting the whole. Sarfatti goes one step further and connects the *quantum potential* to the *super quantum potential*-- a further intangible realm.

> **Sarfatti's superquantum potential is actually equated to the mind field of consciousness.**

These ideas originate with physicists as they try to make sense of unusual and unexpected observations that do not fit classical explanations.

Earlier in this text we have seen how, in *The Self Aware Universe*, physicist Amit Goswami comes to the conclusion that consciousness precipitates the material world by collapsing the quantum wave function. The role of consciousness is also discussed by Petersen in *The Quantum Tai Chi*. From Petersen's perspective, consciousness plays a role in the selection of the phase angle of magnetization that acts to collapse the wave function creating our choice of reality. In his paper *Physical Model of the Biofield*, Detela makes a resounding comment that "there will be a great paradigmatic transformation in modern natural sciences…(and that) physicists will recognize, through intelligent quantum states, the mutual interplay of consciousness and matter".

To believe that the world consists of objects that are totally independent of our human consciousness is a premise in conflict with fundamental advances and observation in Science!

ROCKS ACQUIRE LIFE-LIKE CHARACTERISTICS

In his paper *Self-Organization Within Complex Quantum States* (*see Appendix D*) Detela uses language that you would not usually consider in reference to a rock-like world. For example, Detela begins by stating that quantum states may have some "*inner feeling*". Here he is referring to the ideas of Jack Sarfatti, a physicist we introduced earlier who deals in 'post-quantum' physics of consciousness. Remember that Sarfatti speaks of a two-way relationship and interaction between the subquantum world (consciousness) and the material world [back-action principle]. Detela remarks that not only might quantum states have feelings, but they are able to *care for themselves* in an '*intelligent way*', and certainly one in which they are '*animate*'. "Life is probably at the very basis of our physical reality". [Remember Tiller's proposal of the cosmic atom- it takes on 'physical, etheric, *emotional, mental*, and spiritual parts'!] Many people may be OK with these remarks if they were directed towards their pets— but to speak this way about the rocklike particle world?

INFORMATION PROVIDES INTERCONNECTEDNESS

As Detela continues, we learn that "intelligence is an inherent ability of complex quantum systems" and that "within quantum states there must be some very subtle internal activity responsible for self-organizing phenomena". In order to look at reversing entropy we must consider the relationship between quantum states and information.

Information is what provides the internal interconnectedness of the entangled quantum states. What is the meaning of information? Information is not the same as energy! Exchange of information is not associated with classical exchange of energy. Here we suggest that the reader consult the paper for the full rendition by Detela. It is very intriguing. He explains how information means-"in-*form*"- but that it also means *active information* in his language-- with further connotations. Active information means 'potentially active' everywhere, but active only where it has meaning. A complete meaning of the term information he describes as

"The living bond which maintains the whole world to be complete and sacred"!

DEFINING A NEW TERM

Detela introduces us to a new term, one that relates more specifically to the phenomena of reversing entropy, or putting order back into a disordered state- he calls the term *syntropic* to describe phenomena that do not "obey" the second law of thermodynamics. A syntropic process can lower the entropy (i.e. increase the order) of a closed system.

CONDITIONS O F SYNTROPIC PHENOMENA

What are the conditions that contribute to syntropic phenomena? Here we look for those conditions that trigger the self-organizing syntropic process. We will cite three of these conditions (of the five that must be met) here below.

The first syntropic condition:

A Magnetic Field- The presence of a magnetic field can contribute to triggering the generation of syntopic currents. A syntropic current reverses entropy. The magnetic field provides information about preferred direction of flow. There is a transfer of information, without necessarily having transfer of energy.

A second syntropic condition:

Quantum Coherence-The quantum states of material particles are coherent over one period of chiral structure. Here Detela refers to "an exchange of space-time forms, in the absence of energy exchange....infinitely small energies(in fact, zero energies) can convey considerable amounts of information". Amplification results from quantum coherence. Examples of macroscopic systems that display quantum coherence are laser light and superconductive currents.

A third condition:

Tuning-Up-This refers to an active coupling, getting in-phase, resonance, between the frequency of the magnetic field and the frequency of oscillation at the quantum state. Here, allowance is made for the harmonic coupling between the two because the frequencies can be multiples of each other. When quantum coherence exists, the "sharper are the resonant frequencies". To fulfill this condition Detela explains that the magnetic field should be *"tuned-up exactly, like the frequency of a musician playing his own instrument within an ensemble"*.

A WEB PROVIDING SELF-ORGANIZATION

In his paper *Physical Model of the Biofield* (*see Appendix C*), Detela explains that for living organisms, it is the biofield that provides the mechanism for self-organization of physical processes. The biofield makes a connection at the quantum level to the physical body. As an animate structure, the biofield consists of a stable *informational* component. This stable component exists in symbiosis with an *evolutionary* component. The biofield is capable of syntropic self-organization. Detela suggests that the biofield contains mechanisms for cleansing undesired forms within its field structure. Additionally, it is the *evolutionary* component of the biofield that enables repairs of small defects to the web structure.

It is significant to note that the biofield is one link in a chain that connects the physical state to the subtle fields. We have seen in Tiller's model that the spiritual aspects of our being connect to the mental and emotional aspects, which are linked to the etheric (etheric = biofield[1,7]), and then physical body. *Self-organizational at the biofield level implies a restructuring, or reorganizing, of the internal structures of all the refined subtle states.* In a similar fashion, when we restructure the Universal Calibration Lattice (UCL) through the EMF Balancing Technique©, we affect all refined subtle states. These include the emotional and mental aspects of our being that precipitate positive effects to the physical organism.

SYNTROPIC CONDITIONS IN
THE HUMAN-TO-HUMAN CONNECTION

In the human-to-human interaction [as in the EMF Energy Balancing work] we can conceive of one individual supplying the external syntropic conditions to the subtle fields of the other individual. What are these external syntropic conditions that the human being can provide to another?

- We each carry magnetic fields that have hyperspatial counterparts as hyperfields.
- We each carry the capacity of resonance to the vibrations of magnetic fields and their associated patterns and forms.
- We each can initiate the flow of bio-photonic ordering energy that influences the subtle and subtle levels.
- We each carry the power of INTENT acting through consciousness- Consciousness acts to influence matter and energy.

These elements of our multi-dimensional nature are the very influences that can "trigger" the inherent self-organizing components of the biofield, as well as other subtle field structures. In the process, there is a transfer of *active information*. When we trigger self-organizing processes, we affect a dynamic range within our 'whole' being, from the physical to the spiritual! Affecting the part also affects the whole. The holographic type of interconnectedness that exists within our energy fields ensures that entire energy systems can be tuned towards a new position of 'balance'- even by addressing any one single part of it!

DEFINING THE STRUCTURE OF REALITY

To expand on our view of self-organization, we pose a more general question: "What is the structure of physical reality?" Alex Kaivarainen has developed an extensive general model of physical reality and consciousness. Within this model there is a dynamic layering, or hierarchy that interconnects reality at different levels. Within the model, there exist a holographic type superposition of vibrating waves. Vibrational modes are at the background of the self-organizing process. Each successive level of reality unfolds from, or is related to, a deeper ordered vibrational state.

Vibrational states can be affected by external influences such as cosmic radiation or the electromagnetic field [8]. According to Kaivarainen, any kind of system has the capability of self-organization and evolution.

> In fact "...from atoms to living organisms, galaxies and Universe- (these systems) are tending to conditions of Hidden Harmony, tending to Golden Mean realization" [9].

Examples of the Golden Mean ratio are found in the study of Sacred Geometry [10]. Nature is guided by fundamental and universal, simple yet elegant, formulas of expression!

AN INTER-DIMENSIOINAL PROCESS

Ruth's discussion in *Interdimensional Physics* describes an energy flow from higher energy fields that serve as the regenerative forces of our interdimensional cosmos [11].

> An inter-dimensional vortex connects physical reality to the unseen origins of our Universe, and then beyond.

A similar "vortex" structure applies to physical man. Through it, man is "inter-dimensionally" linked to his higher consciousness. Such a connection would serve to guide the organization of energy and matter, through a sort of hierarchical system.

Unseen energy forces, traveling through this vortex from a higher reality, would certainly account for the observed self-organization phenomena of the various 'lower' systems. We can view such a vortex as being layered like the skin of an onion- a series of tori, one torus inside of another, with each layer interconnecting to the next. A transfer of information and energy takes place from one layer to another. Transformations take place from higher dimensional states that ultimately 'descend' into matter.

CONSCIOUSNESS GUIDES SELF-ORGANIZATION

Jack Sarfatti connects us to the idea that self-organization is linked to consciousness. Self-organization is the result of the mind field (consciousness) interacting with matter in the process he has defined as *back-action* [12]. It is, in fact, the *Intent* of mind that acts on the quantum level of matter. There is a two-way feedback loop that connects mind and matter, and this leads to spontaneously self-organizing system. Through this loop, there exists a top-level control structure that works 'moment to moment', so to speak, and guides the entire constructive processes.

Within this Paradigm, Mind, Consciousness, and INTENT, are inseparable from physical reality. We have the action of consciousness that supplies the geometric *form* (the *in-form* process) that organizes both matter and energy. The process of self-organization becomes an active process where information takes meaning within the organizing system.

A MULTI-DIMENSIONAL INTERACTIVE PHENOMENON

Magnetic field, Coherence, and *Tuning-Up.* . . .these are some of elements that Detala indicates are required to create syntropic currents at the quantum level. When these conditions can be met, then internal self-organization takes place. In doing so, the system tends towards Hidden Harmony, defined by the *deeper-level* mathematical and geometric laws of nature. We find that self-organizing systems are guided by Consciousness that interacts with energies that travel the interdimensional vortex linking the physical world to higher levels of reality.

In the human-to-human connection, we see the existence of syntropic conditions that can influence, and trigger, self-organization within the human energy field of another. These include the magnetic and torsion fields of the hands that carry the patterns and preferred directions, as well as the Intent of Consciousness that interacts with energy systems. Self-organization within any aspect of the human energy field results in the restructuring of the energy system as a *whole.* The EMF Balancing Technique© utilizes the potential of these interactive effects.

APPENDIX C

PHYSICAL MODEL
OF THE BIOFIELD

© Andrej Detela
"J. Stefan" Institute, Ljubljana, Slovenia

First published 1997- reprinted with permission from author

[Note to reader: see Detela's upcoming book "*Magnetic Knots*" (pg. 269)]

ABSTRACT

Biofield (informational and evolutionary components)

Biological living matter displays a variety of subtle phenomena, which most probably cannot be explained merely by biomolecular processes. Among these phenomena, we mention informational processes (transport, procession and storage of information) and evolutionary processes in living organisms (e.g. mitosis and morphogenesis) . Yet such phenomena can be better understood by introducing the concept of biofield. Biofield is a subtle material structure which is permeating biological cells of living beings. It is quite different from the world of atoms and molecules but, however, it is a part of the same material world and can be explained in physical terms.

Here, a theoretical argumentation for biofield is presented. It is assumed that biofield is a three-dimensional web woven of vibrating electric and magnetic fields. Lines of these fields are like tiny threads in a three-dimensional textile. These electromagnetic fields display very complex internal organization.

We find peculiar kind of chiral solutions to Maxwell equations, which do not dissipate energy and lead to stable field structures. This is the so-called informational basis of the biofield. The simplest structures of this kind are toroidal knots.

When electric charge with very light mass enters the informational biofield, non-linear phenomena take place. These non-linear phenomena are based upon bifurcations in internal electric currents and upon resonance effects between currents and fields. We find an evolution of the field structure. This evolution is a syntropic process, oriented in time. There are several obvious conditions for syntropic behavior and one of them is quantum coherence in the states of electric charge.

Biofield always comprises both : the informational basis and the evolutionary component. Both are necessary. The first obeys the linear Maxwell equations and preserves the structural form of the biofield. Linearity leads to superposition of many different non-local states, therefore to a great capacity of information storage. The second is responsible for evolution of the biofield from primitive toroidal knots to very complex forms (with many knots) which show all the features of life.

The structure of biofield is in close correspondence with the molecular structure of living organisms. The discrete knots in the biofield web are in interaction with discrete atoms and molecules in living cells, therefore biofield can regulate many processes in living cells. The most probable candidates for this interaction are chiral molecular structures of proteins and nucleotides, for example microtubules and DNA helices.

INTRODUCTION

Many informational and self-organizing processes inside living organisms can be better understood and explained if we can imagine the existence of a *special self-organizing structure*, woven of *tiny threads of high frequency electric and magnetic fields*. These threads intertwine through the molecular structures inside the bodies of living organisms. The concept of these knotted structures is not new; it was acknowledged inside many old cultures. In classical India, it was called *prana*, while in the modern scientific tradition most commonly the expression *biofield* is in use. Biofield impregnates all living matter, our human body, as well as the animals, plants, *fungi, bacteria*, viruses, partially even in crystals. It is living in *symbiosis* with the *protein structures* of living organisms. Inside living organisms, it provides *self-organization*, for preserving the thermodynamical state with the lowest *entropy* and for the inner *informational interconnections*. The theoretical explanation of the biofield is a great challenge for modern science.

To obtain some basic understanding, it seems that at least several new steps into a new unexplored world must be trodden simultaneously. An understanding of the *syntropic processes* in the state of *quantum coherence* are surely essential [1]. The syntropic nature of the biofield is based upon the probable existence of *electrically charged particles of very small mass* and upon a peculiar *space-time asymmetry* of the biofield structure. Here, the time asymmetry means an *arrow of time* of the biofield vibrations, while the space asymmetry means a *chiral* biofield structure. We shall elaborate further on these two terms presently (see section B).

Although there are not yet direct scientific proofs for the biofield hypothesis, it is attracting a growing support especially within the new interdisciplinary realm between the cognitive science, physics, and biology - the boundaries between these disciplines are gradually disappearing.

Biofield is a three-dimensional (3-D) web with two basic functional qualities:
- It is capable of storing an enormous amount of information (many *bits* of information)
- It is capable of its own inherent evolution (self-organizing process).

In this paper, I will present a hypothesis that in fact biofield is interlaced from two different components: an informational and an evolutionary structure. Both are quite definite material structures with intrinsic mathematical features. Only when both structures are interlaced together can the biofield be made possible. We shall examine several of these features here.

A: INFORMATIONAL COMPONENT OF THE BIOFIELD

Some of the features of a good memory storage system (for instance, a computer memory chip, or our human memory) include:
- The system should be capable of storing a great *amount of information*. If the amount of information is treated in a quantizied sense (as this is usually done from Wiener onwards in cybernetics) then this means a great number of informational *bits*. An informational bit could be defined as the smallest difference (in the material sense, whatever of) that can still be *discerned to the reader* of the information.

This tiny bit of information should be accessible in such a way, that it can be read (or written) without spoiling or changing the rest of the information. Thus, a *separability* between different parts of information should exist.

Inside a computer chip or on the surface of a disk, the different parts of information are separated in space, while in living organisms the separability probably does not exist in *space* terms. For instance, recent investigations of the brain[2] and of other living informational systems show that the functions of the mind are *alocal*. If this is so and if the mutually separable pieces of information are really stored within the same space region, then, regarding the biofield, something is certain: That the component of biofield, which is responsible for information storage, should be expressed by *linear equations*. Only then can different pieces of information be stored independently, because only then the *possibility of superposition* of linearly independent solutions for informational states exists.

Which type of linear equations are convenient to describe the informational component of biofield?

There are many arguments[3] which confirm that biofield is based upon *electromagnetic phenomena* (or at least, is tightly bound to them). The *Maxwell equations* for the electromagnetic field are linear. Let us try to find such a structure of the electromagnetic (EM) field that this field structure will remain temporally stable and that the field energy will not dissipate. Only then can we speak about memory embedded in the field structure. We also wish that the field structure is stable against the boundary conditions. Such boundaries that are distant should only have a negligible influence. In a simplified way, we can imagine an EM field as a 'cloud' that is asymptotically approaching a zero-value in all regions that are distant from the cloud center. If such a field is enclosed into a large box, then at the walls of the box the field is already so weak that the walls do not play any considerable influence upon the field structure.

Such a field structure is a type of *steady wave packet*. It does not move in space. We can already describe it by using ordinary Maxwell equations *in vacuo*. It is easy to show that the solutions described above of the Maxwell equations fulfill the following condition:

$$\text{rot } \mathbf{B} = k \cdot \mathbf{B} \tag{I}$$

Here, B is the vector of the *magnetic flux density* (all through this paper, vector quantities are marked by bold characters), and k is some scalar constant. Let us first pay attention only to the *harmonic* type of solutions, that is the solutions described by

$\mathbf{E} = \mathbf{E}_0 \cdot e^{i\omega t}$ (for the electric field)

$\mathbf{B} = \mathbf{B}_0 \cdot e^{i(\omega+\delta)}$ (for the magnetic field)

We insert this harmonic type of solutions into the first two Maxwell equations for the EM field in vacuum:

$\text{rot } \mathbf{B} = \varepsilon_0\mu_0 \cdot \partial\mathbf{E}/\partial t$

$\text{rot } \mathbf{E} = -\partial\mathbf{B}/\partial t$

Let us try with some peculiar type of solutions: The vector of the magnetic field B is at every moment and at every location *collinear* with the vector of the electric field E:

$$\mathbf{B} = i\,\omega \cdot (\varepsilon_0\mu_0/k) \cdot \mathbf{E} \tag{2}$$

Such solutions satisfy equation (I), but none of the other equations (assuming the solutions are harmonic). *Collinearity* of the vectors E and B is a very important quality of the informational component of biofield. Namely, this is very different from the nature of the usual EM field *in vacuo* or in a homogeneous substance, where vector E is perpendicular to vector B. An important consequence of this collinearity (with regard to the *Poynting vector*) will be discussed later.

Equation (2) also comprises the *imaginary unit i* which means that the magnetic field is phase-shifted (for $\pi/2$, therefore for one quarter of a cycle) with regard to the electric field. At the moment when the magnetic field reaches its maximum (or minimum), the electric field is zero, and vice versa. The energy of the electric field is transferred to and from the energy of the magnetic field, while the sum of both energies remains constant. This fact is similar as with all other ideal oscillators without damping. For instance, in a simple mechanical oscillator the sum of kinetic and potential (or elastic) energy is constant with respect to time.

Let us begin at the instant when the electric field is zero. At that moment, there exists only magnetic energy. The magnetic field has a definite structure which we shall explore later. One quarter of a cycle later, we get an identical structure in the electric field, and again one quarter-cycle later, this is again transformed into an identical magnetic structure (but the field polarity is reversed). The curves which represent the lines of both fields do not change with time (I use the term *field line* instead of *line of force*). The relative intensity of the electric and/or magnetic field is changing. Both fields are oscillating between a positive and negative amplitude. However, the field direction does not change. The qualitative picture of both fields (field structure) preserves its initial shape. This is a special kind of a wave packet – it does not travel at the speed of light, but is static, remaining all the time in the same place! It preserves its internal information (which is in the field structure). Because this standing wave packet obeys linear Maxwell equations, more of them can be superposed. We shall call such a wave packet which does not travel at the speed of light (and therefore has a rest mass) an *informational web*.

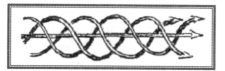

Fig. 1 *(Detela)*

Let us side-track for a moment: The border between an informational web and a classical *photon* is not well defined, however. The derivations on these pages describe an idle informational web, but it can also have a velocity component (yet slower than at the speed of light}. The closer its speed approaches the speed of light, the more it resembles a classical photon.

Following the usual procedures with the Maxwell differential equations, we can easily find the *circular frequency* for an informational web:

$k^2 = \varepsilon_o\mu_o \bullet \omega^2$, or more simply

$\omega = ck$, (3)

where c is the speed of light *in vacuo*.

We want to determine also the *space configuration* of these solutions. We are interested in the shape of the magnetic or electric lines (both have the same shape). Many classes of solutions exist, but firstly, we shall limit ourselves to such solutions which are the simplest of all and which are not too sensitive to the boundary conditions. As mentioned already, these solutions must display the asymp factor. This field can be visualized as a straight, infinitely long rope made of torsionally twisted field lines *(fig. 1)*. The twist in the center of the rope is like that of a right-handed helix if k>0, and like a left-handed helix, if k<0. But observation of the boundary conditions tells us that this solution with regard to the cylindrical coordinate system is not satisfactory. Namely, the field B does not tend to zero when we travel away

Fig. 2 *(Detela)*

in the z- direction. Also, when we travel away in the r- direction, it does not tend to zero enough quickly (the result of loose asymptotic behavior). The complete magnetic energy which can be expressed by the space integral $f_v(2\mu_o) \bullet \mathbf{B}^2 \, dV$ (integration over the whole space V) *diverges* even when only the magnetic energy within a finite length of the rope is being calculated.

Both of these difficulties can be solved by a slightly modified field structure. Let us imagine that the rope described above within the field is of a finite length (then we have a rope section) and curved into a closed loop *(fig. 2)*. In this way we can instantly dismiss of the first difficulty. So what about the second one? Although, due to this new modification, the field does not change significantly in the kernel of the rope, it can change considerably within the region distant from the center of the loop. So totally new solutions can be expected - maybe with finite magnetic energy.

Many features of these new solutions can be found when the equation (I) is analyzed inside a *toroidal coordinate system*[4,5]. The calculus here is very complicated. The solutions *(toroidal solutions)* cannot

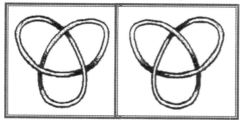

Fig. 3a *(Detela)*   **Fig. 3b** *(Detela)*

be expressed by ordinary analytical functions. But visually, these solutions are very attractive. They resemble the afore-mentioned closed loops from helically twisted ropes. Therefore, the field lines have the same structure as the threads of *toroidal knots*[6]. Toroidal knots can be visualized as a thread that is wound on the *torus* surface. The simplest toroidal knot is shown in the fig. 3.

All toroidal knots are *chiral*, therefore they have a left-handed and a right-handed variant. Chiral structures are those that lack a *center of inversion* which means that their mirror image is not identical to the original. So all chiral structures are in two symmetrical forms, for instance, left hand and right hand (Greek *kiros* =hand), left-handed and right-handed screw, left-handed and right-handed knot (*fig. 3a,b*), etc. It is easy to show that all mathematical solutions to equation (I) *must be* chiral: The differential operator *rot* (= *curl*) transforms a *polar vector* into an *axial vector* (or *vice versa*), therefore k is in fact not a usual scalar constant - it is a *pseudoscalar*[7]. Each pseudoscalar has chiral properties. When the constant k (in equation I) with the opposite sign is used, we get totally equivalent solutions, although not identical - they are the *mirror image* of the original.

It can be shown that for toroidal solutions the above-written space integral *converges*. Toroidal solutions are *good solutions* to equation (I) because they represent non-fictitious field webs, webs with a finite energy and insensitive to distant boundary conditions.

Only the simplest good solutions (toroidal knots) have been observed here because they can be established by moderately simple mathematical tools. But there may also be more complicated solutions to equation (I), for example, knotted structures which are not toroidal and are far more complex. We shall name all these knotted field structures *field webs*.

It is easy to see that *informational webs* do not radiate energy. The *Poynting vector*[8] is, expressed by a *vector product* between the electric and magnetic field, but inside an informational web these two fields are, according to equation (2), entirely *collinear* and the vector product between them vanishes. Therefore there is no radiation inside or outside this web. The web is then *temporally stable*.

Are these structures also stable to perturbations from *outside?* Can such perturbations slowly spoil and destroy our webs? The answer to these questions is not straightforward. Let us provide two pointers:

(I) Informational webs are related to the *evolutionary webs* (more about them later). Syntropic processes in the evolutionary webs provide stability for of evolutionary webs and as a result, also stabilize informational webs.

(2) We have studied Maxwell equations within the classical limit, but actually the magnetic flux in webs is *quantizied*. If nooses of the knotted structure are very tiny and if the magnetic flux density is small, then only a very limited number of the magnetic *flux quanta (fluxons)* pass through each noose. The web could radiate only when a considerable perturbation would change the flux for at least one fluxon.

In fact, both explanations basically mean the same thing: The syntropic nature of matter is the basis for all quantum phenomena. Today we cannot yet speak about an elaborated theory of quantum processes, interpreted through *syntropic activity on the subquantum level* (in a *subquantum vacuum* or, by different terminology, in *ether*). But some preliminary concepts already appear very promising. Such an interpretation is much closer to several alternative interpretations of quantum physics (for instance, in modern times to the *Bohm's school)* than to the already "classical" Copenhagen interpretation.

We have seen that equation (I) leads to extremely interesting solutions and situations. As an illustration of this, let me mention another interesting application of that same equation. When the wire of a toroidal coil follows lines which are solutions to equation (I), then the electric current in this coil is entirely collinear to the vector of the magnetic field generated by this same coil! Such a coil is free from *Lorentz forces*, so it is mechanically very stable. Coils of this type are sometimes used for the generation of very strong magnetic fields, when the mechanical strength of the coil itself could be a limiting factor[9].

B: THE EVOLUTIONARY COMPONENT OF THE BIOFIELD

Here, the EM field has a structure similar to that in informational webs (chiral knots - at least partially toroidal knots). Under certain conditions, an evolutionary web can grow out of an informational web. The basic condition for this is the presence of an *electric charge* in the web region. Until now, we have discussed the EM field *in vacuo*. An isotropic, homogeneous substance could not make a great difference to our equations (only that the dielectric constant c would need to be added), but this would be more realistic because biofield is seldom found separated from biological matter. However, what introduces a crucial novelty into our equations, is the presence of an *electric charge* with high *mobility*, so that this charge is scattered predominantly only on the EM field of the web structure.

When the conditions for syntropic processes are fulfilled in a web (see below), then a *syntropic self-organization of biofield* sets in. This means more than the usual self-organization of protein structures *(autopoiesis[10])* or self-organization in the Prigogine's *dissipative structures[11]*. All three stated phenomena (autopoiesis, Prigogine's self-organization and syntropic self-organization) take place when matter is far from thermodynamical equilibrium. This is obvious for all three self-organizing processes. What makes a difference is that syntropic processes (contrary to other two) *themselves* create this state which is far from thermodynamical equilibrium[12]. The initial disequilibrium can be introduced by a fluctuation that exceeds a certain threshold. From then onwards, the disequilibrium persists, without any outside interference.

Syntropic processes which produce new evolutionary web structures originate under the following conditions:

- the presence of electric charge with high mobility
- low mass of particles which carry charge
- a chiral symmetry to the web structure
- a temporally oriented pattern of EM vibration (arrow of time in the web structure)
- quantum coherence in states of charged particles (the coherence length exceeds the period of knotted structure)
- adequate amplitude of the magnetic field density.

The third condition is fulfilled from the very beginning because already the structure of the informational component is chiral. Yet the fourth condition (time's arrow) is not automatically fulfilled. However, an adequate initial fluctuation creates the time's arrow and from then onwards all the subsequent syntropic self-organizing processes are possible. A little later, we will describe this fluctuation in some more detail. Our description will be based upon the modern theory of *chaos*.

The third and fourth conditions represent the required *space- and time-symmetry attributes of the web structure*. They are prescribed by some basic physical laws *(invariance to unitary transformations of space and time)*. The patterns with the required symmetry of space-time structure should be reflected within the complete quantum state of a charged particle, but this is only possible when the *coherence length* of the quantum state extends at least over the size of discrete knots and the *coherence time* at least over one period of EM oscillation. This fact leads to the fifth condition. Surely, quantum coherence is a pure quantum effect and does not have any classical analogy[13]. The reason for this is a special informational interconnectedness within quantum states; this interconnectedness does not hold in the classical world. Quantum coherence introduces totally new insights into physics - let us remember the Aspect's and other related *EPR experiments[14]*!

The second and the sixth conditions are mutually bound: The necessary amplitude of the magnetic field has some correlation to the mass of charged particles, and to the size of the loops in the knotted structure. The greater the mass is, and the smaller the loops are, the greater the resulting *critical field* (more about the critical field later). All this would only work with electrons when the loops are very large but as a consequence the coherence length should be large also. An effect of this kind could be possible in *superconductive* materials. Thermal coupling between the superconductive *Cooper pairs* and the atoms of matter is negligible, therefore in this case only self-organization of electron gas (without coupling with the lattice) would take place. In spite of this, this hypothetical process in superconductors offers incredible possibilities for information processing. It is not ridiculous that something similar is occurring inside the *melanin protein structures* of nerve tissue (Cope[1]), but we can imagine also many other forms of *quantum computers*[15] on this same level.

In this text, I shall discuss another variant of self-organizing processes. Let us imagine the existence of electrically charged particles with a *very small rest mass.* Numerical estimations hint that in this case the syntropic conditions are very easily fulfilled, even when the magnetic field is quite weak and the coherence length relatively small. Such particles escape our usual observations and measurements. Why is this so? As I have already pointed out in my recent texts, these particles cannot exist independently, but exist only together with the complete web structure. The webs are their home and maybe also their body - the web structure may determine their manifested properties (and, with these properties, the particles themselves). The web structure also obstructs *annihilation* of ultra-light particles and anti-particles by keeping each of these two types within separate regions.

Therefore, detection of these ultralight particles will not be possible until we learn how to detect the biofield (detection by a scientific method). The webs remain in a coherent self-preserving and self-organizing state, without an internal energy transport (the Poynting vector for the informational component is zero). But despite this, there is some internal *informational interconnectedness.* The transport of energy is not the same as the transport of information! information and energy are not the same thing). As soon as the biofield dissolves, the ultralight particles dissolve too. By annihilation and other reactions, they are transformed into photons and other known particles. Ultralight charged particles are in a close connection to biofield; they are created and destroyed together with it. Together with the field, they *are* the web.

To fully understand, it is therefore essential to know that the webs are *animate.* Conventional physics is, on the other hand, based upon *information transport* solely in connection to *energy transport* (for instance, representation of influences with *Hamiltonians* in quantum mechanics). It treats matter as something dead, it measures only dead particles, therefore it first kills the webs - but then the possibility to know something about them is lost[16].

A syntropic process that is preserving a live evolutionary web is an expressively *nonlinear* phenomenon. The evolutionary web (based on the nonlinear syntropic process) is controlling the linear informational web. As we shall see shortly, the reverse is also true: The linear informational web is controlling the nonlinear evolutionary web. The evolutionary component of the biofield is that suffix of the informational component which is leading its evolution. And in the reverse sense, the informational component is the initial information (like the primal seed) for the evolutionary component. The syntropic (evolutionary) process is distinctive only at quite definite space-time patterns *(topologies)* of the web structure. From these syntropic regions, we do not find any syntropic self-organization (for instance, if the field does not exceed some critical field). The syntropic pattern is therefore an *attractor* (known from the theory of *nonlinear system dynamics)* which establishes itself within an evolutionary web. If the web structure is very simple (the simplest syntropic knots that can survive) then this attractor may be *periodic,* but in more complex web structures we find attractors that bear more resemblance to *chaotic attractors.* However, this "chaotic" nature manifests specific features which are characteristic only for the syntropic behavior. (For instance, the attractors in Prigogine's dissipative structures are quite different.) An evolutionary web is vibrating and perpetually transforming itself according to its own inborn laws. Therefore, the attractors of this kind could be classified into a special class: *syntropic attractors.*

Why are the informational and the evolutionary webs so closely related? It is because the chiral field structure of the evolutionary webs is very similar to that of the informational webs. The main reason for this similarity lies in the fact that both webs can be described by *similar differential equations*[17]. In the following paragraphs, I shall present an argument (although very unprecise) that equation (I) which describes the structure of an informational web holds also for an evolutionary web in its early stages of development:

The trajectories of charged particles inside an evolutionary web are, taking an average of many charged particles, aligned along the lines of a magnetic field of this same web:

$$\mathbf{j} = \mathbf{f(B)} \tag{4}$$

Here, j is the *vector of the electric current density*. The vector function f (B) is *nonlinear*, the current density j can have marked extremes at definite magnetic field densities B. In such cases, we can expect a syntropic orientation (a directing) of charged particles.

Now, let us look at what happens if function (4) was *linear*. Surely, this assumption does not hold within the syntropic region of parameters (when field density is greater than the critical value - as we shall see shortly). However, we are interested in knowing where the source of nonlinearity is located (and of the syntropic directing). We begin by observing the early evolutionary stage when field B is still weak (below the critical value), but equation (4) is still valid. At this stage, the linear term in equation (4) predominates:

$$\mathbf{j} = p \cdot \mathbf{B}, \text{ where p is a scalar constant (a pseudoscalar again).} \tag{5}$$

When this j is inserted into the first Maxwell equation (now we have also the influence of matter; electric currents of charged particles), we get

$$\text{rot } \mathbf{B} = \varepsilon\varepsilon_o\mu\mu_o \cdot \partial\mathbf{E}/\partial t + \mu\mu_o \cdot \mathbf{B} \tag{6}$$

Let us assume again that the vibration is harmonic, and let us also assume that the vector fields E and B are collinear (which is true for simple informational webs), and we obtain the already known equation

$$\text{rot } \mathbf{B} = k' \cdot \mathbf{B}, \tag{7}$$

which confirms our assumption about the collinearity of the fields E and B. If the remaining two assumptions were also true (that the function f is linear, and the vibration is harmonic), then the evolutionary web and the corresponding informational web would display exactly the same space-time structure of the EM field (only the *extension* would be different, namely $k \neq k'$). But within the syntropic region of parameters, neither the first nor the second condition can be fulfilled. The function j = f (B) must cease to be linear above the critical point, and also the vibration is no longer harmonic if temporally-oriented evolution sets in. (But it can still be expressed in a *Fourier form* by a sum of harmonic vibrations).

These two complications (nonlinearity, aharmonicity) deform the web structure and make it more entangled. How could we describe this deformation?

First of all, let us deal with the consequences of *aharmonicity*. Each periodic vibration (although aharmonic) can be expressed by *Fourier harmonic components*. The already stated equations are linear (by definition), therefore one can find separate solutions, for each harmonic component separately (the simplest solutions are, as we know, chiral structures in the form of toroidal knots), and then we can sum up these solutions for separate harmonic components. Therefore, the joint solution would be the sum of fields represented by different knots (different k' for different harmonic components). The ratio between frequencies of harmonic components is very regular (ratio between discrete numbers), so equation (3) (together with the assumption on linearity) yields also a regular ratio between the parameters k'. This means that the structure of the collective knot (all the harmonic components combined) appears to be quite regular. Naturally, the collective knot is now much more entangled than a toroidal knot, and moreover, its collective *topology* changes during one period (which is not the case with the knot of one pure harmonic component).

But now we also have the *nonlinearity* of function (4). This condition changes the knot structure even more radically. Let us begin with a web consisting of one pure harmonic component, to make our analysis simpler.

The nonlinear relation (4) can be written in the form of a potential power series (but without the term with n=0, because when B =0, j = 0 also; there is no syntropic directing of particles).

$$\mathbf{j} = \sum p_n \cdot \mathbf{B}^n \tag{8}$$
$$n = 1, 2, 3...$$

Let us observe the conditions as B increases from B = 0. At the beginning, B is small and the linear term predominates. The field B arranges itself into a linear knotted structure (for example, into a

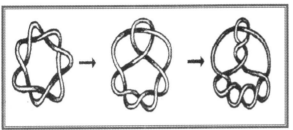

Fig. 4 *(Detela)*

toroidal knot). At higher fields, the linear structure suffers continuous deformation. Still later, at the *critical field*, B_k, an *unstability* [18] occurs and the knot structure suffers an *abrupt* change *(phase transition)*. At a still higher field B, *bifurcations* bring in an additional structural variety. Although these bifurcations are also a kind of phase transitions, they have a special property; from the original phase, the same new phase doesn't always evolve - there are several possibilities available. The line of phase possibilities splits at each bifurcation. The magnetic knot grows evermore complicated, although not less internally ordered *(fig. 4)*. Similar phenomena are known from the non-equilibrium thermodynamics of dissipative structures (e.g., the well-known *Bénard cells* in a turbulent liquid). However, there is also a basic difference: Syntropic structures do not need to be fed from the surroundings (fed, for example, by temperature differences, as in the case of Bénard cells, or by some other gradients).

What is happening to our original web? Due to syntropic directing of electric charge inside the web, increasing amounts of the evolutionary component of biofield is being added to the original informational component. Let us look closer at where the origin of *syntropicity* is lying. Syntropicity is based upon bifurcations in electric currents inside the webs. Bifurcations take place when the field which is growing from the informational field, exceeds successive critical values. Bifurcations always show *hysteresis*, therefore they are an *irreversible phenomenon*. When the field returns to its zero value, the web does not pass exactly the through the same phases as when the field was growing from zero. Thus we get a *temporally oriented* vibration, a necessary condition for syntropicity. From a pure harmonic oscillation, we obtain a time-oriented mixture of harmonic vibrations, from the primitive space structure (which could be represented by a single letter in the alphabet) we obtain a complex structure (which had to be represented by the length of a whole word). An evolution of "words" is taking place here. Some of them are blurred (their energy is absorbed by stronger words). But some of them survive - especially those for which the basic equation (I) holds, because such structures do not dissipate their energy. (However, the parameter k', related to *knot density*, is now probably higher). So we see that also the evolutionary component also controls the informational one, just like the informational component determines the evolutionary one. Thus, the circle is connected.

The described process is time-oriented. Could one then expect that the field energy is being dissipated (into heat), as in other irreversible processes? No, there is no way for dissipation. This is because a simple evolutionary web consists only of EM field and charged particles. The entropy of charged particles cannot grow if equation (4) describes *any* process of particle directing - also that directing which acts upon particles with totally blurred or chaotic movement. A little later, I shall use the term *ether*, a term which can be understood much easier by an eastern (e.g., *Taoist)* rather than by a Western mode of thinking. Now it is essential that ether has, even in its basic quantum state (its state with the lowest energy), a blurred momentum, and equation (4) is sensitive to this. But maybe the entropy of the EM field is increasing? If the field is only of the informational component, then entropy surely does not increase. This informational field is the basis from which the evolutionary component is growing. One part of web structure (one part of knots) is related to growing entropy of evolutionary component; this part quickly decays. The other part is related to diminishing entropy, or to put it another way, to growing syntropy; this part survives and continues its evolution. Therefore, the overall entropy of the web does not grow. Here, the idea of entropy turns out to be of only marginal importance because the classical thermodynamics (with its *second law)* is no longer valid. *Syntropy growth* (and not entropy growth[19,20]) introduce the direction of time into nature, and also irreversibility begins here. Syntropicity has everything to do with the evolution of webs (evolution of letters into words, and these onward into more mature words...). Evolution can also be treated by the *information theory*. The number of *informational bits* grows through evolution. Evolution is a *system phenomenon*, and is known also in modern microbiology. More evolved webs survive, others perish and are instantly absorbed by the survivors. The *direction of time* lies in the direction of growth of internal information, in the direction of cognition, in the direction of (self) organization of material structures.

Another great advantage of the variety of non-linear syntropic structures is hidden in the fact that a single minute period of the biofield vibration (of the order 10^{-15} s for biofield with the frequency of sunlight - more about this in the following chapter) represents one complete *evolutionary cycle:* When, after one oscillation, the field B reaches its amplitude again, then its structure is not the same as it was originally. Maybe we have started with a simple toroidal knot, but now we have a complete cluster of ten mutually interlaced knots. This new structure is the seed for the next period when it may become even more variegated. We know something very similar from the plant life cycle. Each autumn, new seeds are scattered, to give new life a chance in the following year.

The theory described so far includes a hypothetical existence of ultralight charged particles. Maybe these particles do not posses any distinct shape by themselves; only the syntropic inclusion into webs determines their quantum features. I am using the term *ether* for the *unmanifested* collective of these particles, because this name, describing phenomena of just type, has been used for a long time in the European pre-scientific literature. The Sanskrit word *prana*, on the other side, suits more to already ordered syntropic structures, therefore it relates to ether which has already assumed a *manifested form*.

Our discussion of the evolutionary component of biofield is not so mathematically strict, in comparison with the discussion of the informational component. All that we required for the informational component were the Maxwell equations *in vacuo*, while with the evolutionary component this is not so simple. We had to use several assumptions; I shall defend them later, as soon as time and space permit. Much more has to be said about ether itself - what is it, after all? Then, here are the syntropic conditions and syntropicity. More has to be discussed about the relation of webs to quantum states, about quantum coherence etc. The answers to these questions are partially interrelated. I apologize because at this moment I cannot step, with all the required awareness and concentration, out onto this extremely vast range.

C: BOTH COMPONENTS OF BIOFIELD ARE LINKED TOGETHER

The phenomena in biofield are better understood only when we take into consideration both components together - the *informational and evolutionary components*. Biofield is always a *symbiosis* of both. In biofield with a very complex web structure, we can even expect specialization within particular regions, so that we find predominantly informational and predominantly evolutionary regions.

If there was no *informational component*, the evolution in biofield would very quickly *degenerate*. Very chaotic structures would then evolve (far removed from those that can be described by periodic attractors). Probably the ground for quantum coherence would soon become spoiled, and so also syntropicity and evolution in biofield would die away. Moreover, from a simple case (discussed later), we shall see that each stable biofield must be at the outer edge enclosed into an *envelope* - and which is predominantly composed of the informational component.

The *evolutionary component* is also essential. Without it, biofield could not make simultaneous repairs of many small defects in the web structure. (Namely, when biofield interacts with the surroundings, perturbations tend to result in *entropic degradation*.) Furthermore, biofield without an evolutionary component would always remain at its primitive stage of development with the structure of the simplest toroidal knots.

We can imagine that a magnetic field B inside the web structure of an existing biofield looks as follows: The *first part* (the informational component) corresponds to linear equations for informational webs (I). The linear part of the web structure does not radiate any energy. This structure preserves itself.

It is like a firm support upon which, in each period of a new oscillation, the *second part* of biofield (evolutionary component) affixes itself. The *total actual field* in the web is, due to nonlinear effects (equation 4), a little different from the pure informational component. Let us call this difference (between the actual field and the pure informational field) the *nonlinear excess of biofield*. Generally speaking, the Poynting vector of this excess must not be zero (the vectors E and B are no longer collinear). Namely, in the nonlinear portion, more complicated relations hold true than the one expressed by equation (5), so also equations (6) and (7) are valid only approximately. The exact solutions for the web structure are different from those determined by equation (1). Fluctuating levels of radiation between various regions of web structure is present in the evolutionary component. The energy moves about, the structure permanently changing its form. However, syntropicity is vivid only with field parameters confined to quite restricted intervals of magnitude; in particular (as already mentioned), the current density j (equation 4) has well-marked extremes only with definite magnitudes of field density, density of knots, etc. In this way, bifurcations cannot be developed over a certain degree, which imposes limits to the syntropic behavior. Evolution is caught into *regions of dynamical stability.*

Consequently, the entire biofield changes very little within one period of oscillation. The biofield attractor is nearly periodic, especially when we look at only a limited region of space. A special kind of apparent *chaoticness* (chaoticness in terms of modern theories of chaos) is evident only from observations of larger areas of space-time. But this chaoticness is very different from the one used with non-syntropic attractors. However, the word *chaos* is not just a very convenient term to use here, because in its Greek origin, it means confusion, disorder (something negative in the human sense). But the syntropic dance of nature is something totally different. It surpasses the concept of mess already with the first movement.

The informational part also does not remain unchanged all the time. It is also influenced by evolution, for equation (1) which holds for the informational component, is approximately valid for the complete biofield, together with the nonlinear (evolutionary) excess. But through evolution, biofield quickly establishes such structures which tend to preserve energy and information, so that dissipation is limited. This is in the best interest of biofield. Such a biofield which is not capable of storing its own informational patterns quickly decays. Only that one with the correct attitude towards its own *internal information* remains. Most surely, all these concepts are known from biology, and also from microbiology (findings about life patterns of individual cells, or even smaller structures of living matter).

So biofield with a quite definite internal space-time topological structure survives. This means in effect quite definite *space patterns* of threads in the three-dimensional "textile" of biofield, and with quite definite concord of *temporal rhythms* of these threads. Such a biofield is maybe the result of a long evolution which is not at all shorter than evolution of the molecular side of living organisms. Maybe also due to biofield, separate organs (or *organelles)* have evolved, and they exist for very specific functions: Informational lines (from special threads of biofield) like a kind of "nervous system", regions with practically no evolution like a type of memory, mechanisms that cleanse the undesired forms of biofield, etc. Most probably these functions are at least partially affixed to respective functions in the molecular living world - this gives a better stability to biofield. The biofield and molecular structures of living organisms obtain mutual benefit from this *symbiosis*. This is why in the majority of biofield, as soon as it is woven from sunlight, it weaves itself into the *protein structures* of living organisms.

One brief question: How is it woven from sunlight? The most likely scenario is as follows: The photons from the Sun are scattered by the protein structures of green plants. All proteins are chiral, and therefore are *optically active.* The probability for absorption of both *circularly polarized components* is different when a photon is scattered on an optically active molecule *(circular dichroism* or the *Cotton effect)* [21] .Therefore, circularly polarized photons are produced. Such photons have a chiral symmetry. Maybe biofield even has special organelles with which chiral photons can be slowed down better, trapped, and incorporated into the biofield structure. (This would be an analogy of the tentacles, mouth, throat and stomach of a cuttlefish). In early spring (for moderate climate belt, this is in March) when the biofield of trees is still weak, proteins in tree-bark must take over most of this activity. But later these processes become much easier: The proteins in the green leaves then join in this work, and the biofield itself cooperates more as a result.

Most probably, it is the *integrity* of biofield that synchronizes oscillations of newly-formed webs with the time-oriented tune of an existing biofield. The time-oriented vibration gets increasingly more complex, as it gathers more and more information about the existing biofield and about future prospective biofields. This tune is a story-teller and a dreamer, it is the carrier of evolution, it is the self-sensitive *life purpose* that impregnates the pores of all living organisms.

What kind of intuition led Louis Pasteur who 150 years ago assigned *élan vital* (life-giving force and ability of self-organization) exactly to chiral molecules?

The thermodynamical temperature of the Earth's surface is about 300°K, due to dynamical equilibrium between radiation from the Sun and infrared (IR) radiation back into space. But biofield does not tend to this same equilibrium, for it can retain radiation within itself (this is the very nature of biofield). The photons from the Sun get trapped into biofield without any pronounced entropic processes (thanks to the self-organizing nature of biofield), so their temperature is not significantly reduced. The temperature of biofield is therefore approximately the same (or maybe even higher) as the temperature of the Sun's surface (6000°K). But, actually it is somehow difficult to speak about temperature here. Thermodynamical temperature can be defined only within the realm of validity of *the second law* (the Law of Entropy). When syntropic processes are vivid, then different space regions of biofield can have very different "temperatures". When bifurcations in ether spring up, the density of the knots and also the frequency increase (higher harmonic components) - and with this also the apparent "temperature".

Nevertheless, we would like to know the approximate energy of one knot in biofield. A single photon from Sun has the energy of about 2...3 eV (4.10^{-19}J). One knot thus has a rest mass of about 4.10^{-36}kg (4.10^{-6} of electron mass). The mass of charged particles that form ether may also be something similar - on the assumption that photons also give birth to these particles. Maybe these charged particles are even *identical* to some knots (in this case, knots are either charged or neutral).

The *classical radius* of a charged particle with the above stated energy is about 0.6 nm (under the assumption that charged particles carry one *charge unit*). This is for a factor -2π•137 (connected with the *fine structure constant* ∝) less than the wavelength of photons with corresponding energy. This could mean that, up to a certain degree, syntropic processes are still able to weave filigranic details inside a primary informational web. This fine lacework can act upon individual atoms which have approximately the same size (several tenths of nm).

To see things clearer, let us look at the smallest region of biofield that can still preserve syntropic functions; we shall call it a *biofield cell*. In the interior, we find evolution regions that are interlaced with *informational threads* – they retain the required stability. But the outer sheath is (nearly) completely removed from the informational biofield, so that the energy does not leak out. We notice an interesting similarity with a biological living cell which has the outer *membrane* and the inner *protoplasm*. Maybe often there is also an informational *nucleus* inside (like in *eukariotic cells)*?

We have now entered into a wondrous new world, impregnated with the quality of life. Not only do these laws of life exist on the level of *catalytic cycles* in protein structures (as is the case in molecular biology), but they also exist on the level of basic knots in the biofield web structure. We can understand why biofield shows such a remarkable ability in regulating the biomolecular processes in our bodies: It can adapt to them very easily. In comparison with 'clumsy' molecules, it has far better possibilities for self-organization, for the storage and processing of information. We have seen that the biofield structure is markedly chiral, the loops in the knots of three-dimensional syntropic webs are helical. So biofield integrates itself easily into the similarly chiral (helical) structures of *proteins* or *nucleotides*. Two such structures with very regular helicity are the double helix of *DNA* and the helically structured *microtubules*[22,23]. Both types of biomolecules play an extremely important role in informational storage and processing within living cells.

I am grateful to Dr. Marta Klanjsek-Gunde who contributed many useful suggestions, and to Mitja Perus, MSc., who stimulated me to write this paper through fruitful discussions.

References:
1. A. Detela: Sintropni pojavi v biopolju kot osnova informacijskih procesov v zivih organizmih, 2. slovenski forum kognitivnih znanosti, 1996 (Slovene reprint in this book).
2. K.H.Pribram: Some dimensions of remembering: Steps toward a neuropsychological model of memory, in: Macromolecules and Behavior, (ed.J.Gaito), Ac.Press 1966, pp.165..87
 K.H.Pribram: Languages of the brain: Experimental paradoxes and principles in neuropsychology, Prentice-Hall 1971
K.H.Pribram, M.Nuwer, R.Baron: The holographic hypothesis of memory structure in brain function and perception, zbornik Contemporary Developments in Mathematical Psychology, W.H.Freeman, San Francisco 1974
3. B.A.Brennan:Hands of Light (Bantam Books, 1985), chapter 4
4. P.M.Morse, H.Feshbach: Methods of Theoretical Physics (Mc.Graw-Hill, 1953), p. 1301.
5. K.Huang, R.Tipton: Vortex excitations in the Weinberg-Salam theory, Phys.Rev. D, 23 (1981) 3050
6. Lee Neuwirth: The theory of knots, Sci. Am. June 1979, pp 84..96
7. F. Krizanic; Vektorji, matrike, tenzorji (Sigma, Ljubljana 1962)
8. R.P. Feynman: Lectures on physics (Addison-Wesley), vol. II, chapter 27
9. D.H.Parkinson, B.E.Mulhall, The generation of high magnetic fields, Plenum press 1967, p.154
10. F. Capra: The Web of Life (Anchor Books 1996)
11. I.Prigogine, I.Stengers: Order out of Chaos, Bantam 1984
12. M.Jibu, K.Yasue: Quantum Brain Dynamics and Consciousness (John Benjamins, Amsterdam 1995)
13. R. Penrose: Shadows of the Mind (Oxford Univ. Press 1994)
14. L.E. Ballentine: Quantum Mechanics (Prentice Hall 1990)
15. R. Turton: The Quantum Dot (Freeman Spectrum, 1995)
16. A. Detela: Dusevni procesi v zivih organizmih - izziv za sodobno fiziko, 1995 (slovene reprint in this book).
17. R.P.Feynman: The same equations have the same solutions (Lectures on physics vol. II/12-1)
18. J. Gleick: Chaos, Penguin books 1987
19. P.Coveney, R.Highfield: The Arrow of Time (1990)
20. Time's Arrows Today (ed. S.F.Savitt), Cambridge University Press 1995
21. For instance, Applied Optics and Optical Engineering, Vol. 1,ch.9 (R.J.Meltzer), p.347
22. S.R.Hameroff, R.C.Watt: Information processing in microtubules, J.theor.Biol. 98 (1982) pp. 549..61
23. R.D.Allen: The microtubule as an intracellular engine, Sci. Am., Febr. 1987

APPENDIX: OTHER EXAMPLES OF SYNTROPIC BEHAVIOR

Quantitative analysis shows that syntropic conditions are most probably fulfilled in the following natural structures:

- *biofield*
- biomolecules with complex electron states (DNA, microtubules...)
- complex superconductive web structures
- *possibly ball lightning*
- the interior of elementary particles.

Future study of these phenomena is likely to yield new knowledge about very interesting forms of matter, where the events can be described by quite different and yet unknown laws.

The theory of biofield, outlined above, is a possible template for other syntropic structures. Certain quantitative parameters differ (e.g., the structural periods and frequencies) but most of the newly introduced ideas remain.

Complex biomolecules are tiny (but extremely capable) *quantum computers,* similar to the future nanochips, based on coherent quantum states in three-diinensional meshes (knotted structures) of tiny superconductive wires and tunneling switches.

Ball lightning has very strong magnetic field (>10T), and its remarkable stability can be easily explained by the same model, *ie,* magnetic lines and streamlines of electric current woven together into a self-organized tissue.

Curiously, the elementary particles fulfill the same syntropic conditions. Quantum particles are stable syntropic structures, possibly just like ball lightning. The symmetry properties of syntropic structures lead to the well-known *CPT invariance.* Although the *vortex model* of an electron or a photon is not new, this picture now gets a good mathematical basis on the grounds of the self-organizing *ether* (quantum vacuum). Many philosophical questions arise here; if ether is, by definition, without any primordial structure and distinctive qualities, is our manifested world (space-time) then the obvious outcome of an all-embracing syntropic activity, like in the Vedic philosophy the phenomenal world is *maya,* the interplay of Shiva and Shakti?

Questions about the deeper nature of quantum states will not be answered easily. A vast and unexplored field lies before us. One can employ new mathematical tools (like *fuzzy logic* and *complex topologies* of space-time structures) and attempt to observe the syntropic activities in ether. One can find new profound definitions of the *informational interconnectedness* within quantum states. Will they be in accordance with some recent EPR experiments (like Aspect's)? Will this approach yield the von Neuman's axioms and Schrodinger's equation? These are some checking points for validity of the new quantum imagination.

But one thing is already certain; the era when physics dealt solely with dead bodies is clearly over. **Life is at the very base of space-time structures.** In the contemporary world-wide crisis when science must be patiently renewing its inborn transparency by sincere commitment to human ethics and to modern interdisciplinarity, physics will find a new link-up with biology, so that physicists will recognize, through intelligent quantum states, **the mutual interplay of consciousness and matter.** This will be really a great paradigmatic transformation in modern natural sciences.

APPENDIX D

SELF-ORGANIZATION WITHIN COMPLEX QUANTUM STATES

© Andrej Detela
"J. Stefan" Institute, Ljubljana, Slovenia

First published 1998- reprinted with permission from author

I. INTRODUCTION

In the last few years, a growing number of researchers are attempting to understand *complex quantum states* in terms of the *self-organizing processes* at the level of these quantum states. According to these interpretations, quantum state is based upon some *active information* that regulates the internal space-time structure of this state [I]. Such ideas are interesting especially with regard to very complex quantum states that are structured yet still coherent. Examples of such large *coherent quantum systems* are the quantum states in living matter (e.g., in complex protein structures such as microtubules [2]), or complex superconductive structures. If several particles constitute such coherent quantum state, then this state is *entangled*. The quest for a computing quantum chip [3] is also based upon the concept that *sub-quantum* (some call them *post-quantum*) informational fields are able to self-organize in a two-way relationship between the subquantum world and the world of known physical manifestations [4]. Hence, the quantum states may have some *inner feeling*.

Such views are already distinct from the views of the *Copenhagen school*. That school did not admit the existence of quantum states *per se*; it admitted only the existence of data that come to us through our (classical) measuring equipment. (A known Bohr's statement was:

"There is no quantum world. There is only an abstract quantum physical description".

But it is obvious to express deep respect for physical *reality*, whether it be known or unknown - otherwise we could also ignore respect for the most precious essence of this reality, which is *life*.

If we are open to this irrefutable life which permeates everything in nature and which links us together with the world, then we can easily perceive some striking similarities between biological organisms and complex quantum states:

Quantum states are very stable - there is nothing like classical friction to stop their dynamic internal activity. They actively respond to the disturbances from outside in such a way that they preserve their internal space-time structure (*self-organization in space and time*). Information concerning this structure is never lost. Internal order is not dissipated, entropy of the state does not grow, albeit the perturbances from outside. Quantum states care for themselves in an *intelligent* way. The quantum world seems to be *animate*. Life is probably at the very basis of our physical reality. But to grasp some scientific precision, we should first know what life is. Can we define it? Let us leave this issue open for the moment. I hope that this paper will initiate pondering along a fruitful direction.

Modern microbiology and cognitive sciences tell us that the gap between *animate* and *inanimate* matter is no longer apparent. Intelligence is an inherent ability of complex quantum systems. These are *informationally coherent*, so the theory of *information* (long known in cybernetics and in cognitive sciences) is an adequate concept for dealing with these systems.

In this paper, I shall try to elaborate on these views a little further. Strictly speaking, very little has been said about what the quantum self-organizing processes actually are, and what their mysterious inner driving force (*élan vital* if translated into a biologist's terminology) should be at all ? Obviously, within quantum states there must be some very subtle internal activity responsible for self-organizing phenomena.

Firstly, we must be very cautious about the following question; What kind of self-organization do we have in mind? Maybe it is of the type known from Prigogine's *dissipative structures* [5] or Maturana's *autopoietic structures* [6]? If so, then the driving force for quantum self-organizing processes is some initial order within the complete systems, order which is established only if these systems are from the beginning distant from thermodynamical equilibrium. If such systems are left to themselves (isolated from the surroundings), then the source of order (negative entropy) eventually fades out, and with it the internal self-organization.

I do not believe that complex coherent quantum systems belong to this type of self-organization. We cannot imagine any store (*thermodynamical reservoir*) of order (negative entropy) which provides us constantly with the unimaginable variety of quantum manifestations, to persist unexhausted for billions of years, and which still eludes us. The laws of quantum physics are surely among the most basic laws that we are trying to understand today. They should be, if possible, explained without some complicated assumptions (hidden reservoirs of order, etc.).

But if so, then self-organization is possible if and only when the self-organizing phenomena do not obey the *second law of thermodynamics* (the law of growing *entropy*). Many authors claim such a solution. Can such a daring possibility endure? The second law starts microscopically at the level of quantum particles, but some complex quantum particles may already be too clever for obeying a law that was meant and formulated to deal only with very simple, inanimate bodies. Indeed, modern theories of *chaos* with nonlinear dynamics (developed by mathematicians Kolmogorow, Arnold and Moser, among others) do not find a firm support for the second law, not even in "inanimate" matter. Modern physical theories have admitted that *nothing and again nothing* can be proved about the validity of the second law, when the observed system is *far from thermodynamical equilibrium* [7]. Highly organized quantum states may be precisely of this type, although we do not know yet how to define the negative entropy (its distance from thermodynamical equilibrium) of a complex quantum state.

Negative entropy is in a direct relationship to *information* [8]. Therefore, we need some new understanding of the *subtle information* residing within a complex quantum state [I]. The concept of *information* may possibly outgrow the basic concept of *energy* and even discover some new descriptions for *hamiltonians*. Can a quantum state be understood (and maybe even defined) in terms of its *internal informational interconnectedness*? If some *informational structure* is characteristic of a quantum state, on which level should we look for it? Probably, it cannot be expressed with usual space-time forms, but rather it exists on a level with a very different *timeness*, as is evident from instantaneous interconnectedness of entangled quantum states [9]. So our task is quite difficult, and it will be a long time before we can prepare some working mathematical tools.

However, a proper definition for this type of information is the bottleneck of modern quantum interpretations. It is the *missing link* between two ideas: the idea of a *quantum state* and the idea of a *conscious being*. So let us examine the meaning of the word *information*.

The Latin, and also the English, meanings of this word are evident: *in form*, something that is hidden in form or can be expressed by form. But in my native language, which is Slovene (of the Slavic language group) we have an interesting word for it: *vest*. It means a piece or an item of *active information* (information which is being conveyed from one living being to another), but at the same time it also means *conscience*. Consciousness is *zavest*, something which is *behind conscience*. So literally, *vest* is like a guard who takes care that some piece of information (therefore, some passive information in the realm of consciousness) is properly conveyed (which is already an active process), so that there is some life-giving understanding between the giver and the receiver of information. In my language, an active piece of information already comprises a correct *ethical attitude*; only then does it benefit mutual understanding and is able to make connections between various parts of the whole. Curiously, in Slovene, *ves* means *all*, *complete*, and *vez* means *connection*, *bond*. And if we only change the sequence of letters: *Svet* means *the world* but also *holy*, *sacred*. *Vest* is therefore the living bond which maintains the whole world to be complete and sacred [10] . It is something like active information, but with a stressed ethical attitude in the life-giving sense. Accordingly, to our extended understanding of life (expounded above), it would not be difficult to generalize life-supporting ethical attitude even to physical entities like quantum states.

I shall use this Slovene word *vest* instead of *active information*, since I believe that the exact meaning could be a key to a proper understanding.

Let us also introduce other new practical expressions. Here I shall use the expression *syntropic phenomena* for the description of all those phenomena that do not obey the second law of thermodynamics in its strictest sense. The syntropic processes can lower the total entropy of a closed and isolated system. A modern scientist only rarely admits a possibility of their sheer existence (even more rarely one engaged in theoretical physics); and when admitted, it is described very vaguely. However, in the last few years, this view has been undergoing a phase of rapid change [11]. So I think that this point is so important that it needs our full attention. Namely, we cannot understand the self-organizing processes within complex quantum systems without certain knowledge of the syntropic phenomena.

These phenomena deserve a new name because they are very different from other, known types of self-organization, working in the realm of official thermodynamics. The term *syntropy* (which is just the negative entropy) was first introduced by A. Szent-Gyorgy, in connection with self-organizing processes within living cells [12]. Now, when this expression (which was first introduced in biology) is used to specify a kind of physical phenomena, it may acquire new meanings.

2. SYNTROPIC CONDITIONS

Can we tell more about the nature of syntropic phenomena? We introduce the so-called *syntropic conditions* that trigger the self-organizing syntropic processes and are an obvious background for their existence. Altogether, there are 5 syntropic conditions. As we shall see, these five syntropic conditions are based upon the behavior of *informational structures in space and time*. We shall establish the arguments, upon which the five-syntropic conditions are based. The way to a complete proof is extremely long, difficult and complicated. Here I shall describe it in a very simplified light, because everyone must always get some picture about the problem first, before going into the obvious details. We need to develop some new intuitive imagination of the syntropic phenomena first. Only when we know more, can we make generalizations.

The 5 syntropic conditions are:

1. Influence of a magnetic field upon material particles (e.g., electrons)
2. Oriented space : Chiral (pseudoscalar, helical) structure of matter and/or the magnetic field
3. Oriented time : Broken temporal symmetry of the magnetic field oscillations
4. Quantum coherence: The quantum states of material particles are coherent over at least one period of chiral structure
5. Tuning-up : The frequency of quantum oscillations accords with the magnetic frequency (or the multiples of these frequencies are in tune).

Therefore, altogether there are two conditions concerning *space structure* and two conditions concerning *temporal structure*, and all this is with definite regard to the *magnetic field*. Space and time structures must be both *oriented* and *synchronized*. Explanation of these terms will be presented later.

Firstly, we shall limit ourselves to a special class of phenomena (the so-called *syntropic currents*) that probably encompasses the most important syntropic processes. All the members of this class are syntropic phenomena, but there may also exist other syntropic phenomena that do not belong to this special class. As we shall see shortly, it is much easier to show the syntropic conditions for syntropic currents than for some other syntropic phenomena. It seems that other syntropic phenomena (not currents) follow similar rules, so the syntropic conditions will be of a certain value for all possible syntropic processes.

Definition of syntropic currents:

To comprehend syntropic currents, we begin with a class of currents which are known from the thermodynamics of *irreversible processes* : diffusion current, heat current, electric current..., and other transport phenomena [13] . All these currents have their origin in a certain gradient (partial concentration gradient, temperature gradient, gradient of electric potential, respectively). In an isotropic medium, the currents point in the opposite direction to the gradients which give rise to these currents. This is why these currents flow in such a direction that they gradually reduce the gradients. The system thus tends towards thermodynamical equilibrium. All these currents are irreversible and hence, according to the second law, they raise the total entropy of an isolated system.

Let us now imagine a hypothetical *time inversion* of such an event. The directions of the currents are now inverted. The gradients increase with time. The system is very simple; there are only currents and gradients in the system, and it is isolated from its surroundings. But its entropy is diminishing. As we know, such a circumstance is forbidden by the second law.

However, let us assume that under certain additional exotic conditions, such time inversion is still possible! We define just these currents (after time inversion) as syntropic currents, and the "exotic conditions" are precisely the syntropic conditions. The currents from thermodynamics of irreversible processes flow without the syntropic conditions, while the syntropic currents cannot flow without them; therefore, the syntropic currents are not exactly the time reversal of the above-mentioned irreversible currents. The syntropic conditions make the difference.

There are 5 syntropic conditions, and only if all of them are simultaneously fulfilled, then the birth of a syntropic current is anticipated. We shall survey these five conditions one by one.

Reading this chapter (about syntropic conditions) is difficult, and I apologize to the reader for it. After getting some first impression about these conditions, the reader who is interested more in the phenomenological aspect of nature rather than theory, is advised to skip over to chapter 3.

2.1. THE FIRST SYNTROPIC CONDITION:MAGNETIC FIELD

Suppose that a syntropic current is born inside our physical system. What kind of curious physical influences do the individual particles of matter feel, so that they respond with self-organization and order themselves into a syntropic current? They must surely get *information about this preferred direction of flow*. Namely, the symmetry properties of the result (here, the syntropic current) are related to the symmetry properties of the cause (here, the syntropic conditions) [14]. The particles must constantly receive this *information* (or for a better description, *vest*) because the irreversible (classical entropic) processes that want to extinguish the syntropic current are always present, and the source of *vest* should not exhaust itself if the current is to be syntropic. (Let us call such influences *syntropic influences*, and the currents of information *vest currents*.) It can be shown that only such influences are permitted where *the transport of information is not directly connected to the transport of energy*. Therefore, *syntropic influences are those influences that do not act via energy*. In modern physics, a possibility of such influences has been always overlooked or even neglected. But syntropic influences surely do exist. They are the very influences that are responsible for the internal organization of a quantum state. How can we see this? Let us imagine an experiment with two entangled quantum particles. Today we know that the *internal* information within this entangled quantum state travels instantaneously, much faster than the speed of light. If this information was bound to energy, then also energy would travel faster than light. But each energy has a mass, and mass cannot travel faster than light (in as much as we know today). Only *pure information* travels within an entangled quantum state, without energy and mass bound to it.

Can syntropic influences act upon quantum particles also from outside? Can we exert influence upon syntropic currents, and can we tell them in which direction to flow? Can we speak also about macroscopic *vest currents* which are responsible for the generation of syntropic currents? Let us try to express syntropic influence by classical (macroscopic) fields.

It is easy to see that *conservative* (*potential*) vector fields are not an allowed kind of syntropic information-giver (the electric field or the gravitational field are of this type). On the other hand, *selenoidal* vector fields are permitted (a magnetic field is of this type). Every vector field is either conservative or selenoidal (or a combination of these two) [15].

A magnetic field is a *temporally odd* physical quantity, while most of other physical fields are *temporally even*. This fact also plays an important role here; it can be shown that for the birth of a syntropic current, the syntropic influence upon the material particles should be temporally odd. (This argumentation is based upon temporal symmetry of physical influences: at the microscopic scale, the interactions between individual particles of matter are completely *reversible* [16]).

For this reason, the particles also cannot receive the syntropic information about the preferred direction from other types of space conformations. For instance, they cannot get it from the crystal structure (Certain crystals, the so-called *pyroelectric crystals*, have a preferred and oriented direction [17].). They also cannot get it from microscopic valves ("nanovalves") that would permit the particles to pass only in one direction [8].

2.2. THE SECOND SYNTROPIC CONDITION: CHIRAL STRUCTURE

This condition is based upon the symmetry properties of our physical space. The magnetic field is an *axial vector*, while the sought syntropic current is a *polar vector*. Mathematically, there are many possible ways of coupling between a polar and an axial vector, but we must leave aside all those possibilities where a third vector is involved (because only the vector of a magnetic field can have a syntropic influence upon the material particles). One option of coupling is left; multiplication of an axial vector with a *pseudoscalar* gives a co-linear polar vector. Pseudoscalar is, according to its space symmetry, an *alternating tensor of the third rank*. The influences of those space structures that mathematically can be described by a tensor, are syntropic under certain conditions (e.g., when averaged with respect to time).

When a pseudoscalar suffers a space inversion (e.g., by mirroring itself) it reverses its sign. Therefore, each space structure that can be assigned by a pseudoscalar property has a *left-handed* and a *right-handed* form. All such structures are said to be *chiral*. They can exist only in a three-dimensional space (not in two dimensions). Examples of such chiral structures are helices and screws (left-handed and right-handed). Chirality on the molecular scale is related to *optical activity*. All the amino-acids are chiral, and with them, all complex biomolecules. All living matter is chiral. Most *knots* (which can exist only in space) are chiral too. Chirality is *oriented space*; left-handed or right-handed space.

The action of a magnetic field upon chiral structures can manifest syntropic behavior. There are two possibilities; 1. The magnetic field itself has a chiral structure. In this case, the magnetic lines are helical or are woven into a knotted structure; and 2. The magnetic field acts upon a chiral structure of material particles. An interesting possibility is when the carriers of the (syntropic) current themselves are chiral (like optically active molecules, for instance).

When L. Pasteur was exploring *chirality*, he intuitively felt that it has some profound relation to life. He introduced an enigmatic quality *élan vital* (life-giving force) which is a feature of all chiral molecular structures. In fact, chirality is a condition for syntropic self-organization. It is in fact related to life.

2.3. THE THIRD SYNTROPIC CONDITION: ORIENTED TIME

This condition is based upon the symmetry properties of our physical time. The analysis of the influence of a magnetic field upon material particles (which eventually become the carriers of a syntropic current) shows that although magnetic phenomena include some inherent *timeness* (the magnetic field *reverses* if time is reversed, and so do the magnetic moments etc.) this is not enough, because the magnetic field itself is not rich enough in information concerning time. With syntropic phenomena, the complete *time structure* of the magnetic field should be temporally *asymmetric*.

This condition naturally restricts us to time-varying (especially oscillating) magnetic fields. But elementary types of oscillations are still temporally symmetric. Those that are not, are only those which yield a different *sequence of events* when they are read in the inverse direction of time.

The simplest recipe to discriminate time-oriented oscillations from those which are not oriented in time, is as follows: We make a recording of the magnetic field B dependent upon time t. Let this be our original B(t). We then make a copy of the original, which has the reversed direction of time. Let us call it B(-t). We then compare this copy B(-t) to the original B(t). If these two pictures show *inverse orientation of patterns*, then the magnetic field oscillation is oriented in time. The two patterns are usually inverse if each pattern is composed of *at least three different logically separable events*. More precisely, temporal orientation can be tested by *group theory*. Mathematically, the procedure here is slightly similar to finding, from a large amount of crystals belonging to numerous symmetry groups, those crystals that are space-oriented (chiral). In group theory, we replace one *primitive cell* of crystal lattice by *one period* of oscillation. One period should be composed of at least three different events.

Time-oriented oscillation is like a melody with a definite time orientation. Similarly, in the Western music tradition, *the basic tune* (event 1) usually grows first to *quarta* (event 2) and next to *quinta* (event 3), before returning to the basic tune again (so we have the sequence of events 1-2-3), but the melody does not sound so good if we have a quinta first and quarta following it (the sequence 1-3-2).

This condition therefore specifies something like musical rules of the magnetic field oscillations. I should say that *élan vital* comprises both chirality (*oriented space*) and time-oriented melody (*oriented time*).

2.4. THE FOURTH SYNTROPIC CONDITION: QUANTUM COHERENCE

The mutual *vest currents* between material quantum particles and the surrounding field structures have some interesting properties with regard to space-time symmetry of informational influences.

On the classical level, the influence of oriented time, when being passed on to particles (e.g., electrons), only goes through energy exchange. It exhausts the source of information-giver. This influence is not syntropic. (But the influence of oriented space can be syntropic). Those logically separable events which should confer orientation to time are so seriously separated that the direction of time cannot be read from them, except through energy exchange.

This matter is quite different *on the quantum level* - the influence of oriented time can be syntropic, because of temporal interconnectedness in the sequence of logical events. (Surely the influence of oriented space can be also syntropic on the quantum level). In the deepest sense, this means *an active exchange of space-time forms*, yet in absence of energy exchange! Infinitely small energies (in fact, zero-energies) can convey considerable amounts of information. This is an *amplification effect in active information* on the quantum level and can be compared to the amplification of weak radar waves that (through some complex equipment) orient the movement of a great ship [1].

If a particle is to receive some *vest current* of the complete space-time structure (which is here oriented); if the particle is to feel *vest* constantly in its own quantum state, then this state should be *coherent* over at least the span of one period in the chiral structure.

It should be coherent also in time, namely at least over one cycle of the magnetic field oscillation. But since the fifth syntropic condition speaks about temporal synchronicity, the condition of quantum coherence in time is automatically fulfilled when the condition of quantum coherence in space is fulfilled.

Simple (primitive) quantum states are only coherent over a very limited span of space (an atom, for instance). They cannot express some complex structure with orientation in space and time (at least outwardly they cannot express it).

But in the last few decades, we have become familiar with several very different types of quantum states which are far more complex in form. Among them are the states of *complex protein structures* (e.g., *microtubules* - possible biological quantum computers) and the states of *complex superconductive structures* (e.g., *meshes of superconductive knots* - possible artificial quantum computers). Such quantum states may be capable to manifest *vest* with oriented space and time. Then they can also fulfill the remainder of the syntropic conditions.

2.5. THE FIFTH SYNTROPIC CONDITION: TUNING   -UP

An active coupling between the source of temporally-oriented *vest* and manifested behavior of quantum particles is possible, when the frequency of quantum oscillations (of material particles) is *equal* to the frequency of the magnetic field oscillations. If this is not the case, these two quickly "get out of phase", out of *synchronization*, and hence out of their mutual quantum coherence.

Another possibility for coupling; the *multiples* of these two frequencies are equal. A similar situation is well known from music. Two different musical notes always comprise some *higher harmonics* that are approximately (apparently to our ear) equal.

The phenomena of quantum resonance are known in many structures with quantum coherence. The larger the scale of this quantum coherence is, the sharper the resonance frequency and various forms of the resonance effect are more pronounced [18].

To obey this syntropic condition, the frequency of a magnetic field should be *tuned-up* exactly, like the frequency of a musician playing his own instrument within an ensemble. Syntropic structures also resemble self-organized ensembles; there are magnetic fields, there are quantum particles ... and all must be perfectly in tune.

This perfect tuning is possible if there is some *positive amplification* between quantum oscillations and magnetic field oscillations (*positive feedback*). Such phenomena are then declared *non-linear*. With the modern theories of *chaos*, we are increasingly aware that they play a tremendously important role in the whole of nature [19] . We are meeting them now even at the *nanolevel* of quantum manifestations!

The elements in the chain with a positive feedback differ from case to case, it is a matter of the quantum state construction (conformation of quantum particles etc.). One possibility (chiral, time-oriented structures from non-radiating electromagnetic fields and charged particles) has already been described [20] .

3. SYNTROPIC PHENOMENA IN PROTEIN STRUCTURES

A syntropic system is every physical system (closed or open) in which all the five-syntropic conditions are fulfilled, and where syntropic phenomena take place consequently. Here I shall present a well-known system of this kind, so that we get some idea of how the theory outlined above works in practice. In nature, there are surely many other syntropic structures (in fact, an innumerable wealth of them), but we must start with one definite example.

We are going to look closer inside the *cells of living organisms*. It seems very probable that one type of syntropic systems can be found here!

Many protein structures in living cells display quite interesting electric phenomena. They show remarkable semiconducting properties (with a very great mobility of electric charge carriers) or even something similar to a weak superconductivity [21]. The quantum states of electric charge in these molecules are not localized to separate atoms, but rather they are spread to a large part of a biomolecule. They show the features of quantum coherence. Let us call these alocal electron states *Q states*. They dwell in protein structures.

Because of their semiconducting or superconducting nature, the Q states are very sensitive to the electric and magnetic fields (EM fields) that permeate the molecule. Where do these EM fields originate from? They are in a large part produced by the Q states themselves. This is why the frequency of an EM field is often the same as the frequency of Q states.

Like the protein molecules, Q states have a complicated space structure, with the same space symmetry as their host proteins, therefore they are also chiral (like proteins). The same holds true for the structure of the EM field produced by Q states.

At least four of the five-syntropic conditions can be fulfilled in Q states:

1. The electric charge of Q states is largely influenced by a magnetic field.
2. Q state is a chiral system.
   a. Q states are coherent over a large part of the chiral structure.
3. The frequency of the magnetic field is the same as the frequency of Q states.

Little is known about the remaining syntropic condition (#3). Is the magnetic flux oscillation oriented in time? EM structure is oriented in time if Q states are also oriented in time. Although at first sight, time-orientation does not seem to be a feature of primitive quantum states (which show no large-scale quantum coherence), this time-orientation has been proven to exist already in certain elementary particles (for instance, *mesons* K_{20}). So without any doubt, we can expect to find it in many coherent quantum states, for example, in many complex superconductive systems. We shall not go into detail here (a lot of mathematics would be needed to do that!) but we see no reason why complex Q states should not be oriented also in time, like they are oriented in space.

Now let us focus our attention to one peculiar example of protein structure in question, namely *microtubules*. These tiny tubular structures have *helical* arrangement of the building blocks. This is a chiral structure *par excellence*. In the interior, the microtubules appear to be filled with pure water [2].

It seems very probable that microwave EM radiation is trapped inside this interior [22]. This EM field is probably highly ordered; its rich internal structure need not be dissipated [20]. Pure water carries the EM radiation practically without any attenuation. This radiation is in a strong correspondence to Q states in microtubule walls and in the water inside. These Q states show very unusual electromagnetic properties. Coherent quantum states can be formed by a water dipole structure [11]. In a thin layer of water molecules adhering to the inner wall of the microtubule, the Q states are chiral. But Q states are not only in water, they protrude into the interior of the microtubular structure. They are connected to that interesting electron which is lying between the a - and b -tubuline. Through it, EM fields and Q states can act upon manipulation of biomolecules in the living cells.

So the biochemical processes in the vicinity of microtubules are very sensitive to *vest* in both Q states and in EM radiation inside the microtubules. But this radiation also travels through the microtubules all along their length. Consequently, *vest* in the whole living cell is completely coherent. A living cell is interwoven with coherent quantum states that provide for *quantum informational networks*.

When all the five-syntropic conditions are fulfilled in microtubules, syntropic self-organization phenomena can start in the cells of living organisms. As it was stressed in the introductory paragraphs, this self-organization may be very different from self-organization in Prigogine's dissipative structures or in Maturana's autopoietic structures. It may evade the second law of thermodynamics. The total entropy of an isolated physical system may diminish with time, just the reverse to what is known in classical irreversible processes. This situation puts everything into a totally new light, so the importance of this difference cannot be overemphasized.

Let us look at this fact in some more detail. Let us take a living cell that is about to undergo cell-division (*mitosis*). Let us enclose this cell in a tiny box. Let us assume that the walls of this box do not allow any exchange of energy or of matter with the surroundings. The cell is therefore isolated. There is not even an exchange of heat with the surroundings.

Now *mitosis* starts to take place. The microtubules play a very important role during cell division. For example, they pull the genes apart into something that will become two new nuclei. Eventually we have two cells instead of one. It is not necessary that these two cells are identical. A differentiation is possible, like in the early stages of embryo development, for instance.

Then the new system (two cells) is more structured than the original system (one cell). Is the entropy of this new system smaller than the entropy of the original system? The answer is not straightforward. We know many examples where a system develops to a more structured state yet increases its entropy. For instance, such as in the case of the growth of a crystal in an oversaturated liquid. Let us assume that such crystal growth also takes place in an insulated box. Growth of a crystal from oversaturated liquid is a classical irreversible process. Nothing mysterious is here. At the end of the crystal growth, the entropy of the complete system is greater than at the beginning.

But biological processes are very different from simple crystal growth. One big difference is that protein folding is not governed merely by energy changes. A stable protein conformation and an unstable protein conformation can have practically the same energy level [23]. Nobody knows yet why one conformation is stable and another is unstable, why the process of protein folding goes quickly towards a biologically active conformation and not towards an inactive one (which would be, from the standpoint of energy level, just equally favorable). This is very different from simple crystal growth. The growth of internal structure in living matter does not obviously go on the expense of energy exchanges, but rather, as it was stated at the beginning, it may be a manifestation of *vest* in syntropic quantum states.

Maybe very careful measurements of minute energy exchanges (changes in chemical energy, minute heat transport, etc.) could tell us whether the process of *mitosis* still obeys the classical thermodynamics. However, one can hardly expect an orthodox outcome of such an experiment. Life processes are continually expressing wonderful self-originating order. Most probably this order is only partially fed on classical dissipative mechanisms. Those more subtle levels of biological processes are probably led by syntropic phenomena.

REFERENCES

[1] D.Bohm, B.Hiley, The Undivided Universe (Routledge, 1993)

[2] R.Penrose, Shadows of the Mind (Oxford University Press, 1994)

[3] R.Turton, The Quantum Dot (Freeman Spectrum, 1995)

[4] J.Sarfatti, Beyond the Quantum (http://www.hia.com/hia/pcr/vigier/pqm1.html)

[5] I.Prigogine, I.Stengers, Order out of Chaos (Bantam, 1984)

[6] H.Maturana, F.Varela, Autopoiesis and Cognition (D.Reidel, Dordrecht, Holland, 1980)

[7] J.Ford, What is chaos, that we should be mindful of it? (included in : The New Physics, ed. P.Davies, Cambridge Un. Press, 1989, pp.348 ff)

[8] N.Wiener, Cybernetics or Control and Communication in the Animal and the Machine, Wiley 1948

[9] A.Aspect, P.Grangier, G.Roger, Experimental realization of Einstein-Poldolsky-Rosen-Bohm *Gedankenexperiment* : A new violation of Bell's inequalities, Phys Rev. Lett. 48 (1982) 91-4

[10] J.Rozic, private communication. I hope that he soon publishes his very interesting observations.

[11] M.Jibu, K.Yasue, Quantum brain dynamics and consciousness (John Benjamins, 1995)

[12] A.Szent-Gyorgy, his works on catabolic processes

[13] S.R.de Groot, Thermodynamics of Irreversible Processes (North Holland, 1963)

[14] This is a known von Neumann's postulation.

[15] I.N.Bronstein, K.A.Semendiaev, Mathematical Handbook, part 5/II/16, (Nauka, Moscow 1990)

[16] Lars Onsager, his known argumentations on the *detailed equilibrium*

[17] J.F.Nye, Physical Properties of Crystals, Oxford 1957

[18] An interesting example is in : S.Shapiro, Phys.Rev.Lett. 11 (1963) 80.

[19] J.Gleick, Chaos, Penguin 1987

[20] A.Detela, Biopolje : Reprezentacija z informacijsko in evolucijsko komponento, Zbornik Tretji slovenski forum kognitivnih znanosti, 1997. Reprinted in this book, just as also a short English version: Biofield (informational and evolutionary component).

[21] F.W.Cope, Phys.Chemistry & Physics 10 (1978) 233, 11 (1979) 65, 13 (1981) 99, 467

[22] I.Jerman, Osnove spoznavanja v luci nove biologije, Casopis za kritko znanosti 176 (1995) p. 141 ff

[23] R.Rosen, Some epistemological issues in physics and biology (in : Quantum Implications, Routledge 1987).

(Prepared for the 4th Slovene conference on cognitive sciences, autumn 1998)

GLOSSARY
DEFINITION OF TERMS & SUPPLEMENTARY NOTES

Action At A Distance: The existence of a causal correlation between a distant source/cause, and a local effect resulting in an action occurring in a local 3 dimensional space system. No separate local cause exists, or is detected, in 3-dimensional space.

Active Information: Information that is available everywhere (as in nonlocally) or to every part of a system, yet is 'acted upon' or relevant only where it has meaning. This concept implies a relationship between giver & receiver. Information is derived from the word *in-from* – meaning to literally express by form. A resonant response is a response to *active information.*

Aharanov-Bohm Effect: A quantum mechanical effect that demonstrates that electromagnetic potentials, rather than electromagnetic fields, are fundamental quantities. Electromagnetic fields are derived from the electromagnetic potentials. The potentials are the scalar, hyperspatial, higher dimensional entities that connect us to hyperspace, the vacuum, and subtle realm.

Alan Aspect: See *Aspect experiment.*

Antiparticle: A particle of antimatter carrying an opposite electric charge of its matter counterpart. Each elementary particle of our material world is known to have a corollary or counterpart particle in the antimatter world.

Artificial Potential: A polarization of the local vacuum that places specific wave patterns within it.

Aspect Experiment: A landmark experiment in Physics conducted by Alan Aspect in 1982 that demonstrated that two photons remained nonlocally connected as they traveled away from each other. This experiment established quantum *non-locality*. Nicolus Gisin et al recently repeated similar experiments at the University of Geneva. The results were more dramatic in that the observed separation distances were much greater. The conclusions were that even if detectors were separated at opposite ends of the Universe, the results would be the same! These experiments demonstrate and validate that *non-locality* is a property of the Cosmos.

Awareness: Connected to the currents of the mind/body system growing in alignment, calibration, & synchronous relationship with the principal 'whole-being' Consciousness axis. Growing in awareness is growing within, & expanding, this relationship. One can consider that there are minimum configured alignments & balanced states that allow for ongoing & continued 'awakening' of higher levels of awareness. See *calibration.*

Back-Action: A term coined by Sarfatti describing the interplay between mind and the world of matter and fields. See *self-reference.*

Balance: (I) Noun. This notion is best understood by asking what is the "state" of balance? Therefore it is many things. On one hand, balance is a state of equilibrium. In another view, the systems that transform subtle energy into electromagnetic energy, and the systems that encode and decode instructions for physical manifestation are operating at their optimum level. The interrelatedness of the various "components" that make up an energetic structure move toward a state of consonance, whereat if the sounds were heard, it would be the music of the spheres in true Harmony. Life energies flow, experiencing a state of optimum health, and the joy of fulfillment. More specifically, balance is connected to the currents of the mind/body system growing in alignment, calibration, & synchronous relationship with the principal 'whole-being' Consciousness axis. (2) Noun. The condition of balance, in terms of energy, means that your energy fields and energy centers are open to the optimal flow of energies in and out of your system, as you interact with other people and with your environment. Being out of balance is a condition where the energies of the body are out of phase to a point where their natural and graceful of flow is impeded. Dis-ease is the result of an out-of-balance condition. Dis-ease may manifest as a physical ailment if the imbalance is allowed to continue for any length of time. (Greenia, "*Energy Dyanamics*"). (3) Verb. To work with the body's energy fields and fibers to bring about a state of optimal health, equilibrium and energy flow.

Biofield: A hyperfield of a living system. Carries the patterns or blueprints that guide fundamental organization into the formation of the physical biological systems. Woven from light. The biofield is a primary field & is the basis for self-organizing processes in living systems. See also *morphogenetic*.

Bio-Photon: A light particle generated and emitted by a living system. In living systems bio-photons are associated with DNA. They are also aspects of the human energy field. The photon is the basic quantum of the electromagnetic field. Motoyama has determined that the more active & balanced a chakra, the more photons are emitted from that chakra.

Bio-Photonic Prism: A term coined in this text to describe a multidimensional lattice structure that traps, stores or accumulates, translates, or emits light. Such a structure interacts with the living system, as well as the outside universe. Evolutionary process leads to modification and increases the complexity of these devices. Information is stored, accessed, translated and encoded within its structure. By tuning the interdimensional nodal points of these structures, energies can easily communicate across vibrational planes. Such structures interact & relate to physical counterparts.

Bohm, David: An English physicist who made substantial contributions to the problems of interpretation in the field of quantum mechanics. Bohm's interpretations gave us the concept of the Holographic Universe. Bohm's work advocates that a Non-Separability of matter and Consciousness is one of the realities of this Universe. Everything exists as one united and connected Whole. An unseen, or Implicate order, underlies the unfolding of reality in our physical world.

Brain Surface Area: The human brain has a high ratio of surface area to volume. The surface contains *charge*. Increasing charge utilizes more of the brain's surface area and potential. The human nervous system operates at a very high electrical potential. Increasing the brain's charge results in more 'surplus' electromagnetic energy becoming available for higher brain function e.g. multi-dimensional circuits & hyperfunctions. Activating unused brain surface area (i.e. brain cells) is simply exercised through acts of consciousness.

Calibration: A process of establishing minimum, or threshold, symmetries within a system, bringing it into alignment & harmony with its central axis. Such a process may occur through the symmetric internal or external balancing of the centers. During the process of calibration, certain patterns become stabilized within the centers, bringing a harmonious relationship or alignment between all aspects of mental, emotional, psychic, subtle, and spiritual energies. Establishing harmonic symmetries results in internal adjustments to the centers that activate its latent, or undeveloped, potential. This is the "flowering" process. The objective of calibration is to seek and establish alignment with the whole-being consciousness axis. This is the process of growth & expansion of *awareness*, & merging of the spiritual potential within the biology. The attainment of stable and balanced states is required at each level of the calibration process. We are connected to the currents of the mind/body system growing in alignment, calibration, and synchronous relationship with the principal "whole-being" Consciousness axis. A "calibrated" system implies that the necessary "tuning" has taken place and that there is an established harmony between the interrelated patterns. Balance then becomes a natural consequence.

Charge: Everything carries a charge. Charge equals flow. In regards to a fundamental particle, charge is related to the emission and absorption activity of virtual particles. This virtual activity constitutes clouds of patterns that surround particles. Altering this activity may alter the magnitude of charge. A charged particle, a magnetic pole, or a potential, are all versions of special devices that break the symmetry of the vacuum through the emission and absorption activity that they entail. Under this understanding, all mass objects, irrespective of size, are charged. Everything carries a charge. A charged system or particle has energy continuously flowing through it. Increasing the flow increases the charge. Electromagnetic systems are charged, and by definition are *open systems*. They are in constant interaction with the external environment, and they are also linked to virtual reality states. (2) Verb. In regards to torsion fields, to *charge* means to influence, alter, or imprint with a pattern of information.

Chi: Flowing potential energy of life. Also known by dozens of other names throughout different cultures, e.g. qi, ki (Japan), orgone (Reich), prana (India), bioenergy, mana, life force, oki (Huron), Ntu (Bantu), Orenda (Iroquois), biomagnetism, subtle energy, sila (Inuit), Tane (Hawaii), Ankh (Ancient Egypt), Wakan (Lakota), Ton (Dakota), Manitou (Algonquin), etc.

Chi Kung: (pronounced "Chee Gong") Also known as Qi Gong. Chi Kung consists of techniques for dealing with the human energy flows. In utilizing Chi Kung techniques, one employs the use of the human body's chakras and meridians and energy fields. In the view of Chinese medicine, many illnesses are caused by blockages in the energy flow channels. (See also *Tai Chi*).

Chiral, Chirality: Consisting of a 'handedness', right or left version- where one image is not the mirror image of the other.

Coherence: Existence of definite in-step phase relationships between separate waves, patterns, or systems. Coherence allows for interference effects, information transfer, & amplification of signal to take place.

Collapse Of The Wave Function: Action upon a quantum system of all quantum probabilities that determines the selection of one definite and probable outcome to be selected. This outcome becomes manifest in physical reality. Consciousness plays the role of specific and final selection. Consciousness is the agent that collapses the wave function to materialize an event in our physical world.

Crystalline Structures: Geometric forms that may become ordered or aligned to create lattices. Geometric forms may take on varied shapes. Principle geometric forms are the tetrahedron, octahedron, icosahedrons, and dodecahedron. Many primitive ocean life-forms are pure geometric forms. Viruses are geometric configurations with related light wave configurations that could be used to destroy them- eliminating disease. The human energy field consists of a multitude of crystalline structures forming lattices. Certain geometric forms are said to be directly linked to human consciousness. Levels of consciousness relate to alternate or evolving geometric configurations. Crystalline describes a structure of geometric form, developing to perfection. Crystalline (meaning *of crystals*) properties include external form, internal ordering, color, luminescence, fluorescence, phosphorescence, as well as the electrical properties of piezoelectricity, pyroelectricity, and magnetism.

Dimension: An arbitrary coordinate system used to define any range of properties of a vibrational plane. These properties may be scalars, vectors, symbols, tensors, or the flow or exchange of energy. Dimensions do exist outside of what we know as space and time. Modern day Superstring theory of physics incorporates as many as 26 dimensions. Frequency, phase, and amplitude are characteristics that define dimensions within hyperspace.

Dimensioning: A term used by Bearden to describe [deliberately] forming a pattern or template within the virtual photon flux of the vacuum or the virtual photon flux of the scalar potential. A carrier in the vacuum can transport this pattern or template. The quantum potential can also be dimensioned, meaning that the *vacuum engines* that result are instantly transmitted to distant points, acting upon the distant receiver. According to Bearden, the scalar potential can be engineered to access higher orders of dimensional space, i.e. the 5th, 6th, 7th dimensions and beyond, and thus is the origin of the term *dimensioning*. Accessing a higher dimensional space through the scalar potential can alter all levels of "dimensionally" below it. (See *vacuum engine*).

Dipole: A broken symmetry in the vacuum caused by two dissimilar charges [magnetic or electric], resulting in the potential extraction of virtual [free] energy from the vacuum.

Dis-ease: Vibration out of harmony with the whole. A state of separation & fear.

DNA: (*deoxyribonucleic acid*). Organic material within the cell that is now well known as the carrier of the genetic & hereditary material of the living organism. A helical structure, with similar helical structure counterparts found within the biofield enabling communication. DNA is interactive with light, both storing energy derived from photons (quanta of light) & emitting bio-photons. Research has confirmed that chi emission (universal energy from the human being), sound (human voice & music), sound modulated light waves [laser], radio signals [e.g. cellular telephone frequency- not good] conscious INTENT & EMOTION (*Energy in Motion*) can alter or modify the properties & functions of DNA. DNA has natural or resonant frequencies. Matching these can activate, or trigger, its innate functions [i.e. create an exchange of information]. Play the appropriate musical chord, & DNA will sing back to you. These relate to patterns of specific geometry or form. In more generalized notions, DNA is now being considered as a link to decoding or translating information form various universal 'fields' that exist outside space & time. [e.g. morphogenetic, biofield, subtle, cosmic, etc. change the primary fields, & physical reality changes.] This makes DNA a hyperspatial inter-dimensional bridge between normal third-dimensional reality and the unseen reality.

In the exchange of light, in & out of the cell, a universal language of its own would be at play- a 'light based' language. DNA, accordingly, possess the internal 'alphabet' [symbol codes] that translates or decodes outside information into meaningful inner purpose. DNA is considered to be a superconductor (permitting flow without resistance)- flowing light essentially- providing a source of 'electricity'. This property can be enhanced with certain natural atomic elements being present (ORME's) within the cell, & maximized with the cell being free of foreign or 'toxic' substances that degrade its function. Only about 5% of DNA is observed to be active. The remaining 95% may be linked to more evolved hyperfunctions of the brain, & the display of unusual abilities. The geometric configuration of DNA has been given as being resonantly equivalent to the geometry of the global human energy field, & to the geometry of the various electromagnetic & hyperspatial fields that surround the Earth. In such a case, a resonance, or exchange of information- communication, exists between DNA, the human energy field, & the planet. There exist a holographic, fractal, or self-similar inter-related connectedness in these configurations. Consider these to be harmonic relationships between light, sound, & geometry. Altering any aspects of the part, affects the whole. A change to the whole is reflected in any of the parts. Human energy field interactions are one means of altering the whole, and its parts!

Einstein-Rosen Bridge: A region in space, or tunnel, characterized by the shape of a tube with trumpet-like ends that connects one region of reality to another. These regions may be distinct dimensional realities, or distinct points of space-time. A chakra can be characterized as an Einstein-Rosen bridge. An Einstein-Rosen bridge may exist on both microscopic and macroscopic scales. (See *wormhole*)

Electromagnetic Field: (EMF) (I) The externalized structure of an organized reality originating in higher space defined by scalar potentials and patterned substructures. An organized construct formed by the interference of two or more scalar potentials. A field is an organized region of influence. Typically a place to store energy. Electromagnetic systems are open systems, in exchange and communication with the virtual particle flux of the vacuum. Electromagnetic fields are characterized by electric and magnetic vectors. The electromagnetic field is the first hyperfield. (2) In general terms, the vibrational energy patterns emitted from, or surrounding, electrical energy sources. There are a wide variety of electromagnetic fields, ranging the entirety of the electromagnetic spectrum. (See also *electromagnetic spectrum*).

Electromagnetic Radiation: The energy associated and carried by an electromagnetic wave.

Electromagnetic Spectrum: An ordering or arrangement of light, or electromagnetic waves, according to its properties of frequency, wavelength, energy, or some other property. The spectrum spans a range of frequencies from extremely low to extremely high. These include radio waves & visible light, microwaves, X-ray, gamma ray, ultraviolet & infrared.

Electromagnetic Wave: In three-dimensional space, wave-like disturbance characterized by an electric and magnetic vector at right angles to each other- both 90 degrees to the direction of propagation. Electromagnetic waves have hidden substructures that occupy other dimensional space. The substructure can be patterned and programmed with enfolded or hidden information. Electromagnetic waves form three-dimensional spherical wave structures, and an infinite amount of these structures can fit into hyperspace at the same space, and at the same time. See *hyperspace*.

Electromagnetics Of The lst Order: The real component of electromagnetic waves traveling at the speed of light and producing observable signals in physical space.

Electromagnetics Of The 2nd Order: Hyperspatial or 'imaginary' electromagnetic wave components that do not reflect observable signals in the 3-dimensional space. These are longitudinal 'scalar' waves travelling at superluminal speeds. There can be *psychoactive* effects to these waves.

Electromagnetics Of The 3rd Order: Hyperspatial potential that simultaneously affects all the space-time continuum. These travel at infinite speed. Solitons, *Neutrinic* waves, as well as *Tackyon* (takyon) waves enter this category. *Tackyons reportedly respond to consciousness*. There can be *psychoactive* effects to these waves.

Electrostatic Potential: The scalar potential that is the driving force to purely electrical phenomena. The potential is an ordering within the vacuum.

Elementary Particle: Any constituent building block of sub-atomic particles such as the electron, proton, or neutron. Elementary particles have internal or higher dimensional virtual realities.

EMF: (See *electromagnetic field*).

EMF Balancing Technique®: A process of resonant tuning of the (*personal*) Universal Calibration Lattice ("UCL") through the human-to-human connection. The EMF Balancing Technique® was originated and developed by Peggy Phoenix Dubro. It is a new energy system, which accelerates the integration of Spirit and biology.

Energetic Body Preparation: In performing the EMF Balancing Technique®, the preliminary preparation process is called the Energetic Body Prep. It involves series of movements and intents offered by the practitioner, and begins a grand circulation of energy through the UCL. In a sense, the practitioner sets up a resonance with the movements of the procedure, and the client responds accordingly on an electromagnetic level. With the energy now moving more freely through the UCL, the practitioner continues with the rest of the EMF session, delivering whatever Phase is appropriate for the client at that time.

Energy Flux: The passage of any form of energy through any defined unit area omnidirectionally (in all directions). This definition also relates to dimensional communication, transport and translation of energy.

Energy: Physicists know a great deal <u>about</u> energy. What energy actually <u>is</u> remains quite illusive. Is energy ultimately pure potential? Thought requires energy. Is energy a manifestation of consciousness in various forms? Generally, energy is conceived as 'ability to do work' or produce change. Energy is understood as a manifestation of the principle of <u>action</u>. Action is energy times time (energy X time), and action is mediated by the interaction of the photon with matter. (see *light* & *photon*)

Entanglement: The phase locking of two or more particles that produce correlations outside what is normally expected by *locality*.

Entrain: "To get in sync', to bring the pulsations of different systems together. These could be brain waves, heartbeats, etc. To cause to resonate or vibrate at that frequency. A classic example is that of a wall full of pendulum clocks. A grouping of clocks is set to swing randomly. In time, left on their own, they all come to swing together- in 'sync'. Not all entrainment to the human system is positive. For example, if a cellular telephone frequency entrains the brain or DNA at the cellular frequency, it lowers the brain's (& DNA's) capacity to function at its highest potential within its natural rhythm. See *resonance* & *sympathetic vibration*.

Entropy: The measure of the amount of disorder, randomness, or loss of information within a system. Generally connected to concept of steady deterioration within system. In a conventional context, it has for a long time been believed that entropy always increases within systems, and cannot be reversed. In recent years, this concept has been proven inaccurate. Reverse entropy, or syntropic [negentropic] phenomena, are clearly demonstrated within intelligent states from grouping of electrons to complex biological systems.

Evoked Potential: A measurable electrophysicological response produced in the brain due to some sensory, or para-sensory, stimulus.

Explicate Order: A term coined by the late Dr. David Bohm, physicist, to characterize the external, visible universe. The external universe unfolds from the wholeness and connectedness of the *implicate order*. The explicate order is in a constant exchange and interaction with the implicate order. Bohm used the term holomovement to describe the interactive process of the explicate order unfolding from within the implicate order. The external universe unfolds from the wholeness and connectedness that are characteristic of the implicate order. Consequently, the properties of wholeness and connectedness are inherent to the explicate order, or external universe.

Falun Dafa or Falun Gong: A modern day Chinese physical and mental discipline, that is similar to Chi Kung exercise movement. The practice of *Falun Dafa* helps develop an increased awareness of the subtle life force energies ("Chi") of the earth and the body. This practice accelerates the awareness & development of the multi-dimensional nature of the human energy fields.

Faraday Cage: A metallic enclosure that blocks, and provides insulation from, conventional electromagnetic fields. A Faraday cage is unable to block hyperspatial, scalar wave, or torsion field phenomena.

Frequency: The number of complete cycles that a wave undergoes in a second. The first dimension of *hyperspace*. Note how virtually an infinite number of electromagnetic broadcast frequencies (radio, Television, Cellular Telephone, etc.) occupy the same 'space'. Information is carried within each individual wavelength, and is distinct from every other carrier. Tuning into a particular frequency creates separation of information. The empty space within which broadcast occurs is hyperspace. The electromagnetic field is the first hyperfield.

Gingerg-Zylberbaum Experiment: A landmark experiment conducted between two individuals by Mexican neurophysiologist Gingerg-Zylberbaum that established the *non-local nature* of the mind/brain systems in the human to human connection. In this experiment two subjects were in non-local communication as evidenced by the transfer of a brain wave pattern between the subjects. This transfer took place despite the electromagnetic shielding of the two subjects. Each individual was placed in a Faraday cage (see *Faraday Cage*), that shields against electromagnetic radiation or signals. The non-local connection was created in hyperspace. The experiment showed that interaction in hyperspace, such as through scalar wave or torsion fields, cannot be shielded by a Faraday Cage.

Harmonic: In simplest terms, harmonic is defined as an integer multiple of a fundamental frequency. In music, these are called overtones. In music and voice, it is the mix of harmonics that create the distinction or flavor of a particular instrument or voice. The fundamental or basic frequency sustains a form of standing wave resonance. Theoretically, there are an infinite number of harmonics related to any fundamental frequency. In geometry, a specific form may carry a harmonic relationship to other geometric shapes. Harmonic frequencies can superpose, or add up, to form new geometric structures. Harmonics exist everywhere, from atoms to planetary systems. Given the unique mix of harmonics or chords within the vibrations of every individual, we can say that each person has their own unique tone.

Harmonic Relationships: Systems favor harmonic relationships. Harmonic relationships can exists between geometric forms, as well as between frequency patterns and form. For example, a harmonic relationship exists between the frequency of light, sound, and geometry. What may appear as dissimilar entities may contain hidden harmonic relationships. Harmonic relationships lend themselves to tuning and resonance.

Harmony: Relates to two or more systems undergoing simultaneous vibrations. The harmonics of the vibrations do not produce any discords. Complete concordance. The greater the harmony, the less the energy requirement to produce sympathetic vibrations. At oneness.

Healing: To make whole, to restore to original integrity. Harmonize vibration. To eliminate states of separation & fear within one's being.

Hertz: A unit of measure meaning "cycles-per-second." Hertz is the measure of the number of times per second that a wave passes a given point. KiloHertz (KHz) is an abbreviation for "thousands of cycles per second". MegaHertz (MHz) is "millions of cycles per second," and "Gigahertz" is "billions of cycles per second."

Hertzian Wave: A term used for electromagnetic radiation characterized by a cyclical, sinusoidal wave form. Not all electromagnetic waves are Hertzian in nature.

Hologram: An encoded construct within which any part of it contains the information of the whole. A construct that encodes all the properties of the interference patterns that creates the hologram. Each part carries the same significance as the whole. An alternate view is a structure within which every point is in contact with every other point. Hyperspatial phenomena possess properties of the hologram- they reflect patterns of the whole. The human energy field is a hologram. We live in a cosmic hologram. Note how a beam of light within the universe, no matter how small, contains all the information of the universe. Imagine capturing this light with a camera with smaller and smaller aperture setting, yet continuing to obtain the same information! Even one photon of light contains the information of the whole universe!

Holographic Universe: The view that the Universe is like a holographic image- that there are holographic interference patterns existing everywhere in space. Originating with the late great Physicist David Bohm, this concept explains much of our new view of reality. This has gained growing support amongst the scientific community. The physical universe is a projection of holographic interference patterns that originate from a higher, or *implicate*, hidden reality. Holographic structures are defined by their own unique wavelength. Structures outside of the tuning range of our physical bodies are undetectable to us! In other words, the vibrations or frequencies that we can tune into define our reality!

Holomovement: A term coined by Bohm to describe the ongoing unfolding of the external world from its source within the unseen *implicate* hidden order. The *implicate order* is a higher dimensional reality. Holo is derived from the word holograph. Bohm understood that the physical world is a moving, living holographic projection of the *implicate* order. The holographic nature of our reality interconnects everything- living & non-living.

Homeopathy: The applied art of healing based on the principles *of dimensioned potentials* that contain *vacuum engines*. The transference of patterns without chemical residue.

Human Energy Field Interactions: A means of accelerating the transformation and evolution of the individual as well as the collective.

Hyperchannel: A communication channel between frames in hyperspace. These channels allow for scalar wave energies to circulate or 'crosstalk'. *See Interdimensional Nodal Point*, also known as *magic window*.

Hyperfield: A structure or disturbance pattern in hyperspace. Bearden describes the electromagnetic field as the first hyperfield. The next is the neutrinic field, followed by mental or mind field. Hyperfields represent higher levels of nested virtual states.

Hyperfunction: Relating to, or manifesting capabilities, or possessing attributes, of interacting with hyperspace. Capable of bridging the seen & unseen worlds. Abilities outside normal space & time. A higher dimensional capacity.

Hypersonic Waves: Sounds waves in hyperspace.

Hyperspace: Dimension(s) beyond ordinary three-dimensional space and time. In hyperspace there is no time or space- all actions and activities are instantaneous. Mathematically, hyperspace is a space that can contain two or more three dimensional volumes in the same place, and at the same time. Frequency, phase, and amplitude are amongst the characteristics that define dimensions within hyperspace.

Hyperspatial: Relating to a hyperspace dimension, beyond ordinary 4-dimensional space-time.

Ilness/Pain: Vibration out of harmony with the whole.

Implicate Order: A term coined by the late physicist, David Bohm, to characterize the hidden, or enfolded, order of a higher reality. The external universe unfolds from the wholeness and connectedness that are characteristic of the implicate order. The implicate order is a sub-quantum state.

Inception: See *kindling*.

Infrared radiation: Below the red (longer wavelength) - light of frequency less than visible light. Relating to the infrared portion of the electromagnetic spectrum. Invisible (light) radiation of wavelengths in the range of 750 nanometers (near visible red) to I millimeter (microwaves).

Intent: Intent is considered to be a real meta-physical force- a force beyond measurable orthodox physics. Intent acts to influence, alter, shape, modify, or create the 'information' fields & patterns that organize & shape our reality.

Intentionality: We adapt Tiller's perspective in describing applied Intentionality as a process that begins with the placing of a desire at the level of 'Spirit'. This desire, imprinted with Spirit, creates patterns within successive vibrational planes in order that actions ultimately materialize at the physical level. The individual is an active player in the process, and is the observer/participant of the end results.

Interdimensional Nodal Point: Synonymous terms are *magic window* or *hyperchannel*. Bearden describes these as frequency dependent, and the naturally tuned frequency of a hyperchannel. At the natural frequency of the hyperchannel, scalar wave energies can crosstalk or communicate easily between separate frames of hyperspace. According to Bearden, these frequencies represent enhanced channels connecting virtual and observable states [between sub-quantal and quantal states]. Some of these noted frequencies are the infrared and near ultraviolet [life energy frequency]. The ultraviolet is actually the first harmonic of the infrared. Other frequencies for hyperchannels are 38-40 kHz, I50-I60 kHz., I.I-I.3MHz., I.057 GHz. (Lamb shift).

Interference Pattern: Waves of distinct origins intertwine and overlap to form unique patterns. The pattern results in reinforcement in some places, and cancellation in others due to the superposition of two or more waves. Interference patterns create new form and geometry that transcend multiple layers of virtual reality.

Interferometer: An instrument in which a wave is split into two beams, and after travelling different paths are subsequently reunited forming interference patterns.

Kindling or Inception: A term used by Bearden to describe the collecting and condensing of subtle energies into virtual photons or matter. This action couples scalar wave patterns to a living system or object. Activated from the mind field, the kindling process is a cumulative integrative process. As a virtual state pattern is integrated (energy accumulated), it eventually breaches the quantum threshold and becomes a real physical observable event.

Laser: (*Light Amplification by Stimulated Emission of Radiation*)   A device that produces light of one frequency, or wavelength, in which all the photons are in step producing a coherent beam. In such an instance there is a <u>multiplying</u> effect of the strength of the individual waves- e.g. 2 waves superposes to create 4 times the amplitude, 3 waves superpose to create 9 times the amplitude. Laser light is a macroscopic quantum effect. (see *phase relationship*)

Lattice Structure of Vacuum: See *Vacuum lattice structure*.

Lattice: An ordering, arrangement, or periodic structure in two or more dimensions- characterized by unique geometric forms or relationships. In our discussion, a lattice is also a part of a multi-dimensional network. The nodes of a lattice structure become the connectors, or hyperchannels, and the transducers of one type of energy to another. (see *crystalline*)

Light Quotient: A measure of the ability to interact with, process & utilize, light.

Light: A ripple of the 5th dimension. Connects matter to higher dimensional space, because matter is in continuous interaction with photons (see *photons & matter*). An oscillation both in, and out, of time. Generally, visible light is the electromagnetic radiation in the range 400 (violet) to about 800 (red) nanometers. Not all light photons are visible. The light photon is the messenger of the electromagnetic field- the transported & carrier of information. Light carries a hyperspatial substructure- outside space & time. Exhibits wave & particle duality because it straddles physical & hyperspatial dimensions simultaneously. The carrier of bioenergy of living organisms. The brain & nervous system communicate through a light-based transmission system. Biological living things communicate through biophotons. A component of light cannot be shielded with metal screens, because such a component is hyperspatial- traveling outside our 'space-time'. The 'fabric' of the webs that create the human energy field, forming a space-time lattice. Light is harmonically related to sound & geometric form. Light is the constituent of matter. The carrier of neutrinic waves (see *neutrinic wave*). White light carries all colors. Light carries holographic encoded information of the entire universe.

Locality: The notion that interactions and communication between objects or living things occurs through a mechanism of fields or signals that propagate through space-time. The propagation obeys a speed of light limitation. Local interactions leave observable or measurable traces or signals in 3-dimensional space.

Macroscopic Quantum Effects: Phenomena that are visible on human scale, but fail to be fully described and explained by classical physics. Examples include the large scale coherence of lasers, superconductivity, and superfluidity.

Magic Window: See *Interdimensional Nodal Point*, also known as *hyperchannel*.

Magnetic Lines of Force: The result of forming coherent patterns of helical, *hypersonic* waves.

Magnetostatic Potential: The scalar potential attributed to the formation of the magnetic pole and its attendant field.

Magnetic Vector Potential: Generally, a mathematical entity of electromagnetism that defines the nature of the magnetic field. However, the magnetic potential is a real field, and may be separated from the magnetic field. The causative agents of electromagnetic phenomena are the potentials that create the forcefields. Tiller uses the magnetic vector potential as the connector between the physical domain and the subtle domain.

Magnon: A magnetic monopole particle proposed by Tiller to exist in the etheric/subtle/vacuum, realm. It is the pilotwave supplying instructions and guidance to the electron.

Many Worlds: Physicist Hugh Everett has suggested that, according to quantum theory interpretation, a separate world exists for each possible outcome of an event. The implication is that an infinite number of universes, or parallel world, exists. Links exists between these universes through a complex network. The implication is that our local world has multiple copies of itself! Note that the electromagnetic field and the molecular field are parallel universes separated by the speed of light!

Mass: *see matter*

Montessori Education: An educational approach for young children originating with Dr. Marie Montessori. This approach honors the individual & unique needs of our "*Indigo*" children.

Matter: Frozen light- slowed down energy. Standing Scalar wave resonance. Diluted vacuum state. The energy of matter is derived from the vacuum, but its density is significantly less than the vacuum state (see *vacuum*). Matter is in continual interaction with photons (light). There is ongoing absorption & emission of photons. Accordingly, matter is continuously connecting & disconnecting with the 4th dimension of time. Yet light itself is a ripple of the 5th dimension. Light connects matter to higher dimensional space. Matter moves along through time by virtue of quantized pulses or interactions with the photon.

Maxwell's Equations: The original equations or mathematical expressions of James Clerk Maxwell of the late 19th century that described electromagnetic phenomena. The original equations described both the 'real' and the unobserved imaginary-hyperspatial components of electromagnetic phenomena. The final equations that have been adapted in common use in the 20th century do not fully reflect Maxwell's original work-they ignore the imaginary/hyperspatial components that are relevant to 'free energy devices' and Zero Point Physics. Specifically, we note the scalar components that represent nested levels of virtual reality.

Morphogenetic & Morphic Field: A widely accepted concept by developmental biologist that a field of form or pattern is the guiding mechanism for organized life processes. It is the field itself that is primary. It is the morphic field that contains the blueprints or patterns required for bringing physical form into existence. The field interconnects energy & matter. Even crystal growth & molecular structure is guided by a morphic field. This field concept is widely popularized today by the work of Rupert Sheldrake. Such fields exist outside notions of space & time- they are hyperspatial. The information within them is accessible to biological life processes outside & across the limitation of time. Morphic resonance allows the information within the field's structure to become an influencing factor in current organization. A morphic field exists for every level of existence- from atoms to galaxies! As such, there is a layering or hierarchical structure to physical reality.

Multidimensional: Simultaneously possessing properties or characteristics of more than one vibrational plane or coordinate system. The idea that dimensions exists outside of our normal 3 dimensional world , is now a basic statement of our advances theories in physics.

Multiverse: The notion that our Universe is but one of a multitude of separate and distinct universes.

Neutrinic Wave: Consisting of bare neutrinos (*see neutrino*) that behave as a wave, rather than a particle. These waves will 'piggy back' the conventional electromagnetic wave or light photon at superluminal speed (considered to be a speed of light squared, c^2). The ordinary electromagnetic wave is the actual carrier of this superluminal wave, so it is only observed traveling at the speed of light or c. The neutrinic wave is thus a substructure of the light photon, moving in a plane that is perpendicular to the direction of travel of light. Equated to a spin wave that circles around the photon, and is also categorized as a longitudinal scalar wave.

Neutrino: An electrically neutral, massless (zero mass) subatomic or elementary particle. (A member of the lepton family. *Lepton* means 'light thing'. The electron is a member of the lepton family.) In Bearden's approach the neutrino consists of a flux, or flow, of smaller particles within its substructure. The smaller particles are called 'bare neutrinos'. Neutrinos are very plentiful, in fact they are the most common object in the universe. According to Tiller, the population of neutrinos outnumber protons & electrons by approximately I billion to one. (See *neutrinic wave*)

Non-Hertzian: Disturbances that are not defined by a Hertizian waveform- cycles pre second is a term more appropriately applicable to these phenomena. For example, pulsed transmissions are not sinusoidal waveforms, but occur as so many repetitions per second.

Nonlinear Response: Generally, the response to an external influence that is not proportional to the magnitude of the causative agent. For example, some materials or systems possess optical properties with responses that vary with the intensity of light. When illuminated with a single light frequency, the system may create or emit a fundamental frequency along with additional harmonics of this frequency. Bearden suggests that such nonlinear materials or systems also produce a time-reversed signal that traces a path back to the signal source, irrespective of the distance back to the signal source!

Nonlocal Nature Of Mind/Brain System: Established by Mexican neurophysiologist Gingerg-Zylberbaum in a landmark experiment that demonstrated nonlocal (outside 3-D space) connection between two human mind/brain systems.

Non-Locality: The established property of the universe that correlations exist between distinct events irrespective of spatial separation. These correlations or communication occur instantly, in 'no time'. This property has been demonstrated in laboratory conditions for particles (Aspect & Gisin), as well as between human subjects with brain signals (Jacobo Gringerg-Zylberbaum). Non-locality, or non-separability, is a fact of nature, and a dynamic aspect of life of the Universe. Instantaneous influence or communication at a distance occurs without any exchange of signals in space-time. The unbroken wholeness or non-separability that non-locality represents, transcends space-time itself.

Open System: A system that communicates with its external environment. There may be exchanges of energy, matter, or both energy and matter between system and environment.

Order: At some level, a measure of information within a system.

Pain/Ilness: Vibration out of harmony with the whole.

Paradigm: From the Greek *paradeiknyai,* meaning to show side by side. A paradigm is an established pattern of thought or way of looking at things.

Paradigm Shift: A fundamental shift in super concepts and worldview governing scientific work.

Particle: A space-time event that carries information. An alternate manifestation of energy that exists in simultaneous states of reality.

Phase Relationship: A measure of the rhythmic relationship a wave has with other waves. A measure of the difference in angle between two waves. Also, mathematically the 2nd axis of hyperspace. Two in-phase waves create a wave that is 4 times the strength of a single wave. Three in-phase waves create a new wave that is 9 times the strength of the original single wave...etc.!

Photon/Matter Relationship: An electron wave in phase with its antiparticle (antimatter) positron wave creates a light photon. [concept of matter/antimatter collision.] A photon can be turned back into matter & antimatter again at the appropriate energy level.

Photon: The carrier of energy. Light units or quanta of energy existing at 7 basic colors or frequencies. The photon is comprised of a substructure of 'higher' dimensional derivatives such as the neutrinic wave. The photon is the quanta of the electromagnetic field, as well as the messenger particle of the electromagnetic force. Time is connected to the interaction of the photon with matter. The photon is the smallest bundle of light-a piece of electromagnetic radiation. Bearden describes the photon as having aspects that exist in both positive and negative time. A photonic field collapses to form atomic vortices.

Physics: The study of matter & energy, and the interrelationships between the two. The oldest pure science, and the most basic. Known as Natural Philosophy up to the late 19th century. Today's physics has evolved into many specialized fields & disciplines.

Plasma: Highly electrically charged or ionized mass particles.

Potential Energy: Stored up energy that is available for use or conversion into some other format.

Potential: Generally, the concept of energy or work that is locked-in at a point. Artificial potentials may be created that polarize the vacuum and place a specific pattern within it.

Practitioner: In the EMF Balancing Technique®, the practitioner is the one performing the balancing process. The person receiving the balancing is usually called the "client."

Psychokinesis: As described by Bearden, this is the effect of scalar wave patterns that are projected from the two cerebral hemispheres of the brain. This is similar to the action of a scalar interferometer.

Psychoactive: Relating to the mind, mental processes, mood, or influencing emotional stability.

Quantum: From the Latin word meaning *amount*. (Plural = quanta). A quantum is the smallest unit into which something can be partitioned. For example, photons, the smallest bundle of light, are the quanta of the electromagnetic field.

Quantum Physics: A branch of physics that has shown us that there is a fundamental relationship between our thoughts about the world, and the way the world appears to us. According to one of the underlying theories of quantum physics, not only is it impossible for us to measure a particle's position and momentum simultaneously with equal precision, there is no evidence that a particle possesses *any* well-defined properties when it is not being measured. We are part of the world we are observing, and cannot claim to be independent, objective observers of it.

Quantum Potential: A term coined by the physicist Dr. David Bohm defining an information field that interpenetrates, interconnects, and informs the quantum world. For example, electrons are informed of their environment from waves emanating from this information field or quantum potential. The quantum potential is a non-local construct, which is outside space and time.

Quantum Theory: The theoretical basis of modern physics that explains the nature and behavior of matter and energy on an atomic and subatomic level. Basic Quantum Theory dates back to 1900 and the discoveries of physicist Max Planck. Later contributions were made by such scientists as Albert Einstein, Louis de Broglie, Werner Heisenberg, David Bohm, and others. Quantum Theory is the basis for Quantum Physics.

Quantum Wave Function: A pre-matter phase connected to the probability of an event occurring. This faster than light wave moves *backward and forward* in time. It connects our minds to the physical world.

Reality: (I) All encompassing, including both *local* and *non-local* aspects of the Universe. (2) A composite view of existence maintained by an individual based upon belief structures, co-created events, objects and entities.

Resonance: Being in tune, or being in sympathy- vibrating as one. A state existing between two entities or systems of like or similar properties or characteristics that allows for an exchange of information (communication) to take place. A natural rhythm, vibration, oscillation, or frequency of a system that relates to pattern and form. When an external periodic influence, whose frequency is equal to the natural free oscillation of the system, acts on a system, the amplitude of oscillation becomes large. The system is said to be in a state of resonance. At resonance, an exchange of information (in-form) or energy occurs. Systems can be tuned to their resonant properties, at which point vibration or reverberation takes place within the system. Matter is a manifestation of scalar resonance, or standing waves. If you find the appropriate 'ring' for a system, and trigger its particular resonant frequency, it will 'sing' a reflected song back to you. This reflected song can give you information previously locked within the system's structure. The discussion of resonance introduces the notion of sympathetic vibration- that specifically relates to driving a system at its own resonant frequency by the energy of an external system that is vibrating at the same frequency. Energy transference occurs by way of the sympathetic vibrations. When systems are in tune with each other, the energy patterns that are raised in one system induce similar patterns within the second system. The greater the degree of attunement, or sympathy, between the two systems, the greater the facility for this occurring. The tuning between two systems means that harmonious chords exist- concordance. Perfect sympathy, or harmony, between two systems depends not only on the fundamental frequencies being in coincidence. Coincidence must be achieved at the levels of all vibrational components- including the harmonics and partial harmonics. When this situation occurs, the whole systems function more smoothly, with minimum resistance and discord- ultimately creating resistance free circuits and systems. These are systems of greatest efficiency and capability. Resonance established between objects or systems set up standing waves within the objects or systems. In some cases, resonance may set up standing waves between the two systems.

Resonant Tuning: A process of triggering the natural internal, and inter-dimensional unified states of alignment, integration, and balance within a system. Connected to the currents of the mind/body system growing in alignment, calibration, and synchronous relationship with the principal "whole-being" Consciousness axis. Tuning results in expanding states of internal coherence- unification towards the whole. (See *Calibration)*.

RNA: (*Ribonucleic Acid*) Similar to DNA, RNA is a linear, usually single-stranded polymer of ribonucleotides, each containing the sugar molecule ribose in association with a phosphate group and one of four nitrogenous bases: *adenine, guanine, cytosine*, or *uracil*. RNA is found in all living cells. It encodes the information needed to synthesize proteins according to instructions it receives from DNA.

Scalar: In mathematics, scalar refers to a quantity consisting of a single real number used to measure magnitude or size. For example, measurements of voltage, mass, and temperature can be described as scalar quantities. Relating to magnitude or quantity only. Scalar quantities may contain virtual substructures in n^{th} dimensional space.

Scalar Potential: In the particle view, Bearden defines the potential to be virtual particle flux. Engineering the potential is engineering space-time geometry itself. Potentials may be expressed as potentials within potentials- resulting in hidden orders of dimension within the potential. Each successive infolded potential represents a higher dimensional order- e.g. 5th, 6th, 7th etc. dimension of hyperspace. Bearden calls the engineering of the internal potential dimensioning. The scalar potential contains an nth dimensional substructure, each one being a finer, and more subtle region of hyperspace. Potentials represent warps or curvature in the vacuum or space-time. Artificial potentials may be created that polarize the vacuum and place a specific pattern within it.

Scalar Resonance: Standing scalar waves in a resonant cavity. This can be envisioned as two ordinary electromagnetic waves that are coupled together, but exactly 180 degrees out of phase. Externally no electric or magnetic fields are apparent. Mass objects are an example of standing wave scalar resonance.

Scalar Translator: A device that can convert electromagnetic to scalar, and from scalar to electromagnetic.

Scalar Wave: Oscillations in the stress energy of the vacuum. These oscillations contain virtual patterned substructure. These are longitudinal pressure waves of space-time. The scalar wave is able to move in 4 or more dimensions. It may move only in time, altering the flow of time, gravity, or properties of an object; it may move only in space with time remaining stable; or move in combinations of these two modes described. Other references to scalar waves are Tesla wave, gravitational wave, electromagnetic sound waves, electrogravitional wave. Vibrational waves that may be to small to breach the quantum threshold, are, yet real, and are scalar waves. Scalar waves are not limited by speed of light limitation, are hyperspatial and superluminal. Bearden views a scalar wave as the unification of electromagnetics and gravity.

Scalar: Relating to magnitude or quantity only. Scalar quantities may contain virtual substructures in n^{th} dimensional space.

Second Law of Thermodynamics: A 'law' of Physics that states that entropy always increases. See *entropy*.

Self-Directing Energy: During the EMF Balancing Technique® the energy of the Universal Calibration Lattice (*see*) can be felt to be flowing and self-organizes within the field as it is guided by higher dimensional process. Thus, no guesswork, analysis or judgment is needed on the practitioner's part. By simply following the procedure, the most beneficial outcome for the client is co-created.

Self-Organization: An ability of all living things. Spontaneous emergence of order within a system. The greater the degree of complexity or consciousness/awareness of living things, the greater the ability to self-organize. Living things are open systems in constant interaction with their outside environment. Self-organization is a manifestation of a hidden order, be it resonant vibrational modes & states, virtual levels of reality, an *implicate* order, a *biofield*, subtle fields or morphogenetic fields, morphic resonance, continuous influx of 'intelligent' energy, the existence of syntropic conditions, a chaotic attractor, the geometry of life, quantum information fields, '*back-action*', the interaction of mind & matter, nested or embedded self-referencing 'loops', q-bit information waves, an interconnected field of consciousness, the harmonic relationships between geometric form, sound & light, the interaction of the mental field at sub-quantum levels of reality, or the direct intervention of consciousness.

Self-Reference: Communication, interchange, and exchange between the source and the receiver. A double-flow process that is fundamental to every interaction. An interchange between the quantum wave and its reflected space-time correlate or image. Self-reference is an interaction of self with your image, a process that is at the foundation of self-organization. Visually, this concept is depicted by the infinity symbol or "figure 8" loop.

Separability Principle: The idea that things no longer in contact, connection, or communication with each other, cannot affect one another. Nonlocality of the quantum world, and the human brain, has demonstrated otherwise.

Space-Time: The merging or union of space and time that creates the fabric from which the universe is constructed. Events within our 3-dimensional space unfold from space-time. Space-time consists of 4 dimensions. We credit Einstein for adding time as the 4th dimension. Bearden associates space-time with dynamic geometry, potential [trapped or collected energy], vacuum, virtual particle flux, and hidden wave flux.

String: The most fundamental, irreducible, one-dimensional filament entity. The string is at the basis of string theory. Strings assume a variety of modes, patterns, and vibrations. These determine the nature of the forces that are manifested in our three dimensional world.

String Theory: A Unified Theory of the Universe that postulates that the string is the fundamental building block of nature. String theory sees both 11 and 26 dimensional structures of reality.

Subtle Energies: All energies existing in the universe that are either not known or accepted by orthodox science. The term *subtle* was first coined by Einstein to describe energies not directly measurable by science.

Superconductivity: Flow without resistance. Very high conductivity of electrical flow. DNA is said to be a superconductor. Some metals known as ORME's are superconductive at room temperature. [ORME's- monoatomic elements -white powders-some are also constituents of DNA, & assist in the superconductive properties of DNA. Apparently these materials may impact the etheric energy fields.] There is a relationship between electron flow & conversion to light. Superconductivity is associated with diamagnetism- opposing an ordinary magnetic field. This phenomenon is associated with levitation. If the hand is passed over ORME powders, the powders will 'levitate' due to the magnetic field at the hands! Currents induces in superconductive materials remain even after removing the magnetic field that induced it.

Superluminal: Faster than the speed of light in vacuum.

Symbiosis: A relationship that is of mutual benefit to the concerned or connected elements of association.

Sympathetic Vibration: Specifically relates to driving a system at its own resonant frequency by the applied energy of an external system. The external system is vibrating at the same frequency. Energy transference occurs by way of the sympathetic vibrations.

Sympathy: In tune with, or in harmony with another system- see *Harmony*.

Synchronicity: (I) A term originating with Carl Jung referring to meaningful coincidences. (2) Synchronicity describes a situation where our perception of certain events gives us the sense that such events are somehow connected, even though we cannot clearly see the mechanics of such connections. We sometimes experience events in time that seem specifically designed to meet our needs at that precise moment, even though the occurrence of the events would seem on the face of it to be random and not planned by us. Synchronicity implies an unseen force at work that responds to an interconnectivity between all things, and a indication that universal balance is at work, bringing about events in which we are participants and observers as well as co-creators. This is true whether the co-creation takes place at or below our current level of conscious awareness.

Syntropic Phenomena: Causing the reversing of entropy [negentropy], or putting order back into a disordered state. Processess that do not 'obey' the second law of thermodynamics. A syntropic process can lower the entropy (disorder) of a system. Syntropic conditions can be catalyzed by a variety of external or internal factors. These include adding energy or information to a system; providing the external conditions of a magnetic field that establishes syntropic currents; establishing coherence at the quantum state; a tuning-up, getting in-phase, or resonance between the external and internal states. Syntropic processes do not necessarily require the input of energy.

Tackyon (takyon): A superluminal particle that, reportedly, respond to Consciousness.

Tai Chi: An ancient Chinese physical and mental discipline, similar to Chi Kung, the practice of which helps develop an increased awareness of the subtle life force energies ("Chi") of the earth and the body. There are various styles of Tai Chi. The "soft" style looks much like an elegant dance form, and helps one achieve greater balance of body, mind and spirit. The Chinese consider Tai Chi to be a form of Chi Kung (see *Chi Kung*). Practicing Tai Chi is an excellent way to help increase the health of the body and bring piece of mind. Tai Chi is based on the concepts of the Yin-Yang.

Tensor Potential: The accumulation of energy in a precisely contained cavity-characterized by the accumulation of energy with no energy flow.

Tensors: In a biological system, these are the multi-dimensional echoes of consciousness that are capable of generating various [scalar type] potentials. These potentials create fields that are Unified Fields- unified with consciousness and Emotion.

Tesla: Dr. Nikola Tesla, physicist, inventor, mental giant and genius of the 19th and 20th centuries. With over 600 patents & 1200 inventions to his credit, Tesla gave the world the AC electrical system [along with many other contributions]. Discover of the **Tesla wave**, the hyperspatial scalar wave. Strangely, or not so strangely depending upon your point of view, Tesla claimed to be in virtually daily contact with extraterrestrial life!

Time: In relativity theory, time becomes the 4th dimension. Consider *time as a direction relative to matter*. Viewing time as a *frequency* enables the understanding that consciousness can literally "tune-in" to specific or alternate "time" coordinates that co-exist simultaneously. Moving through time is moving through "frequency" within dimensions. Time is a precept that is related to the streaming of Consciousness across its own reality field. Time is a product of three-dimensional reality perception that creates the appearance, and illusion, of a past, present, and future. Multiple things, and events, may exist in time simultaneously. Time enables an ordering of events. The idea of time being 'vertical' rather than linear is a percept that brings us closer to understanding holographic time. In vertical time, the past, present and future are 'stacked' and interrelate through looping cycles. At the quantum level, time is connected to photon interaction. By speeding up the interaction rate, the "flow" of time can also be altered i.e., speed up the "flow" of time. The time dimension allows for multiple objects to exist within the same interval. In quantum mechanics, time is not an observable parameter, nor is it detectable. *Quantum waves move forward & backward in time.*

Torsion Field/Waves: Besides the conventional known classical fields of electromagnetism & gravity, a 3rd field exists that has long-range effects. The torsion field is the consequence of the property of angular spin or rotation. An object's collective spins superpose (add up) to create unique interference patterns around them that are holographic information fields. Hyperspatial (outside space-time), & faster than light phenomenon, a torsion field transfers information without the transfer of energy. Torsion fields are interactive with other torsion fields exchanging information. The aura is described in Russian literature as a torsion field. A torsion field is also referred to as Einstein's Unified Field. The term torsion field is broadly used in Russian literature. In the western world, the term used by Bearden called scalar waves/fields appears to carry analogous meaning. Much more remains to be researched & understood about the torsion field in the western world. The brain interacts with the vacuum- therefore the brain can be called a torsion-field transceiver (receiver-emitter) in similar way that the brain has been called a scalar interferometer. Energy systems forms interference wave patterns that are at the basis of creating holographic information fields. The torsion field may be understood as such a field. Consider the torsion field as a connector field- e.g. connection between electromagnetism & gravity, or a connector to the electromagnetic field.

UCL: (See *Universal Calibration Lattice*).

Ultraviolet Radiation: Relating to the invisible UV radiation of the electromagnetic spectrum. Invisible radiation of wavelengths in the range 380 nanometers (border violet) to 4 nanometers (border X-ray).

Unified Field Energy: Energy originating at a high vibratory plane. This energy is unified with both Consciousness and Emotion. It can be contained in a precisely designed cavity or a structure of precise geometric, harmonic and mathematical configuration. It is infinite, and cannot be exhausted becomes it originates from the Source. When not in motion, Unified Field Energy is pure Potential. When flowing, Unified Field Energy is a flux or flow within the Tackyon continuum. Unified Field Energy flow can be activated by Consciousness. Human Beings are architects and manipulators of Unified Field Energy.

Unified Field: A state in which all energies of a system are in a state of geometrical, harmonic, and mathematical unification.

Universal Calibration Lattice: A structure within the human energy anatomy defined by 12 interconnected principle fibers that form a multidimensional lattice structure. This lattice has principle connections at the chakras, and interconnects the living system to the external universe.

Vacuum: The absence of space and time. The non-material aether- consisting of a plenum of massless charge. The vacuum is the lengthless, timeless spacetime. The energy content or density of one cubic centimeter of the vacuum state is estimated to exceed the total energy of all the matter of the universe [estimated by John Wheeler to be the matter equivalent of 10^{94} gram/cm^3. Compare this to the relatively small energy density of an atom 10^{14} gram/cm^3.] In a global context, the vacuum can be viewed as a background, or fabric, upon which reality unfolds. It is a state of immense vibrational intensity. There are a variety of vacuum states with their respective unique properties and characteristics. The vacuum is a scalar field, and contains an nth dimensional substructure.

Vacuum Engine: As described by Bearden, a vacuum engine is an internal pattern or template that has been deliberately created/engineered within a scalar potential. A scalar potential or a moving electromagnetic wave in vacuum can transport this internal pattern. The scalar potential aspect of either the electric charge or magnetic charge can also become the carrier of the internal pattern or template. A vacuum engine can be implanted in the vacuum, in which case during its creation it has a 'charging-up' time, and also a 'discharging' time. Bearden describes the act of implanting an internal pattern to any carrier [in vacuum] as dimensioning the carrier. Russian work in energetics refers to dimensioning as being the information content of the field. According to Bearden, if a vacuum engine acts upon an object, it has absolutely no choice in that action occurring [unless an exact antiengine is created for it]. As can be construed, this action is distinctly different from an object choosing to act, or not act, upon ordinary signal information. A vacuum engine can alter local spacetime, and results in interaction with objects within that space and time.

Vacuum Lattice Structure: An organization within the aether or vacuum state. Contemporary thought amongst physicists purport that the vacuum is supported through a lattice structure of its own. The geometric structural forms within the vacuum include aggregates of the tetrahedron (like Sierpinski's fractal), the octagon, and the hexagon (Tiller). The icosahedral structure is outlined by Erol Torun. Destabilizing the geometric grids is breaking the symmetry- and results in extraction of energy.

Vector: A mathematical operator that defines both a direction and a magnitude simultaneously, in any given coordinate system.

Vector Magnetic Potential: See *Magnetic Vector Potential.*

Vibration: A change of state going from an energetic positive state, through a neutral state, to a negative state. This occurs over a specific period. Vibrations combine to form unique combinations or chords. In lattice structures, alignments take place according to the directions defined by the vibrational chords. Vibration is the connection link of everything in the Universe. To vibrate is to sound.

Vibrational Pattern: A precise number of peaks and troughs along with defined amplitude. Also the geometry and form of an interference profile that may be a multi-dimensional waveform.

Virtual Particles: Particles that appear or erupt from the vacuum briefly, and then rapidly annihilate. This happens so quickly that they cannot be observed. However virtual particles interact with mass or charge to create very real observable effects.

Virtual Photon Flux: For electromagnetic phenomena, the vacuum can be modeled as a flux or flow of virtual photons.

Virtual State: That part of reality consisting of unobservable and undetectable change, beyond the smallest quantum change. Not individually observable events. Virtual states consist of multiple inner, hidden, and nested levels. Each of these levels is actually a finer, more subtle, higher dimension. Thoughts are virtual events. Charge on a particle is due to virtual events in exchange with the charge or mass particle.

Wave Function: See *quantum wave function*.

Wormhole: A region in space with the shape of a tube that connects one region of the Universe with another-an *Einstein-Rosen bridge*. A warp in the fabric of space-time allowing for the movement and displacement of material things from point to another. Such regions may connect separate points in space as well as distinct points in time. Atoms are wormholes. Every point is in contact with every other point. Thinking and reasoning involves associating ideas that may be very widely separated by logic. This functioning within the brain is a manifestation of the existence of wormholes in the brain.

Zero Point Physics: The applied science & engineering in pursuit of extracting 'free' energy from the vacuum. The principle idea is to alter the symmetry of the 'balanced' vacuum state to cause an energy 'flow' that can be harnessed for terrestrial, and, non-terrestrial, uses.

Zero-Point Energy Of The Vacuum: The vacuum is considered to be composed of an extremely dense quantity of virtual (unseen) energy. This energy state exist even at a temperature of absolute zero degrees, when theoretically, minimum energy states exist. The energy of the vacuum is not related to temperature. One-estimate places the energy contained in one centimeter of empty space to be more than the total energy of all matter in the known universe. No system can have zero energy. See *vacuum*.

INTRODUCTION: Amidst A Time Of Change

1. Braden, Gregg, *Awakening to Zero Point-The Collective Initiation*, Radio Bookstore Press, Bellevue, WA., 1997. *See also his later works.*

2. Chicago Research Group & Associates, *Ancient Wisdom & Modern Physics*, Leading Edge International Research Group, Yelm, WA., 1999, pg. 114

3. Tiller, William A., Ph.D., *Science and Human Transformation-Subtle Energies, Intentionality and Consciousness*, Pavior Publishing, Walnut Creek, Ca., 1997, pg. 181

4. Ibid., pg. 181-*although we quote Tiller's work, we are unable to do full justice in the manner in which he presents his ideas. We recommend the reader consult his original text.*

5. Ibid., pg. 290

6. Ibid., pg. 290

7. Corso, Philip J., Col. (Ret), *The Day After Roswell*, Pocket books, New York, NY, 1997, pg. 192

8. Yao, Dr.George, T.F., *Pulsor Miracle of Microcrystals-A Treatise on Energy Balancing*, Gyro Industries, Newport Beach, Ca. 1986, pg.162

9. Ibid., pg.133

10. Petersen, P. Stephen, Ph.D., *The Quantum Tai Chi-Gauge Theory: The Dance Of Mind Over Matter*, Empyrean Quest Edition, Concord, Ca., 1996, pg. 176

11. Ibid., pg.178

12. Melchizedek, Drunvalo, *The Ancient Secret of the Flower of Life Vol I*, Light Technology Publishing, Flagstaff, AZ., 1998, pg. 185-186

13. Goswami, Amit, Ph.D., *The Self Aware Universe-How Consciousness Creates The Material World*, Tarcher/Putnam, New York, NY., 1995, pg. 126

14. Keepin, Will, Ph.D. , *Lifework of David Bohm - River of Truth*, www.shavano.org/html/bohm.html#Quest

15. Brian Greene, *The Elegant Universe: Superstrings, Hidden Dimensions, And The Quest For The Ultimate Theory*, W.W. Norton & Company Ltd., London, 1999, pg. 18

CHAPTER 2

TOWARDS A NEW PARADIGM: Mind, Matter, & Intentionality

Intentionality in subtitle inspired by William Tiller from his book *Science and Human Transformation-Subtle Energies, Intentionality and Consciousness*, Pavior Publishing, Walnut Creek, Ca., 1997

1. Bearden, T.E., Energetics of Free Energy systems & Vacuum Engine Therapeutics, 1997, Tara Publications Center, Brampton, Ontario, Canada, pg. 54-61

2. Davis, Albert Roy, & Rawls, Walter C., *The Rainbow in Your Hands*, Exposition Press, Smithtown, N.Y., 1976

3. Work of Physicist David Bohm

4. Davis, Albert Roy, & Rawls, Walter C., *The Rainbow in Your Hands*

5. Kaku, Michio, *Hyperspace: A Scientific Odyssey through Parallel Universes, Time Warps, & The 10th Dimension*, Oxford University Press, New York, 1994

6. See Kaku, Hyperspace, & Brian Greene, *The Elegant Universe: Superstrings, Hidden Dimensions, And The Quest For The Ultimate Theory*, W.W. Norton & Company Ltd., London, 1999

7. Bearden, T.E., *Excalibur Briefing*, Tesla Book Company, Box 121873, Chula Vista, CA 91912

8. Tiller, William A., Ph.D., *Science and Human Transformation*, pg. 182

9.   Hunt, Valerie, *Infinite Mind: Science of the Human Vibrations of Consciousness*, Malibu Publishing, Ca., 1989, 1996, pg. 51

10. William Tiller, *Science and Human Transformation*, pg. 59

11. William Tiller, *Science and Human Transformation-Subtle Energies, Intentionality and Consciousness*, ISBN 0964263742

12. Torun, Erol O., *The Complexified Aether*, 1993, www.meru.org/Advisors/Torun/cmplethr.html

13. Tiller, William A., Ph.D., *Science and Human Transformation*, pg. 36

14. Detela, Andrej, *Physical Model of the Biofield*, J. Stefan Institute, Slovenia, 1997

15. Within the 'cavity', standing waves form. These can be considered to be electromagnetic sound waves, or electrogravitational waves- scalar waves. These waves can be 'charged up'. They produce electromagnetic phenomena. The scalar waves establish resonant patterns of vibration in the UCL. In the surrounding vacuum (Cosmic Sea), virtually infinite arrays of hyperspatial scalar wave vibrations exist. Note that resonant circuits require a source of voltage, or charge, to operate.. The field structures at the hand resonate to the whole human energy system. When the human energy systems are tuned to its natural vibrations (circuits or templates), a resonance is established that allows for 'charging' of the energy anatomy as well as exchange of information. This resonance results in free energy at the hand. The frequencies at the hand reflect all those with which the energy anatomy has established resonance (holographic principle). The fundamental frequency in the Universe is the Ryhsmonic , or aetheric, frequency. Its value is 1.855×10^{43} cycles per second. The principle is that interaction with this frequency, or its harmonics or sub-harmonics, under resonance conditions, results in energy exchange, transfer, or extraction. Some of the harmonics & sub-harmonics of this Ryhsmonic frequency also appear in the Schumann resonant frequencies (Earth frequency profile). Predominant to the human system are some of the Schumann frequencies. [Schumann shows peaks in the range: 1.8, 3.7, 7.4-8, 14, 20, 26, 32-33, 37-39, 43-45 Hz.-approximately]. These exist with hyperspatial scalar waves counterparts. Other vast orders of vibrations exist originating from throughout the Cosmos. Many play essential roles to the biological systems. Bearden (Excalibur Briefing) discusses the existence of channels that allow for direct energy exchange, or crosstalk, between frames in hyperspace. These are called hyperchannels, interdimensional nodal points, or magic 'windows'. These windows are frequency dependent and are naturally tuned. Some of the hyperchannel frequencies occurr in the ranges: 38-40 kHz, 150-160 kHz, 1.1-1.3 MHz, 1.057 GHz, and the ultraviolet life energy frequency. Note that resonant circuits require a source of voltage, or charge, to operate[16].Establishing resonance between the UCL and the Cosmic Sea (vacuum) creates a 'free energy generator'.

16. Frolov, Alexander V., *Resonance Effects*, www.padrak/ine/NEN_4_8_6.html

17. Brian Greene, *The Elegant Universe*, & Michio Kaku, *Hyperspace*

18. Walker, Evan Harris, *The Physics of Consciousness- The Quantum Mind and The Meaning of Life*, Perseus Books, Cambridge, Mass., 2000

19. Bearden, T.E., *Excalibur Briefing*, & Mind Matter Unification Project , Cavendish Laboratory, Cambridge, Brian Josephson's HomePage,www.tcm.phy.cam.ac.uk/_bdjl0/index.html

20. Nadeau, Robert, & Kafatos, Menas, *The Non-Local Universe-The New Physics and Matters of the Mind*, Oxford University Press, NY, NY, 1999, pg. 79

21. Ibid. pg. 3

22. Ibid. pg. 5

23. Bearden, T.E., *Excalibur Briefing*, pg. 199-200

24. Reed, Donald, *Torsion Field Research*, New Energy News, www.padrak.com/ine/NEW_6_1_6.html

25. Goswami, Amit, Ph.D., *The Self Aware Universe-How Consciousness Creates The Material World*, Tarcher/Putnam, New York, NY., 1995, pg. 132 & 172 & Grinberg-Zylberbaum, J., M. Delaflor, M. E. Sanchez Arellano, M.A. Guevara and M. Perez, *Human Communication and the Electrophysiological Activity of the Brain*, 1992, *Journal of Subtle Energies*, International Society for the Study of Subtle Energies and Energy Medicine, Abstracts, Vol.3

26. Goswami, Amit, Ph.D., *The Self Aware Universe*, pg. 130

27. Hunt, Valerie, *Infinite Mind: Science of the Human Vibrations of Consciousness*, pg. 50-51

28. Ibid. pg. 93

29. Rollin McCarty, William A. Tiller, & Mike Atkinson, *Head-Heart Entrainment: A Preliminary Survey*, http://www.HeartMath.org/ResearchPapers/HeadHeart/HeadHeart.htm

30. Childre, Doc, & McCraty, Rollin, *Love-The Hidden Power of the Heart:A Scientific Perspective*, Institute of HeartMath, http://www.HeartMath.com/Library/Articles/Caduceus.html

31. Goswami, Amit, Ph.D., *The Self Aware Universe-How Consciousness Creates The Material World*

32. Petersen, P. Stephen, Ph.D., *The Quantum Tai Chi-Gauge Theory: The Dance Of Mind Over Matter*, Empyrean Quest Edition, Concord, Ca., 1996

33. Detela, *Physical Model of the Biofield*, Appendix C

34. Keepin, Will, Ph.D. , *Lifework of David Bohm, Wholeness and the Holomovement*, www.shavano.org/html/bohm.html

35. Ibid.

36. Keepin, Will, Ph.D. , *Lifework of David Bohm, The Implicate Order*, www.shavano.org/html/bohm.html

37. Sarfatti, Jacob (Jack), Ph.D., *Progress in Post-Quantum Theory*, www.qedcorp.com/pcr/index.html, August 7, 1999

38. Ibid.

39. Sarfatti, Jack, *Post-quantum Physics of Consciousness*, Slide Show, www.qedcorp.com/pcr/pcr/pq/pq1.htm

40. Ibid.

41. Sarfatti, Jacob (Jack), Ph.D., *Progress in Post-Quantum Theory*

42. Ibid.

43. Petersen, P. Stephen, Ph.D., *The Quantum Tai Chi-Gauge Theory: The Dance Of Mind Over Matter*, pg. 146

44. Ibid. pg. 169

45. Ibid. pg. 171

46. Bearden, T.E., *Gravitobiology-The New BioPhysics*, Tesla Book Company Box 121873, Chula Vista, CA 91912, 1991, pg. 47

47. See *Vacuum* in Glossary

48. Leaving the South pole, the energy spins to the right (clockwise); leaving the North pole the energy spins to the left (counterclockwise). The energies enter the center of the magnet where they change direction (Bloch wall). Notice the formation of the figure 8 pattern from the circulation of the magnetic energies. At the center there is no magnetism (Bloch wall). At the ends of each pole a cone of energies was detected. These cone shape energies extends outward and shows no point of return. Additionally Davis & Rawls detected a straight-line projection of energy extending outward from each pole-this energy shows no point of return. The new discoveries of Davis & Rawls are principles that apply to all phenomena of magnetism.

49. The charged particle is like a pump absorbing virtual particles- then releasing them. A collection or concentration of massless charged particles in the vacuum state creates a 'potential'. In particular, a grouping of light photons forms the electrostatic (EM) scalar potential. The scalar potential is a (stationary) point of flowing virtual particles. Charge relates to a flow or flux that can be varied, and charge is not a constant. A mass particle is continuously being charged & discharged by the absorption & emission of scalar waves. According to Bearden (Excalibur Briefing), the mind field can interact to alter, increase or extinguish the charge of a particle. Anytime we alter flow (as in energy) we alter charge. In this sense, charge and energy flow, are synonymous terms.

50. The conventional understanding of gravity as 'mass attraction' is incorrect. By definition, whatever curves spacetime is a gravity field- and all the various forces arise from the curvature of spacetime). The

5D gravitational potential is largely expressed within 5D space as electromagnetism. We observe the effects of the primary expression or bleed-off of this 5D potential as our electromagnetic force fields in 3D space. The second expression of the 5D-gravity field is as our ordinary gravity. This 4D-gravity field is actually a very small fraction of the expressed potential energy. The 5D gravitation potential is derived from the sum total of different stress types and patterns (spacetime curvatures or potentials) in the vacuum. These include the contributions of the virtual particles that are in an ongoing state of flux, or flow, within the vacuum state. The virtual photons, neutrinos, charged & uncharged particles, etc. all contribute to the total potential of the 5D gravity field (Concepts from Bearden). Light is electromagnetic in nature. From the above discussion we can see why, from string theory, it is said that light is a ripple from the fifth dimension. Electromagnetism, like light itself, is an expression of a higher dimensional phenomenon. We translate the relevance of this material to understanding the human anatomy in the following. Effectively, a unified 5D-type gravity field (gravity relating to what curves spacetime) surrounds us and is responsible for the expression of our electromagnetic nature. This field can be charged up. Increasing the flow or flux (charge) of the virtual states of our being, increases the potential of this primary field. Accordingly, more electromagnetic energy becomes available for us to use in the NOW. Conversely, undesirable 'bleed-offs' from the personal 5D field would have the opposite effect- less electromagnetic energy available in the NOW.

51. Conventionally, the photon is comprised of the electric field vector E, magnetic field vector H, and velocity vector V. All three vectors (directions) are orthogonal to each other (90°). Underlying each vector is a rich substructure of virtual states that are entering our reality frame from higher dimensional space, and then returning to the virtual state from which it originates. The photon is a non-local phenomenon. Bearden (Excalibur Briefing) describes the electric and magnetic oscillating fields as a rotating etheric or hyperspatial flux (flow). The substructure of the individual vectors can be considered to have an infinite number of virtual vectors. This substructure can be altered, and a virtual pattern can be impressed upon it. The flux within each E and H vector is a neutrino flux- a neutrinic wave is nested within the envelope of the photon. Neutrinos are readily admitted into the E and H fields of the photon. It is the neutrinic wave that is highly interactive with the electric or magnetic field. The neutrinic wave is a hyperfield wave. It's a spiraling wave that circulates around the electromagnetic field. The greater the charge within an electromagnetic field (the greater the potential or voltage), the greater the number of photons available….hence a greater number of neutrinic interactions with the field. Light can be considered to be the conductor of neutrinic waves. According to Bearden, the neutrinic wave is the carrier of the bioenergy or eloptic energy (Hieronymous), and may be the spinning wave known as orgone energy (Reich)[7]. Further, Bearden explains that the neutrino field is the link to the mind field. Motoyama has determined that the more active & balanced a chakra, the more photons emitted from the chakra.

52. Subjects A & B, having first interacted for several minutes to establish a 'connection', were isolated in separate Faraday cages. [The Faraday cages block all conventional electromagnetic means of communication between the subjects.] In the experiment a flashing light is presented to subject A. As a result, an evoked potential is generated in the EEG (brain signal recording) of subject A relating to this flashing light. Subject B has no knowledge of this event occurring, yet a similar signal (transfer potential) 'appears' in the EEG recording of B at the same instant. The mind/brain system, exhibiting nonlocal effects, in fact straddles across multiple dimensions of reality. Its home is in a higher dimension that encapsulates physical spacetime, but is not confined to the spacetime dimension. We can conclude that human to human interactions will always entail, unseen, but real, nonlocal correlations. The appearance of similar signals in the separate subjects can be viewed as establishing a resonance through the human to human connection. The torsion field of the brain is intrinsically nonlocal. This field carries the information patterns that interact with the torsion fields of other individuals.

53. According to Valerie Hunt, every part of an organized field is a hologram where each part contains the pattern of the whole. The human energy field is such a holographic field[27]. Matter, energy, mind & spirit are all part of an expanded reality. Hunt has determined that a person's INTENT can affect another individual's field, & that energy field patterns are related to consciousness[28]. The Heartmath Institute has determined that the heart & brain form a highly integrated system[29]. Emotional activity has an impact on overall system performance. Thoughts & emotion are reflected in the heart's electrical system[30]. The heart is the body's strongest generator of the electromagnetic field, & this field is measurable several feet away from the body. The Heartmath Institute has experimental evidence that when individuals touch, or are in close proximity, one person's heart signal (ECG) is registered in the other person's brain signals (EEG) and elsewhere on the other person's body. We can consider mind/brain signals as holographic parts of the whole human dynamic. Mind/brain signals are established to be nonlocal. We can view these as 'carriers' of emotional wave patterns along with the encoding of other wave patterns of the human dynamic. As is discussed later in text, the heart is the generator of torsion fields that are intrinsically nonlocal. The torsion field carries the information patterns that interact with the torsion fields of other individuals. We can view the emotional aspects of our being as having a home in a higher dimension. This dimension encapsulates physical spacetime, but is not confined to the spacetime dimension. This emotional aspect straddles across multiple dimensions of reality.

54. Sarfatti, Jacob (Jack), Ph.D., *Military Applications of Post-Quantum Physics*, *http://www.qedcorp.com/Q/ChiaoBell.html*

55. Two connecting paths are outlined: 1-Path A, a direct space-time structure, & the path of conventional allopathic medicine 2-Path B, an inverse space-time structure (a frequency domain), & the path of homeopathic medicine. These intervening loops connect the body's biological process to the subtle fields through the magnetic vector potential. Note that the equations of influence functions in both directions! The physical affects the state of the subtle, and the subtle affects the state of the physical! We take the view that the subtle fields can be altered through acts of Consciousness or external 'torsion' fields, or through the human to human connection through energy balancing techniques. All of these influences to the subtle fields ultimately 'filters' its way from the subtle to physical realms as described in Tiller's equation.

56. It exists even in the absence of the observation of the magnetic field (Bohm-Aharonov effect). Shown is the magnetic field of a cylindrical solenoid. The vector potential A exists separate from the magnetic field B. Shielding B, does not eliminate the vector potential in the vacuum state. The spiral threads of the spin/axion/torsion field follow the direction of the vector potential. According to Tiller, the vector potential is the link to the subtle energy fields.

57. Grid dimensions vary for each lattice substructure going from mind lattice (smallest) to physical reality (largest). According to Tiller, there are waves that travel through the network that are related to consciousness. They are inter-dimensional nodal points. These can be viewed as channels of least resistance that can establish a direct correspondence & circulation of energies with other dimensional frames. Establishing such channels is the result of preferential tuning within the structure, and requires coherence within the system as a whole. These points are frequency dependent & naturally tuned. (Bearden calls such points magic windows). It is at the nodal points that these waves of consciousness are converted to energies that interact with matter. The grid points are significant for another reason-they store the 'potentials' that originate from our thought processes. These convert to patterns that are projected into our lives. Altering the patterns and potentials at the nodal junctions will change the events projected into our lives.

58. From William Tiller's perspective, when imbalances exist at the biological level, in order to restore homeostasis, chemical imbalances require adjustments at the electromagnetic level; imbalances at the electromagnetic level require adjustments at the etheric level; imbalances at the etheric level require adjustments at the emotional level; imbalances at the emotional level require adjustments at the mental level; imbalances at the mental level require adjustments at the spiritual level[8]. In this model, the organization at any one level of reality is influenced, and determined, by a higher level of reality. In particular, biological physical reality is under the organizational influence of the electromagnetic field. We can exercise the greatest influence to physical biological function through the 'manipulation' of the subtle structures. These we can alter through acts of consciousness, as well as through intervention with the human-to-human connection.

59. Magnetic polarities are derived from the magnetostatic scalar potentials that are circular, spiraling stresses in space-time. The magnetostatic potentials can be charged up. One quality of energy spirals from North to South; another quality of energy spirals from South to North (sort of Yin/Yang combination).

60. The conventional understanding of gravity as 'mass attraction' is incorrect. By definition, whatever curves spacetime is a gravity field- and all the various forces arise from the curvature of spacetime). The 5D gravitational potential is largely expressed within 5D space as electromagnetism. (See Chapter Note #50.)

61. The nodal points relate to the interconnecdedness of all things in the universe. Additionally, the holographic access to all information, both local & non-local realities is understood from this perspective. Because significant nodal points are located within the physical brain, the key, according to Tiller, is to learn to 'read' and access the information within the lattice structure. In B, we have created an overlay between the lattice grid & the hyperspatial drive mechanism (see chapter 4). According to Jack Sarfatti, an array of 'nano-antennae' formed by electrons within the brain serve to communicate information to the microtubules of the brain[37].

62. Nonlocality is that property that relates to the transfer of information, instantly, no matter how far apart or separated the particles (or systems) are. As the photons traveled away from each other, they continued to 'know' the polarization state of the other photon. This knowing occurred instantly- was not limited by the speed of light, or the distance that separated them. A similar experiment was repeated in 1997 [Gisin et al, University of Geneva], except this time the photons were separated by 11 kilometers (instead of 13 meters in the Aspect experiment). The 1997 experiment verified that the property of nonlocality could be confirmed even if the particles were separated at opposite ends of the universe! Nonlocality suggests the existence of an unseen, or hidden, reality that underlies physical reality. Through this reality there is an undivided connectedness that communicates outside the bounds of time & space.

63. The quantum pilot wave information patterns are non-local. They do not operate on the basis of intensity. Rather, they transfer form – to literally in-form as in supply information. As such the mental field can guide, 'control', or influence even high-energy systems. [The analogy is to consider how radio waves from shore can guide the movements of a large ship at sea.] In the illustration the Explicate order is the external perceived reality. According to Sarfatti, the Explicate order includes the classical fields. The interaction of mind & matter includes the mental field of thought exercising organizing influence upon all the classical force fields-these include the electromagnetic, gravity, torsion and other connecting fields. Bearden elaborates further on this interaction in Excalibur Briefing. Bearden refers to Intent, or what he also calls 'Inception", as an otherwise 'mystery to ordinary science'.

64. Through a process of sufficient pattern coherence, a collection of photons is able to exceed the quantum threshold. When this happens, an observable quantum change takes place. The quantum change reaches the electromagnetic field frame and either creates or alters the electromagnetic field. Observed physical change ensues. Note in the illustration how the virtual photon is the 'carrier' of the thought entity to the electromagnetic field. In fact, we call the photon the 'messenger' particle of the electromagnetic field. If an electromagnetic field could be observed it would be a veritable light show with photonsdancing around everywhere carrying messages between particles. All possibilities exist within the Virtual Reality. The key is to focus sufficient energy & coherence to any particular pattern or possibility in order that it transform into physical Observed Reality.

CHAPTER 3

INTRODUCING THE UNIVERSAL CALIBRATION LATTICE: An Inter -Dimensional Web

1. Introductory remarks by D. Lapierre.
2. Ibid.
3. Dr. Todd Ovokaitys @ www.Gematria.com

CHAPTER 4

MULTI-DIMENSIONAL CIRCUITS: Your Portal To Hyp erspace

1. Bearden, T.E., *Excalibur Briefing, Gravitobiology* & other works of Bearden.
2. Bearden, *A Redefinition of the Energy Ansatz, Leading to a Fundamental New Class of Nuclear Interaction.* 1992
3. Bearden, *Gravitobiology: The New Biophysics*
4. Ibid.
5. Lazslo, Ervin, *Toward A Physical Foundation For Psi Phenomena,* 1994, http://www.goertzel.org/dynapsyc/1996/ervin.html
6. Yao, Dr.George, T.F., *Pulsor Miracle of Microcrystals-A Treatise on Energy Balancing,* Gyro Industries, Newport Beach, Ca. 1986, pg. 133
7. Chicago Research Group & Associates, *Ancient Wisdom & Modern Physics,*Leading Edge International Research Group, Yelm, WA., 1999, (www.trufax.org), pg. 43
8. Ibid. pg.44
9. Falun Dafa, Falun Gong , www.falundafa.org, http://minghui.ca/eng.html, http://www.falundafa.ca/
10. *Ancient Wisdom & Modern Physics,* pg. 45
11. Valerian, Valdamar, *Matrix III, the Psycho-Social, Chemical, Biological and Electromagnetic Manipulation of Human Consciousness,* Vol.I, Leading Edge Research Group, P.O. Box 7530, Yelm, Washington State, 98597 pg. 339
12. Ibid. pg. 346
13. Hameroff, Stuart, www.u.arizona.edu/ hameroff/index.html
14. Leary, Timothy, *Timothy Leary's Eight Circuits of Consciousness,* www.deoxy.org/8circuit.htm
15. www.deoxy.org/eoctave.htm
16. Valerian, Valdamar, *Matrix III,* pg.61
17. Ibid. pg.61
18. Ibid. pg.61-95
19. *Timothy Leary's Eight Circuits of Consciousness,* www.deoxy.org/8circuit.htm
20. See the philosophy & educational approach of *Dr. Maria Montessori,* educator ahead of her time!
21. Explore the potential of *Montessori & Waldorf (Steiner)* as alternatives for today's children. Each child is a unique individual, guided by its own personal development schedule. See *Indigo Children,* by Lee Carroll for further discussion. Today's young children have much to teach us!

CHAPTER 5

GROWING IN CONSCIOUS AWARENESS: Aligning With The Axis Of Consciousness

1. Tiller, William A., Ph.D., *Science and Human Transformation,* pg. 200
2. Sarfatti, Jack, *Post-quantum Physics of Consciousness,* Slide Show www.qedcorp.com/pcr/pcr/pq/pq1.htm
3. Tiller, William A., Ph.D., *Science and Human Transformation,* pg. 178 & 201

CHAPTER 6

RAINBOW HANDS: Your Pot Of Gold

Rainbow Hands *title of this chapter inspired by the book of Davis, Albert Roy, & Rawls, Walter C.,* The Rainbow in Your Hands, *Exposition Press, Smithtown, N.Y., 1976*
1. Brian Greene, *The Elegant Universe- Superstrings, Hidden Dimensions, And The Quest For The Ultimate Theory,* pg.208
2. Bearden, *Excalibur Briefing,* pg. 202
3. Davis, Albert Roy, & Rawls, Walter C., *The Rainbow in Your Hands,* pg.94
4. McGee, Charles T., M.D., Poy Yew Chow, Effie, Ph.D., *Miracle Healing from China-Qigong,* Medipress, Coeur d'Alene, ID, 1994, pg.37

5.   Yao, George, Dr., *Pulsor- Miracle of Microcrystals: A Treatise on Energy Balancing*, gyro Industries, Newport Beach, CA, 1986

6.   Davis, Albert Roy, & Rawls, Walter C., *The Rainbow in Your Hands*

7.   Ibid. Pg.82

8.   Ibid. Pg.9

9.   Ibid. pg. 104

10.   Ibid. pg.84

11.   McGee, Charles T., M.D., Poy Yew Chow, Effie, Ph.D., *Miracle Healing from China-Qigong*, pg.37

12.   Ibid. pg. 37

13.   Guo-long, Liu, M.D., *Infrasonic simulation of emitted Qi from Q-Gong Masters*, www.practicalqigong.com

14.   Xin, Yan, Dr., Dr., *Yan Xin on Scientific Qigong Research*, www.qigong.net

15.   Bunnell, Toni, *A Tentative Mechanism for Healing* www.webserve.co.uk/bunnell/healing.html

16.   Guo-long, Liu, M.D., *Infrasonic simulation of emitted Qi from Q-Gong Masters*, www.practicalqigong.com

17.   Bunnell, Toni, *A Tentative Mechanism for Healing* www.webserve.co.uk/bunnell/healing.html

18.   Popp, Fritz-Albert, , *About the Coherence of Biophotons*, International Institute Of Biophysics ,Neuss, Germany, http://www.datadiwan.de/iib/ib0200e_.htm

19.   Tiller, William, *Science and Human Transformation*, pg.135

20.   Yao, George, Dr., *Pulsor- Miracle of Microcrystals: A Treatise on Energy Balancing*, pg. 21

21.   Ibid. pg. 21

22.   Benveniste, Jacques, M.D., *Understanding Digital Biology*, www.digibio.com

23.   Institute of HeartMath, *The Memory of Water*, http://www.HeartMath.org/Research/water.html

24.   Ibid.

25.   Gerber, Richard, M.D., *Vibrational Medicine: New choices for Healing Ourselves*, Bear & Company, Santa Fe, NM, 1996 & *Vibrational Medicine For The 21ˢᵗ Century*, Harper Collins books, NY, 2000

26.   Bearden, *Gravitobiology: The New Biophysics*

27.   Rein, Glen, Ph.D., *Non-Hertzian Energy and Electromagnetic Energy: The biological Connection*, Matrix III

28.   *The Rainbow in Your Hands*, pg.82

29.   *Excalibur Briefing*, pg. 198-199

30.   Rauscher, Elizabeth A., Ph.D., *Electromagnetic Phenomena in Complex Geometries and Non-Linear Phenomena, Non-Hertzian Waves, and Magnetic Monopoles*, Tesla Book Company, Box 121873, Chula Vista, CA 91912

31.   Additionally, there are energy movements surrounding this area that follow vortex circulating patterns (Dr. George Yao and Davis & Rawls). The circulating vortex fields are indications of primary higher dimensional energy systems. Emission of energy from this area related to both healing & demonstrations of unusual 'feats' is called chi or qi. The energy and fields at the hand are modified by the emotion and expression of the heart.

32.   Magnetic energies spiral from opposite poles. Looking from the North pole end, the North energy is spiraling counterclockwise, with the South energy spiraling clockwise. These opposite magnetic flows contribute to opposite electric polarities. Within the Bloch wall there exists a point where energy is "focused down to an almost microscopically small dimension of constant energy" (Davis & Rawls).

33.   A region called the Bloch wall develops. Using permanent magnets in opposing pole configuration, Davis & Rawls discovered inertial field phenomena (antigravity effects) on matter. The opposing magnetic and vortex fields disturb the local balance of the vacuum state. These hyperfield effects can alter physical constants and produce new forces in 3D space. This can lead to energy flow by tapping into the energy of vacuum (zero point energy source).

34. The South pole is a deficient zone with respect to the vacuum- the energies spiral into the South pole. The North pole has an excess stress with respect to the vacuum- the energies spiral out of the North pole. In the Figure, primary vortex fields are shown. Other vortex fields have also been observed (shown in other illustrations) to be associated with the magnetic poles. These are the hyperfields. Magnetism is associated with unobserved hyperspatial phenomena.

35. This zone is in an area centered at the mid point between the North & South magnetic poles on opposite sides of the hand. Here a phase change of 180° takes place in the primary vorticular, spiraling motion of the field. This forms the figure 8-loop pattern within the Bloch wall zone . A new field phenomenon arises from this pattern. A stress on space-time exists where opposing magnetic and electric poles converge in the Bloch wall zone. A hyperspatial flux, or flow, of 'free' energy enters here. This is tapping into the unlimited universal source of energy.

36. From this oscillation, a current induced in the coil L (inductor) enters the LC circuit. Resonance is established in the circuit by varying C. The signal is detected beyond the amplifier. The human circuitry uses the area of bent spacetime that result from the magnetic fields of the hand. The nervous system/brain network provides the resonant circuit for detection. Human detection of scalar waves is a multi-dimensional process. Tunable human resonance exists on a vast scale.

CHAPTER 7
COLORFUL INTERACTIVE PHENOMENA : Touching The Web Of Life

1. Noteably Jack Sarfatti & Gennady I. Shipov.
2. Of course we are unable to directly explore or verify these claims.
3. Nachalov, Yu. V., *Theoretical Basics of Experimental Phenomena*, www.centuryinter.net/tjsII/hist/shipov.htm
4. Akimov, A.E., & Tarasenko, V.Ya., *Models of Polarized States of The Physical Vacuum and Torsion Fields*, Interdepartmental Scientific-Technological Center of Venture Technologies. Translated from Izvestiya Vysshikh Uchebnykh Zavedenii, Fizika, No. 3, pg. 13-23, March, 1992
5. Nachalov, Yu. V., *Theoretical Basics of Experimental Phenomena*, www.centuryinter.net/tjsII/hist/shipov.htm
6. Nachalov, Yu. V., Sokolov, A.N., *Experimental Investigation of New Long-Range Actions*, www.amasci.com/freenrg/tors/doc17.html
7. Nachalov, Yu. V., *The Basics of Torsion Mechanics*, www.amasci.com/freenrg/torss/tors24.html
8. Poponin, Dr. Vladimir, *The DNA PHANTOM EFFECT: Direct Measurement of A New Field in the Vacuum Substructure*, http://webcom.com/~hrtmath/IHM/ResearchPapers/DNAPhantom/DNAPhantom
9. These may be virtual density waves (VDW), virtual symmetry waves (VSW), or vacuum amplitude waves (VAW) see Kaivarainen, Alex , *Unconventional Consequences of Dynamic Model of Wave-Particle Duality, Hierarchic Concept of Matter & Field : Hypothesis of Biological & Informational Fields, Hierarchic Model of Consciousness, Hierarchic Theory of Complex Systems*, www.karelia.ru/~alexk
10. Nachalov, Yu. V., Parkhomov, E.A., *Experimental Detection of the Torsion Field*, www.geocities.co.jp/Technopolis/1228/torsion_field/doc15/doc15.html
11. Nachalov, Yu. V., Sokolov, A.N., *Experimental Investigation of New Long-Range Actions*, www.amasci.com/freenrg/tors/doc17.html
12. Akimov, A.E. Shipov, G.I., Binhi, V.N., *New Approach to the Problem of Electromagnetobiology*, 1997, www.dataforce.net/~binhi/Torsion/New_app.htm
13. Akimov, A.E., & Tarasenko, V.Ya., *Models of Polarized States of The Physical Vacuum and Torsion Fields* & Nachalov, Yu. V., Sokolov, A.N., *Experimental Investigation of New Long-Range Actions*
14. Nachalov, Yu. V., *The Basics of Torsion Mechanics*, www.amasci.com/freenrg/torss/tors24.html
15. Nachalov, Yu. V., *Theoretical Basics of Experimental Phenomena*, www.centuryinter.net/tjsII/hist/shipov.htm

16. See works of Bearden & Bearden, T.E., *Energetics of Free Energy systems & Vacuum Engine Therapeutics*

17. Norman, Ruth, *Interdimensional Physics-The Mind and The Universe*, Unarius Publications, El Cajun, CA, 1989, pg.165

18. Shpilman, Alexander A., *Physical Properties of Axion (Spin) Fields, Spin (Axion) –Field Generator, Passive Resonators Axion (Spin) Fields, Solar Spin (Axion) Field, Some Effects, Homeopathy & Acupuncture*, www.pmicro.kz/MISC/UFL/Almanach/N1_98/properties.htm

19. Vortex World Of Viktor Schauberger, http://home5.swipnet.se/_w-58759/index.html

20. Shpilman, Alexander A., *Physical Properties of Axion (Spin) Fields*

21. Nachalov, Yu. V., Sokolov, A.N., *Experimental Investigation of New Long-Range Actions* & Kaivarainen, Alex , *Unconventional Consequences of Dynamic Model of Wave-Particle Duality.*

22. Sarfatti, Jack, *Shipov's Torsion Field Theory For Dummies*, pg. 17, 1999, www.stardrive.org/Jack/shipov1.pdf

23. Shipov, Gennady I., *The Theory of Physical Vacuum*

24. The stable tetrahedral structure may become a building block of more elaborate geometric designs, as well as matter itself. The quark, that is the constituent of protons & neutrons, can be defined by the tetrahedral form. In C, we see a 2-D representation of a 3-D structure. The tetrahedral form is found within this self-similar structure- a fractal. The scale of this structure can be extrapolated from microscopic to macroscopic. Resonance within this structure equates to alignment of the geometry, creating perfect symmetry enabling communication & information exchange between cells. Within the vacuum, such a similar structure represents stability, symmetry, and balance. Within the human energy field, such a structure also represents balance. The lattice that is formed can be described as a "geometric collection of harmonic wave-forms of light guided by intelligence" (Bruce Cathie). Tuning is the process of creating resonance between geometry, and the geometric cells. Light, & sound permeate the lattice. Geometry, light, & sound are all harmonically connected!

25. Threads of spirals of high-density energy flow are interlaced within the torsion field, & follow the direction of the Vector Potential (Shpilman). According to Tiller, the Vector Potential is the connecting link to the subtle realm. Torsion fields are hyperspatial-they interact in virtual, unobservable realities and do not respect constraints of time and space. Spin-spin interactions occur between all objects-physical and biological. Spin-spin interactions can occur in resonance like manner. These interactions occur throughout the subtle energy fields. In its interaction, a torsion field can 'charge' (polarize, imprint, influence) another field with its own structure and information content. Additionally, the interaction can alter electrical properties, magnetizability, and other properties of field structures.

26. For example, pyramids, cones, flat triangles, and other shapes or forms have been noted to produce torsion fields with noticeable effects. Passive torsion generators follow the golden mean ratio (1: .618). In the figure, the cone is divided into three equal parts. These three points correspond to the maximum strength of the Left torsion field inside the cone. Certain objects and certain geometric shapes have been discovered to produce resonance interactions with living organisms. Researchers have observed that torsion fields can be 'recorded' on any physical object (Nachalov & Sokolov). A further interesting feature of the torsion field is the effect it has on the physical vacuum. Even after removing an external torsion field from a region of space, the spatial configuration remains as a pattern in the physical vacuum. This is called the torsion field phantom, or simply, a torsion phantom. The vacuum state is polarized by the torsion field, and retains a record of the torsion field for a length of time. Torsion fields are known to transmit information without transmitting energy.

27. It is the torsion fields that interact. An external torsion field can alter the structure of the torsion field of any object. A new configuration of the torsion field remains intact even after removing the source of the external applied torsion field. Any electrostatic, electromagnetic, or magnetic field always exists with a torsion field   (Nachalov & Sokolov). Therefore, the hands manifest torsion fields. These are the hyperspatial fields. The interactive effects of the hands' torsion fields remain even after removing the hands from the region of space. Torsion fields are known to have resonance like interaction. (Of

course the heart and brain qualify as major torsion field generators). Torsion fields have very unusual properties. Amongst the observations of experimental torsion field interaction, is its ability to dramatically alter the characteristics of living things.

28. Cathie, Bruce L., The *Energy Grid-Harmonic 695 The Pulse of the Universe*, America West Publishers, Carson City, NV, 1990, pg. 159-160

29. Torsion fields are associated with all other centers that exhibit vortex or electromagnetic properties: these include the chakras and acupuncture points. All these centers can respond to spin-spin torsion field interactions with the hand. Torsion field interactions exhibit resonance like effects. Torsion fields carry detailed information maps as patterns within their substructure. A torsion field imparts its spatial configuration onto other torsion fields.

30. The interaction results in massless charge polarization. This pattern remains in the vacuum as a metastable state. Each massless charge of the vacuum state consists of a flux or flow of virtual particles. The flux creates potentials in the vacuum that can have non-local effects.

CHAPTER 8

THE MASTER SWITCH: The Heart Of It All

1. Davis, Albert Roy, & Rawls, Walter C., *The Rainbow in Your Hands*
2. Institute of HeartMath, *Subtle Energy Research*, www.webcom.com/hrtmath/IHM/Research/SubtleEnergy.html
3. *Ancient Wisdom & Modern Physics*, pg.114
4. Rollin McCarty, William A. Tiller, & Mike Atkinson, *Head-Heart Entrainment: A Preliminary Survey*, http://www.HeartMath.org/ResearchPapers/HeadHeart/HeadHeart.htm
5. Childre, Doc, & McCraty, Rollin, *Love-The Hidden Power of the Heart:A Scientific Perspective*, Institute of HeartMath, http://www.HeartMath.com/Library/Articles/Caduceus.html
6. Winter, Dan, *Power Spectral Measurements of EKG and the Earth's ELF Magnetic Resonance*, www.danwinter.com/ekgtree/ekgtree.html
7. Bearden, Kaivarainen
8. Gerber, Richard, M.D., *Vibrational Medicine: New choices for Healing Ourselves*, pg. 588
9. Bearden,T. E., *Technical Background on Reguaging a System to Provide Free Excess Energy*, The Virtual Times, 1966, www.hsv.com/writers/bearden/reg01.htm
10. Bearden- *Excalibur Briefing*, pg. 260-265
11. Cathie, Bruce L., *The Energy Grid-Harmonic 695 The Pulse of the Universe*, America West Publishers, Carson City, NV, 1990, pg. 159-160
12. Takashi AOKI, Yasuo YOSHIHUKU And Yoshinori ADACHI, *Influences of Gauge Field on Living Bodies, Journal of International Society of Life Information Science*, Vol.17, No.2, September 1999, www.jssst.or.jp/islis/en/journalE/abst8E.htm
13. Bearden, T.E., *Energetics of Free Energy Systems & Vacuum Engine Therapeutics*, 1997, Tara Publications Center, Brampton, Ontario, Canada, pg. 54-

APPENDIX A

BIOFIELD : Connecting Web Between Physical & Subtle Realm

1. Andrej Detela, personal communication
2. Detela, A., *Physical Model of the biofield*, 1997, J.Stephan Institute, Ljubljana, Slovenia, abstract can be found at Journal of Consciousness Studies, http://www.imprint.co.uk/, 04.07-- Abstract No:1068, http://www.imprint-academic.demon.co.uk/Tucson/4.htm#Physical model of the biofield
3. Robert Bruce, *Astral Dynamics- A New Approach to Out-of-Body Experience*, 1999, & Robert Monroe, Ultimate Journey, 1996
4. Sheldrake, Rupert, Ph.D., www.sheldrake.org, *Interviews*
5. Hemetis, *Torus Knot Topology*, http://hemetis.freeyellow.com/TKTODO.htm,
6. Hemetis, *Quantology*, http://hemetis.freeyellow.com/Quantology.htm
7. Kaku, Michio, *Hyperspace*, pg.11

8.   Greene, Brian, *The Elegant Universe*, '..the fabric of our universe is a richly intertwined multi-dimensional labyrinth within which the strings of the universe endlessly twist and vibrate, rhythmically beating out the laws of the cosmos'. pg.18
9.   Bearden, T. E., *Excalibur Briefing*, Tesla Book Company

APPENDIX B

SELF-ORGANIZING SYSTEMS: Active Information In The Human   -To-Human Connection

1.   Sheldrake, Rupert, *The Variability of the 'Fundamental Constants, Do physical constants fluctuate?*, www.transaction.net/science/seven/constant.html
2.   Detela, Andrej, *Self-Organization Within Complex Quantum States*, J.Stephan Institute, Ljubljana, Slovenia, 1998 (Prepared for the 4th Slovene conference on Cognitive Sciences), copy of paper found at http://ciiiweb.ijs.si/dialogues/r-detela.htm,
3.   Tiller, W., *Science and Human Transformation*, pg. 175
4.   Hunt, Valerie, *Infinite Mind*, pg.69
5.   Bearden, T.E., *Excalibur Briefing*, pg. 273
6.   Andrej Detela- personal communication
7.   Ljubljana, *Quantum Physics Information Consciousness*, Topics of the Second Day, *Interconnectedness of quantum states, information and consciousness*, http://ciiiweb.ijs.si/dialogues/detela.htm, http://ciiiweb.ijs.si/dialogues/page1.htm
8.   Kaivarainen, A., *Hierarchic Theory of Complex Systems*, www.karelia.ru/~alexk
9.   Kaivarainen, A., *Dynamic Model of Wave-Particle Duality: Hidden Parameters, Golden Mean, Eigenmoments, Weak and Strong Interaction*, pg. 6, www.karelia.ru/~alexk
10.   Drunvalo Melchizedek, *The Ancient Secret of the Flower of Life Volume 1,1998 & Volume 2*, 2000, Light Technology Publishing, Flagstaff, AZ 86336
11.   Norman, Ruth, *Interdimensional Physics-The Mind and the Universe*, pg. 171
12.   Sarfatti, Jack, *Post-Quantum Physics of Consciousness*, Slide Show, www.qedcorp.com/pcr/pcr/pq/pq1.htm & Progress in Post-Quantum Theory

SOME REFERENCES & SUGGESTED READING

Bearden, T. E., *Excalibur Briefing*, Tesla Book Company, , Chula Vista, CA 91912, 1988
Bearden, T. E., *Toward A New Electromagnetics, Part III*, Tesla Book Company, 1983
Bearden, T. E., *Toward A New Electromagnetics, Part IV*, Tesla Book Company, 1988
Bearden, T.E., *Gravitobiology-The New BioPhysics*, Tesla Book Company,
         Box 121873, Chula Vista, CA 91912, 1991
Braden, Gregg, *Awakening to Zero Point-The Collective Initiation*, Radio Bookstore Press,
         Bellevue, WA., 1997. See also his later works.
Bryant, Alice, & Seebach, Linda, *Opening To the Infinite- Human Multidimensional Potential*,
         Wild Flower Press, Mill Spring, NC, 1998
Carroll , Lee, *Indigo Children & Kryon* series
Chicago Research Group & Associates, *Ancient Wisdom & Modern Physics*, Leading Edge
         International Research Group, Yelm, WA., 1999, www.trufax.org
Childre, Dac, & Martin, Howard, *The Heartmath Solution*, HarperCollins, NY, NY, 1999
Collinge, William, *Subtle Energy- Awakening to The Unseen Forces In Our Lives*,
         Warner Books, NY, NY, 1998
Detela, Andrej, Look for his upcoming book "*Magnetic Knots*"
Drunvalo Melchizedek, *The Ancient Secret of the Flower of Life Volume 1*, 1998, & *Volume 2*,
         2000, Light Technology Publishing, Flagstaff, AZ 86336
Galimore, J. G., *Unified Field Theory- Using Subjective Response To Psi-Plasma for Analysis
         of Properties Neutral Charge Plasma Fields*, Health Research, Pomeroy, Wa., 1974,
         http://www.healthresearchbooks.com

Gerber, Richard, M.D., *Vibrational Medicine For The 21ˢᵗ Century,*
    Harper Collins books, NY, 2000
Gerber, Richard, M.D., *Vibrational Medicine: New choices for Healing Ourselves,*
    Bear & Company, Santa Fe, NM, 1996
Goswami, Amit, Ph.D., *The Self Aware Universe-How Consciousness Creates The Material
    World,* Tarcher/Putnam, New York, NY., 1995
Greene, Brian, *The Elegant Universe: Superstrings, Hidden Dimensions, And The Quest For
    The Ultimate Theory,* W.W. Norton & Company Ltd., London, 1999
Greenia, Mark, *Energy Dynamics- Conscious Human Evolution,* Unlimited Publishing,
    Bloomington, IN, 2001
Hunt, Valerie, *Infinite Mind: Science of the Human Vibrations of Consciousness,*
    Malibu Publishing, Ca., 1989, 1996
Kaku, Michio, *Hyperspace: A Scientific Odyssey through Parallel Universes, Time Warps, &
    The 10ᵗʰ Dimension,* Oxford University Press, New York, 1994
Leading Edge International Research Group & Associates, & Val Valerian, *Matrix V- Quest of
    the spirit- The Ultimate Frontier,* Leading Edge International Research Group, Yelm,
    WA., 2001, www.trufax.org
Nadeau, Robert, & Kafatos, Menas, *The Non-Local Universe-The New Physics and Matters of
    the Mind,* Oxford University Press, NY, NY, 1999
Norman, Ruth, *Interdimensional Physics-The Mind and The Universe,* Unarius Publications,
    El Cajun, CA, 1989
Petersen, P. Stephen, Ph.D., *The Quantum Tai Chi-Gauge Theory: The Dance Of Mind Over
    Matter,* Empyrean Quest Edition, Concord, Ca., 1996
Pond, Dale, *The Physics of Love,* The Message Co., Santa Fe, New Mexico, 1996
Pond, Dale, *Universal Laws Never Before Revealed: Keely's Secrets- Understanding & Using
    The Science of sympathetic Vibration,* The Message Co., Santa Fe, New Mexico, 2000
Talbot, Michael, *The Holographic Universe,* Harper Collins Books, NY, NY, 1991
Tiller, William A., Ph.D., *Science and Human Transformation-Subtle Energies, Intentionality
    and Consciousness,* Pavior Publishing, Walnut Creek, Ca., 1997
Walker, Evan Harris, *The Physics of Consciousness- The Quantum Mind and The Meaning of
    Life,* Perseus Books, Cambridge, Mass., 2000
Zukav, Gary, *The Dancing Wu Li Masters- An Overview of the New Physics,*
    Bantam Books, 1980

As we go to press we are advised of Andrej Detela's upcoming book

"Magnetic Knots "

Detela is the physicist who authored the two papers featured in our Appendix C & D. Detela has introduced new perspectives in viewing the energetic structure of the biofield, along with advancing new insights into the physics of consciousness. We are advised that this new book will span the fields of physics, biology, & philosophy. We recommend that those readers interested in bridging the fields of science, physics & metaphysics, look out for his upcoming publications!

SOME SUGGESTED WEBSITES

OF THE WORLD WIDE WEB

Aspden, Harold, http://www.users.globalnet.co.uk/~haspdn/

Bearden, T. E., http://www.disclosureproject.org, http://www.teslabook.com/books.html,
http://hsv.com/writers/bearden/tommenu.htm,
http://www.newphys.se/elektromagnum/physics/Bearden/

Consciousness Studies, http://www.consciousness.arizona.edu/,
http://ciiiweb.ijs.si/dialogues/received.htm, http://www.trufax.org/w6.html,
http://www.imprint-academic.demon.co.uk/Tucson/4.htm

Carroll, Lee/ Kryon, http://www.kryon.com/

Dielle Davin: http://home.tiscalinet.be/dielle

EMF Balancing Technique® , www.EMFWorldwide.com

Flower Of Life, http://www.floweroflife.org

Greene, Brian, http://www.phys.columbia.edu/faculty/greene.htm

Greenia, Mark: www.Luminarch.com

Hameroff, Stuart, Consciousness Studies, http://www.consciousness.arizona.edu/hameroff/

Heartmath Institute, http://www.heartmath.com

Hyperspace, http://deoxy.org/hyper.htm

Indigo Children, Psychic Kids, http://www.psykids.net/

Kaivarainen, A., www.karelia.ru/~alexk

Kaku, Michio, http://www.mkaku.org/

Kryon/ Lee Carroll, http://www.kryon.com/

Lapierre, David P.: www.auracom.com/~dpl

Mind Matter Unification Project, http://www.tcm.phy.cam.ac.uk/~bdjl0/mm/top.html

Monroe Institute, http://www.monroe-inst.com/

New Physics, http://www.dnai.com/~zap/, http://www.trufax.org/w6.html

Popp, Fritz-Albert, http://www.datadiwan.de/iib/ib0200e_.htm

Sarfatti, Jack, http://www.qedcorp.com/pcr/index.html, http://www.stardrive.org/library.shtml

Sheldrake, Rupert, http://www.sheldrake.org

Smith, Tony, http://www.innerx.net/personal/tsmith/TShome.html

Spiritweb, http://www.spiritweb.org/

Subtle Energy Studies, http://www.issseem.org/

Tiller, William, http://www.tiller.org

Winter, Dan: www.soulinvitation.com/indexdw.html

Contact Information:

For more information on becoming an EMF Balancing Technique® practitioner or teacher, and for a worldwide schedule of classes please visit the official EMF website.

www.EMFWorldwide.com

Learn to do an EMF Balancing Technique® mini energy session - now on tape. Also available – full size color poster of the Universal Calibration Lattice.

You can also write to The Energy Extension, Inc.
595 W. Main St. Norwich PMB 77, CT. USA 06360, or phone us at 860-889-3451

To Contact The Authors

Your may contact *Peggy Phoenix Dubro* through the publisher, or you may write to

The Energy Extension, Inc.
595 W. Main St. PMB 77, Norwich, CT. USA 06360
or phone us at 860-889-3451

You may contact **David P. Lapierre** by writing to:

Suite 100-125, 1600 Bedford Hwy.
Bedford, Nova Scotia, Canada B4A IE8

email: dpl@auracom.com

For ongoing events, international inquiries, EMF Balancing Technique® teaching schedule, energy dynamic movement workshops, and seminars on expanding your view of reality, visit Dave's webpage at:

www.auracom.com/~dpl

Other contacts:
Ilan Wainer   Cover Design - Ilanwa@netvision.net.il.
Moshe Alembik   Cover Art – Ilanwa@netvision.net.il
Dielle Davin   Artwork-chapter I- http://home.tiscalinet.be/dielle

NOTES

INDEX

NOTES

NOTES